WHO ARE THE CALI CARTEL?

"THE MOST SOPHISTICATED ORGANIZED CRIME SYNDICATE IN HISTORY."

– U.S. Drug Enforcement Agency

"THE RICHEST AND MOST POWERFUL CRIME SYNDICATE in the world, making profits of up to $8 billion a year."

– BBC News

"THE WORLD'S LARGEST drug trafficking gang."

– *The New York Times*

"THE BIGGEST SINGLE DEALER of drugs in the world."

NBC

"THE CALI CARTEL WAS RESPONSIBLE for supplying 80 percent of the cocaine sold in the United States during the 1990s."

– *Miami Herald*

D1514279

"Offers an intimate, never-before-seen glimpse into a shadowy underworld of sophisticated and murderous drug traffickers . . . They eventually met their downfall, as Chepesiuk's vivid portrayal shows, but some cartel leaders have been set free and threaten to rise again." – Tracey Eaton, *Dallas Morning News*

"Chepesiuk's fascinating, factual history of the rise and fall of the world's most extensive illicit drug cartel is a timely, pertinent lesson for our nation's ongoing war, not only against drugs but against the international terrorist network, many of whom derive their resources from drug trafficking." – Ben Gilman, U.S. Congressman (1973–2003) and former chairman, House International Relations Committee

"A well-documented account of the rise and fall of one of the largest cocaine trafficking organizations in history. Relying on interviews, first-hand accounts, DEA records, and documentary evidence the author provides fascinating insight into the reasons for the Cali cartel's entrepreneurial success, in light of the narco-terrorist tactics of its predecessor, the Medellin cartel. It is shown how Cali's growth into a multinational network of immense size and its management failings, ultimately permitted successful infiltration of the cartel. Arguably the most important case in DEA history, the book discusses how the Cali case changed drug trafficking organizations in Colombia and elsewhere, shrinking them in size and altering the measures they now take to insulate themselves from prosecution." – International Association for the Study of Organized Crime

"Ron Chepesiuk is a master of high-octane journalism. This is without a doubt the most thrilling book I have reviewed about Colombia to date. Moreover, I strongly recommend it to all readers who love action-packed crime stories. In the words of Chepesiuk . . . the Cali Cartel would prove to be the most formidable adversary in the history of international drug trafficking. The sophistication of this criminal organization is incredible. The strategy is both simple and brilliant. Communications are state-of-the-art and street level members of the cartel are told to live modestly and to avoid drawing attention to themselves. This is a huge contrast to the rival Medellin cartel that is both violent and audacious. On that note, the author does a commendable job of interviewing all of the major Colombian and American political and law enforcement actors who played a role in the saga . . . On the sad side, this book does document the enormous corruption of government officials in Colombia. The Cali cartel bought off senior members of government and of society. Nevertheless, the Colombian National Police shines in this book with the arrival of its legendary leader General Rosso Jose Serrano, dubbed, 'Mr. Clean' by powerful members of the U.S. Congress. In conclusion, if you have a long business trip to make and need to pack a good book . . . here it is. Buy it!" – Bert Ruiz, author, *The Colombian Civil War*

RON CHEPESIUK is a Fulbright Scholar and the author of several books on crime, including *The Bangkok Connection, Black Caesar* and *Gangsters of Miami*.

Narcos Inc

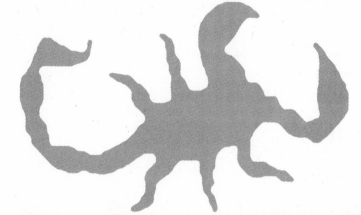

The Rise and Fall of the Cali Cartel

RON CHEPESIUK

The Bullet or the Bribe: Taking Down Colombia's Cali Drug Cartel, by Ron Chepesiuk, was originally published in hard cover by Praeger, an imprint of ABC-CLIO, LLC, Santa Barbara, CA.

This edition published in 2017 by Maverick House Publishers,
47 Harrington Street,
Dublin 8,
Ireland.

www.maverickhouse.com
info@maverickhouse.com

ISBN 978-1-908518-58-3

5 4 3 2 1

Printed and bound by Nørhaven

A CIP catalogue record for this book is available from the Irish and British Library.

For my mother, Anne, and my sister, Diane. We miss you.

And so hubris turns to false certainties, everyone expects to be a winner, and each morning is a mind-blowing experience.

– Stephen Vizinczey, Hungarian novelist

Contents

Acknowledgments

A book of this scope could not have been completed without the help of many individuals who stepped forward and generously provided their time, resources, and sage advice. First, I would like to thank all the knowledgeable sources I interviewed during the fourteen months it took to complete the project. Those interviewees who agreed to talk on the record are listed in the Bibliography's primary sources section.

Many individuals either provided valuable documents or assisted me in finding them. They include Bruce Bagley, Craig Benedict, Billy Bruton, Steve Casto, Cynthia Chase, Rich Crawford, Ken Cook, Gustavo De Greiff, Tracey Eaton, Mark Eiler, Carlos Lopez, Boyd Johnson, Yovanny Lopez, Juan Carlos Esguerra, Michael Evans, Chris Feistl, Cesar Gaviria, Liz Jordan, Ed Kacerosky, Gil Macklin, Bill Mante, Robert Michaelis, Dave Mitchell, Javier Montes, David Scott Palmer, Ruben Prieto, Ken Robinson, Ed Ryan, Jerry Salameh, Ernesto Samper, Bob Sears, Sandy Smith, Richard Weber, and Lou Weiss. The following people assisted me in arranging interviews: Rich Crawford, Monica De Greiff, Lee Granato, Ed Kacerosky, Bill Mante, Bob Nieves, Terry O'Neill, Paul Paz y Minao, Ken Robinson, Ernesto Samper, German Valasquez, and Lou Weiss, and officials from the United States Department of Justice and from the U.S. Treasury Department, who wish to remain anonymous.

I would also like to thank Rogene Waite of the DEA Public Relations Office, who jump-started the project by helping to arrange interviews with key DEA agents who worked on the Cali cartel investigation. Thanks also to the following public affairs specialists for their help in arranging interviews and supplying documents: Maggie Myers, U.S. Customs Department; Neil Schiff, FBI; Liz Jordan, New York Drug Enforcement Task Force; Jamie Mills, New York State Police; Javier Montes, Organization of American States; Karen Ghan and Tim Harms, IRS; Sheri James, Financial Crimes Enforcement Network (FINCEN); Carlos Lopez and Yovanny Lopez, U.S. Attorney's Office, Southern District Of Florida; Herbert Hadad, United States Attorney's Office, Southern District Of New York; and Robert Hughes, U.S. embassy in Bogota.

In researching the book, I made two (special) trips to Colombia and several visits to Miami, New York City, and the Washington, D.C. area. Thanks to the staffs of the following libraries and archives in those locations for their assistance: El Tempo, the New York Public Library, the National Archives, the DEA Library, the Library of Congress, the Dade County Public Library, and the Colombo Memorial Library in Bogota, Colombia. Special thanks to Michael Evans of the National Security Archive for his assistance, advice, and sharing of information.

In Colombia, the following individuals helped me make arrangements, pursue interviews, and get to them on time: Rosa Aranda, Sonia Aranda, Zahadya Aranda Diaz, Camelia Cardona, Jorge Cardona, Oscar Anulfo Casa Mejia, and German Valasquez. Patti Stafford and Jackie McFadden of the Interlibrary Loan Department of Winthrop University, in my hometown of Rock Hill, proved invaluable in locating books, articles, government reports, and other records essential to the project's completion. The following individuals read the manuscript and offered valuable suggestions on how to improve it: Magdalena Chepesiuk, Tracy Eaton, Carolyn Forbes, Bill Mante, and David Weeks. One of the benefits from undertaking the project was finding long-lost Cousin Carolyn. I look forward to her assistance with my future books.

The Winthrop Univeristy Research Council awarded me a grant, and I am grateful for the Research Council's support over the years.

Finally, I have visited and written about Colombia and its nexus with international drug trafficking since 1987. During this period, many kind individuals have shared their knowledge on the subject. For that, I am extremely grateful.

Abbreviations

CI	Confidential Informant
CNP	Colombian National Police
DAS	Administrative Department of Security (*Departmento Administrativo de Seguridad*)
DEA	Drug Enforcement Administration
EO	Executive Order
FARC	Revolutionary Armed Forces of Colombia
FOI	Freedom of Information
KNEU-86055	Cali cartel investigation coordinated by NYSP and NYDETF (also "case 86055")
MAS	Death to Kidnappers (*Meurte a Secuestradores*)
NSA	National Security Archive
NYDETF	New York Drug Enforcement Task Force
NYSP	New York State Police
OFAC	Office of Foreign Assets Control
PEPES	People Persecuted by Pablo Escobar
SDNT	Specifically Designated Narcotics Trafficker
SOD	Special Operations Division (of the DEA)
TAVA	Trans America Ventures Associates

The Cast of Characters

Author's note. Colombians and other Spanish-speaking peoples often use two surnames: their father's surname followed by their mother's maiden name. For example: Gilberto *Rodriguez Orejuela*, Jose *Santacruz Londono*. The general style followed in this book will be to use both surnames on introduction of a character, but usually just the father's surname after that. For example: Gilberto Rodriguez, Jose Santacruz, etc.

Michael Abbell. American lawyer and former U.S. Justice Department official who represented the Cali cartel.

Harold Ackerman. Miami-based manager for the Cali cartel, who was dubbed the "Cali cartel's ambassador to the United States."

Alvaro de Jesus Aguela. Bodyguard to Pablo Escobar.

Freddie Aguilera. Cali cartel operative who, under Santacruz Londono's direction, supervised the cocaine processing labs that the cartel began setting up in the United States in 1984.

Luis and **Mauricio Arboleda**. Brothers and Cali cartel associates arrested in the seizure of a cocaine shipment in Houston, Texas. Gilberto Rodriguez is believed to be the owner of the shipment.

Crescencio Arcos. U.S. State Department official who met with Ernesto Samper in the spring of 1994.

Fanor Arizabaleta. One of the Cali cartel's seven top leaders who was captured in 1995.

Tulio E. Ayerbe. The investigation of this Cali cartel operative uncovered the cartel's operation in Alabama in 1981.

Virgilio Barco. President of Colombia from 1986 to 1990.

Belisario Betancourt Cuertas. President of Colombia from 1974 to 1978.

Alexandro Bernal-Madrigal (aka "Juvenal"). He was a Bogota-based drug transportation coordinator.

Alexander Blarek. American interior designer who worked for Chepe Santacruz and his wife and was later convicted of money laundering for the Cali cartel.

Fernando Botero. Defense minister during the Ernesto Samper administration who was implicated in the narco cassette scandal.

Peter Bourne. Drug policy advisor and special assistant for health issues in President Jimmy Carter's administration.

Bill Bruton. IRS agent assigned to Operation Dinero.

Morris Busby. U.S. ambassador to Colombia at the time that the existence of the narco cassettes was revealed.

George Bush. President of the United States from 1989 to 1993.

Guillermo Cano. Crusading Colombian journalist murdered by drug traffickers in December 1986.

Rafael Cardona. A Cali cartel mole inside the Medellin cartel who, in November 1986, tipped off police that Jorge Ochoa would be in the Cali area.

Amado Carrillo Fuentes (aka "Lord of the Skies"). Carrillo Fuentes was the Cali cartel's most important contact in Mexico until his death in 1997.

Jimmy Carter. President of the United States from 1977 to 1981.

Julio Jo Capriano. Cuban American National who was imprisoned in Colombian jail with Miguel and Gilberto Rodriguez after his arrest in March 1995.

Tom Cash. DEA administrator in Miami in the late 1980s and early 1990s.

Carlos Castano. Brother of Fidel and a Colombian paramilitary leader.

Fidel Castano. Brother of Carlos and a Colombian paramilitary leader who played a major role in the *PEPES*.

Jorge Castillo. Secretary and driver for Miguel Rodriguez.

Bill Clinton. President of the United States from 1993 to 2001.

Tom Constantine. Head administrator of the DEA from 1994 to 1997.

Ken Cook. NYSP detective who investigated the Minden lab explosion in 1984.

Rich Crawford. DEA agent who played a major role in the investigation of the Cali cartel, first as Group Five's detective and later as a DEA agent assigned to the agency's Tampa office.

Alfredo Cervantes. Chepe Santacruz's right-hand man in the United States from 1981 to 1984.

Victor Crespo. Alias for Jose Santacruz Londono.

Oscar Cuevas. Money launderer for the Cali cartel.

Manuel de Dios Unanue. Crusading New York City investigative journalist whom authorities believe Santacruz Londono murdered in 1992.

Gustavo De Greiff. Colombia's Prosecuting Attorney General from 1992 to 1994.

General Guillermo Diettes. The director of the Colombian National Police (CNP) whom General Rosso Jose Serrano replaced in 1994.

Juan Pablo Escobar. Son of Pablo Escobar.

Manuela Escobar. Daughter of Pablo Escobar.

Pablo Escobar. Founding godfather of the Medellin cartel and a bitter rival of the Cali cartel.

Roberto Escobar. Brother of Pablo Escobar.

Victoria Escobar. Wife of Pablo Escobar.

Juan Carlos Esguerra. Colombian Foreign Minister in Ernesto Samper's presidential administration.

Carlos Espinosa (aka "Pinchalito"). Espinosa headed the Cali cartel's communications operation.

Giovanni Falcone. Crusading Italian prosecutor who investigated the Italian Mafia until he was murdered in May 1992.

Chris Feistl. DEA agent in the agency's Colombia office who was involved with the hunt for the Cali cartel leaders.

Victor Figueroa Molineros. Associate of William Rodriguez Abadia who, along with William, is indicted on drug trafficking charges in New York State.

Flaco. The nickname for Alberto Madrid Mayor, Gilberto Rodriguez Orejuela's personal secretary.

Fernando (Fatty) Flores Germandia. A Venezuelan and former Cali cartel operative who was extradited to the U.S.

Myles Frechette. U.S. ambassador to Colombia from 1994 to 1997.

Luis Carlos Galan. Leading Colombian presidential candidate murdered by drug traffickers in 1989.

Fernando and **Mario Galeano**. Brothers and drug traffickers murdered by Pablo Escobar in 1993.

Juan Garcia-Abrego. Major Mexican drug trafficker who collaborated with the Cali cartel until his arrest in January 1996.

Edgar Garcia Montilla. Money launderer for the Cali cartel who was arrested in Luxembourg in 1989.

Rafael Gaviria Herreros. Colombian priest who met Pablo Escobar when he surrendered in June 1991.

Cesar Gaviria Trujillo. President of Colombia from 1986 to 1990.

Robert Gelbard. Assistant secretary of state for Latin American Affairs at the time of the hunt for Pablo Escobar and during Ernesto Samper's presidential administration.

Alberto Giraldo. A Colombian journalist who was a close associate of Miguel Rodriguez.

Hernando Giraldo Soto. The Cali cartel associate that Gilberto Rodriguez sent to New York City in the early 1970s to lay the groundwork for the Cali cartel's distribution network.

Carlos Giron. Cali cartel associate who was captured in 1992.

Vicky Giron. Wife of Carlos Giron and tutor of the Rodriguez Orejuela children for several years.

Luis Hermando Gomez Bustamante (aka Rasguno). Norte Valle Del Cauca godfather.

Nelson Gomez (aka "McCarthy"). Gomez was the Cali cartel operative whose arrest in 1978 gave law enforcement its first indication of the extent of the Cali cartel's operation in New York City.

Bernardo Gonzalez. Colombian lawyer for the Cali cartel.

Nelson Gonzalez. Agent in the DEA's Quito, Ecuador office who met with Ruben Prieto in Bogota in 1995.

Octavio Gonzalez. DEA agent murdered by Thomas Charles Coley in November 1976.

Lee Granato. U.S. customs agent who investigated the financial aspect of Operation Cornerstone.

Jose Gusto Guzman. A regional cell manager for the Cali cartel in the 1990s.

Jesse Helms. U.S. senator for North Carolina and chairman of the Senate Foreign Relations Committee during the time of Colombia's narco cassette scandal.

Archangel de Jesus Henao-Montoya. Head of a drug trafficking group operating out of the Valle del Cauca region.

Orlando Henao-Montoya. Drug trafficker believed to be involved in Jose Santacruz's murder in 1996.

Helmer Herrera-Buitrago (aka "Pacho"). He was one of the four major godfathers in the Cali cartel hierarchy.

Ramon Herrera-Buitrago. Brother of Pacho Herrera and the manager of Pacho's New York drug distribution cell.

Michael Horn. Former DEA agent and current director of the National Intelligence Center in Johnston, Pennsylvania.

Carlos Mauro Hoyos Jiminez. Colombian attorney general murdered by drug traffickers in January 1988.

Frank Jackson. American lawyer who represented Cali cartel operative Gustavo Naranjo after his arrest in 1991.

Orlando Jaramillo. A Cali cartel operative based in New York City until his arrest in December 1992.

Jose Franklin Jurado Rodriguez. Money launderer for the Cali cartel who was arrested in Luxembourg in 1989.

Ed Kacerosky. U.S. customs agent who worked the Operation Cornerstone investigation.

Michael Kane. Head of the DEA's Medellin office from 1981 to 1984.

John Kerry. U.S. senator from Massachusetts and critic of Gustavo De Greiff, Colombia's Prosecuting Attorney General.

Yair Klein. Israeli mercenary who provided weapons and ammunition to Rodriguez Gacha and trained some of his men.

Michael Kuhlman. DEA agent who worked in the agency's Cali office in the early 1980s.

Robert Lafferty. A pilot for the Cali cartel who worked as a confidential informant for the DEA until his death in 1986.

Francisco Laguna. American lawyer who represented the Cali cartel and played an important role as an interpreter and a translator of documents from English to Spanish.

Heidi Landgraf. DEA agent assigned to Operation Green Ice.

Rodrigo Lara Bonilla. Colombian justice minister murdered by drug traffickers after he successfully launched a raid on the mega cocaine-processing lab at Tranquilandia.

Skip Latson. DEA agent assigned to Operation Dinero.

Carlos Lehder. Founding member and leader in Medellin cartel.

Carlos Lemos. Colombian vice-president in the Ernesto Samper presidential administration.

Roberto Levya. El Salvadoran air force colonel who met with the Cali cartel's Jorge Salcedo in El Salvador.

Henry Loiaza (aka "The Scorpion"). Loiaza was a Cali cartel godfather until his capture in 1995.

Raphael Lombrano. DEA confidential informant who the Cali cartel murdered in 1990.

Jorge Lopez (aka "Tio"). A Cali cartel operative who replaced Carlos Torres as the cartel's cell-head in Miami.

Alfonso Lopez Michelsen. President of Colombia from 1974 to 1978.

Alberto Madrid Mayor (aka "Flaco" ["Skinny"]). Personal secretary to Gilberto Rodriguez.

Richard Mahecha-Bustos. Money launderer for the Cali cartel who was arrested in Luxembourg.

Bill Mante. A NYSP detective who was a principal investigator on KNEU-86055.

Raul Marti. He replaced Harold Ackerman as the Cali cartel's chief cell-head in Miami after Ackerman's arrest in 1992.

Miguel Masa. The head of Colombia's *DAS* whom Escobar tried to kill.

Juan Ramon Matta Ballesteros. Honduran drug trafficker who collaborated with the Cali cartel.

Santiago Medina. The campaign manager for Ernesto Samper who later testified against Samper.

Robbie Michaelis. DEA agent assigned to the money laundering investigation of the Cali cartel's operation in Luxembourg.

Dave Mitchell. DEA agent in the agency's Colombia office who was involved with the hunt for the Cali cartel leaders.

Giraldo and **William Julio Moncada**. Brothers and drug traffickers whom Pablo Escobar murdered in 1993.

Maria Montoya. An important Cali cartel distributor in Queens, New York in the 1980s.

Diego Leon Montoya. Norte Valle Del Cauca godfather.

Robert Moore. One of the many American lawyers who represented the Cali cartel's interests in the United States.

George Morales. Cali cartel associate who worked with Miguel Rodriguez while they were incarcerated in Colombian jail in the late 1990s.

William Moran. American lawyer who represented the Cali cartel's interests.

Jaime Munera. Oversaw the cartel's operation in Alabama in 1981.

Daniel Munoz-Mosquera. A *sicario* for the Medellin cartel responsible for bombing a Colombian airliner in 1989.

Oscar Naranjo. Colombian National Police colonel.

R. Richard Newcomb. Director of the Office of Foreign Assets Control, U.S. Department of the Treasury.

Robert Nieves. Head of International Operations for the DEA from 1988 to 1995.

Marta Nieves Ochoa Vasquez. Sister of the Ochoa brothers who was kidnapped by Colombian guerillas in 1981 and subsequently released.

Richard Nixon. President of the United States from 1969 to 1974.

Jorge, **Fabio**, and **Juan David Ochoa**. Brothers and godfathers in the Medellin cartel.

Jaime Pabon. A major cocaine distributor for Pablo Escobar.

Julio Palestino. Leader of the *Palestinos*, a violent group of *sicarios* from Medellin who acted as enforcers for the Cali cartel.

Guillermo Pallomari. The Cali cartel's chief accountant who testified against his former bosses.

Rodrigo Pardo. Colombian foreign minister during the Ernesto Samper presidential administration.

Andres Pastrana. Former mayor of Bogota and president of Colombia from 1998 to 2002.

Victor Patino. The Cali cartel's reputed number-five leader who was captured in 1995.

Gonzalo Paz. Colombian lawyer for the Cali cartel.

William Pearson. Assistant U.S. attorney general for South Florida who was assigned to the Operation Cornerstone investigation.

Frank Pellechia. Interior designer and partner of Alexander Blarek who was convicted of money laundering for the Cali cartel.

Javier Pena. DEA agent in Colombia who investigated Pablo Escobar.

Pina. An associate of Jaime Pabon, a major distributor for Pablo Escobar.

Mario Playo. An alias for Harold Ackerman, the Cali cartel's "ambassador to the United States."

Ruben Prieto. DEA agent assigned to the agency's Colombia office who was involved in the hunt for the Cali cartel leaders.

Jamie Ramirez Gomez. Head of the Colombian National Police who was murdered in November 1986.

Francisco Ramirez. Associate of William Rodriguez Abadia who, along with William, is indicted on drug trafficking charges in New York State.

Juan Carlos Ramirez Abadia. Cali cartel associate who collaborated with the Rodriguez brothers on drug trafficking operations while incarcerated in Colombian jail.

Luis "The Shrimp" Ramos. A Cali cartel associate in the 1980s.

Ronald Reagan. President of the United States from 1981 to 1989.

Alma Beatriz Rengifo. Colombian justice minister during Ernesto Samper's administration.

Janet Reno. U.S. attorney general in the Clinton administration.

Hernando Rizzo (code name "Tio"). Rizzo was, until his capture, an important Cali cartel cell manager in New York City in the 1980s.

Ken Robinson. NYSP detective and later DEA agent who worked on Group Five's investigation of the Cali cartel and who investigated the cartel from 1978 to 1994, which was longer than any other law enforcement officer.

Jorge Elicer Rodriguez. Brother of Gilberto and Miguel Rodriguez, who was captured in 1994.

Jorge Orlando Rodriguez (aka El Mono). Assumed control of Juan Carlos Rodriguez Abadia's organization while he was in prison.

Jose Gonzalo Rodriguez Gacha (aka "The Mexican"). A Medellin cartel godfather until his death in 1989.

Humberto Rodriguez Mondragon. Son of Gilberto Rodriguez Orejuela.

Maria Rodriguez Mondragon. Daughter of Gilberto Rodriguez Orejuela.

Gilberto Rodriguez Orejuela (aka "The Chess Player"). One of the Cali cartel's three principal founders, who played an important role in the mafia's strategic planning.

Jaime Rodriguez Mondragon. Son of Gilberto Rodriguez Orejuela.

Juan Carlos Rodriguez Obadia. Son of Miguel Rodriguez Obadia.

Miguel Rodriguez Orejuela (aka "El Señor" [The Boss]). One of the three founders of the Cali cartel who was responsible for its overall operation from about 1990 onward.

William Rodriguez Abadia. Son of Miguel Rodriguez Orejuela.

Joel Rosenthal. American lawyer who represented the Cali cartel.

Andres Ruiz Rios. A Cali cartel money laundering expert who became a key DEA informant.

Ed Ryan. Assistant U.S. attorney general for South Florida who was assigned to Operation Cornerstone.

Jerry Salameh. DEA agent assigned to the agency's Bogota office who was involved in the hunt for Cali cartel leaders.

Hoover Salazar-Espinosa. An important Cali cartel transportation coordinator and money launderer, who was also a close associate of Amado Carrillo Fuentes.

Jorge Salcedo. Cali cartel operative who became a major CI against them.

Orlando Sanchez. Drug trafficker and reputed "Overalls Man" who is believed to have tried to kill William Rodriguez.

Amparo Santacruz. The wife of Chepe Santacruz.

Ana Milena Santacruz. Daughter of Chepe Santacruz.

Lucho Santacruz Echeverria. Half brother of Jose Santacruz Londono.

Jose Santacruz Londono (aka "Chepe" and "El Gordo"). As one of the Cali cartel's three founders, he played a key role in establishing its U.S. drug distribution network in the late 1970s and early 1980s.

Bob Sears. DEA agent who investigated the Minden lab explosion in 1984.

General Rosso José Serrano. The head of the Colombian National Police who led the assault on the Cali cartel beginning in 1994.

Ed Shohat. American lawyer who represented Harold Ackerman.

Gabriel Silva. Colombian ambassador to the United Nations during the Ernesto Samper presidential administration.

Michael Skol. U.S. State Department official who met with Ernesto Samper in the spring of 1994.

Alberto Soto-Ochoa. A major Colombian money broker who worked with Carrillo Fuentes.

Joseph Stroh. Currency broker for the Cali cartel.

Joe Toft. Head of the DEA office in Colombia from 1988 to 1995 who exposed the existence of the narco cassettes.

Carlo Torres. Replaced Harold Ackerman as the Cali cartel's Miami cell-head after Ackerman's arrest in 1992.

Michael Tsalickis. A Florida importer-exporter who trafficked drugs for the Cali cartel in the 1980s.

Julio Cesar Turbay. President of Colombia from 1978 to 1982.

Jairo Ivan Urdinola-Grajales. A Cali drug trafficker and Norte Valle Del Cauca cartel godfather who had a close working relationship with Miguel Rodriguez.

Julio Fabio Urdinola Grajales. Brother of Ivan and Norte Valle Del Cauca drug cartel godfather.

Alvaro Uribe. President of Colombia from 2002 to the present.

Alfonso Valdivieso Sarmiento. He followed Gustavo de Greiff as Colombia's prosecuting attorney general and launched Process 8000 in the wake of the narco-cassette revelations.

El Pibe Valderama. Famous Colombian soccer player who, in Colombian television ads, wore T-shirts supporting Ernesto Samper's presidential campaign.

John Gavi Valencia. Boyfriend of Pacho Herrera.

Jorge Enrique Valesquez (aka "The Navigator"). Valesquez was the Cali cartel operative responsible for Rodriguez Gacha's death in 1989.

Luis Valez. A NYSP officer who headed KNEU-86055's wiretapping operations.

Wilmer Aliro Varela (aka Jabon). Norte Valle Del Cauca godfather.

Jairo Villegas-Amariles. Associate of William Rodriguez Abadia who, along with William, is indicted on drug trafficking charges in New York State.

Freddie Viva Yangas. An assistant to Patricia Cardona, both of whom, it is believed, the Cali cartel murdered.

Alexander Watson. U.S. State Department's top official for Inter-American Affairs when he and a group of U.S. State Department officials met Ernesto Samper in the spring of 1994.

Lou Weiss. DEA agent assigned to the Operation Cornerstone investigation.

Ann M. Wells. U.S. State Department official who met with President Ernesto Samper in the spring of 1994.

Maria Ximena Wilson Garcia. Wife of Miguel Rodriguez Abadia.

Lucipida Zuniga. Miguel Rodriguez's maid.

Part I

Prologue

Introduction

The Labs That
Made It Snow

It's similar to, maybe, baking a cake.
— David Karasiewski, forensic chemist, DEA

The call came in the dead of night.

Bob Sears groped for the switch on his bed lamp and squinted at the alarm clock on the end table. It was just past 2 A.M. As an agent for the Drug Enforcement Administration in Albany, New York State, Sears was used to irregular hours, but that didn't make it any easier. He fumbled with the telephone and blurted, "This better be important."

The caller was Ken Cook, a longtime friend and investigator assigned to the Major Crime Unit of Troop Six, the New York State Police (NYSP). He had worked with Sears on many joint investigations. This was no social call.

"There has been an explosion at a farmhouse in Minden," said Cook. "We don't know what happened. It could be a bomb factory or a meth lab. Barrels of chemicals are all over the place. It's a mess. Maybe the DEA needs to go out and take a look."

Sears yawned and rubbed his warm bed. He had a better idea. "Come on, Ken, it's almost morning. Can't we sleep on it till tomorrow?"

But Cook persisted. "No, we need to go out there tonight while the scene is still hot." Sears knew well what Cook meant.

Often he would go out to a crime scene only to find that some young cop fresh out of the academy had left his hoof and paw prints all over the place.

So in the early hours of April 12, 1985, Sears dragged himself out of bed, got dressed, and drove out to the state police barracks in downtown Albany to rendezvous with Cook. He had no inkling that he was heading into the biggest drug trafficking investigation in New York State Police history.

During the one-hour drive to the farm, the two men speculated about what had happened. A bomb explosion did not make much sense, but neither did the meth lab theory. Minden was a small, sleepy hamlet of a few thousand inhabitants in upstate New York, about sixty miles from Albany. It seldom gave law enforcement much trouble. In fact, Cook could not recall when an incident in the Minden area looked serious enough to have an officer forsake his sleep and come out in the dead of night to investigate. Yeah, it was some other kind of accident, all right, but what?

At the scene, the bitter smell of chemicals permeated the air and almost singed the hair in their nostrils. About fifty yards away from their car, a house or some kind of dwelling was on fire, and firemen were still trying to hose it down. It was mass confusion, and none of the professionalism they hoped to see was evident. The firemen, Cook and Sears learned, were volunteers from the local county. Sure enough, the cops, who seemed to be auditioning for a remake of a Keystone Cops movie, had not yet secured what could be a crime scene. Meanwhile no crime scene investigators – the kind seen on the popular TV series *CSI* – had yet arrived to find the cause of the chaos and to see if there had been any loss of life.[1]

Sears and Cook began poking around for themselves. In a wooden shed adjacent to the farmhouse they saw dozens of fifty-five-gallon drums filled with chemicals they did not recognize. They took a quick peek inside a couple of the drums. Sears pulled out a pen and began to write down the names of the labels on his notepad. Some labels said acetone, others ether. Several drums had no labels. Nearby, they found case after case of what was labeled hydrochloric acid. There were also fire extinguishers, filter paper, gas masks, and bunches of hoses.

They checked around the back of the shed and spotted a forklift. They also inspected a double-wide trailer about fifty yards away and observed a pot burning on the stove. The pot was hot and the liquid inside was still steaming. Something had been cooking within the last couple of hours. When the two investigators reached the farmhouse, they found walkie-talkies, drying racks, and what looked like financial ledgers.[2]

"What the hell do we have here?" Sears asked Cook. "It's time I call the lab back at headquarters to see if they can tell us what the chemicals are." Sears marched back to the car and made the call. He described the scene and read off the names from his notepad. "What is it? What are we dealing with?" he asked. The answer made Sears wish he had not left his warm bed that night: "Jesus Christ, you're in a cocaine-processing lab! Don't touch anything or smell anything. Get the hell out of there. You can die."[3]

Sears and Cook lived. Later in the day, the New York State Police (NYSP) got a search warrant. During the next several days, the NYSP and DEA worked closely together and began an extensive, professional investigation. DEA lab analysts examined the hundreds of pounds of the brown, burnt sludge found in the double-wide trailer, as well as several pounds of the white, snowy-looking material made soggy by the water from the firemen's hoses. They had a pretty good idea what it was, but it was always good procedure to be thorough.[4]

Their conclusion stunned the two law enforcement agencies. They had uncovered a massive cocaine-processing lab right in their backyard. Based on the amount of chemicals present, the lab could process about 250 kilos of cocaine – at a minimum. As David Karasiewski, supervisory chemist at the DEA's Mid Atlantic Laboratory in Washington, D.C., later testified, "Ether and acetone, the organic solvents used in the cocaine manufacturing process, can be used more times or several additional times. What I mean by this . . . if you have the proper glassware, you can continue to recycle these organic solvents."[5]

But who was responsible for the coke lab? Who had the nerve, the organization, the know-how, the distribution network, and the criminal enterprise to radically change the way drug trafficking was done? Cocaine, after all, was processed at labs in Colombia where the big drug-trafficking syndicates known as cartels operated, not in the rural United States. Traffickers had set up an extensive set of labs in the plains and jungle regions of South America, which they used to convert cocaine base to cocaine hydrochloride, or powdered coke.[6] The realization that the traffickers, wherever they came from, had transported cocaine paste to upstate New York to manufacture cocaine was mind-blowing. Hadn't they got it backward? Shouldn't they first make the coke in Colombia and then ship the finished product to the United States?

That was the way it had been traditionally done. But in 1984, as revealed by the investigation following the Minden lab explosion, the traffickers were changing their strategy, the result of intense pressure from the Colombian and U.S. governments. Rodrigo Lara Bonilla, the Colombian justice minister, had authorized a spectacular raid on a major processing plant known as Tranquilandia, located in the barren southeast Llanos area in the Amazon region and run by the powerful and violent Medellin cartel. The DEA had heard of a major shipment to Colombia of ether, a solvent-like acetone, which was one of the essential ingredients in cocaine production. They secretly attached radio transmitters to two of the drums in the shipment and followed the signal via satellite from Chicago to Tranquilandia. The raid caught the traffickers by surprise. Forty workers were arrested, and 10,000 barrels of chemicals and a billion dollars worth of cocaine were confiscated. Soon afterward, the price of cocaine on the street shot up, a sweet indication that the Tranquilandia operation had hurt the bad guys.[7]

The Medellin cartel leadership was furious, and it ordered *sicarios*, hired contract killers, to murder Lara Bonilla. Colombian president Belaisario Betancourt declared a state of siege and a "war without quarter" on the criminals. The Medellin cartel, with its swagger and high profile, was the obvious target of Colombian government action, but the Cali cartel's operations were disrupted as well. The leaders of Colombia's two biggest drug-trafficking organizations went into hiding and began moving their drug-processing operations to neighboring countries. The

DEA received information that Jose Santacruz Londono, one of the founding members of the Cali cartel – and, as the DEA had learned, a key figure in its distribution network – was in Mexico, where he was trying to establish new processing laboratories.[8]

The U.S. government attacked the cocaine supply by placing restrictions on the number of chemicals used in cocaine-manufacturing processes that could be exported outside the United States. The Colombian drug traffickers adapted when they realized the chemicals were easier to get in the United States than to smuggle into Colombia. In 1985, ether was selling for approximately $400 to $600 per fifty-five-gallon drum in the United States. In South America, the price was somewhere between $1,000 and $2,000. The United States, moreover, had no reporting requirements for chemicals that were manufactured in the United States and stayed there. United States businesses that made shipments to foreign countries, on the other hand, had to report them.[9]

In early June 1984, the Santacruz organization sent a team to the rural town of Gibsonville, North Carolina, about twenty miles from Greensboro, to build a cocaine-processing lab. A lab in the Eastern United States would work out nicely because the biggest market for cocaine was in New York City, and Santacruz and his Cali associates controlled the distribution in the city. Like any good businessman, Santacruz treated the Gibsonville lab project as an experiment to see if it could work.

He put Freddie Aguilera in charge of the project. Aguilera used underling Carlos Gomez and a small team of chancers and opportunists to put the plan in motion. One, petty drug dealer Julio Harold Fargas, had visited a Chevrolet dealership in Alexandria, Virginia, in 1983 and, as he spoke poor English, was introduced to Pedro Canales, a salesman fluent in Spanish. Canales sold Fargas a car; they chatted and became friends. Eventually, Fargas persuaded Canales to help him sell a "little" cocaine. Canales would give Fargas the keys to a car on the lot, and he would put the cocaine in the trunk. A customer would "test drive" the car, and the cocaine would be gone when the car was brought back to the lot.

One day, Fargas was at the dealership when Al Ditto, a farmer from Gibsonville, came by to see his nephew and sell a few T-shirts, moonshine, and other odds and ends he had in his truck. Fargas began to ask questions about Ditto and the area where he lived. Was North Carolina a farming place? Did Ditto have a farm? Did he grow his own vegetables?[10]

Not long after the Ditto interrogation, Fargas offered Canales $3,000 to arrange a meeting between Ditto and Carlos Gomez, Aguilera's point man, so they could discuss a business deal. Canales agreed, and in February 1984 he and Gomez hopped a plane in Washington, D.C., and headed to see Ditto. Gomez toured Ditto's entire farm, checking every detail out thoroughly. "This is perfect for the lab, but we'll need to install an exhaust fan to carry away the fumes made by the chemicals," Gomez told Canales.[11]

Gomez did not speak English, so he asked Canales to tell Ditto upfront what the farm was going to be used for. "No problem," said Ditto, and he agreed to do the work that had to be done to install the fan and convert the outbuildings into a cocaine-processing lab. Aguilera paid $110,000 in cash for the property, no questions asked. Two to three weeks later, Carlos drove to Allentown, Pennsylvania, to pick up the acetone for the lab.

In the summer, Gomez, his mistress Evelyn Dubon, and Fargas, who acted as the interpreter for the group's non-English-speaking members, journeyed to Gibsonville to set up the lab and do a trial run. They were joined by two other Americans: John Wesley Martin, a handyman who was hired to make improvements to the barn and outbuildings, and Thomas Warren Hall, Ditto's brother-in-law, who had brought in seven keys of cocaine paste from Miami for processing. The lab was not sophisticated, but it could get the job done. Later, Karasiewski told a court that an elaborate lab isn't needed to manufacture cocaine. "It's similar to, maybe, baking a cake," was how the forensic chemist described the process.[12]

Once the farm was readied, the lab was set to go. Workers wrapped the processed cocaine in plastic bags and carried it to a U-haul trailer, where it was hidden behind a wooden panel. The cocaine was then moved to New York City and sold for $6,000 a kilo. The amount of cocaine processed and sold was small, but the cartel knew the lab concept could work. They had caught the cops asleep. In no time they would be flooding New York with thousands of kilos of snow. By January 1985, a larger team of at least fifteen workers from Colombia and the United States were working at the Gibsonville lab and manufacturing 200 kilos of cocaine paste that was sold in the Big Apple.[13]

The Cali cartel was now convinced the project should go big-time, and Freddie Aguilera began looking for a location closer to New York City. Why not near his sister, Consuela Donovan, who lived with her American husband, Thomas, in Amsterdam, New York? Aguilera recruited Thomas Donovan, and he arranged a meeting with Carlos Gomez, and a local real estate agent to look at farms in the area around Amsterdam. Shortly afterward, Gomez settled on a 220-acre farm and gave $2,000 to Dubon, instructing her to make the deal. Before the closing, Aguilera gave Gomez an additional $110,000 in cash to pay off the property. Thomas Warren Hall would act as the frontman, and the cartel officially registered the farm in his name. Hall was a U.S. citizen and his ownership of the property would raise little suspicion. Besides, the arrangement would also help shield Aguilera from potential evidence against him should the operation be exposed. He planned to use the farm to raise horses, Hall told his neighbors.[14]

The Hauber family, who lived on Staten Island, owned the farm and had used it as a summer home, but they were ready to sell it. Fred Hauber met with Evelyn Dubon, who claimed to be an exile from Nicaragua, and Thomas Warren Hall, who posed as her infirm gringo uncle from North Carolina. The transaction took place in the second-floor office of an Amsterdam lawyer. The meeting went smoothly until it came time for Dubon to make the payment. She pulled out $110,000 from a cheap-looking airline travel bag and stacked the small denomination bills on the lawyer's desk. Not the brightest of ideas. "At that point everything went out of the window because it was definitely out of the ordinary for that area," Hauber later explained.

Hauber hesitated and then refused to leave with the cash, fearing he might be robbed by the group or somebody working for it as he left the office. "Relax," Dubon said. "I'll deposit the money in an Amsterdam bank and write you [Hauber] a cashier's check."[15]

The cartel could not have settled on a better place to run a clandestine and illicit operation involving many Hispanic workers, almost all of whom did not speak English. The Minden locals kept to themselves, minded their own business, and did not normally contact authorities if something suspicious happened.

"I know it's kind of unusual to have people who looked Hispanic and did not speak English to show up in a small town like Minden," said Pat Hynes, a NYSP officer, who investigated the Minden lab. "The strangers from the farm would show up at the local hardware store and nobody paid them any attention. So yes, it was a perfect place for a cocaine-processing lab."[16]

After the closing in December 1984, the drug traffickers rented a big Ryder truck in Burlington, North Carolina. They loaded it with the chemicals, instruments, equipment, cooking racks, and some processed cocaine and took it to Minden. They built a shed to store the chemicals and a double-wide trailer to house the workers, and they also brought 230 fifty-five-gallon drums of ether, acetone, and other highly hazardous precursor chemicals used in cocaine manufacturing.[17] Aguilera directed his workers to buy the building supplies needed to convert the farm into a lab. He called Bralda International and World Consultants Documentation, the storage company in New York City, where the organization stored the cocaine base and huge barrels of precursor chemicals. The gang outfitted a white 1985 Chevy van with false paneling and began transporting the materials and supplies from the storage companies to the Minden farm.[18]

One day Aguilera called a meeting at the New York City apartment of his mistress, Elizabeth "Nena" Andrade-Londono, and told his associates that the police had followed him on the highway on one of his trips to Minden hauling cocaine base. He was lucky not to get caught, Aguilera told the gathering. In the future, they would have to be careful what they said and where they said it, he warned. Aguilera instructed them to always use pay phones; the cops could be tapping the lines.[19]

On April 1, 1985, the Minden lab was ready. For nine days Aguilera and his associates processed about 1,539 kilograms of cocaine, which, in 1985 value, was worth more than 100 million dollars before being cut or otherwise diluted for street sales. DEA chemists later determined that enough chemicals remained at Minden to produce 5,000 kilograms without restocking.[20]

The Cali cartel believed it had hit the drug traffickers' pot of gold. It could be months, or even years, if ever, before law enforcement would be on to them. But they never factored in bad luck. On its tenth day of operation, an electrical short sparked a fire. The workers frantically tried to put it out, but the extinguishers failed to operate. In a panic they fled on foot into the countryside. When the fire spread to some of the precursor chemicals, the lab exploded. Luckily, only a small portion of the 230 fifty-five-gallon drums were in the lab at any one time. Most of the chemicals were stored in a nearby shed, which the firemen managed to reach just ahead of the flames.[21] "It could have been a disaster," said Craig A. Benedict, assistant U.S. attorney general for the Northern District of New York. "The chemicals at the lab had the explosive power of 63,000 sticks of dynamite. Had they exploded, the workers, firemen, and anybody else in the area would have died."[22]

The police picked up three of the workers trying to flag down passing motorists for a ride. All had cocaine residue on their clothing. Gomez fled on foot to Aguilera's sister's house, and from there, he drove to his apartment in Queens, New York. Aguilera had left minutes before the fire to call his bosses in Cali and report on how well the lab was doing. Returning to the farm, he spotted the fire and immediately headed for the big city.[23]

A fire, an explosion, and cops crawling around their former cocaine lab was not going to deter the Cali cartel. Go ahead and find a good place for another lab, Santacruz instructed Aguilera. The lieutenant gathered the remnants of his Minden team and met in Gomez's apartment. He paid off the members and began making plans for another lab. He directed Julio Fargas to find a new farm. Within two-and-a-half weeks of the Minden disaster, Aguilera had bought another site for $160,000 in rural Orange County, Virginia, under the name of an American, Robert Michael Cadiz. As with the Gibsonville and Minden farms, the traffickers made renovations on the Virginia property. This time workers installed sophisticated surveillance cameras at the farm's entrance, as well as putting exhaust fans into the barn's roof to release the ether and acetone fumes. They installed a large metal building to store the 55-gallon chemical drums.[24]

From mid-May to mid-January, the Virginia lab ran smoothly, producing about 3,864 kilos of cocaine, but now the authorities were hot on Aguilera's trail. The traffickers left plenty of evidence behind at Gibsonville and Minden for the authorities to analyze. Investigators found Santacruz Londono's Cali phone number in the records.[25] They had confiscated record books and computer disks containing the names and addresses of dealers and customers and revealing how the product was being distributed. Evidence at Minden led authorities to Gibsonville. In analyzing the evidence found at the two places, the authorities were able to deduce that another lab was being built somewhere in Orange County, Virginia.[26]

The DEA and the NYSP tipped off police in Orange County, telling them to look for Colombian individuals who had bought a farm in their county between the time period of May and early June 1985, probably in the name of an American. Local police investigated and quickly discovered that a farm fitting the profile had been sold on May 22. They checked out court records to determine who had bought the property and flew over the property to take photographs. They found changes had been made to the property. It looked as if the new property owners had installed two air vents on the roof of the large metal shed.

The police set up surveillance from a fire tower close to the farm and began using binoculars and thirty- and sixty-power spottoscopes to observe activity on and about the farmhouse and metal shed. One day, they spotted workers taking boxes out of the shed and putting them in the back of a pickup truck.

The police had seen enough. On July 1, they obtained a search warrant and the next morning raided the farm. A Virginia state police armored vehicle sped up to the farmhouse, policemen jumped out, and everyone in the house was ordered to get out. When only three people obeyed the order, police used tear gas to force out three others. The police later learned that one person escaped. Inside, police found a computer; telephone; typing equipment; weapons, including a shot gun, an MM-1 rifle, a

.9mm pistol, and a 25 automatic pistol; and a telescope pointed in the direction of the farm's front entrance. In the shed they discovered eighty-six barrels of ether and acetone, more than fifty-five pounds of cocaine base, and a small amount of processed cocaine. Police later learned that, shortly before the raid, the most recent batch of processed cocaine, about 1,000 pounds, had been delivered to Aguilera.[27]

As the investigation continued, the authorities discovered other processing labs. Two days later, they arrested ten Colombian nationals in clandestine cocaine labs in New York State and Virginia: a forty-seven-acre tract at 6805 Sound Avenue in Baiting Hollow, Long Island; a sixty-six-acre site in Fly Creek, New York, located about ninety miles west of Albany; and another property in Gordonsville, Virginia. The labs all fit the same pattern, and the authorities seized another pile of records, 147 pounds of cocaine, 100 pounds of cocaine base, more than 5,000 gallons of chemicals, and the sophisticated equipment criminals use to monitor DEA and police activities. All ten suspects were charged with conspiracy to import and sell cocaine and faced a maximum of fifteen years in prison.[28]

Authorities continued to search for Aguilera and Gomez. Ten months later, DEA agents spotted Carlos Gomez and Evelyn Dubon during surveillance in the Whitestone area of Queens. Using a search warrant, they arrested the two in their home at 1905 Clintonville Street. Inside the house, they found thirty-three pounds of cocaine (which the police later gave a street value of $20,250,000), a wing-master shotgun, equipment for making bricks of cocaine, a machine gun threaded with a silencer, a short-barrel shotgun labeled "law enforcement use only," a New York City police lieutenant's badge, and fake passports and driver's licenses.[29]

In January 1987, Gomez and Dubon pleaded guilty in the Eastern District of New York to distributing and manufacturing narcotics. The following May, Gomez pleaded guilty to the same charge in the Middle District Court of the Eastern District of New York. Freddie Aguilera, the Colombian mastermind of the biggest cocaine-manufacturing lab operation ever uncovered in the United States, fled and became a fugitive.

In busting the labs and keeping thousands of kilos of cocaine off the streets, U.S. law enforcement had won a victory in the War on Drugs. Aguilera and Gomez, however, were two small, irreplaceable parts of a well-oiled criminal enterprise. Jose Santacruz, the mastermind of the labs, would find new foot soldiers and new ways to get his product to the streets of America. Meanwhile, law enforcement had another unsettling glimpse of the enemy that authorities were now calling the Cali cartel. By now, many of the veteran investigators tracking the cartel had concluded it was unlike any criminal organization they had investigated: it combined the best management and marketing strategies of multinational corporations with a mafia's ruthlessness and a terrorist organization's secrecy and compartmentalization.

"Minden reinforced our belief that cocaine was overrunning New York State," said Tom Constantine, who served as director of the NYSP from 1985 to 1992 and later as DEA administrator from 1994 to 1997. "The Cali cartel was running their operation like a legitimate business – getting as close to the market as possible. We stepped up our efforts to go after the cartel."[30]

"The labs opened everybody's eyes," said Bill Mante, a former NYSP investigator who worked on the post-Minden investigation. "Here they were right on top of us," Mante recalled. "The balls. We felt the Cali cartel had a good ten-year start on us. We saw a huge potential for disaster if we didn't hit them hard and aggressively."[31]

During the next decade, law enforcement would use everything in its arsenal to take down this powerful and enterprising mafia. Indeed, the Cali cartel would prove to be the most formidable adversary in the history of international drug trafficking.

Part II

The Rise

_____

Chapter 1

Getting Started

Maybe, people confuse coca with my dealings with Iaccoca.
  – Gilberto Rodriguez, co-founder of the Cali cartel

No one working in U.S. law enforcement in 1975 could have imagined that within a decade Colombian drug traffickers would be setting up processing labs in the heart of the United States and using them to move thousand-pound-plus shipments of cocaine. The scale of the cocaine trade in the mid-1970s is well illustrated in a secret report that the intelligence division of the then-recently formed Drug Enforcement Administration (DEA) prepared in 1975.[1] The report made reference to Operation Banshee, a combined DEA and New York City Police Department investigation into a Colombian coke-trafficking organization based in the city of Medellin and headed by Alberto Bravo and Griselda Blanco. This gang, the report noted, was distributing about 250 kilograms of coke per month in the New York City area.[2] That amount would pale in comparison to the multi-ton shipments hidden in flowers, lumber, concrete fence posts, and by other sophisticated means that became the Cali cartel's smuggling *modus operandi* less than a decade later.

The cocaine kingpins of the mid-1970s relied not on ships, boats and trucks but on "mules" – individuals who carried drugs into the United States in hollowed-out platform shoes, double-bottomed suitcases, stuffed animals or various containers. The cocaine was hermetically sealed in plastic bags and normally packed in half-kilogram units. The mules were usually

Colombians recruited while applying for visas to enter the United States. Some of the future drug barons, such as Pablo Escobar and Jose Santacruz, are believed to have started in the trade as mules.[3] The few petty smugglers the U.S. authorities caught were merely deported to Colombia, where they were seldom prosecuted.[4]

In the mid-1970s, Colombia was making marijuana, not cocaine, a thriving international criminal enterprise. The DEA launched Operation Buccaneer in 1974 to eradicate the indigenous marijuana crop in Jamaica, so the local traffickers simply shifted operations to Colombia's north coast and its Guajira Peninsula. Meanwhile, a paraquat-spraying program in Mexico led U.S. consumers to shun Mexican weed, and that country's drug traffickers moved to Colombia too.[5] By 1979, the South American state supplied seventy-five percent of the marijuana coming into the US, while Mexico's share of the same market fell from seventy percent in 1975 to less than thirty percent five years later.[6]

Heroin, not marijuana or cocaine, was the main illegal drug on the DEA's radar screen in the mid-1970s. As Robert Nieves, a DEA agent who began working for the agency in 1969, explained, "Heroin was considered the dangerous drug, and the statistics suggested that its use was rising. Sure, some people used cocaine, but it was just beginning to become part of the mainstream. There wasn't a huge market for the drug back then."[7]

Heroin use among GIs in Vietnam became a serious problem in the late 1960s, and those who survived the war brought their drug habit home with them. Heroin abuse began to spread from inner-city ghettos to middle-class suburbs, exacerbating public concern.[8] Between 1960 and 1970, the number of users rose from 50,000 to approximately half a million.[9] By 1973 the figure had jumped to 800,000, according to the US Household Survey.[10] Yet signs indicated that the epidemic was beginning to subside. In the fall of 1973, President Richard Nixon proclaimed that the country had "turned a corner on drug abuse," and announced that, after a period of increasing rates of heroin addiction, the statistics were showing a decline.[11]

Still, the DEA remained focused on heroin. "In those days, we were less adept at identifying a change in drug trafficking patterns than we are today," recalled Michael Kane, a former DEA agent assigned in the early 1970s to investigate the legendary French Connection. "It took us some time to see that cocaine use had become a trend."[12] Mark Eiler, an analyst in the DEA's Intelligence Division, said that law enforcement agencies, like all bureaucracies, tend to move slowly. "By the time we identify a pattern, the traffickers have already reacted," Eiler said. "They will always be one step ahead of us."[13]

Times were indeed changing, and the DEA was missing the beat on a major social trend unfolding in America. By the mid-1970s, cocaine was making a strong comeback as a drug of choice for Americans. This changing attitude reflected the drug's history. Cocaine is a powerful stimulant contained in the leaves of the coca shrub, a plant grown primarily in the South American countries of Peru, Bolivia and Colombia. Archeologists have found coca leaves in Peruvian grave sites dating from approximately 500 A.D., along with other important items deemed necessary for the afterlife. Cocaine was first extracted from coca leaves in 1855, and by the late nineteenth century, had become a "wonder drug" used in treating a number of ailments, including asthma, digestive disorders and morphine addiction. It also became the active ingredient in a popular new drink called Coca-Cola.[14]

Enthusiasm for the "wonder drug" waned in the early twentieth century, as evidence suggested that it could be addictive, and it went underground when the 1914 Harrison Act restricted its use. For the next few decades, cocaine was largely the drug of the jazz and Hollywood scenes, and because of its high cost, it became known as "the champagne of drugs." The so-called psychedelic revolution of the 1960s revived interest in drugs of all kinds and people began to view coke as a relatively safe high.[15] Popular culture began to embrace it and that boosted its image. In the early 1970s, rock-and-roll groups such as the Eagles, the Rolling Stones and the Grateful Dead all made subtle references to cocaine in their hit songs.[16]

During this period, US law enforcement became adept at displacing major heroin-trafficking routes, a development that contributed to cocaine's use and growing popularity. After World War II, a number of major French and Corsican drug traffickers associated with the famous French Connection fled France to escape punishment for collaborating with the Nazis during the Occupation. Major traffickers such as August Ricord and his heroin supplier, Joseph Orsini, set up business in South America, where they would be protected by weak narcotic laws and inept, corrupt officials.[17] South Americans joined these organizations as couriers and low-level operatives, but, over time, they rose through the ranks and eventually some of them even established their own heroin networks. By 1970, US law enforcement estimated that up to 35 percent of the heroin produced by the French Connection passed through South America on its way to the United States.[18]

In October 1970, however, Ricord's narcotics empire began to crumble when a heroin bust in New York City led to his indictment in the Southern District of New York. Paraguay, where Ricord was hiding, initially resisted U.S. requests for Ricord's extradition, but after intense pressure, the country yielded and extradited him to the United States in 1972, where he was convicted and sent to jail.[19] In April 1973, Operation Springboard, another major international heroin investigation, led to indict-ments of fourteen major traffickers in the eastern and southern districts of New York for smuggling 5,500 kilos of heroin and cocaine into the United States from 1967 to 1973.[20]

With law enforcement attention riveted on the heroin connection, Colombian cocaine traffickers, based primarily in Cali, Medellin and Bogota, quietly began to transform themselves from nondescript smugglers to the makings of important suppliers. In staking out their turf, however, the Colombians had to muscle out the Cuban mafia. When Fidel Castro came to power in 1959, the entrenched Italian-American Mafia and its local allies had fled the island. Some of the Cuban criminals headed to other parts of Latin America, but many emigrated to the United States and joined a half-million Cuban expatriates, helping to organize a powerful mafia known as La Compania. Not until 1968 did the U.S. Bureau of Narcotics and Dangerous Drugs, the DEA's predecessor, have enough intelligence data to figure out the full extent of the Cuban connection to the South American drug trade.[21] Through the 1960s, the Colombians worked for the Cubans as underlings while learning the business, especially the "cooking" processes for manufacturing cocaine.[22]

The situation changed dramatically in the 1970s, when Colombia became the linchpin of the Latin American drug trade. Many factors contributed to this development. Colombia has a long history of smuggling emeralds and coffee, and the transportation routes it organized for legal products made it well situated to succeed in the drug trade.[23] Colombian attitudes also fostered smuggling. Respectable families made a living bootlegging liquor and cigarettes by sea from the United States and smuggling radios and television sets from duty-free ports in the Colon Free Zone of Panama.[24] As Kevin Jack Riley, a War on Drugs analyst, explained, "Smuggling developed as a natural art in Colombia as a means of evading export duties . . . on most consumer goods."[25]

Medellin in Antioquia province became important in Colombia's emerging cocaine trade after the country's economy nose-dived in the 1970s and the city declined as a textiles center. Asian competition and high tariffs were largely responsible for the textile industry's near-total collapse during the period 1979–1980, according to one DEA intelligence report, and this sparked an economic depression in Colombia that lingered into the 1980s. With their own textile industry in such trouble, thousands of Colombians journeyed to New York City looking for work in the garment industry.[26] Many found employment and led honest lives, but as what became known as the Cali cartel grew in size and power from the mid-1970s through the mid-1990s, members of this expatriate population would help provide cover and support for it, making it a difficult organization for outsiders, especially police, to penetrate.[27]

Developments in Chile also boosted the Colombian connection. Prior to 1973, Chile, not Colombia, was the prime source of the Latin American cocaine trade. It had large numbers of well-equipped cocaine-producing laboratories in place and skilled chemists available to work them. The U.S. government estimated that the cocaine produced in Chile was ninety-eight percent pure, an extremely high level of purity.[28] But in 1973, a military junta led by Augusto Pinochet overthrew the democratically elected government of Salvador Allende in a bloody coup. To improve relations with Uncle Sam, Pinochet launched a campaign against the country's drug traffickers, deporting some twenty-three suspects to the United States.[29] Extradition was illegal in Chile, so the dictator stripped the suspects of their citizenship before putting them on the plane.[30] In 1972, Allende's last complete year in office, Chilean police had seized about one pound of cocaine from dealers. Two years after the coup, Chilean authorities confiscated more than 55 pounds of the drug.[31] The remaining traffickers in Chile got the message and relocated their operations to Colombia.

What became the Cali cartel, the most powerful drug-trafficking mafia in history, has its origins in the late 1960s. The cartel's early history and the biographies of its principal founders – Gilberto and Miguel Rodriguez and Jose Santacruz – are shrouded in mystery, and accounts of their childhoods and family backgrounds conflict and are filled with contradictory details. Some published accounts have the founders coming from middle-class, professionally oriented families; others say they come from more humble backgrounds. Indeed, finding reliable information about the cartel and its leaders became one of the major challenges facing law enforcement during the next three decades.

Santacruz and the Rodriguez brothers were masters of fake identities, especially in the early years, when they carried bogus passports and other fake Colombian documents and traveled under many assumed names as a ploy to confuse investigators. The subterfuge was part of the Cali cartel's brilliant strategy to keep a low profile, portraying themselves as gentlemen and their organization as a gentler, more professional alternative to their violent rival 200 miles to the north in Medellin, led by Pablo Escobar.[32]

In the years ahead, the Cali men would challenge, intimidate – even kill – anyone who attempted to expose this myth. Gilberto Rodriguez, for instance would often get on the phone and leave messages for reporters, chastising them for suggesting that he was involved in the drug trade. Colombian journalist Maria Jimena Duzan, in her memoir *Death Beat*, recalled how Rodriguez once called the newsroom at her newspaper, *El Espectador*, about the publication of an article that described a police raid on his daughter's house. Nothing had been found in the raid, and the police did not charge his daughter with a crime, Rodriguez pointed out. Then he added, "By the way, this violence is really terrible. You and I are both victims of Pablo Escobar. I understand what you are going through because I am in the same situation."[33]

As late as the early 1990s, when the Cali cartel was acknowledged as the leading drug-trafficking mafia in the world, Rodriguez would still coyly play his innocence game with the press. In a rare – indeed extraordinary – interview with *Time* magazine in 1991, the drug lord *par excellence* claimed to be an honest businessman. His only crime, he said, was too much success. He had incurred official displeasure, Rodriguez told *Time*'s reporters, when he was chairman of the board of a bank in Cali and president of the board of directors of a bank in Panama that laundered money. Yes, he owned a Chrysler distributorship in Colombia, but, the godfather joked, in a play on the name of Chrysler's boss, "Maybe people confuse coca with my dealings with [Lee] Iaccoca."[34]

What is certain is that the Rodriguez brothers were natives of Mariquita in the department of Tolima and grew up in the poor Balthazar barrio of Cali. Gilberto was born in 1939 and Miguel in 1943. Gilberto apparently never finished high school. In the 1991 *Time* article, Gilberto provided these details about his background: "I was born between the towns of Mariquita and Honda Tolima. My father was a painter and a draftsman, and my mother was a housewife. We were three brothers [the third was Jorge] and three sisters. When I was fifteen, I started work as a clerk in a drugstore in Cali. By the time I was twenty, I was the manager, and at twenty-five, ten years after entering the business, I quit in order to start my own drugstore."

Rodriguez added that he had seven children, six of whom were professionals and one who was a student. "They all got their degrees at US or European universities; most are now working in our businesses," Rodriguez revealed. In an article in July 1990, *Forbes* magazine reported that Miguel Rodriguez graduated from Colombia's San Buenaventura University, but Colombian investigative journalist Fabio Castillo uncovered proof that Miguel bought that degree.[35] In 1997, Guillermo Pallomari, a Cali Cartel accountant who became an informer for the U.S. government, testified that Miguel Rodriguez had bought a law degree with honors from the University de Santiago de Chile, and in return had donated a library to the university. Rodriguez had also bought personal items for Gonzalo Paz, the dean of the university.[36]

One newspaper reported that Gilberto began working for a drugstore at age thirteen, delivering legal drugs to customers. Younger brother Miguel also worked in a drugstore as a youngster.[37] A decade later, Gilberto would become famous in Colombia as the owner of a chain of drugstores known as *Drogas La Rebaja*. The Rodriguez brothers reportedly began their life of crime as teenagers, and quite early in life they exhibited the leadership qualities that would carry them to the top of the criminal world; not least, it seems, a propensity for violence. According to Castillo, "They commanded the respect of like gangs because they were highly dangerous individuals."[38] Castillo reports how Gilberto and brother Miguel were arrested for counterfeiting money, but the female judge who was to try the case received death threats and let the statute of limitations on the trial run out.[39]

The background details of Jose Santacruz Londono are spotty as well. According to one confidential DEA informant, Santacruz, who was born in 1943, went to high school with the Rodriguezes and became boyhood friends with them.[40] On October 30, 1969, the Bogota-based newspaper *El Espectador* published a biography of Santacruz in which his wife told the reporter that he was the father of one girl and had recently completed four years of engineering at De Valle University of the Andes in Bogota. They lived in Bogota in an apartment building in the Quinta Paredes district, she said. The article revealed that Santacruz had been implicated in the kidnappings of a university student and an industrialist in Bogota and had recently bought three taxis in Bogota for 192,000 pesos in cash.[41] The newspaper made no connection between the kidnappings and the fleet of taxis, but readers must have wondered how an engineering student could afford a taxi fleet.

The three men who would found the Cali cartel were involved in the kidnapping of a fisherman when they were teenagers, according to one source who knew them during the time, but managed to avoid conviction, although Gilberto did spend one day in jail.[42] By 1969 they had become part of a kidnapping organization know as *Las Chemas*, run by a veteran criminal called Luis Fernando Tamayo Garcia. The gang was implicated in the successful kidnapping of two Swiss citizens: diplomat Herman Buff and student Werner Jose Straessle. A June 9, 1995 article in *El Tiempo* newspaper reported that Gilberto was twenty-eight at the time of the kidnapping, and leader of the seven gang members involved in the crime.[43] The three Cali cartel founders reportedly used the twelve million pesos (about $700,000) they were paid for their hostages as seed money to bankroll their entry into the world of drug trafficking.[44]

Law enforcement officials familiar with the mob's history say it is remarkable that for more than thirty years the Rodriguez brothers and Santacruz were able to remain close friends and allies and maintain a relationship not normally found in the cutthroat world of crime. "In all my years of studying the Cali cartel, I never knew the Rodriguez brothers or Santacruz to have any serious disagreement," said Sandy Hill, a DEA intelligence analyst. "They all seemed to know their role and were focused on making money."[45]

Ed Kacerosky, a customs agent who worked on the watershed Operation Cornerstone investigation in the early 1990s (see Chapter Ten), agrees that money was the motivation for their close relationship, but added that the cartel's board of directors banded close together for another important reason: survival. "They realized they had to stick together because the Medellin cartel was out to destroy them," Kacerosky said.[46]

When Helmer "Pacho" Herrera became one of the cartel's key players, Santacruz and the Rodriguez brothers seemed to accept Pacho's homosexuality. "It was very strange," recalled one DEA agent. "From the accounts I heard they tolerated Pacho. They would giggle among themselves about his homosexual behavior, but Pacho would go off and do his thing and business was business."[47]

Interestingly, reports suggest that all three founders had guerrilla sympathies, at least early in their life. One source told British journalist Simon Strong that the three were "friends of the founders of the *ELN* (National Liberation Army), so much so that they took part in the 1969 kidnapping of the two Swiss men to finance the *ELN*."[48] The *ELN* was one of several armed Marxist groups dedicated to the overthrow of the Government; others included *FARC* (the Revolutionary Armed Forces of Colombia) and M-19.

Each of the Cali cartel founders had his own style, which helped them to build their criminal organization. Gilberto, short, goateed and overweight, looked innocuous enough, but he became known as the "Chess Player" for his ruthless and calculating approach to the drug business. In the beginning, the Chess Player would be a hands-on manager, but he eventually stepped back and became responsible for the organization's strategic planning.[49] The handsome but cold-eyed Miguel, his younger brother, was a mircromanager who liked to be involved in the smallest details of the cartel's day-to-day operations and was, by all accounts, a difficult boss to work for. "The people who worked for the Cali cartel looked on Gilberto as being like a kindly uncle," recalled Ruben Prieto, a DEA agent who investigated the mob. "They liked him. On the other hand they were scared to death of Miguel."[50]

Jose Santacruz was stocky, rugged-looking and low key. Known as "Chepe" to his associates and pursuers, he was the most violent of three founders. He was also known as *"El Gordo"* – the fat man – for his love of food. Chepe became invaluable as coordinator of the cartel's international cocaine transportation network. The DEA published a "most wanted" photo of him in the early 1980s, when he was a fugitive. He wore a beard and looked like a dead ringer for Franco Harris, the great Pittsburgh Steelers running back of the 1970s.

Pacho Herrera, who would rise to become number four in the hierarchy, returned to Cali from the U.S. in 1983 after a short prison term and negotiated an arrangement with the cartel founders over supply and distribution rights, which allowed him to build a base in New York City. Herrera was later made a member of the cartel's board of directors, and proved invaluable to the mafia by using his contacts to help open up Mexico for their powders.[51]

The Chess Player, Miguel and Chepe moved into the drug trade as opportunities opened up in the early 1970s. The leading Colombian trafficker of this period was Benjamin Herrera Zuleta, known as the "Black Pope of Cocaine," who had set up a cocaine distribution network based in Cali. In June 1975, he was captured smuggling a huge shipment. Released in March 1976, the Black Pope settled quietly in the Antioquia Department in central Colombia, but by then he had pioneered trafficking routes into the United States that the young, ambitious traffickers of Cali would use.[52]

The cartel founders at first dabbled in marijuana smuggling, but soon saw the huge profits to be made from cocaine.[53] Marijuana, after all, involved a lot of risk, since one had to ship large volumes of the product to earn big profits. On the other hand, cocaine could be bought for $15,000 a kilo in Colombia and sold on the streets of the United States for as much as $50,000 a kilo in the mid-1970s. Moreover, you did not need big ships or planes to do it.[54]

Using the seed money they had made from kidnapping, together with some of their drug profits, the Cali founders bought a small light plane, which they used to ship larger amounts of coca back to the Valle del Cauca, the province of which Cali is capital city. But with little experience in the trade, they quickly ran afoul of the law. In November 1975, Gilberto was captured in Peru with 180 kilos of coca paste aboard a light plane. Released a short time later, he was arrested again in 1977, this time in New York, where he had come to look over the market.[55]

The other partners also had their run-ins with the law as they worked to build their criminal empire. Records indicate that Santacruz was arrested twice during the 1970s, the first time in 1976 while traveling from New York City to Costa Rica and the second in 1977 on a weapons charge in Queens, New York.[56] Pacho Herrera, who started his criminal career smuggling relatively small amounts of cocaine into New York City, was arrested in 1975 and 1979, according to DEA reports.[57]

On September 10, 1975, the Colombian Customs Agency filed this brief report on the state of drug trafficking in Colombia:

Valle del Cauca:
    58 – Rodriguez Orejuela, Gilberto, drug trafficker. Address:
    No. 44E-27 4th Avenue, Cali.
    62 – Rodriguez Orejuela, Miguel, drug trafficker.

Gilberto and Miguel were fifty-eighth and sixty-second on a list of the 113 top drug traffickers in the country. They were certainly moving up in the criminal world.[58]

Gilberto emerged as the gang's early leader, and according to Castillo's investigation, sent his boyhood friend Hernando Giraldo Soto to the United States to make contact. Giraldo Soto ran the organization's operation out of New York City for three years, and during the period from March through October 1978 made at least $2.6 million in drug deals. When law enforcement busted the point man, Gilberto replaced him with another close associate: Jose Santacruz.[59]

As the 1970s progressed, the Cali cartel strengthened and refined its network, became better organized, and began using its family and criminal contacts and the Colombian émigré community in the United States to further its criminal enterprise. Meanwhile, its high-profile competitor, the Medellin cartel, was using gratuitous brutality to eliminate rivals and carve a market niche in Miami and South Florida. By the late 1970s, South Florida was overrun with cocaine and violent crime. In 1978, the US Customs Service seized 729 pounds of cocaine in South Florida, up from 109 pounds in 1970. During the same period, cocaine seizures at Miami Airport jumped from thirty-seven pounds to more than 271. By 1979, illegal drugs had become the state's biggest industry, worth an estimated $10 billion annually. "There is so much money in South Florida that they weigh it instead of counting it," lamented Peter Bensinger, DEA administrator.[60]

One infamous incident known as the Dadeland Massacre gave a startling glimpse of the future of the drug trade in the United States. In 1979, two hitmen entered a liquor store in the Dadeland Mall, Florida's biggest shopping center, and shot two people dead. The hitmen then chased through the mall two clerks from the liquor store, who were witnesses to the killings, as shoppers shrieked in terror. The employees were wounded and the hitmen escaped. Investigators later identified Griselda Blanco, a female drug trafficker from Medellin, as the mastermind of the hit. The two dead people in the liquor store were competitors to whom she owed a lot of money.[61]

The emerging Cali cartel, meanwhile, went quietly about its business creating a market for cocaine in New York City. At the time the city was known as the heroin capital of the United States, and the Cali men had a big jump on law enforcement, whose attention was elsewhere. It was years before the good guys discovered the cartel's presence. "They were big before we knew it," said Rich Crawford, a former DEA agent who investigated the cartel in the late 1970s and 1980s. "It took a long time before we were able to convince the higher ups [in the DEA] that a growing, sophisticated drug trafficking group from Cali, Colombia, was operating in our city right under our noses."[62]

Chapter 2

New York, New York

No one had ever seen forty-four pounds of cocaine in New York City before.

— Ken Robinson, DEA agent

The DEA didn't have a clue about Chepe Santacruz's activities in New York City in the mid-1970s. Once it learned of them, however, the investigation of the Cali cartel would become the longest running in the agency's history. In the summer of 1978, the DEA's New York City branch office received a letter from a citizen's committee representing the Jackson Heights neighborhood in the borough of Queens. "I'm concerned about the violence in our district and the crime wave the cocaine traffic is causing," the letter read. "The DEA is the government agency responsible for investigating drugs. You need to do something about it."[1]

As heroin was the DEA's focus at the time, the letter didn't cause a ripple. The agency, in fact, had yet to do a major cocaine trafficking investigation. "The DEA didn't want to mess with cocaine," recalled Ken Robinson, who was then a member of the New York Drug Enforcement Task Force (NYDETF). "The agency thought the drug was small time, so they turned the matter over to the NYDETF for investigation."[2]

The NYDETF was established in 1970 as a way of better coordinating drug investigations among government and law enforcement agencies. The Bureau of Narcotics and Dangerous Drugs (the DEA's predecessor), the New York State Police, and the New York City Police each contributed to the Task Force, which worked closely with Department of Justice lawyers and support staff. The NYDETF started off with forty-three members; one year later, it had 172.[3]

The NYDETF was split into divisions, with each division consisting of groups. Group Five, which, along with Groups Four and Six made up one division, was given responsibility for investigating the complaint from the Jackson Heights residents. Bill Mockler supervised Group Five's seven members, which included Ken Robinson, a streetwise New York City police detective, and Rich Crawford, a young DEA agent and former Vietnam veteran.[4]

Prosecutors for the Eastern District of New York handled most of the Task Force's cases, but according to former New York prosecutor Jessica de Grazia, they shied away from what they considered to be "kiddie dope" cases, even when a suspect was charged with possessing a kilo of cocaine.[5] The DEA's lack of interest reflected the attitude of the government at all levels toward cocaine at the time. A drug abuse task force established by President Gerald Ford in September 1975 issued a report concluding that it was not a problem. "Cocaine," the report declared, "is not physically addictive . . . and usually does not result in serious social consequences, such as crime, hospital emergency room admissions, or both." The task force recommended that law enforcement focus on drugs such as heroin, amphetamines, and mixed barbiturates, which posed more risk. [6]

Official statistics painted a different picture. By 1974, 5.4 million Americans had acknowledged that they tried using the drug at least once. While law enforcement continued to focus on heroin in the late 1970s, the statistics documenting cocaine use shot up; by 1979, according to one estimate, at least twenty percent of Americans had used cocaine in the past year and 7.3 percent had used it during the previous month.[7]

When President Jimmy Carter took office in 1976, his administration also didn't view cocaine use and abuse seriously. "Cocaine . . . is the most benign of illicit drugs currently in widespread use," wrote Dr. Peter Bourne, drug advisor to President Carter and his special assistant for health issues. "Short acting, not physically addicting and acutely pleasurable, cocaine has found increasing favor at all socio-economic levels."[8]

The government's benign attitude set the tone. "When the public heard government officials like Bourne downplay cocaine, they thought, 'Hey, cocaine is a recreational drug. I have nothing to worry about,'" said Michael Kuhlman, a DEA agent who joined the agency in 1970.[9]

From what he had seen on the street, Ken Robinson concluded there couldn't be much of a cocaine problem in Jackson Heights either. For two years prior to joining NYDETF, Robinson had worked in Brooklyn, and he remembered how the cocaine arrived in the Brooklyn Harbor aboard a shipping line, the Grancolombiana. The cocaine would be thrown overboard and picked up by swimmers, Colombians, who brought it ashore and sold it in the bars of Jackson Heights. That's not the kind of distribution network that can cause a huge problem, Robinson figured.[10]

A few weeks passed and nothing much happened with Group Five and its cocaine investigation. Then, in September, a Colombian walked unannounced into the NYDETF office with some important information. What he told the Task Force would make him one of the most important confidential informants (CIs) in New York City history. He described a big cocaine ring from Colombia that was operating in Queens but had a distribution network in other parts of the country. The ring, the CI elaborated, was well organized and had an unlimited supply. They used beepers to communicate as they moved the drugs.[11]

Robinson was skeptical. He had listened before to CIs who came to the Task Force and spun tall tales. There was no way to corroborate his story. Besides, if the ring was so big, how come the Task Force had not heard about it? "Let us know when something is happening," Robinson told the CI.[12]

A few days later, the CI called again with an urgent message: A drug deal was going down at 5:30 P.M. that afternoon on Queens Boulevard in Jackson Heights. The informant even described the customer: a Colombian, 6'3", 170 pounds, black hair, mustache, and wearing sunglasses. And, oh yes, the CI added, the dealer would drive a red Chevrolet and the customer would drive a white car.[13]

Robinson rounded up three other Task Force investigators and headed for Queens. It was rush hour; the traffic was heavy, but the investigators made it to Queens Boulevard a few minutes before the deal was supposed to go down. Yes, a man fitting the CI's description pulled up in a red Chevy Impala close to where the investigators were parked. Then the white car pulled up about 100 yards away. A man stepped out of the white car with a leather jacket slung over his arm and looked around nervously. He fit the description for the customer that the CI gave. It's a warm sunny day, so why is he carrying a jacket? Robinson wondered.

The man passed Robinson's car, walked over to the driver side of the white car, took a package from inside and stuck it in his jacket. He looked around and walked quickly back toward Robinson's car. The investigators stepped out of their cars and walked slowly toward the man, hoping they wouldn't have to chase him. But he realized they were cops. Turning around quickly, the suspect bolted in the opposite direction. The agents gave chase and caught him. They opened the man's jacket and found a brown paper bag with a one-kilo brick of cocaine bound tight with masking tape. They arrested the man, whose name was Nelson Gomez, and hauled him back to the Task Force office for questioning. Meanwhile, the dealer in the red Impala fled.

The CI called again and told Robinson that the dealer had ditched his Impala. "Don't look for it," the CI advised. "You'll never find it." The dealer had escaped, but Robinson had alertly taken down the Impala's license number during the stakeout. A check of the state motor vehicle records revealed that the car's owner lived on Long Island. Robinson went to the address, but found it to be bogus. In the coming months, Group Five learned that much of what they uncovered during the course of the investigation – names, license plates, addresses – would be bogus.

Robinson was a tenacious cop, who loved the hunt as much as the catch. He never gave up on a case so long as he had a lead. In describing Robinson's relentless pursuit of criminals, one DEA agent who worked with Robinson said, "I'd hate to be a criminal and have Kenny after me." He checked the records at the Parking

Violations Bureau in Manhattan to see if any summonses had been issued for the vehicle. Sure enough, there were over fifty parking violations. Robinson began to check out the places where the Chevy had been parked.

Robinson couldn't find the red Chevy, but a blue Buick parked in one of the spots where the red Chevy had been ticketed caught his attention. It, too, was parked illegally, and a stack of tickets was tucked under one of the windshield wipers. Robinson looked around. Across the street was a six-storey brick building. He had a hunch and walked over to see the building superintendent.

When the superintendent came to the door, Robinson showed him his identification. Using his Irish charm, he smiled and asked in a casual manner, "Would you know who owns that blue Buick on the street?"

"Sure do," said the superintendent. "A couple of Colombians. They keep another car in the basement."

Robinson followed up. "What kind is it?"

"A red Chevy," the super said.

"Do you mind if we take a look at it?" asked Robinson the adrenalin starting to pump.

The car was a red Chevy all right, but something didn't fit. The license plate on the Chevy in the garage belonged to the Buick in front of the building. Robinson looked at the Chevy's VIN, the unique identification number affixed to the dashboard, and got on the phone. He found out that the blue Buick was associated with the license of the red Chevy that had delivered the cocaine on September 28.

Robinson ran checks on the license plates of the blue car on the street and the red Chevy in the garage. Bingo! It all fit now. The Chevy's plates were registered to the blue Buick in the street, and the Buick's plates belonged to a third, unknown car. The red Chevy had not been abandoned as the CI had said. Rather, the driver had gotten rid of its plates and replaced them with the Buick plates.

The investigation began in earnest. For several months, Group Five conducted round-the-clock surveillance on the red Chevy and blue Buick. Robinson began to spend much of his time in Queens, and he could see the cocaine problem that the Jackson

Heights citizen's committee had written about. Dealers prowled the streets, and showed no fear of being busted. Indeed, many sold cocaine directly from their cars.

Despite the problem, the Task Force's brass was still unwilling to allocate resources to the case, and the investigators had to work on it on their own time. They didn't complain because they felt they were on to something big. Finally the long hours and chilly nights spent on stakeout began to pay off. In October, Group Five seized six pounds of cocaine and some financial ledgers. The investigators had their first inkling of the size of the trafficking organization they were up against. It was pulling in at least a million dollars a month. The investigators were stunned. Criminals made that kind of money trafficking heroin, not cocaine.

Group Five continued its surveillance. In January 1979 they identified a man named Jose Patino as a major player in the organization, and tailed him out to John F. Kennedy International Airport. There, he met a stocky man with thick black hair and flaky patches of skin on his face, who had arrived on a flight from Colombia. The well-dressed man left the airport and the detectives stopped him in the parking lot. He produced a passport. His name was Jose Santacruz Londono. The detectives let him go.

The investigators followed the two men to a penthouse apartment in Queens and staked it out for several days. They tailed Patino and his associate to the airport in Farmingdale, Long Island, where Santacruz took a private plane to Philadelphia.

In July Robinson identified one of the apartments Patino was using on Union Street in Flushing, Queens. He befriended the superintendent, an Eastern European immigrant, who let him use the empty apartment facing Patino's for surveillance. The blinds on the apartment's windows were shuttered noon and night and Patino never appeared. Robinson continued to stake out the place, but he had other work to do. He left his card with the superintendent and asked him to call if Patino showed.

One day, Robinson's phone rang. "The man you're looking for is in the apartment right now," said the superintendent. Robinson and Mockler rushed over to Patino's place and stopped him as he was leaving the apartment. The two investigators showed Patino their badges and asked for his identification. "What you got in the bag?" Robinson asked. The bag was black leather and slung over Patino's shoulder.

"Could we search your apartment?" Mockler asked. Incredibly, Patino shrugged his shoulders to indicate, why not? Ignorant of his First Amendment rights, Patino didn't even ask if the investigators had a search warrant. Inside the apartment, the detectives opened the bag. "What's this electric money counter for?" They pulled out a bunch of rubber bands. "Why are there so many of them? What are you going to use them for?"

The phone rang. When they picked it up, they heard a loud, excited voice speaking in Spanish. "Pepe, what's happening? Call me! Call me!" A call-back number appeared on the screen, but the two detectives already had enough to do without trying to trace the call. Robinson figured that the guy who called was expecting Patino to bring him the money-counting machine.

They found a series of rent receipts for a number of apartments. Mockler and Robinson took Patino first to an apartment on Roosevelt Avenue and 82nd Street. When they entered the lobby, Patino began sweating and turned pale. The detectives woke up the superintendent. When Patino saw him, he blurted: "This is where I live, right? Tell them this is where I live." The verbal barrage confused and frightened the super, but he whispered to one of the agents, "No, he doesn't."

The detectives showed the super a photo. "Yeah, that's Victor Crespo," he confirmed. "I've seen him and the guy you're with together. They sure keep strange hours, but they don't cause any problems." The super directed the two detectives to the ground floor apartment, where they found a fake passport in the name of Victor Crespo and discovered he had been receiving mail there. Group Five had hit a home run.

When investigators got to the apartment on Burns Court, they had to kick down the door. The sickly smell of cocaine in the apartment almost knocked them out. The windows were barred and the agents couldn't open them. Some of them left the apartment to get some air. The rugs were infested with coke and the bathtub was crammed with kilo packages of white powder.

The occupants had fled, but the investigators hit another home run. They found forty-four pounds of cocaine in a huge safe, machine guns, thousands of rounds of ammunition, bulletproof vests, drivers' licenses, business cards, an aircraft registration, an automobile registration, coded customer lists, and more financial records.[26] Group Five seized books and manuals that explained how to use firearms, including a Marine Corps manual entitled *Destruction by Demolition, Incendiaries and Sabotage*. "Nobody had ever seen forty-four pounds of cocaine in New York City before," Robinson recalled.

John Fallon, the DEA's Northeast regional director, said the weapons collection was the largest ever taken by authorities in a coke bust. Fallon publicly worried that a war for dominance of the Big Apple's cocaine market, similar to the one going on Miami, would break out among local criminal gangs.[14]

The publicity generated by the Burns Court bust was a wake-up call. "The DEA brass in New York City sent the Washington headquarters information providing evidence that cocaine was becoming a problem, not just in Miami but also New York City," Crawford recalled. "The DEA started to take the drug seriously. It began assigning more agents to cocaine investigations."

While Burns Court was being inspected, Rich Crawford and another investigator checked out The Towers, a high-rise apartment overlooking Long Island Sound in Bayside, Queens. There, they found Santacruz's authentic Colombian passport. And all along they had thought Victor Crespo was Santacruz's real name. The detectives also found bank records of Gilberto and Miguel Rodriguez connecting them directly to drug sales in New York.

Inside the safe houses and stash pads, the detectives found a mountain of evidence: adding machines, money wrappers, coded customer lists, counterfeit bill detection equipment, and adding machine tape with a total of $700,740. Group Five could now begin an in-depth financial investigation of the organization. The investigators hauled the evidence back to headquarters, where they split it up and spent several months going through every scrap of paper, tracing bank records, breaking codes and trying to see what other stashes they could uncover.

When Group Five investigators finally decoded the financial records, they found it hard to comprehend the amount of money involved. In three weeks, Patino had collected $6,932,000 from just thirteen customers, and the organization had made forty-seven cash deliveries to money couriers. The amounts of cash delivered were staggering: $824,000, $722,000, $798,000, and in one instance $1,721,000. And where was the money going? All over the globe, to safe havens in Colombia, Panama, and Peru, as well as banking institutions in Europe, Asia, and the Bahamas.[15]

The investigation uncovered some gold nuggets. The agents had seen a photo of Victor Crespo. He was the man they had stopped in the parking lot at JFK airport. When Crespo's name was put through the DEA's Naddis computer system, routine details of the life of mystery trafficker Jose Santacruz began to emerge.[16] He was an unmarried, thirty-five-year-old Puerto Rican whom the Argentine Interpol had connected to an attempted murder. Authorities also tied Santacruz to another rising drug trafficker named Gilberto Rodriguez Orejuela, who was making quite a name for himself in his native Cali as an entrepreneur, banker and businessman.[17]

The group went back through some of the old cases and began to make connections as early as 1976. For instance, they pulled up a file providing details about the police seizure of 280 kilograms of cocaine paste and a Lodestar aircraft and the arrest of nine members of the Victor Crespo organization.[18] Most important for later in the investigation, the records revealed a stamp for the T.E.A. Manufacturing Company and deposits in the name of a company named Sandra Ana S.A., registered in Panama. T.E.A., it turned out, was the front company, while Sandra Ana S.A. was merely used as a post office box for receiving bank balances. The sole owner? Jose Santacruz.[19]

The surveillance, long hours, digging and persistence had paid off. They had finally uncovered the organization responsible for the growing cocaine problem in New York City. It was based in Cali and its leaders were Jose Santacruz and Gilberto and Miguel Rodriguez. They headed a complex international criminal enterprise, reaching from the coca fields in Peru and Bolivia to the processing labs in Colombia to the streets of New York and other US cities.

As the investigation continued, Robinson, who knew no

NEW YORK, NEW YORK

Spanish, joked that he was getting punch-drunk with all the Spanish surnames swirling around in his head. To add to the confusion, some of the bad guys had more code names than CIA spies in a major intelligence operation. Robinson and Crawford normally didn't have a problem finding confidential informants to further their investigations, but the Colombians didn't trust outsiders, so the investigators had to gather most of their evidence the time-consuming, old-fashioned way: through surveillance.[20]

Group Five continued to make arrests, but they didn't seem to make a dent in the organization's supply of available people. Those arrested and convicted kept their mouths shut and went to jail for ten-to-fifteen years, ignoring offers of lighter sentences in return for cooperation. Even if they'd wanted to sing, they really couldn't tell much. "The organization operated through independent cells, and the members of each cell didn't know each other," Robinson explained. "When we arrested someone, he would say, 'I don't know anything. I've just been dealing with one guy.'"

If suspects made bail, Group Five never saw them again, and this would drive Robinson nuts. The Colombians were flight risks and menaces to society, Robinson would tell the judges. They shouldn't be allowed bail. "It took them [the judges] about a year after we began the investigation to realize this," Robinson recalled. "We named the arrangement 'the Colombian Acquittal Bail.' The bail was automatic acquittal for any member of the organization because they would flee to Colombia."

Arranging the bail for the organization was a group of American attorneys who, beginning in the late 1970s, had no problem taking drug dollars for their services as the Colombian version of house counsel for the mob. In 1979, one attorney met with Santacruz in Miami to discuss a trial in progress in New York City involving Santacruz's men. Santacruz asked the attorney to gather information for him about the arrest of one of his distributors in the city. The two discussed and agreed a fee for the work. This same attorney, according to the US Attorney's Office in the Eastern District of New York, was usually the first to be concerned about any potential names of informants and statements during pretrial discussions with the US Attorney's Office. Four years later, an informant told law enforcement that this same attorney was providing Santacruz with trial and hearing information after gang members were arrested.[21] The lawyers wanted their clients from the Cali organization to go to trial so they could find out during the discovery phase what kind of evidence the prosecutors had.

Agents had to be creative in their investigative techniques, given the limitations of the technology of the day. The NYDETF, for example, didn't have ways of wiretapping public telephones. "You could give us a number and we could tell you it's a pay phone, but we didn't have any technology for it," said Robinson.[22] Group Five made extensive use of pen registers. "We didn't need a court order for a pen register as we did for a wire tap," Crawford said. "We would see that a call was being made and then the person would leave the apartment. We would follow them, get the information off the phone records, check them, and find out where the call was going to."[23]

The organization was clever, to be sure, but it also could be as ruthless as it needed to be. One Colombian suspected of talking to the police returned to her apartment to find her babysitter gone and her three children in the cellar, stabbed to death. Later the Group Five investigation learned that prospective employees had to give the names of relatives in Colombia. There was no doubt that if you betrayed the bosses of Cali, someone in your family was going to pay dearly.

The organization was cocky, too. In September Group Five investigators followed Fernando Carmona and some of his associates to JFK airport, but the Colombians spotted the detectives and in turn began following them. Then they took photos. Robinson's jaw dropped; one of them even had a video camera. It wouldn't be the last time that would happen. "They had no respect for law enforcement, so at times they got sloppy and made mistakes and that gave us a chance to catch up to them," Crawford said.[24]

Over time, the investigators discerned a pattern to the organization's modus operandi, but in its sophistication it was unlike any they had seen in their professional careers. The Colombians used a seemingly endless supply of false passports, they changed phones and residences as often as changing their underwear, and they maintained separate apartments and stash houses for drugs, money and weapons.

By tracing telephone numbers in the records seized in the Patino bust, Group Five was able to connect the airline registration for T.E.A. Manufacturing to a Tulio E. Ayerbe. Further investigation of the airline registration revealed that the plane had been modified for what looked like drug transportation: short runways and long-range flights. Further digging revealed that Ayerbe, under the name of Juan Baez, had bought a Lockheed Lodestar that had been seized in Peru with 192 pounds of cocaine paste. The follow-up police investigation connected the airplane to a Victor Crespo.

Meanwhile, Group Five put Ayerbe under surveillance and hooked a pen register on his telephone. He was making a lot of calls to a condominium complex on Grove Island on the South Florida coast near Miami. In February 1980, Group Five agents went to Miami to follow up. When shown a photo of Jose Santacruz (aka Victor Crespo), the superintendent said, yes, he was with Mr Fernando Guiterrez, the man who rented the apartment when he signed the papers. Crawford pulled out another photo. "Yes, that's Mister Guiterrez," the super confirmed. Mr Guiterrez was none other than Mr Gilberto Rodriguez Orejuela.

Group Five was now on a roll. The investigators uncovered another Ayerbe apartment in Hallendale, Florida, under a phoney name. They connected Ayerbe to the purchase and delivery of two safes to a warehouse near a private airfield in Opa-Locka, a rural community close to Miami Beach. Twenty-six days after arriving from New York, Robinson and other Group Five investigators raided the warehouse. The hits just kept getting better – 285 kilos of cocaine valued at $7.5 million was seized, the biggest bust ever at that time.

Gilberto Rodriguez realized he had a serious problem and decided to move his operation to a much quieter place. He ordered his subordinate Jaime Munera to pay $800,000 for a 622-acre cattle ranch in Hope Hull, Alabama. Munera built a 3,600-foot airstrip on the Bar-J Ranch, but he blew his cover by doing a stupid thing: buying 200 head of cattle for cash and at a price well above the herd's market value. The man who sold Munera the cattle mentioned the sale to his cousin, who just happened to work for the Alabama Bureau of Investigation. A computer check revealed that the DEA was investigating Munera, so Alabama police notified the NYDETF, and once again Group Five detectives left New York City for long hours, boring nights, and no extra pay to help their colleagues in Alabama pursue the Colombian connection.

In September 1981, authorities seized the ranch, charging that the property had been bought with money generated by a multi-million-dollar Colombian drug trafficking gang and was intended to serve as a base for shipping cocaine. The seizure included machinery, equipment, livestock, a private plane and the proceeds of two bank accounts belonging to Munera. The property was valued at $1 million.

Group Five had much to show for its hard work: an impressive list of successful inroads into the cartel's drug operations. Since September 1978, NYDETF had been responsible for seizing $2 million in cash, seventy weapons, and more than 430 pounds of cocaine with a street value of $50 million. Law enforcement officers had identified some forty members of the organization and prosecutors had convicted many of them on cocaine trafficking charges. Group Five had exposed a drug ring with the organization, resources and nerve to turn their fair city into Cocaine Central of the United States. The three major godfathers – Gilberto and Miguel Rodriguez and Jose Santacruz – had been identified and their carefully woven cover was blown.

But three years after Group Five had followed up on the confidential informant's lead that took them to Nelson Gomez and the red Chevy Impala, the reality was this – they had stung the men from Cali but not crippled them.

Chapter 3

Chepe Does His Thing

Do you know how lucky you are to work for me? You'd be broke! You'd have to get a real job.
   – Jose "Chepe" Santacruz Londono, co-founder, Cali cartel

Gilberto Rodriguez left the mess behind in Alabama and returned to Colombia and the safety of Cali, where his younger brother Miguel had been overseeing the organization.[1] Jose "Chepe" Santacruz remained the point man in the United States, and continued working to establish New York as its cocaine beach-head. "From the records we seized, we could see that Gilberto handled the money end and Chepe the distribution," said Ken Robinson. "We had no doubt that Chepe came [to the U.S.] for that purpose."[2]

Chepe did not have any problem traveling via commercial airlines to and from Colombia to New York and other points in the United States, most frequently Miami and Los Angeles. Using the intelligence it was gathering on the Santacruz organization, the DEA told its offices that Chepe could be entering the country on flights from Madrid, Spain, and the Bahaman Islands, as well as by private plane from Colombia. The drug trafficker felt so secure in his travels that he would visit one of his daughters, Ana Milena, who was attending Pine Manor Girl's School in Boston, Massachusetts. By April 1984, the police were receiving reports that Chepe was using private planes to set up a distribution ring in Houston, Texas, and to transport family and friends to the U.S. from Colombia.[3]

To hide his identity, Chepe would wear a full beard or a mustache and, at times, glasses and a wig. Chepe was like a chameleon, and, as late as 1984, law enforcement had yet to learn his correct weight and height. In a report distributed to several of its U.S. branch offices, the DEA noted that "the description of the subject (5' 7" tall and 170 pounds) is not accurate."[4] Still, Chepe did not believe in taking risks. He traveled with several bodyguards who were heavily armed, sometimes with submachine guns.[5] He constantly reminded his associates to take every precaution to ensure the cops were not following them when they met with him.

Chepe's near arrest in 1979 at JFK airport, however, suddenly made him wary of flying. Alfredo Cervantes, Chepe's right-hand man in the United States from 1981 until his arrest in Waycross, Georgia, in 1983, recalled that his boss traveled by air only once during their association. Cervantes would drive Chepe everywhere, and all the boss carried was a paper bag containing a toothbrush and some cash. While the Cali cartel was growing, it still was not the complex organization that later drew comparisons with multinationals and Fortune 500 companies. Cervantes did everything for Chepe: picking up merchandise (cash, dope and equipment) and taking it to a stash pad; collecting the money; preparing it for laundering and transport out of the country; and dealing with customers, lawyers and anybody else important to the organization. He acquired the nickname "*Mochila*," which means "Pocketbook" in Spanish.[6]

Born in Barranquilla, Colombia, Cervantes had emigrated to the United States with his family in 1963. After graduating from high school in Queens, New York, Cervantes joined the U.S. air force, receiving a health discharge in 1979. He attended commercial art school and then went to work for his cousin, Alberto Cavallero, in Miami, Florida. Soon after, however, cousin Alberto was killed in South America. One of Alberto's clients, a Mr Tamayo, who operated a company named American Distribution and Export, persuaded Cervantes to manage a warehouse near Miami. The company was supposed to be exporting automobiles and farm equipment to South America, but it never did ship anything overseas. Instead, it became a stash house for cocaine and money, and Cervantes continued doing the same job that his cousin had done for Tamayo: trafficking in cocaine.

A few weeks after the warehouse opened, Tamayo introduced Cervantes to a gentleman named Jose Santacruz, informing him that Santacruz would be his new partner. "I'm leaving for Colombia for an indefinite period of time," Tamayo explained. "You'll be reporting to Mr Santacruz Londono."

Who is Mr Santacruz? Cervantes wondered. He had never met the man.

Cervantes had a meeting with his new boss, who came with an engineer from Colombia. "He is going to build an underground safe in the warehouse," Chepe told Cervantes.[7] During the safe's construction, Santacruz came by constantly to supervise the project. Three weeks after its completion, Cervantes received a call at 3 A.M. from a Chepe associate, who needed to put something in the warehouse. The associate arrived with three duffle bags containing 175 pounds of cocaine. "You are going to make some money now," the courier told Cervantes. "We are going to be using the warehouse as a safe house, so keep your mouth shut." In subsequent meetings, Chepe kept reminding Cervantes how dangerous his business was. "You need to keep a low profile," he advised.

In the following months, Cervantes traveled to New York City with as much as thirty kilos of cocaine hidden in a well-concealed compartment in the car. Upon arriving, Cervantes made a call to a beeper number that Chepe gave him and then went back to his hotel to wait for a courier to pick up the load. The courier arrived, took the keys to Cervantes's car, drove off, and returned in an hour, minus the load. "Drive back to Miami," the courier instructed. Once back in Miami, Cervantes waited for the next phone call and instructions for another trip to the Big Apple. From 1980 to 1983, Cervantes drove to New York City about 100 times with thirty to thirty-five kilos of cocaine on each trip. The street value at the time was about $30,000 per kilo, so the amount of cocaine transported by Cervantes during this period was worth at least $90 million.

Chepe had Cervantes on standby twenty-four hours a day,

seven days a week. Initially they communicated via beeper and pay phone when Cervantes was in New York. The organization had designated numbers for phone booths. One booth on Queens Boulevard, for example, had the number six. When Chepe beeped the number, Cervantes walked to the phone booth, and about fifteen minutes later received a call from the boss. The two discussed when they should have their next meeting or other details important to their business, especially the matter of picking up money from customers. Chepe required his people to carry $100 worth of quarters at all times so they wouldn't have any problem making calls from booths. When Santacruz gave his people a phone number, they were expected to add one number to it, so that if someone saw the number it wouldn't be the correct one.

The combine set up the same system for its other three major markets – Miami, Houston and Los Angeles – putting a tight cell structure in place. The guiding philosophy of the emerging Cali cartel was that the less a member knew, the better it was for the organization. Every employee, however, was given a code number, a record of which was kept at the Cali headquarters. The cell's head beeped the dealer, who would then go to a pay phone to receive a list of customers and the times he had to meet each of them. The dealer contacted the next customer and then the next, and so on, until he finished the list of names. The dealer already knew the locations for the buys, but the times changed from week to week.

The dealer normally delivered two kilos to each customer, but the customer usually didn't have to pay at the buy. The cartel sold on a consignment basis, meaning that two to three kilos were distributed to a customer on credit, and he had a specific period of time to pay. They delivered on Saturdays and Sundays because they believed the majority of the police were off work on those days. As Cervantes later told the court, "It's a thin shift . . . for the police."[8]

After selling the cocaine, the dealer returned to the stash house to count the take, using money-counting machines (like the one that Jose Patino had on him when he was arrested by Group Five detectives Ken Robinson and Bill Mockler in 1979). The types of stash houses the Cali men used evolved as they expanded and refined their distribution network. In the late 1970s, Santacruz, now in charge of the New York branch of Cocaine Incorporated, liked to keep the drugs, money and arms in stash houses in heavily populated Hispanic neighborhoods such as Washington Heights or the Lower East Side of Manhattan. However, these were high-crime areas, and the local hoodlums would kill many of his workers and steal the money and drugs. Looking out for the police was tough enough without having to watch your back, so Chepe began locating the stash houses in middle-class neighborhoods, first in Queens and Manhattan, and later in Westchester and Long Island, where the chance of being ripped off was less.[9]

Chepe bought realty companies with access to a large number of properties in New York City, especially in the Queens borough. One such, Mechizzo Realty, even supplied Chepe's organization with cellphones and false identifications. As former New York prosecutor Jessica de Grazia described the relationship between the Cali cartel and the realtors, "They [the realtors] had permanent residence status and spoke perfect English; no one suspected that they were involved in a criminal enterprise. They would prepare the rental application, sign the lease, pay the rent, obtain electricity and gas, arrange for the phone and prepare all the documents in false names." The realty companies were part of a vast support network of corrupted sources from the business and government communities that the Cali cartel built in the Big Apple in the late 1970s and early 1980s. On its payroll, for instance, were car dealers who took cash, no questions asked, as well as bureaucrats in the department of motor vehicles who supplied phony tags and IDs.

Not yet in the computer age, the transactions were recorded in ledger books. Each of the organization's four major markets used the same kind of ledger books, as well as stash pads. Based on their analysis of the Santacruz group's financial records, police figured it was pulling in about a million dollars weekly from each of the four major markets.[10]

The couriers beeped Chepe on his phone or, if the boss was in Cali, made a long distance call to his secretary, Esmeralda and left a message. When Chepe and his courier made contact, they checked each customer's name with the amount of money received. If the money was short, no problem. Chepe could wait to balance the books. "He never had any problem with us, thinking that we took the money or anything else like that," Cervantes later explained.

The bosses vetted employees carefully before hiring them. It was not easy getting a "job" with the cartel. One applicant named John Harold Mena was typical. He had to have an interview with a Cali-based representative of the organization via pay phone. Successful applicants were faxed a list of rules, a company contract so to speak. "Live modestly" and "avoid attracting attention to yourself" were two of the major stipulations. Even people operating stash houses were expected to leave the house in the morning and return at night like any typical working-class person. After the applicant had read the list, he was ordered to cut it up into little pieces.[11]

By any measure, Chepe was a tough, demanding boss. No one becomes the head of distribution for a major drug trafficking mob by being Mr Nice Guy. Santacruz employed a group of hit men who were known as the Palestinos, street-tough Colombians who came from Medellin under the leadership of Julio Palestino.[12] The Cali cartel brought the Palestinos to the United States, and they were suspected of being involved in the killing of numerous people in New York, Chicago and Miami.[13] "The Palestinos are legendary for their violence," said Bill Mante, former NYSP investigator. "Anybody crossing Santacruz or the Cali cartel could be gone in a heartbeat. They were almost impossible to track. We would receive information that a hit was about to go down. The problem was that we couldn't determine the location. We would spend many nights trying to locate every possible location where we believed the hit would happen. No luck. The next day a Hispanic would be found dead. The Palestinos were a major distraction [to U.S. law enforcement] for many years."[14] Santacruz had no qualms about killing people close to him. Marely Fuquen, his mistress and the mother of several of his children, would later be one of the unlucky targets.[15]

The cartel also used couriers to smuggle money out of the

United States. They carried the money in square briefcases like the ones pilots used. In the late 1970s, the cartel had its couriers fly on Braniff Airlines because it had a contact there. The Braniff employee would check Cervantes in, give him a ticket, and get his baggage through security. Once past security, the employee gave Cervantes his baggage and he would be on his way. The money smuggled per trip varied between $100,000 and $300,000, depending on the size of the bills. Small bills weighed too much, Chepe would grumble. Unfortunately for the organization, Braniff Airlines went out of business in 1981, and the Cali men had to use private planes to help launder their money.

In addition to shipping money out of the country, they smuggled automobiles, household goods, construction materials and heavy-duty machinery back to Colombia. These goods were usually bought under fictitious names, if there was no need to show ID. Otherwise, Cervantes would use his own name, since he was an American citizen. Everything was paid for in cash. "This is a good way of getting money out of the country," Santacruz told Cervantes one day. "Smuggling money to Colombia is a lot riskier than, say, buying a machine for a quarter of a million dollars and shipping it to Colombia."

In the early 1980s, a lot of the dirty money was funneled from the United States to Panama, where Gilberto Rodriguez co-owned a bank. Cervantes never knew who would meet him upon his arrival in Panama City, but whoever it was would give specific instructions about what to do.[16] Cervantes estimated that between 1980 and 1983, he personally traveled to Panama about twenty times, smuggling around $500,000 on each trip.

One day, Cervantes heard Chepe talking on the phone to a customer who wanted to exchange pesos for dollars. The drug lord was explaining how the caller's accountant could transfer money in pesos from his account in Colombia into Chepe's account in New York. Chepe could then arrange to have the dollars deposited to the caller's account in Colombia. Cervantes didn't understand how that could be possible, but he had just overheard a discussion about Colombia's Black Market Peso Exchange. As law enforcement gradually tightened the screws on money laundering techniques throughout the 1980s, the Black

Market Peso Exchange became an increasingly popular way for the Cali cartel to get its dirty dollars out of the United States.[17]

Chepe had to do something with his money besides put it in stash houses and banks. Like all crime godfathers, he loved the good life – the luxuries, the opulence, the women, and the social status that his illegal business brought. In 1979, Chepe and his wife Ampara met interior decorator Alexander Blarek in Colombia. The couple needed an interior decorator, and Blarek, who was working in Miami at the time, was looking for clients. He saw that a lot of South Americans had extra cash, and they were becoming a lucrative market for his profession. The Santacruzes looked like the kind of wealthy clients he should cultivate. In their initial meeting, Blarek later recalled, Santacruz was "kind of quiet" and Ampara was a "bit Rubenesque" but had a great smile.[18] In his diary, Blarek wrote that the Santacruzes' house was "fantastico." Chepe and Ampara were also gracious hosts, who took Blarek to the Country Club Shalom in a ritzy residential section of Cali.

They then had a business meeting where Blarek showed his prospective clients photos of some of his work. Chepe and Ampara liked what they saw and agreed to Blarek's request that they pay a $25,000 retainer so he could begin decorative improvements to their house. Blarek spent the next three days with Ampara, and she showed him the various properties that they owned in Cali: banks, shopping centers, a construction company, an office, a ranch, a sugar cane plantation, and an apartment complex with two towers connected by a commercial space. The two parties agreed to meet again in Miami to further discuss the business arrangement.

In April 1999, Ampara introduced Blarek to her two daughters, Sandra and Ana Milena, at the Omni Hotel in Miami, where they were staying. Blarek had brought the drawings he had for their home. Ampara liked them. "I've budgeted three hundred thousand dollars for the project," Blarek explained. "Why don't I give you some time to think about my proposal."

Several days later, Ampara called Blarek. "My husband is not happy with the budget," she said. Blarek backtracked. "I put these figures together quickly," he explained, adding, "it's very time consuming to select all the elements we need for the project, put them together, estimate what you need for particular items and then price them out."

After Ampara called, Blarek reviewed the figures again and then arranged a dinner meeting with Chepe, presenting to his client a revised budget of $200,000 for the project. Chepe liked the new budget and the project proceeded. However, another problem arose. Someone had shown Chepe an issue of the *Florida Designers Quarterly* that had a photo of his house on the cover. Chepe was livid and confronted Blarek. "Who gave you permission for this?" he demanded. Chepe cooled off and the project proceeded. Blarek ordered everything he needed for the project and sent it by freight to Cali. Then he waited . . . and waited. The Santacruzes didn't call to give the go-ahead to do the final installation, nor did Blarek recover full payment for his work on the project. Chepe still owed him $10,000.

Blarek wasn't worried that Chepe didn't call. He was busy with other projects and in 1981 he found a partner: Frank Pellechia, another interior decorator. They became lifelong lovers and business partners.

Then in July 1981, Ampara called Blarek out of the blue. "How have you been doing, Alexander? Would you be available in an hour?" she asked cheerfully. "We have a surprise for you." At the meeting, the Santacruzes brought out floor plans for Chepe's office. They wanted to make design changes and buy new furniture for it.

Blarek agreed to redesign the office, but said, "What about the ten thousand dollars you owe me?" Chepe let out a little chuckle. "Consider it a discount," he said. "You didn't fulfill your final obligations on the installation."

Blarek wanted the job, so he flew to Cali to complete the project at a cost of about $350,000, which included his $120,000 commission. Blarek received some of his commission through wire transfers, but most of it was paid in cash by a well-dressed Colombian named Fred, who would often meet him accompanied by his beautiful Puerto Rican wife and two young children.[19]

On September 3, 1981, detectives Ken Robinson and Rich Crawford from Group Five, NYDETF, paid a visit.

"Do you know a Mr. Jose Santacruz?" the detectives asked.

"Yes, I do," Blarek answered nervously.

The detectives couldn't help but notice that Blarek was trembling. In all his years of interrogating witnesses, Robinson had never seen one who looked so scared. "Would you mind looking at some photos?"

"Sure."

"That's Mister Santacruz," Robinson said, pointing at a photo. "Did you know Mister Santacruz was a drug dealer?"

"No, I didn't," Blarek said, not certain where the questioning was headed.

"Well, you better be careful," Robinson advised. "He's smart and probably dangerous."

The two detectives left their business cards and asked Blarek to call them if he ever saw Santacruz again.

The next day, Blarek was alone, upstairs in his house, working, when the door bell rang. He went downstairs, crossed the entry hall to the front door and looked out the window. He froze. There, standing and looking at him, was Chepe Santacruz. Blarek couldn't believe it. No bodyguards, just Chepe. What was he doing there?

He let his client in. "Greetings, Frank, how are you doing," Chepe said cordially.

"Sit down, please. Do you want a drink?" Blarek asked, trying to act calm.

"No, I don't have much time. How is the project doing?"

"Well, it's much too soon yet," Blarek said feeling a little better now that he knew Santacruz had come on business. "I won't be able to give you a presentation until I get the custom prices, probably sometime at the end of the year."

"Oh, I see. I'll be happy to see it." Chepe smiled and then he got to the point. "By the way, did some government people come to see you?"

Blarek's heart began to pound. The man obviously knew something he did not. "Yes," Blarek said, not knowing what to expect. Chepe smiled and stood up. "Well, I have to go."

Blarek watched his client leave the house. How did he get here? How did he know the cops had visited him? Didn't he want to know what the cops asked? Bewildered, Blarek walked to the front door and looked out. There were no cars on the street. He felt queasy. Did the man fall out of the sky?[20]

Blarek proceeded with the project. Chepe had told him to work directly with his wife, who would approve the design, carpets, and furnishings. Meanwhile, Blarek and Chepe were to meet in November 1981, but he got a call from Chepe's secretary. "Mister Santacruz wants you to meet him in New York City, not Miami," she instructed. "Fred will pick you up."

Fred met Blarek at La Guardia airport and took him to the Waldorf Astoria, where he checked in before they headed for the meeting. The two drove back toward the airport and to a motel located directly across from La Guardia. In the motel room, waiting patiently, was Chepe Santacruz, who, after the usual pleasantries, told Blarek to go ahead and make his presentation. The decorator did, but then he thought about the DEA visit and the drugs. He had an idea. No real money had been exchanged on this project at this point. "Let's end our relationship," Blarek suggested to Chepe. "I'll give up the plans, the specifications . . . and let's say that my services are free because of the inconvenience I've caused you."

Chepe's mood changed; the smile evaporated. Blarek got anxious. He noticed the gun on the nightstand next to the bed. Fred had also taken off his jacket, revealing a small gun in the shoulder holster. "You need to fulfill your obligations," Chepe said firmly. "You have a contract. I'm looking forward to the finish of the project. You'll be contacted."

Blarek was not the only employee who had problems with Chepe. One Sunday morning in 1982, Cervantes left his boss standing on the corner of a Manhattan street. Cervantes was fed up with drug dealing and being on call all hours of the night. He wanted out. The next day, Chepe called Cervantes and they agreed to meet. Chepe gave Cervantes the figure for the amount of money he owed him and followed up with a sermon. "Do you know how lucky you are to work for me? You'll be broke. You'll have to get a real job!"[21]

Then Chepe showed his employee the door. "Don't tell anyone about the warehouse," he warned his now-former employee. "I don't exist, get it?" Cervantes knew how bloodthirsty Chepe could get when he felt betrayed. Cervantes didn't really fear for himself, but he did for his family, so he quietly began moving them out of Queens.

Cervantes's former boss was right. He found that working at a real job was no fun. So in January 1983, he went back to work for Santacruz, helping him move cocaine from Colombia and merchandise back to the country. Chepe was delighted. Business was booming and he needed Cervantes's experience.

The combine owned a front company in Jacksonville, Florida, named the Maserik Trading Company, which it used to import a fungicide from Barranquilla manufactured by Dupont. Its name was Maneb-80.[22] Santacruz had workers at the port of Barranquilla on his payroll, and they put cocaine, instead of fungicide, inside the pallets. The organization was betting that because Dupont had been shipping the highly toxic fungicide for thirty years, the U.S. Customs Service would not inspect the pallets too closely. The organization had undertaken surveillance of Customs' practices before beginning their product switch to see how the agents reacted when they inspected the legitimate shipments. Later, they conducted a few dry runs to see if the smuggling method worked. It did – for a while. Cervantes helped move four or five shipments of cocaine to the United States before the sheriff's department in Waycross, Georgia, busted him.

Cervantes was on his way from Jacksonville to Waycross with sixty-seven kilos of cocaine to meet a pilot. They were to travel together by plane to Houston on cartel business. The pilot was in Waycross a few days before Cervantes arrived. He had a conspicuous-looking high-tech, loaded plane and walked around the small town, acting suspiciously, which drew the attention of the Waycross police. They placed him under surveillance. A background check indicated the pilot was a fugitive. They waited to see who he would meet and then made their arrests, catching both Cervantes and the pilot in the act.[23]

It took several calls from the jailhouse in Waycross to Santacruz's house and office in Cali before Cervantes was able to contact him. The anxious employee asked his boss, "Are you going to put money up for my bail? Are you going to pay me any money?"

The answer was, "Don't say anything. Keep your mouth shut. Don't forget the ship is coming in and that [it] needs to be protected?" In the next phone call, Chepe explained that the Waycross bust had cost him a lot of money, too. "The money I owe you will cover that cost, as well as the cost of your attorney's fees," Chepe said coldly. "Have a good day."[24]

Authorities seized 230 pounds of cocaine in the Waycross bust and another 1,391 pounds in Tampa, Florida. On October 19, 1983, a federal grand jury for the Southern District of Georgia indicted Santacruz.[25] Chepe would have to pay a bond of $10 million, if law enforcement ever caught him. The following February, the DEA officially declared Chepe a fugitive. Authorities estimated that between March and September 1983 the gang from Cali, under Santacruz's direction and using the Maneb-80 fungicide as a cover, smuggled about 7,000 pounds of cocaine into the United States.[26]

Authorities had linked the smuggling operation directly to Chepe Santacruz and made a connection to the NYDETF's investigation of the Cali cartel. As a result of the Waycross bust, the DEA developed valuable intelligence about the way the Cali men smuggled coke into the United States. The intelligence, in fact, was accumulating from a number of different investigations. On February 23, 1984, the DEA had a meeting in Washington, D.C., to coordinate the activities of the various branch offices involved in investigating the Santacruz mob. The DEA brass wanted the branches to "collectively determine the most advantageous judicial district for prosecution."[27] By this time, Group Five investigators felt like they were breathing and eating information about Santacruz's operation. Indeed, they had become so obsessed with Chepe Santacruz and the case that they began to refer to themselves as "Chepe Chasers."[28]

But Chepe was still operating in their backyard. In March 1984, Group Five searched the Queens home of Jose Justo Guzman, the head of one of the cartel's cells, and found more evidence, including a 100-page ledger filled with codes and aliases. When they took the ledger back to the office for analysis, they found clues linking the Guzman safe house to Santacruz. They also identified several entries relating to the schooling of the drug lord's daughter, Ana Milena. She was now attending Harvard University, and Chepe Santacruz, like any good father, was doing the right thing – helping to pay her way through the university.[29] Ana Milena rented an apartment, which was large enough to accommodate her mother and brother when they visited her. Blarek helped Milena find the furniture for the apartment. The cost was $30,000.[30]

Chapter 4

Growing the
Criminal Enterprise

Our sense was that the thugs from Medellin were more insidious. Escobar was your typical gold-chain, fancy-car gangster
who liked the flamboyant lifestyle. The traffickers from Cali,
on the other hand, were low key and manipulative. We called
them "criminals with Gucci slippers."
— Crescencio Arcos, U.S. deputy assistant secretary
for Latin America, 1987–1989

In the early 1980s, the world had no better place than Colombia in
which to build a criminal enterprise. During the Alfonso Lopez
Michelsen presidential administration (1974–1978), the government established the so-called *Ventanilla Siniestra* or "Left-Handed
Window," which allowed U.S. dollars earned from illegal activities
to enter the economic system and be converted into pesos, thus
boosting the nation's international money reserves. From 1978 to
1980, the foreign exchange reserves produced by the Left-Handed
Window jumped from 14.3 billion pesos to 28 billion pesos. In
1978, *Business Week* magazine noted that Colombia's central bank
had showed service exports of $924 million in 1977, but, of that
figure, the government could only account for $100 million in
legitimate business.[1]

Millions of the illegal dollars from smuggling coffee and
marijuana – and, increasingly, cocaine – flowed into the

Colombian economy.[2] By the late 1970s, illegal drug sales were netting the government one billion dollars annually, thanks in large part to its reluctance to close the Left-Handed Window.[3] Drug trafficking expert Peter A. Lupsha noted that "not only had the Left-Handed Window become an increasingly crucial part of the Colombian fiscal policy by 1980, but, by the summer of that year, the Colombian bank superintendent announced that about half of Colombia's international reserves (slightly more than $21 billion) originated from narco dollars and contrabandista activity."[4]

The Colombian government's indifference toward the Left-Handed Window's introduction showed how lightly it took the threat posed by the thriving drug trade. The U.S. government, on the other hand, was becoming concerned, and sent two fact-finding missions to Colombia in 1977 and 1979 to learn more about the drug situation there.[5] When President Julio Cesar Turbay (1978–1982) met with members of the 1979 mission, he made references to critics who described Colombia as a nation busily producing drugs for the rest of the world. This description is unfair, said Turbay, because the drug trade is "encouraged and financed by Americans."[6]

The U.S. government had a different notion. It began suspecting that the Colombian government was part of the problem, not the solution, in the battle against drugs. A March 29, 1978, study by the U.S. General Accounting Office identified corruption as the major reason for Colombia's growing trafficking problem.[7] Four days later, Morley Safer, a correspondent with CBS television's *60 Minutes*, revealed the existence of an explosive memo from drug policy advisor Peter Bourne to President Jimmy Carter, charging that three prominent Colombian politicians including Julio Cesar Turbay – then the front-running Liberal candidate for president – had dirtied their hands in the drug trade.[8] The Colombian response was swift and angry. General Abraham Varon Valencia, Colombia's minister of defense and one of the three officials identified in the so-called Cocaine Memorandum, told U.S. Ambassador Diego Asencio that the charges were based on "false information, which has caused enormous damage to the prestige of the country, its government and its armed forces."[9] U.S. officials fueled more Colombian anger a couple of months later when Dave Burnett, special agent in charge of the Bogota office, confided to *New Republic* magazine that Jaime Serrano Rueda was the only Colombian official in which the United States had complete confidence.[10]

Again came the indignant responses from Colombian officials, but protestations notwithstanding, the drug trade was booming, and cocaine, with high profit margins, was starting to eclipse marijuana as the Colombian smuggler's preferred product. The huge profits to be made from cocaine spurred the growth of highly organized, dynamic networks of traffickers. They had once used mules to smuggle their product to market, but now, to meet the increasing demand, they began using more sophisticated means, including private airplanes that ranged from old DC-3s to Cessna 210s to ultramodern Lear jets, as well as ships from the Colombian merchant marine fleet.[11] U.S. and Colombian law enforcement reported that smuggling routes were expanding to include not only flights directly from Bogota to Miami but also indirect routes involving Cali, Medellin, Barranquilla, and Buenaventura to places in Canada, Mexico, the Caribbean Islands, Central America and even Europe.[12]

By 1980, two distinct trafficking groups centered in Cali and Medellin were emerging as the major players in the country's drug trade. The leaders of the Medellin cartel – Pablo Escobar, Carlos Lehder, the Ochoa brothers (Jorge, Fabio and Juan David) and Jose Gonzalo Rodriguez Gacha – became known as *"Los Hampones"* (the Hoodlums) because of their backgrounds and rough criminal style. They came from the lower- and blue-collar classes and clawed their way up the road to riches, using intimidation and violence.[13]

Born in 1949 in Rionegro, a town twenty-five miles from Medellin, Pablo Escobar was the son of a night watchman and schoolteacher. Legend has it that he got his start in crime by stealing gravestones, rubbing off the inscriptions and then selling them to bereaved relatives at bargain prices. In the early 1970s, Escobar worked as a thief and bodyguard, and made a quick $100,000 on the side kidnapping and ransoming a Medellin business executive. In 1976 he was arrested for possessing thirty pounds of cocaine, but never went to trial. Later, the drug trafficker had a *sicario* (paid gunman) murder the arresting police officers in what became a vicious pattern throughout his criminal career. Escobar killed anyone who crossed him, stood in his way, or posed a threat. By the late 1970s, he was making so much money from drugs that he had invested in U.S. real estate, including an $8 million apartment complex in Florida.[14]

The charismatic Carlos Lehder was born in Armenia, Colombia, but raised in the United States. In 1976, he was deported to Colombia because of his criminal activities. In a short time, he was playing a pivotal role in pioneering an ingenious plan for smuggling large shipments of cocaine into the United States. In 1978, Crazy Carlos, as he became known for his unpredictable behavior, paid $4.5 million for Norman's Cay, an island in the Bahamas strategically located between Colombia and the United States and perfect for smuggling cocaine into Florida. Soon, the emerging Medellin cartel was loading big shipments onto planes in Colombia and flying the loads to Norman's Cay, where the planes would be refueled, before heading to the United States.[15]

Jorge, Fabio and Juan David Ochoa came from a family with a long history of smuggling. Jorge, the oldest brother, was mainly responsible for turning his family's business into a modern drug-trafficking organization. The DEA first discovered his role in drugs in 1977 when it seized sixty pounds of cocaine in Miami.[16] Jose Gonzalo Rodriguez Gacha, known as "the Mexican" for his love of all things from Mexico, served as a bodyguard to Gilberto Molina, the godfather of Colombia's emerald-smuggling underworld, before joining Escobar in drug trafficking in the mid-1970s.[17] Later, the Mexican became prominent in the Medellin cartel as an enforcer. He also bought up and converted large tracts of jungle land that the cartel used for cocaine processing labs.[18]

Never were the styles of two major criminal organizations operating in the same space so different. While the Medellin cartel tried to bully and bribe the state, the Cali cartel worked quietly behind the scenes to corrupt it. "We learned that the Cali godfathers loved the fact that the Medellin cartel was always in the spotlight," said Ken Robinson.[19]

The Medellin cartel godfathers really believed they could be a part of the political system, and for a time, it looked like they could. Escobar was elected an alternate delegate to Congress, representing Medellin from 1982 to 1984. Both Lehder and Rodriguez Gacha organized their own political parties, and Lehder even had his own newspaper, *Quindio Libre*. Colombian officials told U.S. Senate investigators in 1989 that Gacha wanted to rid his country of all left-wing politicians and guerrilla groups.[20]

The Medellin godfathers, however, never realized their political ambitions. When the Colombian state bureaucratic machinery began to breathe down their necks in the mid-1980s, they dropped out of mainstream politics and turned to the terrorist's way of doing business – murdering hundreds of police, judges, prosecutors, state officials, and ordinary citizens who got in the way or who happened to be in the wrong place at the wrong time.

In reality, of course, the Cali cartel was not the kinder, gentler mafia that their propaganda machine brilliantly portrayed them to be. They could be just as ruthless as Medellin when necessary. Miguel Rodriguez, for instance, had no qualms about killing the husband (a fellow drug trafficker) of a woman he desired. Claudio Endo, an associate of Miguel Rodriguez, had killed a couple of guerrillas, one of whom owed him money. Unfortunately for Endo, one of the guerrillas was a friend of Pacho Herrera. Pacho received permission from the other three cartel godfathers (the Rodriguez brothers and Santacruz) to kill Endo.

About 2 A.M. on an early March day in 1994, Endo was sleeping at his ranch near Jamundi when a couple of carloads of gunmen arrived, on orders of the Cali cartel. They surprised Endo and proceeded to torture him and mutilate his body with submachine gunfire. Claudia Endo was there but was taken away unharmed. Six to eight months later, Miguel Rodriguez and Claudia were lovers.[21]

Santacruz murdered Marely Fuquen because she was a pain in the butt, even though she was the mother of some of his children.[22] A confidential informant told DEA agents that Chepe had Fuquen killed because she was planning to leave Colombia for Miami with the kids. The drug lord thought she was planning to take them away from him and he would never see them again. "The CI told us that Marely was always yelling and screaming and complaining, and Chepe was not the type of guy who would put up with that forever," said Robinson.[23]

It was just that the self-styled gentlemen from Cali usually did their violence without much noise. Pacho Herrera would invite guests whom he believed had betrayed him to his sprawling hacienda, El Desierto, outside Cali. There he would feed them, take them into a room, put a bag over their head, torture them until they confessed, kill them, and then dump their bodies in the Cauca River at night, all neatly done without waking up the neighbors.[24]

The gentlemen from Cali had another unique way of dealing with some of their suspected traitors and screw-ups. They would invite them to come to Cali by airplane, and then kill them. Rather than dump their bodies in the Cauca River, they would find somebody that looked like them, give the substitute the dead person's papers and plane ticket, and then send them back to where the dead person had come from. When the dearly departed was reported missing, the cartel could always say, "Hey, don't blame us. He took the plane and went back to where he came from."[25]

The two cartels had starkly contrasting philosophies toward criminal enterprise, but initially, during the period from the late 1970s through the early 1980s years, they were on basically good relations. According to intelligence sources, Cali and Medellin collaborated on making joint shipments, setting up processing labs, planning assassinations, coordinating their operations, and working together to corrupt the political process.[26] As Rennselaer Lee, author of *The White Labyrinth: Cocaine and Political Power* and *The Andean Cocaine Industry* and an expert on the drug trade, pointed out, "Cocaine barons share a common political agenda that includes blocking the extradition of drug traffickers, the criminal justice system, and selectively persecuting the Colombian left."[27] Former DEA agent Michael Kane, head of the DEA's Medellin office from 1981 to 1984, said that the Cali and Medellin cartels were friendly competitors through the mid-1980s. "They were not at each other's throats in those days," said Kane. "They had their own markets and there was enough room for both of them."[28]

At this time, the leaders of the Cali and Medellin cartels mingled, enjoying their growing wealth and moving freely in society. Both Pablo Escobar and the Rodriguez brothers, for instance, got involved in auto racing – Escobar and a partner owned a share of a Renault team and the Rodriguez brothers owned two racing circuits. Drug traffickers heavily patronizing motor racing and, always looking to make more money, attempted to smuggle cocaine to the United States inside racing cars involved in competitions. Colombian police, acting on a tip from the DEA, thwarted their plans and seized thirty kilos of cocaine.[29]

A November 1981 meeting of the "who's who" of Colombian drug trafficking was the high point of this Cali-Medellin collaboration. On November 12, the leftist guerrilla group April 19 Movement, more commonly known as M-19, swooped in on the University of Antioquia, kidnapped Marta Nieves Ochoa, the sister of the Ochoa family, and held her for ransom.[30] Earlier, leftist guerrillas had tried to kidnap Carlos Lehder, wounding him in the attempt. The traffickers were incensed. They also had no intention of paying the outrageous ransom of nearly $15 million that the guerrillas were reportedly demanding for Marta's release.

Historians disagree about where the watershed meeting was held (Cali or Medellin) and how many attended (the numbers range from twenty to 223), but it's certain that the drug traffickers adopted a strategy that would not only free Marta Ochoa but also deal with the guerrilla threat. Leaflets were dropped at a soccer field in Cali, announcing the birth of a new organization, *Meurte a Secuestradores* (Death to Kidnappers), or *MAS*, as it became commonly known, and warning that their common defense group would see to it that those responsible for the kidnapping were "hung from all the trees in public parks or shot and marked with the sign of our group – MAS."[31] The guerrillas got the message and released Marta unharmed, although it's unclear whether any ransom was paid.

At a second meeting of *MAS*, the drug lords reached agreement about how coke shipments would be regulated and coordinated to increase their profits, and what group would control which market. The Cali cartel would have New York; the Medellin cartel would have Miami and South Florida. California was left up for grabs. According to journalist Fabio Castillo, the California market eventually ended up in the hands of Cali.[32] The Ochoas and Escobar dominated the two meetings of *MAS*, and it appears at this point the Cali men was willing to defer to the Medellin leadership.

The relationship between Jorge Ochoa and Gilberto Rodriguez in the early 1980s illustrated well the groups' coexistence. Jorge Ochoa grew up in Cali, where he became a boyhood friend of Gilberto. In the late 1970s, the two became business partners and founded their own bank, the First InterAmericas Bank, as a way of laundering their money. According to Castillo, "The drug traffickers are said to have made a tacit pledge to the Panamanian government not to collect interest on deposits that they made in Panamanian banks. The earnings of these banks are simply handed over to the local government."[33]

In 1984, Gilberto Rodriguez and Jorge Ochoa journeyed together to Spain to escape the pressure that the Colombian government was exerting on the country's drug traffickers and to explore the European market for cocaine. The two friends and associates assumed aliases and posed as respectable businessmen, but they began enjoying an opulent lifestyle that was bound to attract attention. Gilberto lived in a plush hotel and bought two Mercedes and two apartments, while Ochoa purchased four Mercedes and an 8,000-square-foot mansion with a discotheque, swimming pools and tennis courts. The Madrid authorities took notice of the wealthy visitors from South America and began investigating. Discovering that warrants had been issued for their arrests in the United States, they began wiretapping their residence in September 1984. On October 17, the police arrested Ochoa and Rodriguez. The U.S. Ambassador in Spain immediately requested their extradition to the United States.[34]

Early on, the Medellin cartel became the main focus of U.S. law enforcement efforts. Alexander F. Watson, the deputy chief of missions at the U.S. Embassy in Bogota from 1981 to 1984, said that the mission viewed Cali as a relatively quiet city during that period. "The drug trade was just starting to explode," Watson recalled. "Back then, if you were an American, you could drive to

Cali from Bogota any time you wanted without fear of danger."[35]
The U.S. government maintained a benign view of the traffickers
from Cali all through the 1980s. In explaining why the U.S.
didn't pay more attention to Cali, Cresencio Arcos, a career
foreign service diplomat and the U.S. deputy assistant secretary
for Latin America from 1987 to 1989, said, "Our sense was that
the thugs from Medellin were more insidious. Escobar was your
typical gold chain, fancy-car gangster who liked the flamboyant
lifestyle. The traffickers from Cali, on the other hand, were low
key and manipulative. We called them 'criminals with Gucci
slippers.'"[36]

The DEA had opened branch offices in Cali and Medellin in
1981. Working as an agent in Colombia was not without risk. In
November 1976, Octavio Gonzalez, the DEA chief in Bogota,
was shot dead. The assassin, Thomas Charles Coley, an American
citizen, was able to walk into Gonzalez's office at DEA headquarters on the top floor of the Ugi Building without anyone
checking his identity. Coley killed Gonzalez with a .9 millimeter
pistol. The brazen assassination was a foreshadowing of the
violence that the Colombian drug trade would later generate.

The two DEA offices kept a low profile and neither had more
than two agents. The DEA received bits of intelligence about the
MAS meetings and began trying to gather information and
cultivate sources and informants from the local drug smuggling
scene. According to Michael Kuhlman, a DEA agent who worked
in the agency's Cali office in the early 1980s, "At this time there
were all kinds of traffickers in Colombia who didn't work for the
Medellin or Cali cartels. They were small timers who trafficked
in ten- to twenty-kilo shipments to the United States, as well as
Canada and Europe."[37]

The DEA's office in Cali also spent time trying to verify the
intelligence that Group Five in New York City had gathered in
their investigation of the Santacruz organization. "There was all
kinds of misinformation about Chepe Santacruz – his physical
appearance, his false passports – and one of our jobs was to sort it
out," said Kuhlman. One day, Kuhlman went to see the principal
of a high school that Chepe's daughter had attended and graduated
from eighth grade. The principal gave him a videotape of the

graduation ceremony. It included some footage of Santacruz. Looking at the videotape, Kuhlman figured that he was about 5'8" tall and 180 pounds, very different vital stats than Kuhlman had seen in the reports. A little while later, the agent learned that he didn't have to go far to find Chepe. He had an office on the twelfth floor of the largest building in Cali, located about 100 yards from the DEA's office.

In 1983, the Colombian authorities began wiretapping Chepe's telephone calls to the United States.[38] By October, the DEA verified that Santacruz had three Colombian bank accounts and his wife, Ampara, had an account at the Banco de Ponce in Miami.[39] One of Santacruz's lawyers visited all the antinarcotics agencies in Colombia to warn them that he was planning to obtain an order from a local judge that would prohibit the police from intercepting any or all telephones belonging to Santacruz. By this time, the Cali cartel had on their payroll a team of talented lawyers handling their legal affairs. The Colombian authorities believed an employee in a telephone company had compromised their investigation by telling Santacruz about the government's wiretaps.[40]

On April 17, 1984, the head of the Cali antinarcotics unit received a letter, written by Chepe Santacruz and addressed to the manager of the Cali telephone company. "I am aware that three telephone numbers in my name are being intercepted and I want to know if the intercepts have been authorized by a judge," Chepe demanded. The Colombian authorities believed that a telephone company employee on the cartel's payroll had once again compromised their investigation. The authorities instructed the telephone company to discontinue the wiretaps, while they made plans to install wiretaps at points other than the central telephone switching station.[41]

As shown by the Colombian police's experience in trying to monitor Chepe's telephones, the godfathers were privy to anything happening in their city that impacted on their business interests or threatened their freedom. During the 1980s, the Cali cartel developed a formidable security and intelligence network that corrupted the state and made it difficult for Colombian authorities to investigate.[42] Their communications expertise was such that they were able to intercept police and military phone calls within the government and even to intercept phone calls made from the United States embassy.[43] Carlos Espinosa (aka "Pinchalito") was the head of the cartel's communications. In his Miami courtroom testimony in 1997, Guillermo Pallomari, the cartel's chief accountant, noted that Espinosa had great influence at the telephone company in Cali, which allowed him to intercept about 400 calls a month.[44]

At its height of power in the early 1990s, the cartel was said to control the public telephone lines in Cali and as many as 5,000 taxi drivers, who were paid to be its eyes and ears in Cali. "As soon as your plane landed in Cali, they knew who you were," said Chris Feistl, a DEA agent who investigated the cartel in the 1990s. "It was impossible to do anything in Cali without the cartel knowing it."[45]

That was the frustration in investigating the gangsters in Cali, which the DEA was learning fast. The phone company was not the only local institution that their money and power had compromised. In the early 1980s, the cartel began turning Cali into a company town. The Rodriguez brothers and Santacruz controlled Cali in the way that feudal barons once ruled medieval estates. Miguel and Gilberto Rodriguez's base was the center of Cali (Normandia, Juanabu, Los Cristales) and the center of the downtown area around the Intercontinental Hotel, as well as a large portion of the upscale Ciudad Jardin area. Santacruz controlled the southern area of Cali (Ingenio 1 and Ingenio 2), and Pacho Herrera controlled a city south of Cali, Jamundi, and the areas around Yumbo and Palmira north of Cali.[46]

Inside their enclaves, the godfathers built palatial estates that flaunted their success as "businessmen." In 1989, *Money* magazine described Miguel Rodriguez's four-bedroom home (not including servant's quarters) as having "it all." The magazine provided details: "Seven living rooms, each in a different style, are packed with expensive furniture, a real stuffed lion and lion-skin rug, plus hundreds of Lladro porcelain figurines that cost $2,000 to $3,000 each. A curtain of clear glass beads hangs from the ceiling on the second floor down to an indoor reflecting pool. Spiral staircases at either end of the house lead down on one side to a

Jack Lalanne size sky lit gym and [on] the other side to a bar with an underwater view of the outdoor pool."[47]

The overlords had money and power, but they wanted status too. So they began working hard to have Cali's movers and shakers accept them. Chepe, for instance, liked to throw lavish parties for government officials, providing food, drink and entertainment for 6-700 people at a time.[48] But it wasn't easy at first. Club Colombia, an exclusive social club for businessmen and industrialists, rejected Chepe's application for membership. The enraged drug lord didn't go out and murder the snobs. Instead, he built an exact replica of the club on a hillside in the upscale subdivision of Ciudad Jardin and named it Casa Noventa. Chepe also built his own country club outside the city, Villa Brenda, complete with a bridge, statues of Cali's heroes, and three large white religious crosses.[49]

By the mid 1980s, the combine had decided that its strategy should be economic in nature. Buy Colombia, rather than terrorize it, became their guiding philosophy. Spread the money around and everybody accepts you. Back a political candidate and he is in your pocket. The drug money pouring into Cali ignited an economic boom. The city was once a slow-paced hamlet of low-rise buildings, but now the cartel built dozens of high-rise offices and apartment buildings as a way of laundering their money. The Cali skyline changed and thousands of jobs were created. Their money permeated the city economy, and the natives became addicted to laundered cash and conspicuous consumption. "The good citizens of Cali were willing to look the other way, as the godfathers curried favor by spreading their wealth around town," said Jerry Salameh, a DEA agent who investigated the cartel in the 1990s. "Later on, that made it much more difficult for us when we tried to take the cartel down."[50]

The Rodriguez brothers used their cocaine profits to build a business empire that penetrated every section of Cali's economic life. Their organization employed about twenty tax accountants, economists and financial consultants, who worked exclusively on its business and money-laundering activities.[51] In 1974, the Banco de Trabajadores was founded with a $500,000 grant from two foundations that were created to strengthen and organize labor in

Latin America. Gilberto Rodriguez managed to gain control of the bank and was appointed chairman of the board of directors. He then gave shares of stock to local leaders as a token of friendship, appointed some of them to the board of directors, and granted loans and allowed overdrafts on their checking accounts. In return, the godfather expected favors. Police investigations later learned that the Rodriguez brothers, as well as other narco-traffickers, including Pablo Escobar, laundered millions of dollars through the bank.[52]

They used the Banco de Trabajadores to forge a key relationship with Eduardo Mestre Sarmiento, the senator from Santander, one of the most powerful members of the Liberal party and a member of the bank's board of directors. *El Espectador* linked Mestre to the Cali cartel and a loan from the Banco Trabajadores, which allowed him to buy shares in the financial corporation of Boyaca. After *El Espectador*'s exposé, two companies owned by the Rodriguez brothers paid back the loan.[53] Pallomari later testified that Miguel Rodriguez was in the habit of giving expensive gifts to Mestre for services rendered.[54]

Drogas La Rebaja, a drugstore chain that included more than 250 outlets across Colombia, was the heart of the Rodriguez brothers' business empire. The chain distributed pharmaceutical products manufactured by Laboratorios Krassfer. Through the use of frontmen, the Rodriguez brothers also owned Tecno-quimicas Laboratory, the producer of Alka Seltzer in Colombia, whose annual sales in 1987 were estimated to be four billion pesos.[55]

By the late 1980s, the Rodriguez holdings included at least two exclusive urban developments in Cali; the Los Fundadores shopping center; a housing development called La Aurora; two computer service companies; more than fifty bars, apartments and restaurants; two upscale discotheques, one for the older Rodriguez clan and another for the younger set; a Chrysler dealership under the name of Chrysler Discor; and a Bogota company called Financieros Asesores Asociados, which owned a fleet of aircraft used in drug smuggling operations.[56] The DEA reported that the Colombian National Police had verified several Santacruz-owned companies that had previously been identified by the DEA's Cali office, as well as a farm called La Novillera, which was located near the towns of Lamundi and Santander de Q, Valle.[57]

The Cali godfathers loved sports, especially soccer, and they used their passion as an effective corrupting tool. The Rodriguez brothers owned the Cali-based Club America, one of the most popular soccer clubs. According to Fabio Castillo, "The government agency in charge of monitoring sports, Coldeportes [Colombian Institute for Youth and Sports], has never made any move to clean up Colombian sports. All of its directors have preferred to live with the mafia, or, rather, ask them for help."[58]

Manuel Francisco Barrera was a board member of Club America for several years. He was also an education minister during President Virgilio Barco's presidential term (1984–1988), as well as a senator and governor from the Valle del Cauca Department. While serving as auditor general, his most important underling was Maule Pinzon, head of internal audits and husband of Claudia Pilar, Gilberto Rodriguez's daughter.[59]

The cartel used the press to promote its phony image of respectability. In her book *Death Beat*, Colombian journalist Maria Jimena Duzan concedes that the Colombian press paid more attention to Medellin because it was always considered the more violent of the two. "Cali's operatives were less bloody, more businesslike, and therefore less obviously newsworthy," Duzan writes. "In addition, the members of the Cali Cartel were and still are part of the traditional wealthy business class, owners of major businesses and even media outlets, and thus had seemed untouchable."[60] On occasion, when a news story made reference to the suspicious sources of their wealth, the Cali team of high-priced lawyers would be on the phone to the publisher's office, threatening them with lawsuits for "defaming legitimate businessmen."[61]

The media outlets that Duzan referred to were a part of the Colombia Radio Group (GRC), which Gilberto and Miguel founded in 1979. The GRC consisted of twenty-eight outlets in Cali, Medellin, Bogota and other Colombian cities. When the press published stories about the cartel's presence in the media, Gilberto Rodriguez quietly transferred his shares in 1984 to newsman Renteria Jiminez and another frontman, Alvaro Gutierrez Cerdas.[62]

The cartel put journalist Alberto Giraldo in charge of their public relations machine, and he eventually became a close associate of Miguel Rodriguez. Miguel and Giraldo, for example, became partners in a front company named Conapar Ltd.[63] The cartel put media members on its payroll. In 1997, Guillermo Pallomari, the cartel's accountant from 1989 to 1995, told a Miami court that Miguel Rodriguez made monthly payments to "news media, news people who would cooperate with the Cali cartel, as far as keeping out the news that would hurt their image, or they were willing to present news in order to improve the image of the Cali cartel." The media employees the godfathers bought off included presidents, directors, and other executives of media outlets, as well as reporters and broadcasters.[64]

By the mid-1980s, the Cali cartel had corrupted all the key sectors of Colombian society. Its members felt untouchable; they *were* untouchable. The authorities were not going to go after them; they were too busy chasing the rampaging Medellin cartel. The men from Cali could now focus on transforming their mafia into a multinational criminal enterprise.

Chapter 5

Heating Up

Nobody can tell me what to write. If they want to kill me, they
know where to find me.
> – Manuel De Dios Unanue, investigative journalist

Cali was well on its way to becoming a company town by the
mid-1980s. Nevertheless, Jose Santacruz and Gilberto Rodriguez
no longer felt secure enough to travel to the United States
to micromanage their operations. Group Five and other law
enforcement agencies working in the cartel's major markets
began putting together small pieces of the Cali puzzle and building evidence that led to arrest warrants and indictments. In
February 1983, a warrant for Gilberto Rodriguez's arrest was
issued in the Eastern District of New York based on a complaint
of Group Five investigator Rich Crawford.[1] Meanwhile, in New
Orleans, a grand jury had indicted Santacruz and the Rodriguez
brothers on drug trafficking charges.[2]

By 1983, however, the NYDETF's Cali investigation was more
disrupted than its target. The DEA transferred supervisor Bill
Mockler to headquarters in Washington, D.C., and Rich Crawford
to the Tampa office, and the remaining Group Five personnel
were reshuffled within the Task Force. Of Group Five's original
members, only Ken Robinson remained on the Cali probe,
working on it as a New York City police detective until 1986,
when he retired and went to work as an intelligence analyst for
the DEA. Robinson loved working the streets, but his age
disqualified him from serving as an agent.[3]

No other law enforcement officer in the country had Robinson's institutional knowledge of the Cali cartel. Whenever possible he shared what he knew with his colleagues through workshops and seminars. "I know the DEA likes to move agents around and it's a good move for the ambitious agent who wants to get promoted," Robinson explained. "But the Cali cartel was a long-haul investigation, and it hurt us not having that experience that comes with having agents work a case for an extended [period of] time."[4]

Robinson was amazed at how openly Santacruz had operated right under Group Five's nose. The NYDETF now knew that Chepe had assumed three different aliases in his frequent travels to the United States in the early 1980s and had kept three apartments in the upscale Manhattan neighborhoods of Central Park West, the Upper East Side, and Lincoln Center. Interestingly, his Lincoln Center pad was just a few blocks from 11th Avenue and West 57th Street, where the Task Force's office was located. When not attending to business, party animal Chepe spent several hours a day at his favorite hangout, the nearby Martin's Bar on Broadway and 61st Street. When asked by inquisitive barflies why he flew to Miami, Los Angeles, and Houston so often, Chepe responded, "I'm in the vending machine business."[5]

The drug lord had found the Big Apple to be a lot like home. For one thing, Chepe had his own enclave – the Queens borough, which served as the distribution hub and money laundering center of a network that now covered the entire Eastern United States. Jackson Heights and the surrounding area in Queens, especially Roosevelt Avenue, was the heart of the hub and a whirl of drug trafficking activity in the late 1980s. But one would never know that the Cali cartel was the power behind the crime scene. True to its disciplined style, its members kept a low profile and operated out of public view. Cocaine dealing was indeed rampant in Jackson Heights, but as Francisco Diaz, a senior investigator with the NYSP, explained, "Street crime has never been a big problem in that area. There's no serious money in muggings."[6] Diaz has worked on several cases involving the Cali mafia.

More than one million Colombians live in Queens, making them by far the borough's largest ethnic group. "I think it's quite possible for Colombians to spend a great deal of time in these twenty to thirty blocks," one Colombian said in reference to Roosevelt Avenue and the surrounding area. "They can eat Colombian meals, catch Colombian television, listen to Colombian radio and talk to other Colombians. Maybe it will snow once in a while and that will make it different from Colombia. But that's about it."[7]

While most Colombian residents in Queens worked hard each day to earn an honest living, the district had plenty of people willing to join the Cali payroll. The corrupted came from many walks of labor. The cartel, for example, recruited bank tellers and some of their supervisors for money laundering purposes, and Chepe Santacruz used bureaucrats in the motor vehicles bureau to help him get fake driver's licenses.[8] In the 1980s and early 1990s, you could walk along Roosevelt Avenue and see a large number of travel agencies, whose true purpose was to serve as wire-transfer operations; retail stores, where one could buy beepers and cell phones; and real estate agencies that not only rented apartments the dealers used for stash houses but helped pay the bills as well. In front of most storefronts were rows of telephone booths available not only for Colombian immigrants needing to call home, but for gang operatives who used them to evade wiretaps.[9] In 1993, one journalist estimated that Jackson Heights had 200 travel agencies, check cashing agencies, and international telephone companies.[10]

As early as 1978, concerned residents had sent a letter to the DEA's New York office to complain about the impact of cocaine trafficking on their neighborhood. A decade later, the Jackson Heights residents were still concerned, and one of them felt compelled to do something personally about it. His name was Manuel de Dios Unanue, and he worked as a crusading journalist. As an investigative reporter and former editor of the Spanish-language El Diario-La Prensa newspaper, de Dios wrote numerous books and articles about the drug trade and published several photos of drug kingpins and their street operatives. His writings included exposés of the Cali cartel. Colleagues knew he was a dead man walking, and even stayed clear of his car for fear of getting killed by a car bomb. "Nobody can tell me what I can write," de Dios told his nervous friends. "If they want to kill me, they know where to find me."[11]

On March 11, 1992, de Dios was sitting in the bar of the Meson Asturias restaurant in Jackson Heights when a man walked in, took a good look around and walked out, only to return a few minutes later wearing a hood over his head and accompanied by another man. The masked man walked up to de Dios, and, without saying a word, shot him twice in the head with a .9 mm handgun. De Dios slumped to the floor and died almost instantly. Santacruz had ordered the hit, putting a $20,000 contract on the journalist's life, testimony at the 1994 trial of de Dios's killers revealed. Chepe was so upset with de Dios's persistent digging that he was willing to risk the heat and the attention that would surely come with killing an American journalist.[12]

By the mid-1980s, the NYDETF was no closer to breaking the cartel and incarcerating its members than it was when the confidential informant first walked into its office in September 1978 and jump-started the investigation. Robinson had been the only Group Five member to have actually seen Chepe when he stopped him in the JFK parking lot back in 1979.[13] "Que pasa? Que pasa?" Those words, which Robinson heard on the phone in Patino's apartment, still haunted him, for he believed the person trying to contact Patino was none other than Chepe Santacruz.[14] Group Five had seized plenty of records shedding light on the cartel's finances and structure, but they still didn't have the CIs who could help them penetrate it from within. Cali associates knew the price of squealing, and the tight cell structure prevented members from telling much after they were arrested.

In 1983, Group Five had managed to cultivate one valuable CI: a likable, overweight gringo named Robert Lafferty. A former marine officer in the Vietnam War, Lafferty was a pilot for the cartel. He contributed valuable intelligence, providing a sobering insight into the powerful mafia the investigators were up against. Lafferty told Robinson and Crawford that the cartel had actually conducted video surveillance of Group Five members. Robinson smiled. So it wasn't an isolated incident when they videotaped at the airport back in September 1979. The cartel, moreover, had wiretapped their phones, kept photos of Ken Robinson and Bill Mockler in their Cali headquarters, and knew about the DEA's Naddis system. Lafferty remained a valuable CI until he died accidentally in a 1986 plane crash.[15]

At this point, the cartel may have known more about the various teams investigating them than those investigators knew about each other. As Rich Crawford put it: "Law enforcement agencies have a long history of not talking to each other."[16] The events surrounding the Minden lab investigation graphically illustrate this fact of government agency life. From using the financial ledgers they seized in 1982 and 1984, Group Five traced a telephone number to an apartment in the Whitestone section of Queens owned by Fred Aguilera. On April 3, 1985, Ken Robinson and two members of the Task Force were conducting surveillance on a building in Acorn Drive, Rosyln. About 7:15 P.M., the surveillance team observed a brown, four-door Chevrolet enter the underground parking lot at the address. Ten to fifteen minutes later, the Chevy's driver left the building in the company of a Hispanic female. The two drove to an area near the airport and stopped in front of warehouse buildings owned by Bralda International and World Consultants Documentation. Ten minutes later, they left the building driving a white truck. Just before entering the Triborough Bridge in Queens, the truck stopped at a diner, giving Ken Robinson a good look at the driver. It was Fred Aguilera.

The surveillance team continued to follow the white truck. They went through the tollbooth at Exit 29 on the New York State thruway. The truck turned left; the surveillance team turned left. The truck suddenly made a U-turn and went in the opposite direction. The detectives were forced to follow. Once the truck reached Fort Plain, it began driving around in circles with the two surveillance cars on its tail. No other vehicles were on the road, so the investigators figured that Aguilera had made their surveillance. Aguilera now knew he wasn't being paranoid when he made that speech to his Minden lab associates in 1985, warning them to be careful: the police did have them under surveillance. Aguilera never did go to Minden; instead, he went to Amsterdam and the home of his sister, Consuela Donovan. At about 5 P.M. the

following day, the Group Five investigators called off their
surveillance.[17]

Neither the NYSP nor the DEA office in Albany knew the
Task Force had Freddie Aguilera under surveillance. If they had,
a connection to the Minden lab might have been made. "After
Minden, our agency and the DEA began to see the scope and
reach of the Cali cartel," said Ken Cook, a former NYSP detective
who investigated the Colombians. "That's when we really saw the
importance of coordinating our efforts."[18]

The NYDETF and Troop K of the NYSP became the lead
agencies on the investigation that followed the discoveries at the
Minden and Fly Creek labs. Tom Constantine, the NYSP's
director, called a meeting in the agency's Albany office to discuss
strategy. The brass decided it would be best if the law enforcement
agencies pooled their efforts on the investigation. The cartel's
base appeared to be in the Queens, so the Troop K narcotics unit
was assigned to lead the investigation. The case was given the
prosaic code-name KNEU-86055 (known as case 86055 for short),
and a special office was created and staffed by twenty-five state
police officers and three attorneys from the New York Organized
Crime Task Force.[19] "Constantine knew that if you want a group
of police officers to be extremely proactive, you can't inundate
them with paperwork," said Bill Mante, a former investigator and
member of Troop K, NYSP, and a key member of the case 86055
team. "A key part of the strategy was to have us in the street and in
their face."[20]

From what they had learned so far about the cartel's structure
and modus operandi, case 86055 investigators knew that traditional
law enforcement tactics wouldn't be effective against the
formidable drug mafia. They would have to apply continuous
pressure, twenty-four hours a day. "We knew we couldn't focus
on the bust per se – that is, seize a 100-kilo load and then taking a
couple of days off to celebrate," Mante recalled.[21]

The NYSP had a computer information system called Napper,
a huge database containing addresses for mail drops in Jackson
Heights, case file information, driver's license records, beeper
and pay phone numbers, and other valuable information. The
NYSP's crime analysis unit at headquarters in Albany began to

use it for data analysis and to see if they could establish connections between cases. The analysis quickly began to pay off. Investigators linked a cocaine supplier in the Utica area to the Cali cartel in the New York City area, then to its operations in Miami, and, finally, to its headquarters in Cali. Acting on a tip from the Maryland state police, detectives began investigating drug activity in Yonkers, New York, to see if it connected.[22]

The investigators also knew that their target had in place a sophisticated communication system of telephones, beepers and pagers to help it direct operations from Cali. The cartel was well ahead of the police in adopting state-of-the-art technology, but investigators decided that wiretapping, not surveillance, would be the principal investigative tool. "Surveillance is important, but you need a lot of manpower working eighteen hours per day to be effective," said Mante. "We had many discussions as to whether eavesdropping was the most effective approach to investigating this case in the long term. We agreed that it was."[23]

Eavesdropping had its challenges, too. As we have seen, the cartel knew that the Colombian police were wiretapping their calls, and no way did they trust the public telephone system. Cartel managers in Cali began instructing their cell heads in the United States to use pay phones and stay off the private lines. Investigators would see operatives leave a comfortable apartment and walk two blocks in the pouring rain just to use a pay phone. The cartel's workforce knew the potential cost of failure and thought it wiser to be wet than dead.

The Cali men lived and worked by the phone system. Police had wiretapped the Cosa Nostra, but that was like wiretapping the Boy Scouts compared to what was involved in bugging the Colombians. It turned out that wiretapping, especially of pay phones, would require a lot of manpower – interpreters, technicians, detectives – to watch the pay phones to see when the suspected criminals got the call, and people to sit around and tap the phones at the right moment.[24] There were legal considerations as well. The police needed a court order to wiretap a public telephone, and the wiretap conversation had to be related to the persons named in the court order. "If a certain part of the phone conversation was irrelevant to our investigation, we had to shut down the wire," explained Louis Velez, a former member of the NYSP, who headed case 86055's wiretapping operation. "We could go back on the wire tap when the parties started talking about the alleged crime again," he said.[25] Calls between the caller and his counsel were privileged.

The strategy was to identify and gather evidence against customers, couriers, and managers. "Very difficult decisions had to be made as to when to arrest and seize contraband, said Terrance Kelley, the attorney the NYDETF assigned to the investigation. "We had to be careful not to expose too prematurely the existence of electronic surveillance on a particular phone."[26]

The investigators on the street were free of paperwork, but the wire-intercept crew had to document all the calls they made by writing a short synopsis of each call and noting the time it was made and where.[27] Case 86055 set up a huge wiretap room in early 1986 in the Whitestone section of Queens. The Organized Crime Task Force had identified the Cali cartel as an emerging organized crime syndicate and provided funding for the wiretap operation. The Whitestone building was where Velez and his seventeen-member wiretap team operated for the next six years, twenty-four hours a day, 365 days a year. In some years they got lucky and made it home for Christmas dinner.

Mante's and Velez's close working relationship helped to coordinate better what was happening in the wiretapping room and on the street. Mante, the son of a New York City police officer, joined the NYSP in 1974. Velez, the son of a chief who grew up in the tough Lower East Side of Manhattan, joined three years later. They both started out as uniformed officers at the Somers Barracks in Westchester County, about thirty miles north of New York City. In the late 1970s, the two were assigned to the Troop K narcotics unit as undercover detectives, initially investigating street-level drug operations involving mostly heroin, PCP, marijuana and pills.[28]

"As undercover cops, we also bought illegal guns on the street, sold fenced stolen property, and bought the real proceeds from burglaries," Mante recalled. "We propositioned hookers and pimped them. Basically, we did whatever our cover required." At the time, Mante noted, "cocaine was fresh on the streets and was selling for a hundred dollars per gram, but most of our targets could not afford the luxury."[29]

Over the years Mante and Velez continued to work the streets undercover until they joined case 86055. "We clicked and kicked some serious ass when it came to narcotics enforcement," said Mante.[30]

The investigation had a chronic problem that was giving Velez headaches. Reports of the intercepts needed to be written, but almost all of the cartel operatives spoke in Spanish. New York in the mid-1980s lacked police officers fluent in Spanish who could translate the intercepts. Finding them wouldn't be easy. Indeed, Velez could identify just one Colombian on the NYSP force, and he was stationed on an Indian reservation near the Canadian border. The officer was transferred to Velez's unit overnight and began working as a translator.[31]

Through documents obtained by its lawyers in discovery, the cartel learned that the authorities were bugging the pay phones. So, as it did throughout its history, the cartel adjusted its strategy, and by 1985 it was using faxes to communicate with headquarters and to conduct business. The cartel used so many faxes, in fact, that they actually had apartments whose sole purpose was to serve as stash houses for their fax machines. The switch prompted the NYSP to begin wiretapping faxes, becoming the country's first law enforcement agency to do so.[32]

The investigation became a cat-and-mouse communications game, as the Cali cartel tried to outfox the authorities and stay one step ahead of them. About four years later, the cartel switched again – this time to cell phones. "They started using banks of cell phones and we said, 'Oh shit!'" Mante recalled. He explained: "Wiretapping cell phones was really tough at first because NYNEX [the New York Telephone Company] had only seven ports available at a time. So imagine the number of people in the New York metropolitan area and then consider that only seven phones at a time could be tapped. Also, the U.S. government had set aside a number of the phones for national security purposes, and it never allowed anybody else – including law enforcement – to use them."[33]

Fortunately, that barrier was an issue only for about a year. The government started using a different system, and law enforcement had unlimited access for court-ordered eavesdropping. As a result of the fax wiretaps, Hernando Rizzo, an important Cali cell manager, whose codename was "Tio" ("uncle" in Spanish) and five other traffickers were arrested in Queens for possession of 2,014 kilos of cocaine and about $2.3 million in cash. "To this day, it's the largest cocaine bust ever by U.S. law enforcement without the use of CIs," Mante said.[34]

The Rizzo bust was only one of two times that Bill Mante saw the price of cocaine jump during the investigation. "Making the price jump was a sure sign we were hurting them," Mante explained. "The Rizzo bust drove up the price of cocaine to thirty thousand dollars from about fifteen thousand dollars a kilo for six to eight months. It has a trickle-down effect and can make their business customers go to other suppliers. It doesn't kill their business, but it lets them know that we're on to them."[35]

By 1987, the investigation began to broaden, as the Cali cartel network expanded, and the DEA, NYSP, and NYDETF co-ordinated intelligence, surveillance, and wiretap operations.[36] "We realized that we couldn't just rely on the wiretaps," said Robbie Michaelis, who joined the NYDETF right out of the DEA academy in 1987. "We also had to use the knowledge of the old-timers who had worked the investigation, such as Ken Robinson and Bill Mockler. We did surveillance and continued trying to develop informants."[37]

As the wiretaps revealed, the flow of cash and cocaine never slowed. Jaime Orejuela, who had overseen the U.S. processing labs for Chepe Santacruz, fled the United States after authorities uncovered them in 1985. Now he was working the phones from Cali, giving instructions to the regional managers. In early 1986, the first wiretap intercept relating to the cartel's dis-tribution in New York City involved a call between Jaime Orejuela and Marina Montoya, a distributor for the cartel in Queens. Orejuela informed Montoya that he was sending her ten kilos of cocaine. On June 5, Nelson Tapias delivered approximately $1.2 million in cash to a buyer in Queens. On January 2, 1987, Gerardo Garcia, also known as "Puntillon," told Jaime Orejuela that he had "something," meaning money, to give to Orejuela. On February 29, 1988, Orejuela instructed Jorley Arbelaez to "change your house, don't go back there, go and move now! Move from where you live, grow a mustache, a beard, whatever."[38]

Kenny Robinson, now working closely with the case 86055 investigators, was getting so familiar with the financial records that he could tell from Guzman's ledgers that Freddie Aguilera was next in line to take over as the cartel's regional manager. That was why he had him under surveillance and tailed him to a location near the Minden lab in 1985. In September 1987, the NYSP received information that Aguilera had reentered the country and was in the Miami area and, most likely, was hanging out at a bar called the Bakery Center. Robinson, Mante and three other agents from the Task Force and the DEA began surveillance of the Bakery Center. On September 28, the investigators followed Aguilera to several bars into the wee hours of the morning. Aguilera emerged from the bar blind-drunk, and, when they moved in to arrest him, he struggled violently. The officers had to pull him out of his 1987 Cadillac Seville. They brought him back to the DEA's Miami office for questioning and got a warrant to search his apartment on Biscayne Boulevard. There, they found forty-one kilos of cocaine stashed in various places and a Colombia passport in the name of Victor Martinez. On October 7, the U.S. Attorney's Office indicted Aguilera for possession of cocaine with intent to distribute.[39]

When the NYDETF seized the Jose Justo Guzman ledgers in 1984, they identified two brothers, Humberto El Pintor Sandoval and Francisco Sandoval, as cartel members. Twenty-four-hour surveillance of Francisco (Humberto was out of the country) over several days led them to an individual who they identified as Luis "the Shrimp" Ramos, a forty-year-old Colombian illegal alien whose real name was Alvaro Ivan Neira. Task Force investigators followed him to quiet residential streets in middle-class neighborhoods, a cemetery, street corners, and several other locations, where they saw various people give Ramos suitcases and duffel bags. They believed the Shrimp was handling the money for the cartel's drug sales, and they applied for a search warrant for his house, located in a well-to-do section of Bayside, Queens.

On February 20, 1988, the Task Force decided it was time to execute the search warrant. The detectives hit the apartment door, rushed into the living room, and hooked left to the master bedroom. There was the Shrimp coming out of the shower. He dove for the bed, but two officers tackled him and put him in handcuffs. Underneath the bed was a fully automatic and loaded Uzi machine gun. Also within Ramos's reach was an AR-15 assault rifle and an automatic pistol. Both the Uzi and AR-15 had the safety off and were in fire mode. A search of the house revealed several other weapons – a .44, two .38s and Chinese martial arts throwing stars – and a drug ledger on the coffee table in the living room. They found the duffel bags that Ramos had received and discovered that they contained $7.8 million in cold cash. Back at the office, investigators had to push four desks together to stack the money.[40] An analysis of the evidence connected Ramos to Santacruz and the Cali cartel.[41]

Using the windfall of records and documents confiscated in the Ramos arrest, investigators continued to identify the cartel's operatives and customers in New York City. Meanwhile, law enforcement in other areas of the United States, especially Miami and South Florida, were also targeting Cali smuggling operations. "Any ongoing investigation in New York City had a South Florida connection on it," said Tom Cash, an administrator at the DEA's Miami office in the late 1980s. "South Florida became Cali's staging area for getting their drugs into the country and their money out of it. It seemed that, at times, we had more people in South Florida from Cali than there were people living in Cali."[42]

When Gilberto Rodriguez was arrested in Miami in 1984, he had the name of Michael Tsalickis, along with his home and work phone numbers, in his address book. Tsalickis, a Florida business-man from Tarpon Springs, owned an import-export business and had sold monkeys from Colombia's Amazon jungle to research laboratories. "CIs had told us that Tsalickis had been involved in importing cocaine since 1983, and we suspected him of using his business to launder money for the Cali cartel," said Rich Crawford, who was assigned to the case.[43] As part of the investigation,

Crawford journeyed to the Amazon region of Colombia, about 150 miles east of Leticia, to a Tsalickis-owned sawmill, which informants told the DEA was a major center for cocaine production and distribution.

In February 1987, an anonymous letter written in Spanish and postmarked from Cali arrived at the DEA's Miami office. The letter claimed that a shipment of 4,000 kilos of cocaine valued at a mind-boggling $1.7 billion would be arriving in St Petersburg, Florida, aboard a ship named *Amazon Sky*. On April 20, customs agents boarded the ship to inspect the cargo. One of the cedar boards broke and an agent became suspicious. He got a power drill from his office and drilled into the broken board. Pay dirt! The drill came out tainted with cocaine. They discovered that the boards holding the cocaine were holed out to neatly hide one kilo in each hole. The authorities decided to stay put. They carefully glued the boards back together and sanded them down to hide the seams. Federal agents knew that the traffickers had been shipping their cocaine in lumber since 1976, but they still marveled at the sophistication of the organization. "You had to look hard to find the seams," Crawford recalled. "It was unbelievable how professional the job was."[44] Tom Cash later estimated that it must have taken an army of about 800 to 1,000 workers to load the boat.[45]

The authorities watched as the *Amazon Sky*'s crew moved the boards over a period of four days to Tsalickis's office and warehouse complex in St Petersburg. The authorities obtained a search warrant allowing them to videotape the warehouse and wiretap the telephone. Federal agents saw about 700 boards of the cocaine-filled lumber being carried into trucks for the drive to Tsalickis's warehouse. Two weeks after the surveillance began, authorities arrested him and two Colombian associates for cocaine smuggling.[46]

By the end of the 1980s, authorities had a good understanding how the Cali cartel operated. From its headquarters in Cali, the high level "executives" would direct the managers and other traffickers, which federal officials estimated to number between five and six thousand.[47] The executives kept in daily contact with their people in the United States. "Decentralization is not a word in their vocabulary," Tom Constantine, administrator of the DEA, told Congress in October 7, 1994.[48]

The cartel sold its cocaine wholesale through the use of cells or "customer groups," each headed by a manager. Overseeing the cells were regional managers, such as Jose Justo Guzman, who oversaw the distribution of cocaine, the collection of money from customer groups, and the acquisition and maintenance of storage and commercial facilities.[49]

The regional managers had to attend periodic business meetings in Cali. In 1984 Jorge Salazar became head of the cartel's Los Angeles office. In January 1988, he attended a meeting in Cali presided over by Jaime Orejuela. Arriving with twenty bodyguards, Chepe Santacruz greeted Salazar and told him to relax while he made some calls to the United States. "How are things going in L.A.?" Chepe asked Salazar when he had finished making the calls.

"Everything is going well," Salazar replied.

Chepe then took out the books and did a check to be sure there was no missing drugs or money and no money owed. Good, the books were in order.

"You're in Cali for a short time, so enjoy it," Santacruz told Salazar. Then he gave his employee a $12,000 check in Colombian pesos as a bonus for having done a good job.[50]

The NYSP compared the cartel in its style of management to a fast-food chain, such as McDonald's or Dairy Queen, which provided franchisees with supplies of hamburgers or ice cream.[51] Cell managers were treated like the employees of a franchise in that they were given financial incentives to sell the product. Santacruz, for instance, paid Salazar $500 for each kilo he distributed.[52] Just as a corporation would, the Cali cartel transferred its workers from one city to another. "If the heat was on one of their employees in New York City, the cartel would move them to L.A.," Diaz said.[53]

Employees would get regular vacations and other company benefits.[54] In return, they were told to act like regular Joe and Jane America. For instance, those workers maintaining stash houses were expected to leave the house every day, as if they were going to work.[55] On December 11, 1992, investigators hit a home on a quiet street in the city of Yonkers, New York. It was the residence of Orlando Jaramillo, a Miguel Rodriguez operative. Jaramillo left his home every day just like many of his neighbors. His wife shopped in the local supermarkets and his children attended the local Catholic elementary school. Jaramillo told his neighbors that he worked on Wall Street.

Inside the Jaramillo residence, police found the typical financial ledgers showing that Jaramillo had collected $5 million over the previous few weeks. They found a large box in the basement containing more than $100,000. They looked for the Cali cartel's trademark hidden vaults, and, when they moved a flowerpot, a door opened, allowing access to a room, approximately three feet by twenty feet. Inside were U-Haul boxes, floor to ceiling, each stuffed with cash and marked on the outside with amounts totalling $5 million.[56]

Still, there was a big difference between the Cali cartel and a franchise. Each cell or franchise operated with little or no knowledge of other cells. So the takedown of one cell would not compromise another.[57]

Once inside the United States, the cocaine was transported from a central distribution point to markets throughout the country. The mob used trains, buses, private vehicles, airlines, the postal service, and concealed compartments within vehicles, such as trucks and vans, much in the manner that the Aguilera gang moved cocaine from Minden to New York City in 1985. Using perishable cargo to conceal and move the cocaine inside the U.S. was a favorite smuggling method. In June 1994, 1.3 metric tons of cocaine was discovered behind the false wall of a tractor-trailer transporting thirty pallets from Edinburg, Texas, to Immokalee, Florida.[58]

The drug lords retained a team of "corporate" lawyers in the United States to handle legal problems and a team of private investigators to vet potential business partners. When the Task Force busted Hernando Rizzo, the cartel made him go to trial to see what it could learn from the discovery phase. "They analyzed us like we analyzed them," Mante observed.[59]

Still, despite the cartel's well-planned organization, law enforcement was taking down its cells with regularity by the early

1990s. "The cartel was having to send substantial numbers of Cali operatives to the U.S. from Colombia," Robinson said. "That showed we were making a dent in their organization."[60] By 1991, the Case 86055 investigation had resulted in the arrest of nearly 200 defendants and the seizure of more than 5,700 kilos of cocaine and nearly $24 million in cash. Additional property confiscated included seventy-five vehicles, numerous weapons, and property valued at $1 million.[61] The NYSP had done a major hit on the gentlemen from Cali.[62]

Other major cartel distribution rings in New York City and Miami went down hard. Two of the most successful investigations focused on the Pacho Herrera and Ivan Urdinola-Grajales organizations. Like the other three Cali godfathers, Herrera kept a tight rein on his business through the use of coded telecommunications from Cali. But over the course of a one-and-a-half-year investigation, the NYDETF broke most of his codes and penetrated Herrera's wireless communications through the use of eighty-four court-ordered wiretaps. In all, they investigated 71,403 calls, 40,000 of which pertained to drug trafficking activities.[63] At one point, in what turned out to be the largest eavesdropping campaign ever waged by U.S. law enforcement against an international narcotics trafficking organization, the NYDETF simultaneously bugged twenty-one cellular phones, five pay phones and thirty-five pagers.[64]

The Herrera crew became paranoid about the eavesdropping and tried to further encrypt their communications using aliases, cryptic language, and numeric codes. The names of their distribution centers were coded. "The Towers" was used for New York; "la Tia" (the aunt) for Los Angeles; "la Playa" (the beach) for Miami; and "the Town" for Cali. The drug business was going so well for Herrera's people that they had no time to change their modus operandi. They got sloppy and kept using the same words, phrases, and code names over and over again. Micromanager Pacho Herrera was referred to in the wiretapped phone calls as "Abuelo" (grandfather) and "Don Pacho." Over the course of an hour's conversation, several of his team would continually refer to cocaine as "shoes," "checks," or "shirts."[65]

On November 26, 1991, the NYDETF arrested Ramiro Herrera

Buitrago, and a federal grand jury in the Eastern District of New York indicted Ramiro and his brother William Herrera Buitrago, who remained in Colombia. On December 8, 1991, Ramiro Herrera was sentenced to thirty years in prison. Eleven months later, Pacho Herrera and brothers William and Alvaro were indicted in the Eastern District of New York, and the United States presented warrants to the governor of Colombia for their extradition.[66]

Meanwhile in Miami, law enforcement took down the network of Jairo Ivan Urdinola-Grajales, a Cali drug dealer who had a close business relationship with Miguel Rodriguez. He regularly purchased a part of Miguel's multi-ton shipments. The DEA in Miami wiretapped lengthy conversations among Urdinola's cell workers to build its case. In 1992, its High Intensity Drug Task Force concluded Operation Wizard 11, seizing 13,000 kilos of cocaine and $15 million in U.S. currency, and indicting and arresting sixty-five people in the U.S. and Colombia who worked for the Urdinola-Grajales organization.[67]

Authorities had found the Achilles' heel of their target. As the Cali cartel grew into a multinational enterprise during the 1980s, it became more reliant on telecommunications to coordinate its activities. Yes, they used the best and latest technology available on the market, but law enforcement was not standing still either. It, too, refined its investigative techniques and methods as it learned more about the organization. The bosses in Cali, however, couldn't let go, and as the criminal enterprise expanded not just in the United States but globally, their management style became a major liability.

"All important decisions were made from Cali – whether it involved distribution, security or whatever – and that made the cartel dependent on communications technology," said DEA agent Michael Horn. "They were planting the seeds for their own downfall."[68]

Chapter 6

Dirty Laundry

The greed factor came into play. The Cali cartel loved money
and they loved how fast we were able to hide it.

— Billy Bruton, retired IRS agent and
investigator on Operation Dinero

Getting drugs into the United States was one of the two major
challenges facing the Cali cartel as it expanded its criminal empire.
The other challenge was getting the money out of the country
without being detected. The U.S. General Accounting Office
defines money laundering as "the process through which the
existence, illegal source and unlawful application of illegal gains
is concealed or disguised to make the gains appear legitimate,
therefore helping to evade detection, prosecution seizure and
taxation."[1]

The Cali cartel's network of businesses in Queens – travel
agencies, realty agencies, and mom-and-pop convenience stores –
served as a front for its illegal activities, including the wire
transferring of money abroad. The cartel needed this elaborate
network because the hundreds of millions of dollars it made
comprised the lifeblood of the organization. As Harold Wankel,
a former chief of operations for the DEA, explained to
Congress, "Without it, they can't finance the manufacturing, the
transportation, the smuggling, the distribution, the movement,
and the murder that are essential to their illegal trade. Drug
money laundering organizations are essential to the cash flow of
these illegal entrepreneurs."[2]

As the cartel grew, its expenses mushroomed, and it needed to smuggle a lot of money back into Colombia to pay the bills. Expenses included a sizable payroll of informants and gofers who worked in key national institutions – the armed forces, the police, the courts, the government, the legislature, the news media, and the telephone system. In 1989, the DEA estimated that a private from the Colombian National Police (CNP) who was on the cartel payroll received about $1550 a week; a captain, $5,000; and a general, $15,000. These were enormous sums of money, but the drug lords relied more on silver than lead – the bribe, not the bullet – and considered it money well spent, the necessary cost of doing illegal drug business.[3]

From the 1970s to the mid-1980s, money laundering was a relatively simple process. The cartel's associates would open a series of bank accounts and hire couriers to deposit the money and then wire it to Colombia, where it was "washed" into legitimate money. But the U.S. enacted laws that made it increasingly more difficult for traffickers to launder their money this way. Currency Transaction Receipts (CTRs), for example, had to be filed with the U.S. government for every cash transaction over $10,000. Then the U.S. introduced the Currency Receipt of International Transaction of Currency or Monetary Instruments (CMIR), which had to be filed for every foreign deposit of $10,000. Americans also had to file an IRS Foreign Bank Account Receipt for every foreign bank account they maintained.

To circumvent these financial requirements, the cartel recruited "smurfs" out of the poor barrios of Colombia and brought them illegally to the United States and its major markets: Miami, New York City, Houston and Los Angeles.[4] They were named smurfs after the small blue cartoon characters who performed routine tasks. The smurfs would buy money orders for an amount that would be just under the $10,000 CTR reporting requirement. In purchasing the money orders, buyers needed no identification or forms to complete, and the money orders could remain blank until they were deposited or cashed in a bank. Once the money orders were purchased, they would be packed in a cardboard box or some other container and shipped out of the country to Colombia or another money-laundering destination, such as

Panama, the Cayman Islands, or a country that had an absence of legislation regulating wire transfers.[5]

With so much money to move, the Cali barons did not hesitate to use any associate available. Santacruz's interior decorators, Alexander Blarek and Frank Pellechia, helped launder Chepe's drug profits by buying lavishly expensive items, such as a $100,000 dining room table and a $250,000 entertainment system, and having them sent to Colombia.[6] In an audiotape prosecutors presented as evidence in one trial involving the cartel, a witness described a Colombian warehouse filled with appliances and other American goods as being like a "Home Depot."[7] According to Richard Weber, the assistant district attorney for the Eastern District of New York who helped prosecute the Blarek-Pellechia trial, "The tremendous amount of money that the cartel was making became difficult for them to move from the United States. That's why Santacruz turned to interior decorators from San Francisco."[8]

In another case, Oscar Cuevas owned a money exchange house used to launder dollars. Cuevas was in charge of shipping money inside the United States and making deposits to existing accounts in Great Britain and Switzerland. Authorities discovered Cuevas's money-laundering operation when they arrested one of his employees at a New York airport with a suitcase containing $543,000 shortly before he was to fly to Switzerland. On September 13, 1986, Cuevas was convicted of laundering $25 million.[9]

The smurf system was cumbersome and risky, so the cartel began smuggling cash to Colombia in bulk. Jumbo planes, such as Boeing 727s, Caravelles, and Turbo Prop Lockheed Electras, were stripped and used to ship cocaine to the States from Colombia. Once the shipment was unloaded, the planes would be reloaded with U.S. cash amounting to $20-30 million, or more.[10]

Moving drug money in bulk may seem a simple task, but a kilo of cocaine weighs less than the money used to buy it. In fact, if the money consists of U.S. dollars in denominations of fives, tens, and twenties, it will weigh ten times more than cocaine. As Bill Bruton, a financial investigator and former IRS agent, pointed out, "The figures involving weight are even more dramatic when you consider that a single trafficker can earn as much as $500 million in the United States from the sale of cocaine. The weight of that amount of illicit currency would exceed 125,000 pounds."[11]

During its history, the Cali cartel continually looked for better ways to hide its money so it could stay ahead of international law enforcement. As authorities intensified their investigation of the cartel, its schemes became increasingly more sophisticated. The Rodriguez brothers had a team of launderers in charge of identifying mechanisms in Colombia that could help them smuggle their money into the country.[12] One clever operation involved Colombian front companies in Cali and the Colombian National Bank of Miami. In 1985 the cartel used the Miami-based Irving Trust Company to transfer money orders totaling some $40 million from Continental to the Banco Cafetero de Panama. Irving Trust sent a credit memorandum ordering the funds in the Banco Cafetero de Panama to be placed on the books for conveyance to the First Interamericas Bank that Gilberto Rodriguez and Jorge Ochoa controlled.[13] "The absence of effective anti-money-laundering laws made it easy for the cartel to get their money back into Colombia," explained Greg Passic, a former DEA agent and expert in money laundering.[14]

The Cali cartel, like Colombians from all walks of life, used the country's well-established Black Market Peso Exchange to launder.[15] As Al James, a money-laundering expert and former financial investigator with the Financial Crimes Enforcement Network (FINCEN), pointed out, "The problem for the drug traffickers is that they are paid in U.S. dollars, but the medium of exchange in Colombia is the peso."[16]

In the 1980s, however, it wasn't easy for Colombians to exchange their pesos for dollars. In fact, it was virtually impossible, according to money-laundering experts who testified at the 1998 trial of Jose Santacruz's interior decorators. "Colombia had very strict currency controls in place on the peso," said Charles Morley, an expert who has taught money-laundering training symposia for the DEA. "It was illegal for most people, virtually all people, to have dollar accounts in them either in Colombia or in the United States. Those that would be allowed dollar accounts were very tightly regulated, and it was only select industries that were allowed to have dollar accounts for trade purposes."[17]

The case Cali associate Jose Stroh graphically illustrates how the Black Market Peso Exchange worked. In becoming a currency broker for the drug lords in 1986, Stroh negotiated the currency exchange from dollars to pesos for several cartel representatives. In return, he received a commission for each cash currency transaction.

In transacting the currency exchange, Stroh provided the cartel representatives with code names and beeper numbers of individuals in the United States who they could contact for the pick-up of U.S. currency. Stroh's associates in the United States would convert the cash to checks, money orders, and wire transfers, which would then be transferred within and outside the United States. To meet the U.S. currency reporting requirements, the transactions did not exceed $10,000. To further the scheme, Stroh set up two front corporations in August 1986, which were used to open bank accounts in Panama so that checks, money orders and wire transfers could be transferred to Colombia.[18]

Stroh and other bent brokers would arrange currency transactions of dollars to pesos with legitimate Colombian businessmen who would buy such goods as cigarettes, liquor, dishwashers, and television sets. The rate for exchanging dollars for Colombian pesos would usually be about twenty percent of the official exchange rate, and this would be Stroh's commission. The Colombians paid Stroh in pesos, and he, in turn, would use dollars to pay the Colombian debt in the United States.[19]

By using brokers like Stroh to manipulate the Black Market Peso Exchange, the cartel avoided legitimate banks and the challenge of having to deal with tougher money-laundering laws that the United States and other governments were legislating. "The Black Market Peso Exchange took the work of money laundering away from the drug traffickers and made it the responsibility of the money broker to get the drug money back to Colombia," Passic explained.[20]

By the early 1990s, the Cali mob and other drug trafficking groups were laundering an estimated $5 billion annually in the Black Market Peso Exchange. Today in Colombia, an estimated

10,000 Colombians make their living as brokers for the system.[21] The entire process of smuggling drugs to the United States and getting the pesos back to Colombia has become known as *La Vuelta* or "The Round."[22] "The Exchange has been devastating to the Colombian economy," said Robert Grosse, professor of international business at the Thunderbird Graduate School in International Management in Glendale, Arizona, and author of *Drugs and Money: Laundering Latin America's Cocaine Dollars.* "The Colombian government really can't do anything about the system because it's such a pervasive part of their economy and so many Colombians depend on it."[23]

The Cali cartel did get more sophisticated in developing its networks of front companies and money brokers during the 1980s, but authorities in other countries also began finding success going against the money-laundering operations. In 1989, the DEA launched Operation Pisces, an undercover investigation in which agents posed as money launderers. The DEA handled more than $10 million for the Cali cartel during a two-year period. When the DEA finally closed the operation, forty-three people were indicted for laundering, including Cali godfather Gilberto Rodriguez, and $2.5 million in U.S. currency and 5,360 pounds of cocaine were seized. U.S. Attorney Dexter Lechtinen unsealed the indictments on March 15, 1991, at a news conference in Miami. "What we have here is the federal reserve of the money-laundering system," he boasted to the press. "It's the blockbuster of money-laundering indictments, especially against the Cali cartel. This is the essence of money-laundering indictments."[24]

Such operations did get some good publicity for law enforcement in the War on Drugs, but in terms of hurting the enemy, all they actually did was to confiscate some of the cartel's pocket change. After all, the seizure of $2.5 million pales in comparison to the billions of dollars that the drug lords were earning annually. What the DEA needed to do to disrupt the cartel's money supply was to undertake a concerted attack on its financial infrastructure.[25] In 1992, Robert Nieves, who was with the DEA's cocaine investigations section at the time, proposed that investigations of kingpin drug-trafficking targets be directed and funded from the agency's headquarters in

Washington, D.C. Not surprisingly, the proposal wasn't popular with DEA field managers and regional offices. "Every investigator and every DEA manager wants to have the capability of setting and funding his own priorities and to be able to pursue cases he thinks are more important to his area of operations," commented Nieves.[26]

The DEA realized a change to a kingpin strategy could not be done cheaply. The cost of wiretapping alone would exceed the annual budgets of most DEA field offices. Nevertheless, the agency pushed ahead with the strategy, establishing the Special Operations Division (SOD) to coordinate all kingpin cases involving wiretaps. Many of the cases covered multiple jurisdictions, not just in the United States but also in other countries. "It sounds like an easy thing to do, but prior to SOD's establishment, it wasn't done efficiently," Nieves explained. "Having the SOD, for example, would ensure that wiretaps were being pursued in Houston that otherwise wouldn't be pursued and that important lead information was passed to the Bogota office that otherwise wouldn't be passed by the DEA office in Los Angeles, et cetera."[27]

The mechanics of the Kingpin Strategy were simple. For a case to be included as part of the program and to qualify for financial and personnel support, a clear connection had to be made to one of the identified and targeted bosses. "That nexus had to be established and demonstrated through investigative reporting," Nieves said. "Once an investigation was included in the kingpin program, its financing became the responsibility of DEA headquarters, as did the national and international coordination of the case."[28] The initial kingpin targets included Chepe Santacruz and the Rodriguez brothers, as well the Medellin cartel's Pablo Escobar and the three Ochoa brothers.

The CIA had a parallel program, which was known as the Linear Strategy. The program's initial targets were identical, as was the goal – to help bring all the resources of the federal government to bear on those criminal groups, not only in the United States, but throughout the hemisphere and wherever the activity of drug distribution was identified.[29] "The Kingpin Strategy showed that there is no better way to go after a drug trafficking

network than by disrupting its ability to finance the production
and movement of drugs," Passic said.[30]

The DEA had its first major success with the Kingpin Strategy
when it launched Operation Green Ice (Freeze the Money) to
attack the Cali cartel's financial networks. Operation Green Ice
began in 1989 when the DEA established its own front company,
Trans America Ventures Associates (TAVA), and put it in an
upscale office in La Jolla, California. The DEA selected agent
Heidi Landgraf, a beautiful blond in her early thirties who spoke
perfect Spanish, as head of the operation. She was given a cover
background and a crash course in money laundering, set up in a
fancy mansion, and provided with luxury cars seized from previous
investigations. To get the money back into Colombia, TAVA set
up a series of leather companies to circumvent the country's
currency laws. The DEA then put the word out on the street that
TAVA was a full-service laundry ready to wash drug profits.[31]

The TAVA was so successful that it was named one of the
country's top 100 Hispanic companies.[32] Soon, it outgrew
California, as the good news about the bank appeared in the
underworld and other crime bosses began looking to have their
money laundered through the TAVA network. The DEA's front
company established a complex import-export scheme in Rome
to help move the drugs and money generated by the alliance
between the Cali cartel and the Italian Mafia. By the time
Operation Green Ice ended, the DEA's coordinated international
law enforcement effort involved Canada, the Cayman Islands,
Colombia, Costa Rica, Italy, Spain and the United Kingdom.
Operation Green Ice was the first coordinated international
operation against drug trafficking in history.[33]

In 1992, undercover agents arranged meetings with some of
the Cali cartel's financial managers at locations in the United
States, Italy, Spain and Costa Rica, where they were arrested.
Police involved in the operation worldwide did a sweep, arresting
more than 150 people and seizing $42 million in illegal profits.[34]
At a news conference, a senior Italian investigator said, "I would
not hesitate to define this operation as the most important ever
carried out in Italy and Europe against drug-trafficking and
money-laundering."[35]

Operation Green Ice would impact on drug trafficking long term, the DEA assured, because it disrupted the Cali cartel's methods of communication, flow of information and money, and trafficking patterns. Critics of the War on Drugs, however, questioned whether Operation Green Ice justified the allocation of the country's limited resources. "Those charged in the operation weren't the kingpins," editorialized the St. Louis Post Dispatch. "The money managers who were charged won't be missed by the Cali organization, in as much as the cartel is said to employ dozens of the key money managers. This nation shouldn't expect, and shouldn't even try, to stamp out drug cartels around the world."[36]

Nevertheless, U.S. law enforcement, led by the DEA, pushed forward with other multiagency operations involving lots of man-hours and resources. Through Green Ice II, for instance, the U.S. was able to identify about forty Colombian and Panamanian bank accounts used by the Cali combine for laundering drug money.[37] More than twenty federal and local agencies participated in Green Ice, besides the DEA, including the FBI, IRS, RCMP (Royal Canadian Mounted Police) and Italian agencies.[38]

The most innovative sting by the U.S. against the cartel came in 1993, when an informant revealed to IRS and DEA agents during a debriefing that what the Cali godfathers really wanted was their own personal bank to wash their dirty cash. "We knew the cartel valued the banking relationship, so we decided to be bankers," said Billy Bruton, a retired IRS agent with twenty-three years of experience investigating financial crimes. "A kilo of cocaine weighs 2.2 pounds and may be worth a million dollars, but the money can weigh a couple of hundred pounds. A bank is the best way to move that kind of weight. We knew by putting a full-service bank in place and then conning the Cali to use it would provide us with the best way to get a close look at their complex finances."[39]

The Office of the U.S. Attorney General authorized the operation, which became known as Dinero, and the DEA and IRS were put in charge of coordinating it. To avoid charges that U.S. taxpayers' money was being used to finance illegal drug operations, the two agencies had to assure the Attorney General's Office that they would only use previously seized drug money to finance the bank.[40] The DEA and IRS bought a failing bank, renamed it the RHMT Trust Bank, and then began laying the groundwork for a fictitious bank to be located in Antiquilla, a British dependency and secret-bank haven that appealed to criminals. The governor of Antiquilla was the only person on the island who knew about Operation Dinero, and he was told not to tell anyone else. It took about a year for the IRS and DEA to set the bank up.

To get the bank approved, the federal agencies made a formal application to proper Antiquilla authorities just as any normal bank would do. The Antiquilla authorities were skeptical of the plan, but after several months, they gave it the go-ahead in the summer of 1993 and issued a Class B British banking license. The "bankers" joined a business association, printed slick brochures advertising their services, and set up accounts with correspondent banks in other countries. They rented phones and connected fax lines from the phony bank to Atlanta. They set up posh front offices, where Spanish-speaking assistants, who actually worked for the federal agencies, answered the phones. They set up toll-free numbers in Colombia, Mexico and Venezuela. They didn't miss a detail. The fake bank even had its own stationery in English, Spanish and French. Bruton and his partner on the sting, Skip Latson, a DEA agent and money-laundering expert, assumed new identities and put the word out on the street that they were ready to do some dirty business.[41]

The bank charged outlandish fees to scare off legitimate customers, but that didn't bother the men from Cali. The first customer who walked through the bank's door was a cartel associate who wanted to wash the drug money he had made the previous year.

"How much would that be?" one of the agents asked.

"Oh, about five hundred million dollars," was the answer.[42]

"The greed factor came into play," Bruton recalled. "The Cali cartel loved money and they loved how fast we were able to hide it."[43]

In Dinero's first two weeks of operation, the bank accepted more than $8 million in deposits. More importantly, the federal authorities gathered valuable intelligence on how the cartel moved its money.[44] "We got a wealth of data on the Cali cartel's assets, their financial accounts and their drug shipments," Latson said.[45]

In November 1994, a Cali cartel drug trafficker told an undercover agent in Colombia he had three paintings valued at nine million dollars that he wanted to sell and launder the proceeds. "Can I put it on consignment with your bank?" the drug trafficker asked. "By all means," the phony banker told him. The three paintings were Joshua Reynolds's *Portrait of a Gentleman*, Peter Paul Rubens's *Saint Paul*, and Pablo Picasso's *Head of a Beggar*.[46]

On December 14, 1994, a cartel representative took the paintings to the United States to sell. She arrived at the Miami airport and met a man and a woman – undercover IRS agents posing as a banker and an art expert – who were there to negotiate the purchase of the paintings for a client. The three boarded a Lear jet, ostensibly on their way to meet the buyer; instead, they landed in Atlanta and the cartel rep was led away in handcuffs.[47]

When the U.S. Justice Department finally shut down the RHMT Trust Bank in 1994 and all the other storefront operations it had in place, the DEA and IRS had set up 12 front corporations and 51 corporate bank accounts; it had handled 92 cash transactions totaling $39.5 million and 29 noncash transactions of $8.1 million; it had seized $4.3 million from money launderers and about 9 tons of cocaine; and it had arrested 60 people in the United States, 80 in Italy, and 22 in Spain.[48]

Operation Dinero was a big change in the way the U.S. government handled money-laundering operations, and it showed how innovative federal agencies can get chasing the criminals. The U.S. Justice Department, however, never had much faith in sting operations like Operation Dinero. "We were shocked when Janet Reno said we had less than three months to close Operation Dinero," Bruton recalled. "It's true that some of the storefront operations had been around too long and served their purpose, but we got thrown out with the bath water."[49] Al James added, "The [Justice Department] said we were funding drug trafficking by laundering money for drug traffickers, and that we weren't prosecuting enough of them. The bottom line, though –

the systematic disruption of money-laundering operations is a justifiable operation for a police investigation."[50]

But perhaps the most successful of the money-laundering operations against the Cali cartel didn't involve elaborate stings or substantial resources or have a lot of bureaucratic red tape to cut through. All it took was some luck. In 1989 in Luxembourg, an apartment dweller complained to the police that a neighbor down the hall was sending and receiving phone messages and faxes at all hours of the day and night. He didn't seem to have a job either, the source noted. The police investigated, and, using wiretaps, they found that one of the faxes had been sent to Miguel Rodriguez Orejuela, none other than the prominent Colombian drug dealer. It turned out that the neighbor, Jose Franklin Jurado-Rodriguez, was educated at Harvard and had worked as head of the Cali stock exchange. The Luxembourg authorities contacted the DEA to ask if it had information about the suspicious Colombian. The NYDETF files showed that Jurado had served as a director of the Rodriguezes' Interamericas Bank in 1984.[51] Police arrested Jurado and two associates, Edgar Alberto Garcia Montilla and Richard Mahecha-Bustos.

As soon as the arrests were made, Miguel Rodriguez called a big meeting with his brother Gilberto, Chepe Santacruz, and Pacho Herrera. Santacruz apologized to Miguel because Edgar Alberto Garcia Montilla was a very important person in the cartel and was arrested while running a personal errand for him without Miguel's permission. Garcia Montilla was trying to move some money to one of Chepe's accounts out of Colombia that U.S. and Colombian authorities were investigating. Miguel accepted Chepe's apology and said he would split the cost of defending Garcia fifty-fifty with him.[52]

Through further investigation, Luxembourg police uncovered a remarkably complex arrangement of money-laundering transactions that Jurado had undertaken for the Cali cartel. He and his partners had opened hundreds of bank accounts throughout Europe in the names of family members, friends, and associates of Santacruz, which he used to deposit large amounts of checks and wire transfers.[53] Through wiretaps, police found that the three Santacruz money launderers deposited about $180,000 in the account of Herberto Castro-Mesa, who turned out to be Chepe's father-in-law.[54] Anticipating that the arrests would lead the Cali cartel to move their money from Luxembourg to Colombia before they could seize it, Luxembourg authorities asked several countries to freeze the money they suspected was in cartel accounts. Sure enough, a flurry of electronic transfers from suspected accounts ensued, but European authorities did manage to seize $30 million in Europe, $16 million in Panama, and $12 million in the United States.[55]

When police arrested Jurado, they seized a twenty-page memorandum titled "phasing," which he had written. It outlined a plan to money-launder Santacruz's finances and enterprises.[56] Phasing included a five-step process (phases zero to four) in which a phase, Jurado wrote in his memorandum, is "a transition period during which assets move from a higher to a lower level of risk."[57]

Phase one essentially involved money from street drug sales that the cartel had managed to move from the United States to its banks in Panama. In the mid-1980s, couriers deposited $64 million in small bills from U.S. drug deals into the First Inter Americas Bank in Panama, but when Panamanian authorities discovered that Gilberto Rodriguez and Jorge Ochoa owned the bank, they froze $28 million that could be directly linked to it. The cartel quickly moved the rest of the money to other Panamanian banks. The cartel hired Jurado in 1987 to launder the other $36 million through the soft-on-money-laundering European financial institutions.[58]

In phase two, Jurado moved the money into the European accounts, putting them in the names of Santacruz's family and associates. Jurado used the Panamanian financial institutions to convert the money into money orders, which were then wired to the European accounts.[59] At this point, Jurado traveled all over Europe to see which financial institutions had the most favorable conditions for his client's money. Jurado checked out Austria, Scotland and the Channel Islands, but he avoided Switzerland because of "a lack of trustworthiness in reference to confidentiality."[60]

In phase three, Jurado moved the money from Panama to the

European accounts, transferring from more than 100 accounts in sixty-eight banks in nine countries. In the final phase, Jurado moved the money to Colombia where it could be converted to pesos and used to pay expenses, buy goods, and invest in the local economy – in other words, laundered. Here again, the Black Market Peso Exchange went to work. The final phase was actually the easiest to complete because many Colombians wanted to get their money out of the country and were more than willing to work with the cartel.[61]

But Santacruz still had lots of money in banks that the authorities hadn't frozen, and he began looking for a way to get it back. Chepe's lawyer, Michael Abbell, told his client that the best way to do that was to claim the frozen funds actually represented legal profits that were flight capital from the United States. On December 28, 1990, Abbell set out the strategy in a memorandum that he faxed to Santacruz. Abbell and Donald Ferguson, another cartel lawyer, traveled to Cali and met with Santacruz at the Intercontinental Hotel to discuss it. Chepe gave Abbell the go-ahead. Santacruz retained a German attorney named Raphael Barber Llorete, who was able to get some of Chepe's money released in Germany, which has no money-laundering laws. Meanwhile, Chepe's lawyers got another $15 to $18 million released from accounts in Panama.[62]

Santacruz blew his top when he learned his lawyers couldn't get the other $48 million released, $3 million of which was in the United States and the rest in Europe.[63] "I really believe that Santacruz was planning to use the money for his retirement," said Robbie Michaelis, a DEA agent who worked the Luxembourg investigation. "We really upset his plans."[64]

Meanwhile, the trial of Chepe Santacruz's three money launderers was scheduled for the summer of 1991. The U.S. Attorney's Office for the Eastern District of New York also announced that it planned to pursue a prosecution in New York City. Although it would take years for the authorities to unravel and pursue the Luxembourg money-laundering case's many ramifications, law enforcement had begun to disrupt the Cali cartel's smooth-running enterprise.

Chapter 7

Going Multinational

The major drug of choice in Europe in the late 1980s was heroin supplied by the Asians. But the Cali cartel showed up on the DEA's radar screen, and we began seeing substantial increases in cocaine seizures.

– John Constanzo, retired DEA agent

Successful money-laundering investigations in the early 1990s exposed the global reach of the Cali cartel. Federal agents working undercover on Operation Green Ice provided laundering "services" for the cartel in Europe, Colombia and the Caribbean. In the United Kingdom, authorities seized about $6 billion, arrested three cartel members and confiscated forty-three kilos of cocaine. Italy's Servicio Centrale Operativo (SCO) and the Internal Security Service (SISDE) seized $1 million and arrested twenty-one members of two Italian Mafia families who worked with the Cali cartel. The Spanish National Police arrested four cartel members, while the Royal Canadian Mounted Police arrested one individual and seized another $1.6 million.[1] The international community had never cooperated on drug trafficking cases as it had on Operation Green Ice, and the investigation showed that more of that type of cooperation needed to be done in the future, given the growing reach of the Cali cartel.[2]

In Operation Dinero, authorities in the United States, Italy, Spain and Great Britain had used a clever sting to follow the cartel's money trail and unravel a web of organized crime syndicate connections in Italy, Russia, Great Britain and several other European countries, and as far away as the Orient. Dinero also exposed a strong alliance between Cali and the Italian Mafia when authorities arrested Italian crime boss Pasquale C. Locatelli in Spain on September 6, 1994. The Locatelli organization, which had operations in France, Romania, Croatia, Spain, Greece, Italy and Canada, sent ships to the Colombian coast to pick up cocaine and transport it to North Africa, where it was transferred to smaller boats and smuggled into Europe.[3]

By the early 1990s, the cartel had grown into a true crime multinational. It made its money illegally, but that was about the only difference between the Cali cartel and an IBM or any other multinational corporation. In terms of structure, marketing, and distribution, the drug mafia had as much in common with the giants that made *Fortune* magazine's annual list of top 500 companies as it did with its rivals in the drug trade. The Cali cartel, in fact, became the poster syndicate for multinational crime. It had the ability to challenge state authority. It employed a workforce spread around the world. It was constantly opening up new markets.

As a multinational commonly does, the cartel began decentralizing and moving some of its operations out of its home base of Colombia. By the early 1990s, it had cocaine processing and distribution operations in a dozen Latin America countries.[4] Tom de Renenteria, a drug expert with the Andean Commission of Jurists, told *Newsweek* that "Latin America as a whole is sliding into the drug war. Argentina and Brazil can see their future in Bolivia. Bolivia sees its own 'future' in Peru . . . Peru in Colombia . . . it's an endless cycle." *Newsweek* also noted that "Bolivia and Peru, which have long been prime sources of raw coca for Colombia's cartels, were becoming major producers of finished cocaine as well."[5]

The Cali drug lords began using Latin American and Caribbean countries in a variety of dynamic ways. Guatemala became the largest warehouse for cocaine in Latin America, and, according to U.S. officials working in the country, most of the cocaine trafficking there was Cali-related. Analysts at the U.S. Department of Justice and the U.S. State Department's Bureau of International

Narcotics Matters calculated that traffickers were using Guatemala to move fifty to seventy-five tons of cocaine annually to the United States.[6]

In 1990, customs officers began seeing a significant increase in the number of Haitian couriers smuggling large quantities of cocaine out of Haiti for the Cali cartel on commercial airlines and air cargo planes. In one three-month period, they arrested about thirty Haitian drug couriers, or mules, trying to smuggle sixty kilograms of cocaine into Miami and San Juan, Puerto Rico.[7] Ecuador became a drop-off point for precursor chemicals, while in Brazil the cartel worked closely with Italian organized crime groups based there to form dozens of bogus companies that they used to launder drug money.[8]

In Venezuela, the cartel worked with the Contrera family, which had moved to the country from Sicily in the 1970s and made it an important conduit for the Colombian-Sicilian drug connection. One Venezuelan official, Guillermo Jiminez, the head of the country's organized crime unit, estimated the Contrera network was responsible for eighty percent of all the cocaine being exported from Colombia.[9]

In terms of marketing strategy, the alliances the Cali cartel forged with Mexican traffickers were its most important in Latin America. Mexican and Colombian drug traffickers had collaborated on a small scale since the early 1970s, when the Colombian traffickers "piggybacked" their drug loads on smuggling routes that their Mexican counterparts had set up for heroin and marijuana.[10] Still, most of the Colombian cocaine entering the United States from the 1970s through the mid-1980s came by way of the Caribbean. As the United States stepped up its so-called War on Drugs in the 1980s, law enforcement intensified the pressure on this smuggling corridor, forcing the cartel to seek new routes through Central America and Mexico and across the United States's Southwest border.[11] In reality, the shift was inevitable. Mexico had what the cartel needed – a 2,000-mile expanse of border that offered unlimited smuggling possibilities, experienced smugglers eager to collaborate, and a ready-made infrastructure to meet its needs.

To further its changing distribution strategy, the Cali cartel helped organize a crime federation in Mexico, which consisted of experienced traffickers who could provide safe and reliable smuggling services.[12] According to DEA intelligence, to meet the cartel's transportation needs, "major Mexican traffickers united their operations, which resulted in the formation of a loose federation."[13]

By the early 1990s, sixty to eighty percent of the cocaine entering the United States came through the Mexican connection, while only twenty to thirty percent continued to be smuggled via the Caribbean.[14] The 1989 seizure of more than twenty-one tons in Sylmar, California, illustrated how important the Mexican connection had become in the Cali cartel transportation scheme of things. The shipment, at the time the largest cocaine seizure on record, crossed the Mexican border at El Paso, Texas, and then was moved by truck to the West Coast. In making the big bust, law enforcement officials boasted that they had prevented an even larger amount of cocaine from reaching the streets, but on further investigation they learned that it had merely dented the drug smuggling. "We realized our encouragement was premature when we analyzed seized records," conceded Tom Constantine, the DEA administrator from 1994 to 1998. "What we found was even more astounding. We learned that during only a three-month period, the organization had succeeded in smuggling fifty-five tons of cocaine into the United States. This cocaine had been trucked to the United States and had already been distributed on the streets."[15]

Several Mexican drug traffickers became key players in the cartel's Mexican connection, but one of the first was actually a Honduran named Juan Ramon Matta Ballesteros, who, from the mid-1970s to the mid-1990s, worked with the Guadalajara cartel, the group responsible for kidnapping and killing DEA Special Agent Enrique Camarena in 1985.[16] Matta Ballesteros was arrested and jailed in Colombia, but he escaped after paying a bribe estimated at between $1 million and $2.5 million. He fled to Tecucigulpa, Honduras, where he bought a home and moved openly in public. The drug lord thought he was safe in Honduras because it didn't have an extradition treaty with the United States, but Honduras, under pressure from the United States, deported him in 1988. Two years later, he became the first person convicted of Camarena's murderer. The following year, Matta Ballesteros was sentenced to three life-terms in prison.[17]

Until his arrest in January 1996, Juan Garcia-Abrego, the first international drug trafficker to be included on the FBI's Most Wanted List, smuggled drugs for the Cali cartel from the Yucatan region in Mexico to South Texas and on to Cali's New York market. Garcia-Abrego also helped move bulk shipments of cash. During one four-year period, from 1989 to 1993, U.S. authorities seized $53 million from the Garcia-Abrego organization.[18] The personal fortune of Garcia-Abrego, nicknamed "the Doll" because of his youthful appearance, was placed at $2 billion, and he reportedly owned eighty-six homes. He had close ties to leading Mexican politicians, including Raul Salinas de Gortari, the brother of former Mexican President Carlos Salinas de Gortari. Salinas was seen at a lavish party given by Garcia-Abrego at his ranch near Monterrey in 1992.[19] The authorities captured Garcia-Abrego in Mexico, and, since he was an American citizen, Mexico extradited him to the United States. In October 1996, Garcia-Abrego was convicted on federal drug trafficking charges in Houston and was given a life sentence.[20]

The cartel forged its most important alliance in Mexico with Amado Carrillo Fuentes, nicknamed "the Lord of the Skies" because of his pioneering use of old passenger jets to move multi-ton loads of cocaine from Colombia to Mexico.[21] Carrillo Fuentes was born in 1953 in Mexico's northwestern state of Sinaloa, an area from which many traffickers came. Legendary Mexican drug kingpin Pablo-Acosta Villareal schooled Carrillo in the basics of the trade, and as part of his training he had to work with the Colombians to develop them as a source of supply. Carrillo Fuentes's mentor was his uncle Ernesto Fonseca Carrillo, who was jailed in 1985 for the murder of DEA agent Enrique Camarena. The drug lord assumed leadership of the so-called Juarez cartel in 1985 after its leader, Raphael Aguilar Guajardo, was gunned down in Cancun.[22] Carrillo played an important role as liaison between the Mexican Federation and the Cali cartel. As one analyst told *Time* magazine, "He has the ability to form alliances."[23]

Alberto Ochoa-Soto, a major Colombian money broker who operated in Mexico, was one of the first Colombians to work with Carrillo. They began collaborating when Carrillo operated in the Ojinaga, Chihuahua area, and maintained close ties as Carrillo-Fuentes's organization grew in power and he became the "premier patron [boss] in Mexico."[24] The DEA arrested Ochoa-Soto on July 9, 1994 for conspiracy to distribute six tons of cocaine, but U.S. authorities released him from their custody on February, 11, 1995. Ochoa-Soto walked across the Stanton Street Bridge in El Paso and was never seen again. According to a DEA intelligence report, "recent reporting indicates that ACF [Amado Carrillo Fuentes] may have had Ochoa-Soto killed shortly after he returned to Mexico because Ochoa-Soto was moving large quantities of cocaine through Ciudad Juarez without coordinating the movements with Carrillo."[25]

Hoover Salazar-Espinosa, an important Cali transportation coordinator and money launderer, was also Carrillo-Fuentes's close associate. The Lord of the Skies provided protection for cocaine shipments that Salazar-Espinosa brokered and transported and even helped to move the coke to crossing points along the U.S.-Mexican border and across the border with the help of appropriate members of the crime federation. Once the cocaine was in the States, Salazar-Espinosa assumed control of the load and continued moving it to its destination. According to DEA intelligence, this scenario "showed ACF's power and the flexibility of the Mexican drug trafficking alliances. With ACF's approval and protection, Salazar-Espinosa has the ability to smuggle and stage drugs along the entire length of the United States-Mexican border."[26]

Carrillo-Fuentes allowed Grupo Union, a Mexican money-laundering group, to operate in his area. Grupo Union members reportedly traveled to Colombia to coordinate the arrival of aircraft on their ranches in the Mexican State of Tabasco. The group then used Mexican rental vehicles to transport the cocaine across the U.S.-Mexican border. The traffickers sealed the powder in plastic and sprayed it with butane gas to mask the odor from cocaine detection devices.[27]

As perhaps Mexico's most powerful drug lord, Carrillo-Fuentes established a close working relationship with another patron – Miguel Rodriguez. The two reportedly talked about business almost every day.[28] Rodriguez paid Carrillo-Fuentes a "transportation charge" of one kilo for every two kilos of Colombian cocaine successfully delivered to the United States. Despite their relationship, the two bosses constantly haggled over money, largely because Carrillo-Fuentes was chronically overdue on his payments for cocaine that he bought from Miguel. Once Carrillo-Fuentes had to send three Mexican hostages to Miguel as a guarantee that he would pay him for a lost shipment. The Mexicans were freed after Carrillo-Fuentes paid Miguel millions of dollars and turned over some property in Mexico to him.[29]

Carrillo-Fuentes adopted the Cali cartel's use of high-tech gadgetry, including beepers, fax machines, cell phones and encryption, as well as its terrorist-like cell structure, which compartmentalized each of the organization's functions.[30] "Amado Carrillo-Fuentes learned from the Cali bosses," said Tracey Eaton, a former Mexico City bureau chief of the *Dallas Morning News* who has written extensively about Carrillo-Fuentes. "He ran his operation much like a corporation and got into profit sharing before it was fashionable. He bribed Mexican police chiefs and politicians. He also had the touch of Tony Soprano of the HBO TV series, *The Sopranos*, in that he could go from polite gentleman to ruthless thug in a minute."[31]

By the mid-1990s, however, Carrillo-Fuentes was under intense pressure from Mexican and U.S. law enforcement. He tried to disguise his appearance through cosmetic surgery and planned to retire after relocating some of his operations and resources to Chile. In July 1997, he went to Mexico City to have some plastic surgery done. His surgery appeared to have gone well, but then he was injected with Dormicum, a post-operatory medicine. The drug lord's blood vessels contracted and he had a fatal heart attack. After his death, a violent struggle broke out in Juarez for control of his drug empire.[32]

The U.S. market for cocaine was starting to become saturated by the mid-1980s.[33] The street price had dropped nearly two-thirds, while cocaine was selling for four times as much in Europe. The Cali cartel saw that the European drug market was ripe for penetration.[34] When Gilberto Rodriguez and Jorge Ochoa moved to Spain in 1984, they bought a large ranch in Badajoz, near the border with Portugal, to serve as a base of operations from which they could analyze the potential for trafficking cocaine in Europe. The Cali cartel reached out to tobacco smugglers from Galicia in Spain, who had a good knowledge of the region's coastline and storage facilities that could be used to smuggle drugs. The cartel began to use boats to pick up the drugs from ocean-going vessels and bring them ashore. To launder its money, it set up a network of accounts between Spanish and Panamanian banks and invested in real estate.[35]

Jorge Ochoa sent one of his key lieutenants, Teodoro Castrillon, to England, Germany and Holland to establish contacts with the local Colombian communities and to see if they could develop the infrastructure and distribution networks similar to those they had in the United States.[36] Gilberto and Jorge and their wives, however, were arrested near Rodriguez's apartment in Madrid. The United States sent a lawyer to Madrid to secure the extradition of Rodriguez and Ochoa, but the Spanish court extradited the two to Colombia instead.[37]

Another important potential market was the United Kingdom, which had seen an explosion in heroin consumption from the late 1970s onwards but did not as yet have a significant coke problem. In 1985, a female cousin of the Ochoas opened up a supply line with her English husband Keith Goldsworthy, a pilot. Goldsworthy would fly hundreds of kilos into the U.S. in his private Cessna and then ship it to England. A parallel supply route was opened up by Fabio Ochoa personally on a visit to London. Within a year, cocaine seizures in the UK had doubled.[38]

Goldsworthy was eventually caught in Miami and jailed for twenty-two years, but by then the genie was out of the bottle. Four years after the arrival of Rodriguez and Ochoa in Spain, the Cali cartel had made significant inroads in a drug market long dominated by heroin. "The major drug of choice in Europe in the late 1980s was heroin supplied by the Asians," said John Constanzo, a DEA agent who worked in Italy in the 1980s. "But the Cali cartel showed up on the DEA's radar screen, and we began seeing substantial increases in cocaine seizures."[39]

Surveys conducted in the countries of the European Community verified these observations. Cocaine seizures skyrocketed from 900 kilograms in 1985 to thirteen tons in 1990. Two years later Miguel Solans, a government delegate for Spain's National Plan on Drugs, commented, "Although it is obvious that even if heroin is the drug that produces the most instability and deaths in Europe, the level of cocaine traffic and cocaine consumption has been rising at an alarming rate in recent years."[40] Three years later, the cartel had so refined the European smuggling network that they were using many of the major commercial ports in Europe, including Hamburg, Liverpool, Genoa and Rotterdam.[41]

Operating on foreign terrain, the Cali godfathers, being the shrewd businessmen they were, understood their limitations and the importance of strategic alliances for getting a foothold in the European market. To meet their strategic objectives, they established a close working relationship with the Italian Mafia. "The Cali cartel and Italian organized crime had an understanding," said Michael Horn, a former DEA agent and the current director of the National Drug Intelligence Center in Johnstown, Pennsylvania. "Cali supplied the cocaine and the Italians would handle wholesale distribution."[42] The Italian mob and the Cali combine got along well, their relationship strengthened in part by their common love of soccer and the Cali men's respect for the Italian Mafia's criminal style. "The Cali cartel modeled its organization on the Italian Mafia," Constanzo said.[43]

Group Five's investigation revealed that the cartel had cultivated the Mafia connection for some time. When Rich Crawford searched Chepe Santacruz's apartment in Bayside, Queens, in 1979, he found some shirts and original wrappers with the sale tags showing that they had been bought in Italy. In 1981 the DEA discovered that Santacruz had spent several months in Milan learning Italian and setting up the infrastructure for the cartel's cocaine pipeline from Colombia to Europe.[44]

According to Constanzo, it was the Camorro branch of the Mafia that worked the closest with the Cali cartel. "The Camorro had a well established heroin network in Europe that could handle cocaine," Constanzo explained. "The Cali cartel didn't have to invent the wheel."[45] The Camorro services for the cartel included money laundering. In one case, authorities discovered that the Camorro had laundered $40 million for the Colombians by first depositing the money in the account of an elderly grandmother in Mantua and then having her transfer the funds to a dummy corporation in New York. From there, the money was moved to an account of another firm in Brazil.[46]

Several cocaine busts documented the budding relationship with the Italian Mafia. In 1989, the dismantling of two laboratories in Italy resulted in the seizure of 267 kilos of cocaine base and cocaine hydrochloride and confirmed that Colombian traffickers and the Italian mob had established links.[47] In the same year, the FBI convinced Joseph Cuffaro, a Sicilian drug dealer, to become an informant and he confessed to arranging a 1,300-pound shipment of cocaine from Colombia to Sicily.

The growing ties between the Mafia and Cali concerned U.S. legislators and Italian authorities. "If these two criminal organizations successfully join forces, the results could be disastrous in the U.S. and Europe," warned Charles B. Rangel, chairman of the Select Committee on Narcotics Abuse and Control at the House of Representatives, in a letter to Secretary of State James A. Baker.[48]

One of the last cases that legendary Mafia investigator Giovanni Falcone supervised involved the smuggling of 600 kilograms of cocaine from Colombia to Sicily. In May 1992, Falcone, his wife and three bodyguards were blown to bits on a road outside of Palermo. In the following weeks, speculation abounded about who was responsible, and there were even suspicions about a Colombian connection. The FBI, Falcone's close ally in previous transatlantic mafia investigations, sent a team of six agents to help with the investigation. "We had our suspicions," said John Moody, an FBI agent, in reference to the Cali cartel's suspected involvement in Falcone's murder. "But the connection was never made."[49]

Ironically, it was their love of soccer and connection to Italy that almost did in the cartel. In June 1990 the DEA, in collaboration with the Italian police, set up an elaborate sting operation called Offsides during the World Cup in Italy. The objective was to catch several fugitive traffickers who had fled to Colombia after being charged and convicted in the United States. The Colombian national soccer team had qualified for the World Cup for the first time since 1962, and the DEA had received intelligence from sources in Colombia that several important figures, including perhaps Chepe Santacruz and Miguel Rodriguez, were going to attend.[50] Ken Robinson went to the World Cup as part of the investigation, and thought he had spotted Chepe, but lost the surveillance of him.[51] Miguel's wife and mother-in-law came to Rome but Miguel and the other Cali godfathers were no-shows, evidently scared off by the threat of capture.[52]

By 1992, two important events dramatically increased the cartel's potential for expansion in Europe. The first was the collapse of Communism, which followed the fall of the Berlin Wall in 1989 and the dissolution of the Soviet Union on January 1, 1993. Second was the advent of a continent without borders after European trade barriers were erased in 1992, in accordance with the terms of the Single Europe Act of 1987. Immediately after the fall of the Berlin Wall, the first links established between East and West were those of organized crime syndicates. "Western Europe crime groups are better organized than those in the East, and they forged alliances for certain activities," said Robert Moroni, the former interior minister of Italy.[53] The Cali cartel and other major crime groups, such as the Russian and Italian mafias, began holding summits in the early 1990s to see how they could better cooperate to further their criminal interests.[54]

It took a little while for the collaboration to bear results. "European law enforcement have been warning the United States for some time about the coming cocaine blitz of Western Europe, but that blitz didn't materialize until 1993 and 1994," wrote Professor Phil Williams, director of a think tank, the Ridgeway Center.[55] "In the first three months of 1993, about 2300 kilograms of cocaine were seized. In a corresponding period for 1994, that figure jumped to 4200 kilograms of cocaine."[56]

In the United Kingdom, the Colombians formed a particularly lucrative alliance with enterprising criminals from the tough seaport of Liverpool, led by a former street hooligan of mixed-race called Curtis Warren. Warren was a natural drug trafficker:

hard working, engaging, street smart, fearless and ruthless when he needed to be. Through personal contacts, he met a young South American called Mario Halley, a kind of European salesman for the Cali cartel, in the Dutch city of Amsterdam, and was soon organizing mammoth shipments of cocaine sealed inside hefty lead ingots. In 1992, customs officers seized a spectacular load of 905 kilos, the biggest single haul found in the UK up to that time. Warren, however, was acquitted at court and relocated to the Netherlands, from where he continued to flood his home country with cocaine, heroin, Ecstasy and cannabis until his eventual capture in October 1996. Dutch police say the source of his cocaine was high-ranking Cali boss Arnaldo "Lucho" Botero, who would himself be arrested not long after. [57]

Law enforcement agencies also began to express concern about drug trafficking developments in Russia and Eastern Europe in this period. In testimony before Congress in May 1994, Hans Ludwig Zachert, president of the German Criminal Police, noted the growing significance of Eastern Europe in international cocaine trafficking. "The traffickers come . . . taking advantage of the political process and fundamental economic restructuring in order to transport drugs to Western Europe, circumventing the former transit routes and transit countries," said Zachert. He added, "At the same time, these Eastern European states are increasingly being used as transit countries for drug deliveries to Western Europe, [and] the consumption of all kinds of drugs in these countries has risen considerably."[58]

The proof of Russia's and Eastern Europe's growing significance was evident in the type and amount of cocaine seizures in the region. On February 21, 1993, some 1,092 kilograms of cocaine were seized and seven people were arrested near Saint Petersburg in Russia.[59] In September and October 1991, Czechoslovakian and Polish authorities seized two 100-kilogram loads of cocaine hidden in beer shipments.[60] The following year, Russian officials said they seized 4.6 kilograms of cocaine. Another year later, that amount had increased to 1,000 kilograms.[61]

There seemed to be no geographical limits to the level of international criminal cooperation. European traffickers were even traveling to Colombia to exchange information with local traffickers about the methods of refining and producing heroin.[62] This reflects one of the major developments in Colombian drug trafficking in the early 1990s: the country's increasing importance as a producer and distributor of heroin. By 1992 law enforcement had no doubt that Colombians had the "capacity to competently produce high quality heroin."[63]

There is disagreement among analysts and officials, however, over how involved the Cali cartel was in the heroin trade. Some experts said there was a strong connection. Robinson believes that Cali began dealing in heroin in the early 1980s. He recalled that informant Robert Lafferty had even brought the NYDETF heroin samples from Colombia.[64] The cartel had a Japanese chemist to teach them how to manufacture heroin, according to Ken Robinson.[65] There were press reports, too, that they had cooperated with heroin distributors in New York and invested in heroin shipments smuggled to the city, although they did not get directly involved.[66]

In 1994, Tom Constantine told Congress that "DEA intelligence suggested that the Cali cartel would be the dominant group in trafficking South American heroin. The Cali cartel had better access to the predominant opium poppy growing areas in Colombia. The Cali cartel has displayed a significant involvement in the South American heroin trade from its outset. It appears likely that large-scale involvement of the Cali cartel would make it difficult for small independent, trafficking groups with limited resources to compete for the market."[67]

Some DEA analysts, on the other hand, said that the cartel godfathers were not active in the Colombian heroin trade and that it most involved traffickers from the Valle del Cauca under the leadership of Ivan Urdinola-Grajales, who was associated with the Cali men but was not a member of their inner circle.[68] According to one cable from the U.S. Embassy in Bogota, "Urdinola-Grajales became the driving force in the young heroin trade."[69] But other DEA agents say Urdinola and other heroin traffickers in the Valle del Cauca could not have dealt in the drug without approval from the Cali godfathers. "It would have been impossible to survive without the Rodriguez brothers' approval," said Joe Toft. "The Cali cartel controlled the valley. I'm sure they got a cut of it."[70]

By the beginning of 1993, nearly a decade after Gilberto Rodriguez and Jorge Ochoa had journeyed to Spain, the Cali cartel had a global reach that was perhaps unparalleled in organized crime history. In Colombia, the Medellin cartel was on the ropes. Pablo Escobar was in hiding, the Ochoa brothers were in jail, and Rodriguez Gacha was dead. The Cali cartel, on the other hand, looked untouchable. It dominated cocaine trafficking and it appeared to have no limits on its growth as a crime multinational.

In successfully flooding the world with the white powder, the cartel had steadily expanded, opening up new markets. Its ambitions were boundless. The criminal entrepreneurs had even begun moving into the lucrative Japanese market. "Why go to Japan?" said Robinson. "They are like successful businessmen. They need to conquer new markets to thrive."[71] One Joint Intelligence Center report noted that the main factors for targeting Japan are "almost certainly excesses of cash in Japan and excesses of cocaine in South America."[72] But the Center doubted the Colombian cartels could make inroads into the Japanese market, given the power of the local mafia, the yakuza. Agents who had investigated the Cali cartel for years weren't about to bet that it couldn't happen.

Chapter 8

The War of the Cartels

Mr Escobar is sick, a psycho, a lunatic . . . he thinks that a criminal can win a war against the state. I think that is absurd.
— Gilberto Rodriguez, Cali cartel "chairman"

During the Colombian drug trade's formative period, the Cali and Medellin cartels operated in their home country with virtual impunity. However, by the mid-1980s the United States government was pressuring Colombia to abandon its laissez faire policy. President Ronald Reagan had declared the War on Drugs in 1982, and the U.S. shifted the focus of its interdiction efforts from heroin in Asia to cocaine in Latin America. Uncle Sam recognized Colombia as the hub of the region's drug trade.

Two years later, Rodrigo Lara Bonilla, Colombia's justice minister, reopened the case involving Pablo Escobar's arrest in 1976 on drug possession charges. Escobar was at the time serving as an alternate delegate to the Colombia Congress, but he had higher political aspirations. As a criminal with a fervent desire for acceptance by Colombia's elite social class, Escobar presented himself as a sports promoter, industrialist, philanthropist, building contractor and defender of natural resources. For many poor people in Medellin slums, he was a folk hero, a kind of Robin Hood who stole from the rich and gave to the poor. Escobar shrewdly curried the common man's favor by doing good works. In the early 1980s, he built 1,000 small brick houses complete with plumbing, electricity and gardens in a poor barrio that bore his name.[1]

The Rodriguez brothers and Santacruz, on the other hand, kept such a low profile that few knew who they were. They tried to blend into the Cali business community and quietly established legitimate ventures as a means of forging ties with key people from the country's media, politics, legal system and business community. They enjoyed their wealth but didn't make a public spectacle of it, unlike Escobar, who led a flamboyant lifestyle that made him a celebrity. His sprawling 7,000-acre estate, Hacienda Napoles, was the stuff of royalty, a country house that could accommodate 100 guests, surrounded by twenty-four artificial lakes, a swimming pool flanked by a marble Venus, and a zoo populated with hippos, giraffes, elephants and other exotic animals. At the entrance to Hacienda Napoles, the owner arrogantly displayed the aircraft that reputedly carried his first load of cocaine to the United States.[2]

When the 1976 case was reopened, Don Pablo, as many now respectfully called the drug baron, suddenly found himself in the harsh and uncomfortable glare of public scrutiny. Stripped away was the image of Don Pablo, leading citizen. Exposed was the reality – Pablo Escobar, drug lord. Escobar sued Lara for libel, sniffing, "I'm a victim of a persecution campaign," but eventually dropped out of public life, humiliated and fixated on revenge. Lara Bonilla received death threats, but ignored them. He was determined to investigate Escobar and go after the country's mafia.[3]

In 1984, Lara authorized the spectacular raid on Tranquilandia, the major cocaine processing plant in the Amazon region. He paid for it with his life. A few months later, *sicarios* machine-gunned him to death on a residential street in Bogota. The justice minister's murder compelled president Belisario Bentacourt to declare a "war without quarter" against all drug traffickers, and the Medellin cartel godfathers did a disappearing act from public life. The Cali godfathers didn't approve of Lara Bonilla's assassination, but they were forced to go underground as well.[4] That's when Gilberto Rodriguez and his friend Jorge Ochoa left for Spain, and Santacruz traveled to Mexico and sent some his lieutenants to the United States to investigate possible locations for new cocaine processing labs.

At 11.40 A.M. on November 6, 1985, approximately thirty-five M-19 guerrillas stormed the Colombian Palace of Justice, located on Bogota's central Plaza de Bolivar. Within minutes, the guerrillas had 250 hostages, including Alfonso Reyes Echandia, the chief justice of Colombia's Supreme Court, and many of the twenty-four Supreme Court justices. For the next twenty-four hours, thousands of soldiers and police tried to retake the building, but the heavily armed and well-entrenched guerrillas fought them off. When the government finally prevailed, twenty-five hostages lay dead, including Chief Justice Reyes, and apparently all the guerrillas.

It is widely believed the Medellin cartel paid the guerrillas to take the Palace and burn the extradition case files in the court archives, which contained incriminating evidence against them. The justices, many of whom favored upholding the extradition treaty with the United States, were scheduled to vote on the issue in the near future.[5] The shocking attack on the heart of the Colombian legal system set the tenor for the rest of the decade. By 1990, more than 200 court officials and at least forty Colombian judges had been murdered.[6]

Colombian President Virgilio Barco, who took office in 1986, implemented the Colombia–United States extradition treaty. The Medellin cartel responded by launching a ruthless terrorist campaign against the state. Calling themselves "the Extraditables," the cartel vowed, "better a grave in Colombia than a jail in the United States" and began to target prominent supporters of extradition, as well as get-tough-on-drugs officials. On November 17, 1986, *sicarios* murdered Colonel Jaime Ramirez Gomez, the head of the Anti-Narcotics Unit of the Colombian National Police.[7] The following month, a killer on a motorcycle wove through the downtown Bogota traffic and shot to death Guillermo Cano, the crusading anti-drug editorial writer for *El Espectador*, Colombia's second largest newspaper.[8] In January 1988, near the Medellin airport in Rionegro, gunmen ambushed an automobile carrying Carlos Mauro Hoyos Jiminez. After killing Hoyos's bodyguard and chauffeur, the thugs dragged the bleeding attorney general from his limousine, put him in a car, and sped away. President Barco ordered a manhunt, and authorities found

Hoyos's body a few miles away from where security forces a few hours earlier had freed the kidnapped Andres Pastrana Arango, the Conservative party candidate for mayor (and future president of Colombia). Pastrana told the author in 1988 that Hoyos's killers had planned to kidnap Hoyos and others to dramatize their opposition to extradition.[9]

The Medellin cartel did not direct its warring efforts on the Colombian state alone. In 1981 the Cali and Medellin cartels had participated in a meeting that organized *MAS* to deal with the guerrilla threat (see Chapter Four), and for the next three years, their members met in Colombian bars, discos, and haciendas to discuss business. When Gilberto Rodriguez and Jorge Ochoa left for Spain together, they trusted each other and worked together to explore new markets without fear of a double cross. But relations went steadily downhill as the two powerful mafias expanded their operations and tension developed between them.

Colombian and U.S. officials are unsure as to what caused the rift, but relations were not helped by the events following the extradition of Gilberto Rodriguez and Jorge Ochoa from Spain to Colombia in 1986. Rodriguez went to trial in March 1987 on cocaine smuggling charges that could have led to his extradition to the United States, but it took place in the company town where the Cali cartel owned everything, including the legal system. Agent Rich Crawford, who was now in the DEA's Tampa office, traveled to Colombia to testify. He had no illusions about the trial's outcome but was eager to testify as a way of showing that the DEA wasn't afraid to go into the cartel's home territory and rip off its phony cover of respectability. Crawford arrived in Cali on March 17 and became the only DEA agent ever to testify at a trial in Colombia. His testimony was never allowed in court, however, and after three days, the judge acquitted Rodriguez.[10] As a result, Rodriguez could not be extradited to be tried for the same offense, thanks to the double jeopardy clause of the U.S. Constitution.[11]

Jorge Ochoa returned to Colombia in July 1986 to face a tougher legal situation than his friend Gilberto. He would first have to stand trial in Cartagena for smuggling 125 bulls into Colombia in 1981 and then face a drug charge in Medellin. If convicted, he could be extradited to the United States. Ochoa was found guilty and sentenced to two years in jail, but pending the appeal, the judge released Ochoa on $11,500 bond, conveniently overlooking the fact that he faced a more serious criminal charge in Medellin. The judge ordered Ochoa to report to the court every two weeks. The drug lord thanked the judge and opted to walk away.[12]

Ochoa remained a fugitive until November 1986, when police stopped him at the tollgate near Palmira in the vicinity of Cali. He was on his way to a summit meeting called by Pablo Escobar to work out the details for creating a single, supercartel that Escobar would head. According to reports, Rafael Cardona, one of the Cali's contacts to the Medellin cartel, tipped off police that Ochoa would be driving a white Porsche in the Cali area. Cardona wanted to get even with Ochoa for having an affair with his girlfriend. When a police officer stopped Ochoa's car, Cardona's girlfriend was seated in the front seat. The drug lord casually offered the officer a $10 bribe; he refused. The bribe offer climbed to $400,000, but to no avail. Ochoa was arrested and put in a maximum security prison in Bogota. Meanwhile, the United States requested his extradition.[13]

The police had arrested Ochoa while the drug lord's surveillance helicopter circled above. Obviously, the threat of arrest didn't concern Ochoa. He was in Cali country, and his good friend Gilberto Rodriguez would get him out quickly.[14] The Cali godfathers knew everything that went on in their stronghold, so they must have been aware that Ochoa was in the area. Yet they made no attempt to get him released. Ochoa was finally freed on December 30, but the damage was done and the seeds of distrust were planted. The Medellin godfathers wondered: Did their Cali friends supply the information that got Ochoa arrested? And why didn't they try to get him out of jail quickly?[15]

Meanwhile at his "supercartel" meeting, which included the men from Cali, Escobar laid out his proposal. Under his leadership, the unified cartel would coordinate political and economic strategy for all drug traffickers in Colombia. Moreover, he would not only approve every shipment made, but would get thirty percent of the wholesale value of each one. Two to three years earlier, such a proposal made by the powerful and ruthless bully might have intimidated the Cali godfathers into agreeing to such an outlandish arrangement. But that was then. The Cali men were now in a much stronger competing position to reject Escobar's demands categorically and tell the Medellin boss that they wouldn't pay him anything. According to journalist Simon Strong, "Almost speechless with rage, Escobar was reported to have simply muttered, 'But this is war then,' before he immediately left the ranch."[16]

Several scenarios have been put forth to explain why the deteriorating relations erupted into open warfare. One theory popular with many sources is that the two mafias were locked in a power struggle over the New York market. They say Cali had dominated the cocaine market since the mid-1970s, but when the market was glutted and prices began to drop in the late 1980s, Medellin's more aggressive element, led by Jose Rodriguez Gacha, started muscling into the lucrative New York market. It is known that Rodriguez Gacha visited New York City in 1988, but other sources say that he went to Queens to mend fences, not to break heads.[17] The Colombian government may have tried to encourage the feud. One communiqué from the United States embassy in Bogota to the U.S. State Department stated that General Jaime Ruiz Barrera, commanding general of the Medellin army brigade, and the mayor of Medellin, "are strongly pushing this line, perhaps to keep the cartels at each other's throats."[18]

Bill Mante, a former New York detective who spent ten years investigating the Cali cartel, believes it was the Medellin cartel's anger at Cali's decision to shift their distribution network to Mexico that led to war. "We can't say for sure; it's purely speculation," Mante said. "But we knew that the Cali cartel had meetings with the Guadalajara cartel about shifting their distribution route to Mexico. That was Jaime Orejuela's brainchild. He had a good relationship with the Mexicans. It was a business decision but it led to war."[19]

The mutual hatred of Pablo Escobar and Pacho Herrera, the result of a dispute over a worker for one of Escobar's New York distributors, is another plausible explanation for why the cartels went at each other's throats. While in prison during the early

1980s, Herrera befriended a Colombian named Pina, a worker for Jaime Pabon, who was a major cocaine distributor for Escobar. But Pina angered Pabon when he philandered with a member of his family and had to flee and seek support from the Herrera organization. At first, Pacho Herrera balked at hiring Pina because he knew Pabon was a close associate of the powerful and violent Escobar. He didn't need to rile the Patron.

That didn't satisfy Pabon, though, who wasn't going to be happy until he had Pina killed for dishonoring his family. He asked Escobar for help. No problem. Escobar figured that a single call to Chepe Santacruz to complain about Pacho Herrera's protection of Pina would be enough to persuade him and the other Cali bosses to use their influence on Herrera and get him to turn Pina over to Pabon. The Rodriguez brothers, Pacho Herrera and Santacruz had a meeting. They knew the consequences of defying Pablo, but they decided that maintaining a united front was the best response to his intimidating threat. "We have no quarrel with Pina," was their terse reply to Escobar.

Pina wouldn't let the matter go. He lied to Escobar. The Cali cartel plans to kidnap you, Pina told Escobar. The enraged Escobar called Herrera and demanded that Pina give up Pabon within 24 hours or he would kill Herrera's entire family. Rather than being intimidated, Herrera took Escobar's demand as a slight to his honor. There are times in the cutthroat world of drug trafficking when honor takes precedence over business. Pacho called his brother Ramon, who was managing his cell in New York City, and ordered him to hire Pina immediately.[20]

Just before dawn on January 13, 1988, a huge bomb exploded outside the Monaco, a luxury eight-story apartment building owned by Escobar in the upscale El Poblado barrio of Medellin. The drug lord was not home, but his wife Victoria and their twelve-year-old son, Juan Pablo, and daughter, Manuela, were sleeping in the penthouse apartment. The blast killed two nightwatchmen, dug a thirteen-foot hole in the street, and smashed the windows of nearby buildings.[21] Remarkably, Escobar's family was unhurt, although the explosion partially deafened daughter Manuela.[22]

The attempted assassination shocked Escobar. No one had ever challenged his authority before. All he had to do was threaten and bully and people would knuckle under. At first he thought the DEA was responsible, but then he concluded that his upstart rivals from Cali were making a power play to take over his distribution networks. Escobar sent *sicarios* to Cali to find his enemies and kill them. Figuring that the best defense is a good offense, the Cali godfathers sent their own hit squads to Medellin. The war of the cartels was on.[23]

In the following months, the casualties inexorably mounted. On July 11, authorities discovered the bodies of five ex-military men outside Medellin with a note explaining that the mercenaries were killed because they were *sicarios* for the Cali cartel. Three weeks later, police captured Jose Luis Gavria, Escobar's cousin, and charged him with participating in the killings. On August 18, arsonists torched the biggest Medellin outlet of Gilberto Rodriguez's Drogas La Rebaja chain of drug stores. In mid-August, Colombian military intelligence officials reported that sixty members of the Cali cartel and eighteen of the Medellin cartel had been killed since the Monaco bombing.[24] The U.S. embassy noted in a cable that "their intelligence against each other appears to be very good, especially that of the Medellin cartel against the Cali cartel."[25]

Both sides realized that war was bad for the drug business and tried to negotiate a truce, but there was too much bad blood. "They tried to meet several times, but it never happened," revealed Javier Pena, a DEA agent who played a major role in the hunt for Pablo Escobar. "They were just too big for the same territory."[26]

Instead of working toward peace, the two mafias got increasingly vicious in their attacks. One 200-pound bomb planted inside a Renault exploded outside a Rebaja outlet in Cali, killing seven people, wounding twenty-four more, destroying a supermarket and damaging twenty other business and seven houses.[27] The war spread to the United States, and, in the last week of August, the media reported on several dozen bombings in New York and Miami.[28] According to the *New York Times*, law enforcement officials were saying that "there was evidence that the two cartels . . . had begun informing the police about each other's shipments" and that, "as a result of the anonymous tips, police made several large seizures during the year."[29] The Cali cartel also sent more than ten professional killers to the United States from Colombia, according to the *New York Times*.[30] New York City officials worried that their city would experience the same kind of out-of-control violence that ravaged Miami in the late 1970s and early 1980s.

Both cartels went even further and hired foreign mercenaries. Yair Klein, a retired Israeli defense force colonel, helped arrange a shipment of 100 Uzi submachine guns, 460 Galil automatic rifles and 200,000 rounds of ammunition to Rodriguez Gacha, and trained some of his men, including his son Freddy. The Cali cartel, meanwhile, brought in a team of eleven British mercenaries in August 1988 to plan an operation that would kill Escobar. The mercenaries trained for three months in preparation for an assault on Escobar's ranch, Hacienda Napoles, but the operation turned into a fiasco when a helicopter carrying the assault team crashed into a mountain, aborting the mission.[31]

As the war dragged on, the attitude of Colombia's security forces increasingly frustrated and angered Escobar. Rumors circulated that Escobar believed Gilberto Rodriguez had worked out a deal with the DEA.[32] In April 1988, General Ruiz told the press that Escobar was plotting to eliminate the top members of the Cali cartel, but he failed to mention the similar plan the Cali men had for Escobar and his associates.[33] From Escobar's perspective, the Colombian government seemed interested only in taking down his cartel, not the one in Cali, and he suspected that the security forces were in bed with his bitter rivals.

Today, former Colombian officials confirm what Escobar suspected, but make no apology for focusing their attention and resources on him and his Medellin associates. "We viewed Escobar and the Medellin cartel as the worst of two evils," explained Cesar Gaviria Trujillo, the president of Colombia from 1988 to 1992, and currently the president of the Organization of American States. "That's why the Colombian government directed all its attention and resources against the Medellin cartel."[34]

The DEA office in Colombia had to follow the Colombian

government's lead, said Joe Toft, a DEA agent who joined the agency's office in Bogota in 1988. "We were concerned about the Cali cartel, of course," he said. "We had agents working on both cartels, and the group assigned to the Cali cartel worked just as hard as the Medellin group. But the Colombian government's focus was on Medellin, which had declared war on the state. So we couldn't get the Colombian government to do much on Cali."[35]

Escobar saw plenty of evidence documenting the collusion. In June 1989, for example, police seized government documents from former army captain Luis Javier Wanomen and Jose Rivera, a civilian, showing that top government officials Raul Orejuela, the interior minister, and Colonel Oscar Pelaez, director of the F-2 intelligence agency, were collaborating with Cali by passing on information from agencies staffed by high-level Colombian officials.[36]

The Colombian government could have cared less about such revelations, so Escobar decided to take care of his problems. He targeted Miguel Masa, the head of DAS (Administrative Department of Security), Colombia's equivalent of the FBI, whom he believed was on the Cali payroll. Escobar flooded the streets with leaflets, offering $1.3 million for Masa's head.[37] When Escobar seethed, Colombia shivered. On May 25, 1989, a 220-pound car bomb exploded near a convoy carrying Masa and his bodyguards through downtown Bogota, killing six people and injuring more than fifty.[38]

Three months later, Escobar and his allies elevated their terror campaign to another level, murdering leading presidential candidate Luis Carlos Galan, despite his sixteen bodyguards. Many Colombians believed the charismatic Galan would win the 1990 election and continue Barco's tough policy toward drug trafficking. His death was a turning point. Using his powers under the state of siege, Barco reinstated the U.S.–Colombia extradition treaty, which the Colombian courts had suspended, and launched an all-out war against the Medellin cartel. Between mid-August and mid-December 1989, the government arrested 497 people, seized $250 million in drugs and property, and extradited nine suspects to the United States. Escobar struck back during the same period, killing 187 officials and civilians, carrying out 205 bombings, and causing $501 million in damage.[39]

The terror blitz culminated in two spectacular attacks. On November 27, Daniel Munoz-Mosquera (nicknamed "Tyson"), a Medellin *sicario* believed responsible for killing fifty police officers, judges and other officials, arranged to have a bomb planted aboard Avianca's Flight 203, en route from Bogota to Medellin. The plane exploded over Bogota, killing all 107 passengers aboard, including two Americans.[40] The "official" explanation of the bombing was that Escobar wanted two informants on board the plane dead, but sources revealed that the shocking incident happened because Escobar wanted to kill a girlfriend of Miguel Rodriguez, who was aboard the plane, in revenge for the bomb blast that partially deafened his daughter Manuela.[41] Law enforcement identified Munoz-Mosquera as the bombing's mastermind. He went on the run, but authorities captured him in Queens, New York, in 1991. Three years later, he was convicted of the slaughter.

Another bomb in December outside the headquarters of DAS killed fifty-two people, injured 1,000, gouged a thirty-foot-deep crater and damaged buildings forty blocks away.[42] It was the biggest narco-terrorist attack in Colombian history. The Cali cartel retaliated, showing that spies and intelligence information could be more effective than outright carnage. In early 1989, the cartel leadership hired Jorge Enrique Velasquez, nicknamed "the Navigator," to infiltrate the organization of Jose Gonzalo Rodriguez Gacha. Velasquez did such a good job that Rodriguez Gacha entrusted him totally with his security. "The Cali cartel paid Velasquez a million dollars to get the Mexican," said Pena. "Velasquez led the police right to Rodriguez Gacha."[43] Rodriguez Gacha learned that the police knew he was hiding at his ranch near Tolu, some sixty miles south of the coastal town of Cartagena, but he suspected son Freddy, not Velasquez, as unintentionally being the source of the lead. No problem, Rodriguez Gacha figured. He had an escape route. Unfortunately for the trafficker, he shared it with the Navigator, who gave it up to the police. On December 15, 1989, security forces killed Rodriguez Gacha, son Freddy, and several bodyguards in a shootout.[44]

In March 1990, bombs exploded in Cali, Bogota, and Medellin simultaneously, killing twenty-six people and injuring 200 more. Escobar increased the bounty he was willing to pay for the killing of a police officer to $4,000, plus a bonus of $8,000 for the killing of any member of the security forces. Within three months, 108 policemen had been murdered.[45]

By 1990, President Barco had spent four years trying to bring Escobar down, but the drug lord remained on the loose and narco-terrorism was still a way of life in the country. That May, Cesar Gaviria Trujillo won the presidential election, becoming the youngest president in Colombian history. Gaviria had begun his political career by winning election to Congress at age twenty-five, and one year later was mayor of Pereira, his hometown in the coffee-growing region. While climbing the political ladder, Gaviria gained a reputation as a competent technocrat, and he served in the Barco administration, first as minister of finance (1986–1987) and then as minister of the interior (1987–1989). In 1989 he left the government to manage the presidential campaign of Senator Luis Carlos Galan. After Galan's shocking assassination, the Liberal party selected Gaviria as their presidential candidate. His campaign stressed a get-tough platform that granted no concessions to the traffickers. Once in office, however, Gaviria did an about-face and began pursuing a policy of compromise rather than confrontation.[46]

On August 7, Gaviria made a generous offer to the drug barons: turn yourself in and you will receive light sentences and immunity from extradition. Escobar sensed weakness and increased the pressure on the government to wring more concessions from Gaviria. In September, he kidnapped journalist Francisco Santos, a member of the family that owned *El Tiempo*, the country's largest newspaper, and Marina Montoya, the sister of German Montoya, former secretary of the presidency. Escobar shrewdly concluded that making the country's elite a major target of his terror campaign was the best way to change government policy.

On September 25, Escobar renewed his two-front war with a bold attack at an estate outside Cali near Candaleria, reputedly owned by the Rodriguez brothers. Eighteen people were killed and several others wounded. The CNP later captured four men who confessed that Tyson Munoz-Mosquera had hired them to make the attack.[47]

The wave of kidnappings and killings continued into late October. The Cali cartel sent two men and a woman to Bogota to carry out hits on Medellin targets, but they were captured, gagged with their feet and hands bound, wrapped in mattresses, and tortured before each was shot fifteen times. Before fleeing, the killers sprayed the scene of the crime with slogans: "Death to the Cali Cartel," "Here are three killers from Cali," and "War is war, and, if you do not believe it, look at the bodies."[48] In another incident, twelve men were hauled from their rooms in a hotel in Medellin. Four of them were found shot to death, while the other eight remained missing. Two of the dead had signs pinned on their bodies, reading, "Because they are from the Cali Cartel. War is war."[49] Authorities predicted the war of the cartels would get uglier.

A few weeks after the kidnappings of Francisco Santos and Marina Montoya, Gaviria issued the first of two decrees giving further concessions to the drug traffickers. Now, all a trafficker had to do when he surrendered was confess to just one crime and he would avoid extradition, if any new charges were brought after the surrender.[50] Escobar responded by offering another carrot – the release of three hostages. President Gaviria issued a third decree in December, offering traffickers "full judicial benefits" if they confessed to a single crime.[51]

The Ochoa brothers were the ones who finally took the government's offer. The deal was simply too good to turn down. Serve a few years in jail, with no possibility of being extradited to the United States, and they could get out and still have their fortunes to spend. On December 17, Fabio Ochoa, accompanied by his mother and sisters, surrendered to authorities at a church located about twenty kilometers south of Medellin. "I feel the same happiness entering jail as someone else feels when leaving it," Fabio told the press. "I only wanted to end the nightmare of my life."[52] Following their brother's lead, Jorge surrendered the next month and Juan David in February.

With Rodriguez Gacha dead and the Ochoas in jail, Escobar

was now alone in his two-front war. He feared extradition if he turned himself in. Nothing guaranteed that he would get the same concessions as the Ochoas. After all, he had not stopped murdering and kidnapping after Gaviria had issued his first decree. In the end, he continued fighting the state the only way he knew how: narco-terrorism. In January, Marina Montoya's body was found in Bogota with six bullets in her head. During a raid near Medellin, police accidently killed another of Escobar's kidnapped victims, Diane Turbay, the offspring of another prominent Colombian family and the daughter of a former presidential candidate.

Gaviria sensed that Colombians were tired of living under the siege of narco-terrorism, and he continued to pursue the surrender policy he had sweetened and proposed to the traffickers. He issued a fourth decree guaranteeing immunity from extradition for all offenses committed from the date of surrender and not just from the first decree. Meanwhile, in early 1991, as part of its effort to reform the country's constitution, the Constitutional Assembly debated its extradition policy, giving consideration to banning it completely. Since 1984, the extradition treaty had been used to send at least forty-nine suspected drug traffickers to the United States.[53] The Extraditables, an unidentified group opposed to the extradition of Colombian nationals to other countries for trial, released a statement in Bogota, saying that the recent killings of Turbay and Montoya were not meant to intimidate the Constitutional Assembly and "respectfully requesting that extradition be prohibited by the new constitution."[54] Escobar freed the last of his kidnapped victims as part of his clever campaign to bring Colombia to its knees.

The vote on extradition was never in doubt. Reports were rampant that the drug traffickers had bribed and intimidated the Constitutional Assembly. One of its members, Augusto Ramirez, collaborated with the police and arranged for one of Escobar's lawyers to offer him 4,000 pesos while police filmed the exchange. The lawyer told Ramirez that Escobar had given him the money and that thirty-nine other members had already taken the same amount.[55]

The drug traffickers threatened those members of the

Constitutional Assembly who couldn't be bought off. Juan Carlos Esguerra, later a foreign minister in the Ernesto Samper administration, received a letter reminding him what had happened to others who supported extradition. The list included such names as Luis Carlos Galan, Guillermo Cano and Diane Turbay, a "who's who" of assassinated Colombians.[56] "The cartels put a lot of pressure on us," Esguerra recalled. "It wasn't just the Medellin cartel. The Cali cartel spread its money around and its lawyers were always hanging around during the debate on extradition."[57]

In 1997, Guillermo Pallomari, who worked for the Cali cartel as its head accountant from 1990 to 1994, testified that it set up a "structure" of bribes and payoffs to the Constitutional Assembly through Mario Ramirez, the secretary of the Assembly. According to Pallomari, Ramirez "had the task of contacting members of the Constitutional Assembly to relay to them the wishes of the Cali cartel regarding various laws, including the new extradition law."[58]

The cartel also had its house lawyers working hard to influence the extradition vote. In 1989, Miguel Rodriguez directed Michael Abbell to draft and forward a memorandum to be used in Colombia. It included a comparative study of standards of extradition then existing in U.S. treaties with various countries in South America. The following year, Miguel had Abbell draft and forward a memorandum to a Colombian congressman, which contained language prohibiting the extradition of Colombia nationals in the proposed redrafted constitution.[59] In effect, the Cali cartel was trying to rewrite the constitution. Around November 29, 1991, a Cali courier delivered $86,000 to a member of the Constitutional Assembly for his work in nullifying the extradition treaty.[60]

Despite the intense pressure, Esguerra voted for extradition, even though President Cesar Gaviria provided little support. "One could see where the [Gaviria] administration stood on the extradition issue," Esquerra recalled. "No one represented the government when it came time for the Assembly to debate. That made it difficult for those members who wanted to support extradition."[61] Carlos Lemos, later Colombia's vice-president during the Samper presidency, was another Assembly member who voted for extradition. "Members were afraid," Lemos recalled. "The cartels had too many resources – money, guns – at their disposal and too much influence. The vote was never in doubt."[62] The vote was fifty-one against extradition and thirteen for, with ten abstentions.

Pablo Escobar never doubted the outcome either. In late May, he had announced he would give himself up in exchange for the promise from President Gaviria that he would be treated leniently and not extradited to the United States, where he faced at least ten indictments for drug trafficking and murder. The drug lord now had everything he wanted. It was time to turn himself in and join the Ochoas in jail. On June 19, 1991, the most-wanted man in Colombia – perhaps the world – was picked up from an undisclosed location and flown to his hometown of Envigado, where he was incarcerated in a plush prison especially built for him. Wearing military fatigues and dark glasses, Escobar was accompanied by Father Rafael Gavria Herreros, an eighty-two-year-old Roman Catholic priest who had mediated the godfather's surrender. When the helicopter arrived at its destination, Escobar fell on his knees before Father Gavria Herreros and begged the priest for his blessing. The Colombian people breathed a collective sigh of relief. They were exhausted by all the killing, the fear, and the destruction. They believed that narco-terrorism had ended with Escobar's surrender and that there would be peace in their time. In a poll held close to the extradition vote of the Constitutional Assembly, eighty-two percent of Colombians said they opposed extradition.[63]

While Escobar warred with the state, the Cali cartel continued to grow in power, wealth and reach, solidifying its U.S. base and expanding into Europe and Latin America. By 1990, U.S. officials, who, a few months earlier, said that the Medellin cartel was responsible for most of the cocaine smuggled into the United States, now revealed that the Cali syndicate had grabbed the lion's share of the traffic. "Precise figures are difficult to ascertain, but a little more than a year ago, the Medellin cartel was believed to be responsible for about seventy-five percent of the cocaine shipments to the United States and Europe," Douglas Farah, a reporter with the *Washington Post*, wrote in 1990. "Now, say officials, Medellin's share is below fifty percent."[64] The Cali share of the U.S. market had jumped to around seventy percent, according to U.S. officials, and they estimated that it now controlled ninety percent of the European cocaine market.[65]

In its July 1, 1991 issue, *Time* magazine devoted nine pages to "The New Leaders of Coke," centred around a lengthy interview with Gilberto Rodriguez himself. The avuncular drug baron had consented to meet two reporters as part of a charm offensive – *Time* called it "a nine-hour public relations blitz" – designed to portray himself as both a legitimate businessman and an innocent target of the psychopathic Escobar. As a white-coated butler offered a variety of beverages and a secretary took verbatim notes, the reporters noted that the Chess Player's curly black hair was now flecked with white and he had gained at least thirty pounds in the past few years. His *élan*, however, was undiminished. Smartly casual in pink-striped cotton shirt and dark trousers – offset by a thick gold crucifix on a neck chain, a gold-and steel Cartier watch, and his small, manicured hands – Gilberto denied any involvement in drug trafficking and protested that if the authorities ever arrested him, Escobar would have him killed. He labeled his Medellin rival "sick, a psycho, a lunatic. He knows he's lost the war against the state. He lives now only to destroy."

He blamed the conflict on Escobar's tendency to see anyone who didn't back him as an enemy. "All this started when Mr Escobar called me and asked me to help him commit violent acts to get the Colombian government to abrogate the 1979 [extradition] treaty. Mr Escobar thinks that one must take justice into one's own hands. I don't agree. He thinks that a criminal can win a war against the state. I think that is absurd. The crimes he has committed in Colombia on the pretext of narco trafficking have been very grave mistakes." Rodriguez dismissed the Cali cartel as "a poor invention" of General Jaime Ruiz. "He chased Mr Escobar and his partners pesistently and yet failed in all his attempts. He didn't succeed in gaining immortality with the Medellin cartel. Thus the Cali cartel was invented, and with it the war over the New York market. Of course, this tale about the Cali cartel has been helped along by my differences with Mr Escobar."

Even though Escobar was in jail, he was still trying to kill him,

Rodriguez claimed. So he continued to take extraordinary security measures, such as dividing his time between six or seven houses in Cali, not spending Christmas with his seven grown children, and having to celebrate the birthdays of family members on the wrong days.[66] For all the smooth bravura of his performance, the Chess Player must have been nervous. Like many other Colombians, he must have doubted that Escobar would stay in prison and pay his debt to society. And with good reason.

Chapter 9

Exit the King

The Colombian government wasn't going to get information about Escobar from the Vatican. Sometimes, having to deal with scumbags is the nature of the beast. Sometimes, you have to get into the sewer because that's where you'll get the best information.

– Robert Nieves, the DEA's chief of international operations, 1989–1995

To attack the powerful drug cartels, the Colombian government had organized the Bloque de Busqueda (Search Block), a combined police-army-marine antinarcotics force of 1,500 personnel, which had received training from the United States. In reality, Pablo Escobar was the only drug trafficker Search Block seemed interested in pursuing. In his typical style of always going on the offensive, Escobar tried to relieve the heat by putting a $27,000 bounty on each Search Block member.[1] His exploits during his years on the run had made him a legend in Colombia, and even while in prison, he remained the King of Cocaine. Like the proverbial cat with too many lives, Escobar had escaped time and again, often dramatically, as he stayed one step ahead of his relentless pursuers. Sometimes Search Block would get so close that Escobar had to use such clever disguises or tactics to flee, such as dressing as a woman or riding in a coffin in a carriage.[2]

His legend grew as the press reported on the drug lord's "imprisonment." Indeed, Colombians began to wonder if he was really the jailer. "It is a prison that's no better than any for a similar criminal in the United States," President Gaviria assured his countrymen. "I do not think any of us would like to spend time there."³ Cynical Colombians scoffed, and dubbed the prison holding Escobar "La Catedral" – the Cathedral. Escobar's new home stood high on a hill, part of a ten-acre spread that included a soccer field, a gymnasium, a recreational center, a discotheque, a bar and a sweeping view of the Medellin Valley below. Don Pablo, in fact, had supervised the prison's construction. His 1,000-square-foot "cell" was bigger than the warden's accommodations, and had a king-sized bed and a private bath with Jacuzzi, as well as fine furnishings handpicked by the prisoner.⁴ For company, Escobar had six of his top lieutenants, including his brother Roberto. The police were not allowed inside the prison, but the press reported comings and goings from the Cathedral at all hours of the day and night. It soon became evident that Escobar was still running his empire from within the prison walls; yet, the government did nothing. As the truth about the Cathedral leaked out, Gaviria's popularity plummeted and his strategy for getting the drug lords to surrender became a national joke.

In the following months, mutilated corpses, including those of some of Escobar's most trusted lieutenants, began turning up in the vicinity of the Cathedral. According to rumors, the victims had been kidnapped and taken to the prison, where, under Escobar's supervision, they were tortured and killed. The brazen killings showed that, even while incarcerated, the drug lord had lost none of his arrogant swagger. The king felt that Colombia's drug trafficking industry owed him big-time. After all, he was the one who had stuck his neck out against the state in the fight against extradition, and his terror campaign had benefited all of the country's traffickers. He began referring to his war against the Colombian state as "my struggle" and demanded that his associates in the Medellin cartel pay him "taxes" – as a fee for every shipment they made.⁵

"The problem with Escobar is that he began to kidnap all the people closest to him," Gabriel Toboada, a U.S. prisoner and former Medellin cartel member, told the U.S. Senate Subcommittee on Terrorism, Narcotics and International Operations in 1994. "He became a person who wanted to do evil to everybody.

From his compadres he knew how much each politician had earned, how much each member of the Medellin cartel had earned, and he began to demand money from them, because he said that he was the one who put his name forward in the fight against extradition, and this thing went out of control."[6]

Giraldo and William Julio Moncada and Fernando and Mario Galeano were among the Escobar associates who refused to pay. They, too, were lured to the Cathedral and, in July 1992, authorities found their mutilated corpses on a roadside a few miles from the prison. After the press reported the killings, the Gaviria administration launched an investigation to find out what was going on at the Cathedral. To no one's surprise, the government reported what every Colombian knew – Escobar was actually running the place. He had to be moved to a high-security prison, Gaviria decided, but Escobar learned of the government's plans while watching the evening news on television. It was time to check out.

By this time, Escobar was also concerned about his personal security and whether the Cathedral was as safe as he thought. A lot of planning had gone into constructing the custom-built prison, but the drug lord hadn't thought of everything. The Cali cartel offered $10 million to a British mercenary, David Tomkins, to drop a bomb on the prison from the air. Tomkins, a risk-addicted former safecracker who often cropped up in hotspots around the world, had been part of the failed helicopter attack on Escobar in 1988. This time he was trapped in a sting in Miami trying to buy a Vietnam-era attack aircraft from federal agents. He also attempted to buy bombs and a Bell helicopter to survey the prison. Tompkins fled the U.S. before he could be arrested, after receiving a telephone tip-off, but was finally caught over a decade later and jailed for thirty-three months.

In September 1991, Jorge Salcedo, codenamed "Richard" by the Cali cartel and later "Sean" by the DEA, met with Roberto Leyva, a colonel in El Salvador's air force.[7] Salcedo was an important member of the Cali cartel's intelligence and security team and typical of the type of talented employee it liked to hire. The son of a retired brigadier general in the Colombian armed forces, Salcedo had studied economics and mechanical engineering in the United States and was fluent in English. After joining the Colombia military, he became a member of the Brigade of Cali, where he acquired expertise in arms, communications and explosives. He distinguished himself in the government's fight against M-19 guerrillas during the 1980s, until the group disbanded and integrated itself into Colombian society in 1990. Through his contacts in the Cali-based Third Brigade, Salcedo became good friends with Mario del Basto, the Cali cartel's head of security. Salcedo had excellent skills, which included the use of computers, and the cartel recruited him. Between 1990 and 1991, Salcedo became head of the cartel's security and a trusted intimate of the Rodriguez brothers. DEA agents who later worked with Salcedo described him as cultured, highly intelligent, charismatic and remarkably cool under pressure.[8]

Arriving in El Salvador, Salcedo posed as an entrepreneur who wanted to invest in the country and was looking for partners. Leyva was interested in what Salcedo had to propose, since he was about to retire from the air force and wanted to make some money. Salcedo and the colonel hit it off and became friends. Three months went by before Salcedo told his friend the real reason why he had come to El Salvador. He represented an officer in the Colombian military who worried about the Colombian guerrillas' growing power, Salcedo explained, and he wanted to find some bombs that the officer could use against the guerrillas.

"Could you help out, Colonel?" Salcedo asked. "We don't expect a decision right now. Let's meet in the New Year."[9]

Salcedo and Leyva met again on January 7 at the Hotel Charleston in El Salvador. This time, Salcedo came prepared to tell the truth. He was actually representing the Cali cartel, he told Leyva, which was urgently looking for bombs that it could use to destroy the jail where Pablo Escobar was imprisoned. The cartel emissary laid out the operation's main details. They planned to use a UH-212 helicopter to carry a bomb and drop it on Escobar's jail.

"We are willing to pay four million dollars for the bombs," Salcedo said.

"I can get the bombs," the colonel assured him. They agreed to meet again in San Salvador.[10]

The details of what happened next remain a mystery, but authorities know for certain that the cartel and its associates in El Salvador flew three of the four bombs out of the country from a remote coastal airstrip.[11] However, Salvadorian agents foiled the plot, arresting nine people, including some Salvadorian air force members, and seizing one of the bombs and almost $400,000 in cash.[12] To protect Escobar against possible future aerial attack, Colombian authorities mounted aircraft guns at the Cathedral and banned air traffic over the complex.[13]

In July 1993, Escobar sneaked away into the night, even though 500 soldiers surrounded the prison. He first fled to a ranch, La Romelia, and waited in a hiding place until the initial search patrols left the area and the commotion surrounding his escape subsided. Then Escobar moved to Llanogrande, close to Rionegro, and renewed his life as a fugitive. Once again, the Patron had embarrassed the state.[14] Gaviria knew he had to recapture the drug lord or forget about having an honorable place in Colombian history.[15]

This time Escobar would have a much more difficult time eluding his enemies, for Search Block was just one foe among many he had to worry about. The families of the Moncadas and Galeanos had vowed revenge and were scheming to exact it. The associates who still remained alive were tired of his bullying ways and of having to put up money to finance his wars with the state. They didn't want to be next to be lured to a meeting with El Patron, only to be summarily tortured and killed.

Even his powerful paramilitary allies began to wonder if they could trust Pablo. Paramilitary leader Fidel Castano, who was good friends with the Galeanos and the Moncadas as well an associate of Escobar, was on the "guest" list at the Cathedral the night they were killed.[16] So Escobar had few allies upon whom he could count for strong support. And he also had to worry about the godfathers in Cali, who knew they would never have a good night's sleep until they removed their bitter enemy from the scene.

On January 30, 1993, a bomb exploded in downtown Bogota, killing twenty people. It was narco-war as usual in Colombia. The country's public enemy number one had sent a message to the nation: Brace yourself. I'm back in the business of attacking the state and unleashing mayhem. But then there was a surprise. The following day, two bombs – one containing an estimated 100 kilos of dynamite and the other containing eighty kilos – exploded in Medellin in front of apartment buildings where Escobar's wife, two children, his sister and his mother-in-law were staying. Meanwhile, five men showed up at the weekend country retreat of Escobar's mother, located about forty-five miles from Medellin, ordered the lone caretaker out and blew up the place.[17]

In a communiqué released to the press on February 2, a new group calling itself "Persecuted by Pablo Escobar" (*Los Pepes*) claimed responsibility for the attacks. The communiqué declared that *Pepes* were working toward "the total elimination of Pablo Escobar, his followers, and his assets to give him a taste of his medicine, which he unfairly dishes out to so many."[18]

Escobar struck back. Mid-morning on February 15, two powerful bombs exploded five minutes and twelve blocks apart in downtown Bogota, killing four people and injuring more than 100 others. They were the fifth and sixth car-bombs since Escobar's mid-January declaration of war against the state. But a few hours later, in Medellin, unidentified men traveling in a blue Toyota camper torched an Escobar-owned luxury house in the exclusive El Poblado section. It was the *Pepes* again, showing they meant what they had vowed – tit for tat each time Escobar committed a terrorist act.[19]

Two days later, gunmen killed Carlos Mario Ossa, a high-ranking Escobar financier who was helping to pay for Escobar's terrorist campaign. The same day, Carlos Alzate, a coordinator of Escobar's *sicario* groups, surrendered. Ossa was a key person in passing instructions from Escobar to Alzate, and with Ossa's death, Alzate had no way of communicating with the Patron. Better to come out of the cold than to end up in a morgue. The *Pepes* were starting to disrupt Escobar's organization.[20]

But on March 5, the *Pepes* declared a ceasefire, giving no reason for their action, although the press speculated that it was done to give Escobar time to surrender. That didn't happen, and exactly one month later the *Pepes* issued another communiqué, announcing their "commitment to the total annihilation of Escobar," even if "he was captured and put in jail." In other words, the *Pepes* were saying, "We will get you, Pablo, no matter what you do."[21]

The *Pepes* continued to attack Escobar's infrastructure, causing anyone associated with him to fear for their lives. Assassins gunned down two lawyers employed by Escobar's brother Roberto and associate Carlos Alzate. The same day, the *Pepes* killed Escobar's most important attorney, Guido Parra, and Parra's eighteen-year-old son in retaliation for Escobar's north Bogota car bomb that killed eleven and injured over 200.[22]

It became obvious that the *Pepes* were actually trying not only to kill Escobar but also to humiliate him. That was evident when they stole "Terremoto," a stallion owned by Escobar's brother Roberto and valued at more than $1 million, and then returned it in a slightly altered condition – gelded. Terremoto was tied to a sign that read: "We return the horse to the terrible Escobar and his brother." The *Pepes* also murdered Roberto's horse trainer, Oscar Cardona Zuleta. In a cable, the U.S. embassy noted, "The loss of Terremoto as a sire is seen locally as a grave insult to the Escobars."[23]

The carnage caused by the *Pepes* was unremitting. By mid-November, they had assassinated fifty of Escobar's people, including his brother-in-law, and destroyed some twenty properties belonging to his relatives and associates. The vigilantes couldn't catch the big fish, but they were slowly poisoning the sea in which it swam.[24] They were embarrassing the Colombian government as well. Why wasn't the Gaviria administration getting control of the situation, Colombians wondered? Are the *Pepes* and government working together? Gustavo De Greiff, the country's prosecuting attorney general, said that his office seriously tried to investigate the group, but it was never able to get any good information or leads on the people behind it.[25]

When the Gaviria administration issued a $1.39-million-dollar reward for the capture of the *Pepes'* leaders, the group once again announced its intention to disband. Escobar, however, was not impressed. The drug lord suspected the government and the *Pepes* were in cahoots against him, and he didn't believe the administration had any real intentions of identifying the people behind *Los Pepes*. In a letter to the government dated August 29, Escobar charged that "the government offers rewards for the leaders of the Medellin Cartel and for the leaders of the guerrillas, but it doesn't offer rewards for the leaders of the paramilitaries, nor for those of the Cali Cartel, authors of various car bombs in the city of Medellin." He identified the individuals whom he believed to be behind the *Pepes*: the four leaders of the Cali cartel (the Rodriguez brothers, Santacruz Londono, and Herrera) and paramilitary leader Carlos Castano.[26]

Were the *Pepes* and the Colombian government working together? During the period that the *Pepes* launched their campaign against Escobar, U.S. and Colombian officials publicly denied the Cali cartel had supplied them with information that was helping in the hunt for Escobar. Today, officials readily acknowledge that the men from Cali played the key role in taking down Escobar. "As soon as Escobar killed the Galeanos and Moncadas, their people saw themselves as vulnerable and they ran to the Cali cartel and said, 'We want to change sides,'" said Joe Toft, chief of the DEA's Bogota office from 1988 to 1994. "The Cali people said, 'Okay, if you want to change sides, you need to pay us.' A lot of money changed hands."[27]

The Colombian government was in a death struggle with Escobar and it didn't care where information came from, so long as it was credible. "The Colombian government wasn't going to get information about Escobar from the Vatican," explained Robert Nieves, the DEA's chief of international operations from 1989 to 1995. "Sometimes, having to deal with scumbags is the nature of the beast. Sometimes, you have to get into the sewer because that's where you'll get the best information."[28]

The Cali intelligence operation rivaled those of many governments, and this was a major factor in taking down Escobar, sources confirmed. As Ernesto Samper, Colombia's former president explained, "The cartel's intelligence network was the 'key element.'"[29] The Cali mafia had a highly sophisticated computer system that they used to gather information on the Medellin cartel, which helps to explain why the *Pepes* were able to find and kill so many rivals when they were most vulnerable. The cartel kept its computer system in Bogota before moving it to Cali. Always in step with state-of-the-art technology, the cartel replaced it with a more sophisticated and expensive system that Santacruz bought in the United States and kept in one of his businesses.

Still, some former U.S. officials remain ambivalent about the cartel's assistance. "No question the [Colombian] government was getting intelligence about Escobar from the Cali cartel," said Robert Gelbard, who served as assistant secretary of state for Latin American affairs during the hunt for Escobar. "In some ways that was all right, but it wasn't all right that the Cali cartel bought off some members of the Colombian government."[30]

After the *Pepes* episode, reports were published alleging that the United States had turned a blind eye to the ruthless actions of the group. In an article in the *Miami Herald*, Colonel Oscar Naranjo, the director of the Colombian police intelligence services during the search for Escobar, said that "American drug agencies knew of the direct channel of communications existing between the police and the *Pepes* and that American antidrug agencies knew of its existence and took advantage of it." A source known as "Ruben," who had been a *Pepes* member, asserted that the group had actually kept in contact with DEA agent Javier Pena, who worked in Medellin as the DEA's liaison to Search Block.[31] *Time* magazine also reported that Carlos Castano visited Disneyland as a reward for his work in getting Escobar, which Amnesty International characterized as a euphemism for his work for the *Pepes*.[32]

In his autobiography, *My Confession*, published in 2001, paramilitary leader Carlos Castano said he met with Gilberto Rodriguez seven times and loaned him helicopters. "They were the bosses," recalled Castano in reference to the Cali godfathers. "It's normal to have these types of relations in a country like Colombia."[33] Paul Paz y Minao, a spokesperson for Amnesty International, said that revelations about the U.S. connection to the *Pepes* raise the question as to whether the U.S. government acted within the law. "The organization was illegal and it committed criminal acts," he explained. "U.S. law forbids government agencies from collaborating with them." Amnesty

International has filed lawsuits to get access to CIA records relating to the *Pepes*.[34]

Both the Cali cartel and U.S. government intelligence helped get Escobar, along with input from the elite Delta Force unit of American special forces troops, but U.S. officials stressed that good police work done by Colombian security forces on the case should not be underestimated. "I know Delta Force is credited with being the difference, but we shouldn't give it too much credit," Pena explained. "To do so is to short-change the Colombian National Police. The Delta Force is good at what they do and they did train the Colombian police how to read coordinates and plan the operations, but Delta Force was never directly involved, although they did provide logistical support."[35]

As the *Pepes* and the Colombian government destroyed Escobar's infrastructure, he became desperate for his family's safety and tried to get his wife, Maria Victoria Henao, and their children out of Colombia. Colombian immigration authorities, however, denied his wife permission because she didn't have Pablo's written approval.[36] Morris Busby, U.S. ambassador to Colombia, noted in a cable that Escobar's "continued efforts to get his children out of Colombia and to re-constitute his terrorist bombs suggest that he has not given up on his war against the government, but consistent police work that target his trafficking and terrorist infrastructure are threatening his plans."[37]

Colombia's nightmare ended on December 2, 1993, when the alliance of the CNP, U.S. law enforcement and the *Pepes* achieved their objective of poisoning the sea around the big fish. When all the escapes and violence had ended, Escobar was alone with a single bodyguard, Alvaro de Jesus Aguela, in a middle-class, two-story house in a Medellin barrio. Using the high-tech equipment supplied by the United States, Search Block intercepted a call Escobar made to his family, who were holed up in room 2908 of the Residencias Tequendama in Bogota. Security personnel surrounded the house and cut the telephone lines in the barrio so no one could warn the drug lord.[38]

Escobar never had a chance. Authorities knocked the door down and stormed the apartment. Dressed only in a T-shirt and jeans, Escobar tried to flee to the roof, but his pursuers gunned him down. Autopsy reports later showed that he had been hit three times, with a shot to the head killing him instantly. Escobar's death raised a relevant question. Had he been killed trying to flee or was he executed? Most Colombians could care less. A Bogota radio station reported the news of Escobar's death in mantralike fashion, while in the background, carolers sang "Joy to the World." Colombian newspapers, once bludgeoned into timidity by Escobar's power and violence, printed in bold headlines, "Escobar has fallen!" "The King is dead!"[39] When Cali radio stations broadcast the good news, residents celebrated by forming caravans of horn-tooting automobiles and waving white flags from the Rodriguez-owned Drogas La Rebaja pharmacies.[40]

An elated Cesar Gaviria called Ambassador Busby to thank him for all the assistance the U.S. gave Colombia in its hunt for Pablo, and Busby, in turn, called Colombia's defense and foreign ministries to congratulate them. The U.S. embassy in Bogota issued a press release congratulating the Colombian government.[41] A spy in the CNP called Miguel Rodriguez from Medellin to inform him of the good news. Miguel immediately called his brother Gilberto, and during the conversation, he began to cry. Later he hugged his startled accountant Guillermo Pallomari. The uncharacteristic gesture from the normally intense and businesslike Patron frightened the accountant and revealed how much strain the gentlemen from Cali were under in their war with Escobar. According to Pallomari, Miguel then got on his private line and called Gustavo De Greiff to inform him.[42]

On December 18, less than ten days after being put in isolation in Itagui Prison in Medellin to protect him from his enemies, Pablo's brother Roberto received a package. As he tried to open it, it exploded in his face. The package had the seal of the prosecuting general's office, and prison officials hadn't opened it because they believed it carried privileged information. The package should have been x-rayed as part of normal security procedures, but the equipment curiously malfunctioned about an hour before the package arrived. Roberto suffered severe damage to both eyes, and he was transferred to a hospital for surgery. Colombian authorities launched an investigation the day after to see if the three guards who handled the letter had any link to the perpetrators.[43] In a report to the State Department, the U.S. embassy in Bogota assessed, "while no one has yet claimed responsibility for the attack on Roberto Escobar, the *Pepes* are the most likely suspects."[44]

Escobar's family remained in seclusion at the Tequendama Hotel in Bogota, still looking for a country to accept them. Pablo's eight-year-old daughter Manuela made an emotional appeal on television to the *Pepes*, imploring them to stop their attacks on her family, and another one to President Gaviria, asking him to help them leave the country. "What have I done for this to be happening to me?" Manuela asked.[45]

Cali's godfathers felt relieved that their bitter enemy was finally buried in a grave, but they were uncomfortable with being crowned "the New Kings of Cocaine" by the press. What course of action the Colombian and U.S. governments would take in the War on Drugs remained uncertain. Some U.S. officials, such as Robert C. Bryden, the head of the DEA's New York regional office, pointed out that the Cali cartel now had no competition, "so they can go on any corner of any city in this country [the U.S.] and nobody in the drug business can oppose them."[46] Other analysts and law enforcement officials wondered how aggressively the Colombian government would pursue a more peaceful breed of drug trafficker not known for narco-terrorism. The Colombian government announced it would keep Search Block together to begin their pursuit of the Cali cartel.[47]

In its hunt for Escobar, the U.S. and Colombian governments had not totally ignored Cali. Even as the pursuit of Escobar intensified, authorities were working to penetrate Cali's infrastructure. They conducted a series of raids on drug processing labs, official residences, and office residences belonging to the godfathers, destroying nearly twenty tons of processed cocaine and 100 laboratories. In January 1992, the Colombian security forces conducted their first operation against the cartel's money-laundering operations, carrying out thirty-two simultaneous raids, not only in Cali but also in Bogota and Baranquilla. They seized numerous computers, floppy disks and 20,000 other financial records and uncovered information that led to three arrests and the freezing of $15 million in bank accounts in Colombia, Britain, Germany, Hong Kong, and the United States.

By March 1992, U.S. officials began to see a change in the cartel. In a cable, the U.S. embassy noted, "The Cali cartel is very concerned about the capabilities of the U.S. government to interfere with their operations. They appear to be paranoid."[48] As evidence of their paranoia, the report noted that the godfathers were living less ostentatiously and driving cars built and sold in Colombia as an effort to keep a low profile in an environment that was increasingly hostile to them.[49]

Through Operation Belalcazar III, authorities arrested Diego Martin Buitrago on September 18, 1993, one of the cartel's major contacts in Cali.[50] On December 1, police raided an estate near Cali belonging to Jose Santacruz Londono.[51] Ambassador Busby told his superiors in Washington D.C. that "Pablo Escobar's death and the disabling of the Medellin cartel are great successes for Colombia, but now they should continue with the Cali cartel."[52]

On December 13, the U.S. embassy announced that 120 U.S. army engineers were arriving in Colombia in late December to undertake a ten-week construction project in the jungle village of Juanchaco, about seventy-five miles from Cali. Officials from both countries insisted that the troops were there solely to build schools and roads, but many Cali residents believed the project's true purpose was to construct a major base to gather intelligence and stage raids on the cartel infrastructure.[53]

In late December, the press reported that lawyers for the Cali cartel and officials from the office of Prosecuting Attorney General Gustavo De Greiff's office had made contact and were negotiating. A special jail was being built to accommodate up to 300 gang members, including three of the godfathers, who were planning to surrender, or so the story went. Under an agreement, said the rumor mill, the godfathers would keep their assets and get light sentences, as little as two years.[54]

Meanwhile the cartel was exploring its options in the post-Escobar period. Its leaders held an important meeting to discuss their future and how they could increase drug trafficking to the United States and grow internationally. "We need to control the drug trafficking market at the world level," Miguel told his partners. "We need to be able to set the price and to control the price."[55] The cartel had big dreams and big plans, but its next nightmare was already taking shape.

Part III

The Fall

Chapter 10

Breakthrough

I can't. I won't. Besides, they will kill me. They will kill my family. I will never consider it!
— Gustavo Naranjo, jailed Cali cartel associate

By the early 1990s, the Cali cartel had become history's most sophisticated drug trafficking organization, but in one important way it was just like all the others. It eventually settled into its own tried, true, and pet ways of smuggling their product to the marketplace. In the end, it was these discernible smuggling patterns that brought the cartel to the attention of the law. The cartel preferred using big merchant vessels to evade U.S. radar planes, as well as naval vessels deployed in the Caribbean to smuggle cocaine in a variety of products, including lumber, wood, coffee and frozen vegetables. In 1979, for instance, Group Five investigators searched the Atlantic Lumber Company in Baltimore, Maryland, and discovered that the Santacruz organization had smuggled cocaine to the United States in shipments of mahogany.[1]

In June 1988, federal agents were tipped off about a shipment aboard the *Amazon Sky*, and found 4,000 pounds of cocaine stuffed in thousands of hollowed-out Brazilian cedar boards. In another case, the cartel attempted to ship their cocaine through Miami in merchant ships containing tropical fish.[2] "Federal agents noticed all the dead fish," recalled DEA agent Lou Weiss. "We discovered that the cocaine had dissolved in the water and liquefied."[3]

Federal investigators hot on the Cali trail noticed that the cartel preferred using a third country as a transshipment point rather than ship the cocaine directly from Colombia. "We began to put the pieces together, applying our investigative techniques," said Ed Kacerosky, a U.S. customs agent who investigated the cartel. "After awhile, we began to see patterns that made their smuggling techniques almost predictable."[4]

In 1991, the DEA office in Caracas, Venezuela, notified the Florida Joint Task Force in Miami to look out for a shipment of cement fence posts that could be carrying cocaine from Venezuela. Such a shipment would not have normally piqued the curiosity of customs inspectors monitoring ports of entry. After all, the Venezuela-Colombia border area had a legitimate concrete industry and such shipments were not uncommon.[5] On August 23, 1991, a battered tramp steamer called the Mercandian tied up at the port of Miami, and a team of DEA and U.S. customs agents boarded the ship to inspect its cargo of concrete posts. They discovered what looked like a huge load of cocaine hidden in the hollowed cores of the concrete posts stacked in the hold.

A drug bust of such magnitude makes great copy and could have been the lead story on the evening television news, but the agents decided to let the shipment go through to see where it was headed. Perhaps they could catch the big fish behind the operation. They followed the shipment to two warehouses owned by a Miami company called Tranca, Inc., which was immediately put under surveillance. On March 15, agents watched as traffickers loaded about 1,075 kilos of coke from the warehouse onto a truck. A platoon of federal agents picked up the surveillance and followed the load to its final destination, a warehouse in Longview, Texas. "The load was so big that none of the agents [involved in the surveillance] wanted to flush their career by losing it, so they stayed way too close," Ryan said.[6]

The traffickers had strong suspicions they were being followed. The area around the warehouse was flooded with agents and they could see DEA surveillance planes circling overhead. One of the traffickers spotted a command post the agents had set up close to one of the storage facilities where the cement posts were stored. To confirm his suspicions, he telephoned the business and told the person who answered that he was an agent with an emergency and that he had to talk to the agents in the command post. The worker promptly transferred the call to the "secret" command post in the back of the business, thus confirming the traffickers' suspicions.[7]

So why did the traffickers go ahead with the operation? "Miguel was threatening them and the traffickers were scared," Ryan explained. "They felt they had no choice but to try and get the load to Texas."[8] When Cali cartel employees tried to move the cocaine, federal agents swooped in and arrested four individuals, including Gustavo Naranjo, the operation's leader.[9]

Ed Kacerosky, an intense, aggressive, boyish-looking U.S. agent who was assigned to the investigation soon after it started, flew to Tyler to interrogate the four drug traffickers. Kacerosky was able to pry out some interesting information. Naranjo identified the head of the smuggling operation for which he worked as a Colombian named Miguel Rodriguez Orejuela. Naranjo had never met Rodriguez, although he communicated with him directly. Kacerosky laid out Naranjo's options: He could either go to jail for a long stretch or he could cooperate and the authorities would put in a good word for him to the judge.

Making a decision was not easy, for Naranjo knew well the possible consequences if he informed. Naranjo, however, was in bad health, addicted to Mexican brown-tar heroin, and after twenty-four hours in custody, he went into severe withdrawals. At one point in his cell, Naranjo was so weak that Kacerosky literally had to hold him up. It took the addict five days to come out of the nightmare. During that time, Kacerosky developed rapport with the inmate by supplying him with cigarettes and letting him call his wife.[10]

Finally, Naranjo agreed to phone Miguel while the agents monitored his calls. On November 2, Naranjo made contact with the boss. Miguel didn't know yet that something had gone wrong and thought it was business as usual. He gave Naranjo instructions for the delivery of 800 kilos and told him to expect the arrival in Texas of additional concrete posts containing more coke. The following day, Miguel paged Naranjo and inserted his Cali telephone number. When Naranjo called, the boss was angry and agitated, for he had learned that the authorities had busted his warehouse in Tyler. He blasted Naranjo for failing to detect the surveillance and ordered him to close the cocaine storage vault in the East Texas area and to do some counter-surveillance to see if the authorities were monitoring him.[11]

Federal investigators had heard enough. The phone conversations implicated Rodriguez in the fence post smuggling case. There was no question that Rodriguez was running the drug business in Cali. Brother Gilberto had been instrumental in setting up the distribution network in the United States, but Miguel was now the day-to-day boss, overseeing directly from Cali the cells in the United States, Mexico, Central America and South America. Luis Carlos Galan's murder in 1989 had changed the entire managerial staff of the cartel, most of whom went into semihiding. In early 1990, the case 86055 investigation (see Chapter Five) began intercepting a new voice in Cali that was directing the day-to-day activities of 86055's upper-echelon Cali targets. The voice was later identified by informants and confirmed by DEA as that of Miguel Rodriguez, using the code name "Don Manuel." "He was a micromanager beyond belief," Bill Mante recalled. "He was demanding, decisive, and articulate. In my opinion, his managerial skills institutionalized the distribution future of the Cali cartel."[12] As the investigation proceeded, it became clear that Miguel also had responsibility for protecting the business by paying bribes to Colombian politicians.[13]

On November 25, law enforcement went public with the arrests in Texas, and then coordinated a series of raids that led to the seizure of an additional 12,250 kilograms of cocaine.[14] The raids shook up Cali cartel headquarters, and the godfathers had to call an emergency meeting to discuss the unexpected headache. They were upset with the loss of the huge load and worried that Naranjo might talk if he was convicted. The cartel liked to have its lawyers visit incarcerated associates and threaten them. This time, the godfathers decided to use Abbell, the lawyer who would defend Naranjo, as the carrot and Gonzalo Paz, one of their Colombian lawyers, as the stick – the emissary who would travel to the United States and intimidate the inmate into silence.[15] Miguel knew it was also important to have someone visit Naranjo as soon as possible to assure him that the cartel would pay his legal expenses.

Miguel Rodriguez called Joel Rosenthal, one of the U.S. lawyers he kept on retainer. Rosenthal got involved with the cartel in 1989 when the authorities arrested Lucho Santacruz Echeverria, the half-brother of Chepe Santacruz, in Miami. At that time, longtime Cali cartel lawyer Michael Abbell had approached Steven Hartz, a lawyer with whom Rosenthal shared office space, and asked him if he could recommend someone to help with the Lucho Santacruz case. Hartz recommended Rosenthal, who agreed to work as Lucho Santacruz's lawyer. In previously defending Pablo Escobar, Rosenthal had gained valuable experience representing drug lords.

Miguel liked the way Rosenthal handled the Lucho Santacruz case, so he called to ask for some advice. He had a plan he hoped would make him part of mainstream Colombian society without having to pay the price for being a drug trafficker.

"Could you arrange a meeting with the FBI?" Miguel asked Rosenthal. "I want to establish a dialogue with the U.S. government."

"Could this be done without making direct reference to me?" asked Rosenthal, being candid with the powerful drug boss. He added, "The FBI will expect you and the other cartel leaders to admit that you are drug traffickers before that could happen." [16]

Rosenthal had also worked briefly for Abbell when Abbell was a prosecutor for the U.S. Department of Justice and provided the department with expertise in extradition law. Colleagues remembered the Harvard-educated Abbell as a reserved but brilliant lawyer who preferred researching extradition cases to prosecuting them.[17] Abbell decided he could make more money in the private sector, so he left the Justice Department in 1984 and joined a law firm. When the Justice Department gave him a waiver of potential conflict of interest, Abbell was free to represent suspected cartel figures, such as the Rodriguez brothers and Santacruz Londono, and he became a valuable legal counsel to the drug mafia. Ironically, Abbell had investigated Santacruz while he was at the Justice Department.[18]

Abbell attended the trial of Gilberto Rodriguez after his 1984 arrest in Spain. In a court case to decide whether Rodriguez should be extradited to the United States, Abbell testified before the Spanish judges that he would not have approved the extradition request as it was presented to the court if he still worked at the Justice Department.[19] DEA agent Rich Crawford remembered seeing Michael Abbell at Rodriguez's trial in Cali in March 1987. Abbell was an American attorney who represented the cartel's interests. "When I testified, I could see Abbell in the courtroom huddling with some of Rodriguez's defense lawyers," Crawford recalled. "He was with another lawyer from New York who had also done work on Cali cartel cases. I asked the judge: 'Who are those guys and why are they here?' The judge said, 'They are Rodriguez's lawyers.'"[20] During the late 1980s and early 1990s, Abbell was a frequent visitor to Cali. "We never monitored him, but we knew when he came to Cali," said Joe Toft, head of the DEA's office in Bogota from 1988 to 1995.[21]

Rodriguez gave Rosenthal $10,000 and instructed him to go to Tyler, Texas, and give Naranjo the money. The two met in a bare interview room at the local jail where Naranjo was incarcerated. Joel Rosenthal introduced himself to Naranjo. No response. Rosenthal tried again: "I'm the lawyer you sent for." Still no response. "I am the lawyer from Miami that your wife told you about," Rosenthal said. Naranjo looked warily at his visitor and still did not answer him. In frustration, the Cali cartel's counsel finally blurted, "Well, your brother and Miguel Rodriguez had sent me to get you a lawyer."

At that point, Rosenthal later recalled, "it was as if the air had been let out of Naranjo." He slumped and relaxed, stood up, went around the table and gave Rosenthal a big handshake. "Thank God, you've come," Naranjo said.[22] Naranjo's wife had failed to tell him that Rosenthal was coming. "There might be a conflict of interest if I represented you because I am Mr. Rodriguez's lawyer," Rosenthal told Naranjo. "A lawyer named Frank Jackson, who comes well recommended, will be seeing you. We are going to get you the best lawyer that money can buy in the state of Texas or anywhere else. If you don't like Frank, call me back on Monday and I'll come and find you someone else."

Rosenthal added, "You know, if you are planning to fight this,

I may have a problem being involved with this, and I won't be able to assist you."[23]

"What do you mean?" Naranjo asked.

"Well, if, for instance, you choose to cooperate, it's going to create a conflict of interest for me."

Naranjo put his hands up like a man being paralyzed by fear. "I can't. I won't. Besides, they will kill me. They will kill my family. I will never consider it!"

Rosenthal reassured Naranjo. "Wait a minute! Right here and now, I am not here to give you a message. I am here to get you a lawyer who will represent you the way you want."[24]

Naranjo relaxed and said: "Okay, I just want you to know."

Frank Jackson became his lawyer, and on December 9, Miguel Rodriguez gave Rosenthal $75,000 in cash to pay for Naranjo's legal representation.[25] Naranjo had lied to Rosenthal. He was cooperating with the feds, and Miguel had no idea that his telephone conversations with his cell manager were being wiretapped.

Rosenthal had brought the carrot, and eight days later Gonzalo Paz, using the alias "William Jo," came with the stick. He warned Naranjo of the consequences of cooperating with the U.S. government. The same day, Rosenthal issued a $25,000 check from his trust payable to Frank Jackson.[26]

As usual, the Cali style of intimidation was effective. Naranjo got the message from the Señor and clammed up, refusing to have anything to do with authorities. Kacerosky quickly returned to Texas to convince Naranjo to cooperate again, but despite all the agent's talent at cajoling and coaxing informants, the prisoner didn't talk again for three years.[27]

The federal investigators had to go back to the drawing board and find some new evidence to further their investigation. Naranjo had given them the name of the main cartel contact in Miami, who went by "Mario Playo." Naranjo had received a few phone calls from him, but had no other contact. Kacerosky went to work. One of the phone numbers Naranjo gave the investigators was still active.

As he proceeded with his investigation, Kacerosky learned from the DEA that the combine had smuggled a large shipment of cocaine hidden in frozen broccoli from Guatemala to the United States through the Port of Miami to a warehouse, which the agency now had under surveillance.[28] Customs and the DEA discovered they were after the same man. This lack of communication between federal agencies in the War against Drugs was nothing new. They had a dismal history of not working together and of distrusting each other. One of the best examples of the failure to cooperate was the large number of separate drug task forces that the DEA and FBI had set up. As Jim McGee and Brian Duffy explained, "The FBI had theirs. The DEA had theirs. Sometimes, there was a third set, sponsored by the Treasury Department's Bureau of Alcohol, Tobacco and Firearms."[29]

This investigation, however, would be different. The Florida Joint Task Force had grown out of the South Florida Task Force, established by President Ronald Reagan in 1982 when he declared the War on Drugs, and it worked hard to coordinate what became known as Operation Cornerstone.[30] "We needed cooperation because once a drug shipment arrives in port, it can't be left alone," Kacerosky explained. "We had twenty-four-hour surveillance, with DEA and Customs – eighty people – working on the case in three shifts a day. Tom Cash, the top administrator in the DEA's Miami office and my superior, William Rosenblatt [U.S. Customs Special Agent in Charge for South Florida], had a good working relationship and respect for each other, which helped to move the case forward."[31]

When the dust settled after the cement post bust, Kacerosky locked himself in a room with the mountains of telephone records that were seized when the authorities arrested Naranjo. Trying to make sense of the evidence was like trying to complete a giant jigsaw puzzle. After countless hours of digging, he concluded that Mario Playo was the cartel's big player in the city. The phone associated with Mario Playo was dumped the day of the cement seizures, but Kacerosky managed to follow a trail of telephone calls from cellphones to beepers to more phones and came up with a live number that he concluded belonged to Mario Playo. With a little more work, he determined that the live number belonged to a "Mario Robertson" and then nailed down that Mario was really Harold Ackerman.

Ackerman was such an important cell head that he was known as "the Cali cartel's ambassador to the United States." He was the prototypical Cali manager and the type of employee who helped make the cartel the world's most powerful and successful criminal multinational. Born in Palmira, Colombia, in 1941, Ackerman graduated from a university in Cali where he studied industrial engineering and business administration before joining a clothing manufacturing business. He came to the United States in June 1981 and opened a dress shop in the Dadeland Mall. "I was living well, but one day some Colombians started coming by my shop and hanging out," Ackerman recalled. "They kept telling me that I could make a lot more money working for an organization based in Cali."[32]

One of the Colombians, Cesar Velez, introduced Ackerman to Jorge Lopez (aka Tio or Pana), an important person within the organization. "Lopez was an old Miguel Rodriguez guy who had become too hot by 1990 because of a money seizure related to him," said Ed Ryan. "So Miguel ordered him back to Colombia. But, first, he needed to pick his replacement."[33]

Lopez and Ackerman met at a Miami restaurant in early March. "My organization needs a corporation to import frozen food, specifically frozen vegetables," said Lopez. From his conversations with his new friends, Ackerman gathered that it wouldn't be a corporation for a legitimate business, but he listened.

Lopez explained the deal and said, "If you're interested, we will provide you with false identification. You will report to me and follow my instructions."

"I want in," Ackerman told Lopez, who now had his replacement.

"That's good, but you have to go to Cali and meet the Señor," said Lopez.[34]

In March 1990, Ackerman journeyed to Cali, where he met with Miguel Rodriguez over a four-day period. Ackerman stayed at a hotel the cartel liked to use for out-of-town visitors, and he was given sunglasses to wear on his way to the meeting. To passersby on the street, the glasses made it look like Ackerman had a problem with sun glare, but the lenses were pitch black and he couldn't see a thing. In effect, Ackerman went to the meeting blindfolded. It was a favorite security technique of Miguel Rodriguez that he used when people came to call on him. [35]

The meeting was a job interview and both employer and job seeker liked what they heard. The cartel hired Ackerman, and he went to work when he got back to Miami, establishing a number of front companies that could ease the flow of cocaine and money into and out of the United States. The most important of these companies was Southeast Agrotrade (SEA), a small warehouse with storage bays on Northwest 89th Court. Ackerman began wheeling and dealing, using four cellular phones to coordinate the movement of multiton shipments to at least sixteen distribution groups in the Miami area. [36]

It wasn't the kind of job where the boss gave the employee a lot of latitude. The Señor was constantly phoning Ackerman, micromanaging virtually every aspect of the operation. "I would get at least one phone call a day from Miguel," said Ackerman. "He was always on top of every little thing that was going on." Ackerman deserved the title of "ambassador" because he became the most important executive the cartel had in the United States. "Harold was involved with everything, which was not typical of the way the cartel liked to do things," said Ed Kacerosky. "It liked to compartmentalize everything, usually by having different people handle different tasks, the money, the distribution, et cetera. Harold handled everything. It had a lot of confidence in him, but this is where the cartel's tight cell structure broke down and it made a strategic mistake." [37]

At their meeting, Miguel had lectured Ackerman about the importance of not bringing attention to oneself, but, in Ackerman's case, the cartel made another exception to its rules. "I was different; I had money from means other than drug trafficking," Ackerman explained. "The cartel was flexible and allowed me to live a good lifestyle." [38]

When a cocaine shipment arrived in Miami, Miguel called Ackerman and gave him instructions on how to deliver it. Miguel was a stickler about having his managers keep good records, so his ambassador kept a notebook on him at all times in which he wrote down the instructions. He then passed them to one of his assistants, who would, in turn, contact the person designated to receive the contraband, and they would agree on the location for the deal. Once the delivery was made, Ackerman received a phone call or a code was placed on his beeper. After recording the transfer in the notebook, Ackerman called Miguel.

In handling the money, Miguel would receive a call from the associate who had the money and then call Ackerman to give him the phone number he needed to make the arrangements for the pickup. Once the money was counted, Ackerman wrote the amount in his notebook and called Cali again to notify Miguel. Ackerman later entered all the financial information into his computer at home. Every two weeks, Ackerman sent a "flow statement" to Miguel, providing his boss with information about gross profits and expenses. After reviewing the statement, Miguel passed it on to his chief accountant, Guillermo Pallomari. Ackerman also sent faxes to the Cali headquarters containing information about expenses and income. Jorge Castillo, Rodriguez's secretary, received the faxes and passed them on to Pallomari, who reviewed them and checked the figures to make sure they balanced, before handing them over to Miguel for his review.[39]

Ackerman's notebooks and computer-generated financial records were later seized when federal agents arrested him and searched his house, and they proved to be a bonanza for law enforcement. Not only did the records reveal how the cartel operated, but they also provided valuable information about how it spent its money. One entry, for example, showed a payment to Rosenthal of $492,000, which included the $75,000 paid for Naranjo's representation.[40]

Soon after joining the Cali cartel, the money began to roll in for Ackerman. In October 1991, Ackerman earned his first $120,000 by helping to smuggle to the United States a 5,000-kilo cocaine shipment concealed in frozen broccoli. Two months later there was a second shipment, an importation by Southeast Agrotrade into the port of Everglades, Florida, of 5,000 kilograms of cocaine, once again hidden in frozen broccoli; this second shipment earned him another $200,000. Ackerman earned another $400,000 for a third shipment of 2,000 kilos of cocaine in early February, using the same route as the first one. Ackerman estimates that he earned $3 million during the two years he worked for the organization.

On April 23, federal investigators raided Harold Ackerman's luxurious home in North Miami. They were amazed at what they found – $462,000 in cash in a safe, $200,000 worth of jewelry, and a Lexus, a Toyota Tercel, a Mazda RX-7 and two BMWs, all uncovered after a search of the property. "It was obvious that he liked the good life and needed a lot of money to keep up his lifestyle," said Lee Granato, a U.S. customs agent who investigated the financial aspect of Operation Cornerstone.[41]

Keeping his mouth shut and not cooperating with the U.S. government, if the authorities arrested him, was one rule Ackerman knew he couldn't break. He had too many family members in Colombia, vulnerable to retaliation. Just in case, Miguel used Moran to relay messages to Ackerman. Some were reassuring. "Don't be concerned, Harold. Take it easy. Your family will receive a monthly payment." But Moran also relayed this message: "Mr. Rodriguez told me to remind you that as a friend, he is a very good person, but as an enemy, he will be a very bad person. Think of cooperating and not even your dog will remain. Remember, you still have family in Colombia."[42]

One day cartel counsel Robert Moore went to see Ackerman to inform him that he had prepared an affidavit for his signature, which stated he had never heard of Miguel Rodriguez or had any business dealings with him. The godfathers thought they could use such documents to shield them against any trafficking charges they might face in the Colombian and U.S. courts. "They were, in some way, I imagine, for use in Colombia, but their real use was for here in the United States, which is why they were all in English, citing U.S. laws, cases, et cetera," said Ryan. "It was a true sign of their arrogance and power. They thought nothing of reaching into this country and exacting their will and having their hired mules sign utterly false documents for the benefit of the Rodriguez family. And to do this dirty work, they used lawyers who were willing to sell their professional souls for a piece of the mountain of drug money controlled by the Rodriguezes."[43]

The cartel also sent Michael Abbell and Francisco Laguna, two of its most important lawyers, to see Ackerman and discuss with him the importance of signing the affidavits. If the cartel had an award for Most Valuable Employee, Abbell would have won it hands down. He seemed to show up any place where the combine had a major headache. In 1990, for instance, Abbell fielded a civil suit on behalf of Ampara Santacruz, Chepe's wife, claiming that the funds seized in the Luxembourg case were actually an inheritance from her father. Santacruz's wife lost the case. In a post-trial opinion, Judge Jack B. Weinstein ruled that the authorities had properly seized the money because it was the drug money of a "well-organized multi-national organization based in the city of Cali, Colombia, and led by a fugitive named Jose Santacruz Londono." Abbell went the extra mile and wrote a letter to the judge, complaining that the judge had "mis-characterized the evidence."[44]

Abbell had come a long and crooked way from his days as a young lawyer in the U.S. Justice Department. Then he had written the Swiss government seeking access to Swiss bank records because Jose Santacruz Londono was involved in a large cocaine trafficking organization that was laundering millions of dollars in profits from the illegal distribution of narcotics.[45]

Bogota native Francisco Laguna was a member of Abbell's law firm and ran its Florida office. Fluent in Spanish, Laguna had the important responsibilities of translating legal documents into Spanish so the firm's important clients in Cali could read them and of serving as an interpreter when Abbell and the other cartel house counsel went to Cali.

Ackerman was puzzled, though, about their visit. Neither Abbell or Laguna represented him, so why did they come?

Abbell got right to the point. "Mr. Ackerman, do you understand everything representing the affidavit[s]," Abbell asked.

"Yes, sir, I do," replied Ackerman. "Mr. Moore explained it to me."

"Are you going to sign them?"

"Yes, I have no other alternative and I will sign them."

"Okay," Abbell said. "In a few weeks, either myself or Mr. Laguna will come over to bring them to you."[46]

By now, the cartel had too many Ackerman-like mistakes sitting in jail, who probably could be damaging witnesses against their enterprise. The godfathers were getting desperate, and they held several more meetings to figure out what they could do to repair the damage. Ackerman's legal counsel had obtained copies of the indictment, both in English and Spanish, pending against their client, as well as copies of documents from the Prosecuting Attorney General that U.S. prosecutors had sent to the office.

The cartel was making use of the extensive contacts it had within that office and other regional prosecutors' offices, particularly in Cali. Its bosses became aware that the attorney general's office in Bogota was planning to file exactly the same charges filed in the United States, so it could now plan a strategy to defend itself in Colombia against possible charges. Miguel met with one of the assistants in Prosecuting Attorney General De Greiff's office and asked him to "lose" the documents. If they screwed up the process, the charges would be delayed.[47] This was a normal tactic the drug lords used when faced with a possible prosecution against their organization.[48]

The legal problems were not the only matter Miguel and his associates had to worry about. The broccoli-smuggling route through Guatemala had taken years to establish, but now it was exposed, making the cartel's distribution network even more vulnerable. It needed to develop a new smuggling route to keep moving the huge loads of white powder manufactured in its clandestine labs. But with Ackerman in jail, the organization had to find a new cell head to direct operations in Miami.

Miguel chose Raul Marti, an ambitious Cuban, who had shown a lot of talent working with Ackerman. The Señor summoned Marti to Cali to give him his instructions. Marti was to set up a coffee exportation business using a company in Panama as the supplier. The cartel planned to use the coffee shipments to smuggle cocaine in the same manner it did with the concrete fence posts and frozen broccoli. Miguel showed Marti some of the documents his American lawyers had given him. They revealed how federal authorities had intercepted Ackerman's cellular calls and had used the financial records they confiscated from Ackerman's house to gather incriminating evidence. "Study these records so you can learn from them," instructed Miguel, who warned in his typical stern fashion: "Be careful!"[49]

After studying the documents obtained in the pretrial discovery phases of the cases involving his busted lieutenants, Miguel knew it was time to make operational changes. Using cell phones and beepers, talking in coded language, and changing phone numbers frequently had been the Cali modus operandi, but the documents revealed that federal agents had successfully wiretapped his organization's phones. Now, no one was to talk on cell phones, the Señor ordered. "When Marti took over from Ackerman, he began using prepaid phone cards," Weiss revealed.

The Panama smuggling route, however, was not the best one the cartel could have chosen. "It didn't make sense because Panama is not a coffee producing country," said Weiss. "It would have made more sense to establish the route through Brazil, the world's major coffee producing country." The cartel had made another strategic mistake. It looked like law enforcement was finally beginning to disrupt its well-oiled distribution network.

Federal agents continued to analyze phone records and financial information from the Ackerman case. "The records gave us a pretty good idea of how the cartel worked," said Weiss. "Ackerman was not only the cartel's wholesale distributor and the distributor for South Florida, but he also handled the money. The cartel broke its own rule about keeping the parts of its operation compartmentalized. Federal authorities were able to examine three sets of records at once and get a better understanding of its operation." In August 1993, the authorities put a coffee shipment that arrived in Miami from Panama under surveillance. The following month they seized the ship's containers containing 5,600 kilos of cocaine. Raul Marti and three others were arrested.[50]

The cartel's lawyers worked hard to shore up the leaks. After Marti hired the independent lawyer, Francisco Laguna met with the lawyer.

"I'm representing Miguel Rodriguez and he wants Mr. Marti to sign an affidavit," Laguna said.

"No way am I going to get my client to sign a false document," was Marti's lawyer's response.

"Well, Mr. Rodriguez won't be paying Mr. Marti's legal bills if he doesn't sign," Laguna warned.

Laguna met with Marti without his lawyer's permission, and

then called Marti's lawyer to inform him he was transferring $160,000 to him for his services in representing Marti. The lawyer was outraged and contacted the U.S. government after receiving the money.[51]

By the end of 1992, the Cali cartel was reeling from some heavy blows. Too many of its associates were sitting in jail and too many of its cocaine shipments had been discovered. Yet all was not bleak. Harold Ackerman was so frightened for his family's welfare that he could be counted on to not betray his employers. His testimony would have been devastating, but the former cartel ambassador to the United States dutifully went on trial on January 25, 1993, in Miami federal court for smuggling twenty-two tons of cocaine into South Florida.[52] On August 23, 1993, the court found Ackerman guilty and sentenced him to six life terms. Ackerman had kept quiet, but as he went off to jail, the thought of spending the rest of his life behind bars began to haunt him. The ex-cartel ambassador wondered if the federal authorities could really do what they told him: protect his family if he talked?

Chapter 11

Submission to Justice

We had a complex relationship. De Greiff was meeting with some [Cali cartel] people behind the scenes, but he kept that from me. I don't blame him for not telling me everything. We would have been all over him, and later we were.
– Joe Toft, head of the DEA office in Bogota, 1988–1994

Harold Ackerman had a simple and direct answer when asked to explain why he changed his mind and decided to cooperate with U.S. prosecutors. "Six life sentences," he said with a laugh.[1] After some reflection, he elaborated, "I also had to take care of my family, and I couldn't do that spending the rest of my life behind bars. I agreed to testify because the prosecutors said they could protect my family if I testified, and I believed them."[2]

The U.S. government froze Ackerman's assets, but, as was the case with the other cell managers who were arrested, the cartel provided him with one of its lawyers, Robert Moore. True to Cali form, the first thing Moore did was deliver a message from Miguel: Do not cooperate with the authorities or else your family will die and not even your family dog will live.[3]

But Ackerman had begun to have doubts about the wisdom of not cooperating with the authorities. He was in jail for the rest of his life. He had a bad heart. Worry about his family was eating him up. Who will protect my interests when I go to court and to jail, Ackerman wondered? Can I really trust the house counsel? Ackerman's family was also concerned about Moore's representation, and in October 1992, they convinced Ackerman that he should retain a criminal defense lawyer who would be independent and outside the drug barons' control. Their choice – Ed Shohat, a top-flight Miami-based lawyer with drug-case related experience defending such high-profile clients as former Medellin cartel godfather Carlos Lehder.

Shohat was the type of lawyer who was not afraid to protect the interests of his client against powerful forces. Michael Abbell visited Ackerman in the Tallahassee prison after Ackerman had retained Shohat and told him to sign a false affidavit denying that he had ever known Miguel Rodriguez. When Shohat learned what the Colombians were pressuring his client to do, he urged Ackerman not to sign. "It's the most unethical and unprofessional behavior I've ever seen," Shohat told Ackerman. But Ackerman was still intimidated by the cartel's power, and he signed not one but three versions of the affidavit, all of which Francisco Laguna delivered to Miguel.[4]

Abbell later told Shohat that Miguel had agreed to pay Ackerman's legal fees, but that he needed his client to sign still another affidavit. Shohat was outraged. "It's another false affidavit," Shohat said, scolding Abbell. "I'm not going to have my client sign it."[5]

The cartel's house counsel obstructed Shohat as he tried to pursue the best defense strategy possible for his client. For instance, Moran also represented Carlos Giron, another Cali member who, until his arrest, operated in a front warehouse, which stored guns, dope, and other items for the cartel. Shohat wanted to pursue a coercion defense for Ackerman, which Abbell challenged. "Have you received permission from Miguel Rodriguez to do so?" Abbell asked Shohat.[6]

To turn or not to turn against the richest and most sophisticated criminal organization in history – that was an agonizing decision for Ackerman. The thought of six life sentences aside, the cartel's chilling admonitions about adhering to its code of silence haunted him. Ackerman, however, finally made up his mind. He met with Shohat and told him to give federal prosecutors this discreet message:

"I will testify against the Cali cartel if you guarantee the protection of my family."

"No problem," assured the U.S. Attorney General's Office when Shohat delivered the message.

Shohat met with Bill Pearson, the assistant U.S. attorney general for the District of South Florida, to begin the negotiations. The son of a distinguished former state appeals court judge, Pearson had worked for several years as a public defender before switching sides to become a prosecutor. Pearson arranged a secret meeting with Ackerman and Shohat in a cramped area of the underground section of the Miami federal courthouse.[7] Ed Ryan, Ed Kacerosky, and Lou Weiss also attended.[8] The investigators took every precaution to ensure that people in the courthouse and jail would not know Ackerman was talking to federal authorities. Ackerman did not speak English, so Kacerosky, who was fluent in Spanish, did the translating. "Ackerman was a high-profile defendant," Ryan recalled. "If he flipped, he would open the floodgates and other jailed Cali people would be willing to flip as well."[9]

Kacerosky was also impressed with Ackerman, whom he found to be polite, soft-spoken, and obviously smart, and he certainly had a lot more going for him than the typical cartel thug. Despite his criminal past, Ackerman was a family man who loved his wife and was putting his son through medical school. Ackerman would be a convincing witness, if they could get him to turn against the cartel.[10]

After the group took their seats and exchanged greetings, Pearson didn't waste time. "We want to make you a deal, but you have to tell the truth and nothing but the truth," the prosecutor told Ackerman. "You have to tell us everything. If we find out you're lying, the deal is off." Shohat wanted to have a formal agreement of cooperation signed before his client started cooperating, but Ackerman said it could wait.[11]

This gesture impressed Kacerosky, but he wanted to make sure Ackerman could be trusted. The customs agent pulled out a big notebook full of photos, most of which were taken by a government surveillance camera with a long telescopic lens. In the financial ledgers that investigators had taken from Ackerman's house were repeated references to the number twenty-four. The investigators believed the number was code for an important person in the organization. "Pick out number twenty-four from the photos," Kacerosky instructed Ackerman. Kacerosky felt that Ackerman shouldn't be trusted if he picked out a minor player in the organization. Ackerman flipped quickly through the book, then stopped. "That's him," Ackerman said, pointing to a photo of a Latin man with slick black hair. "He's called 'Jesus.'" Number twenty-four was Raul Marti, the important cartel manager who had refused to cooperate with prosecutors after his arrest.[12]

Ackerman became one of the most important witnesses ever to testify against the Cali cartel, and his testimony helped make Operation Cornerstone one of the most significant criminal investigations in U.S. history. "Most flips are either sneaky or stupid or both," Ryan explained. "But in interrogating Harold, it was like talking to a sharp businessman. We never caught him in a lie. He probably spent three weeks on the witness stand over the course of two trials. He was the most important witness I ever worked with and the best as well."[13]

In noting his personal contribution to the Cornerstone investigation, Ackerman later testified, "My cooperation with the United States provided a detailed, minute and true narration of my activities in narcotics smuggling. I was involved with the Rodriguez Orejuela organization. This cooperation also included the explanation of the organization's flow chart, the structure of the Cali organization, its operation methods, as well as providing the positive identification of other persons involved in the organization, the identification of other routes of importation and distribution of cocaine in the United States, and a precise and exact analysis of the participation and the activities of the U.S. attorneys who worked on behalf of the cartel. And as a result of this information, a number of investigations and operations were begun against the Cali cartel."[14]

When Ackerman began to cooperate secretly, prosecutors Ryan and Pearson were confident he would affirm the theories they presented to the jury at Ackerman's trial about the amount of cocaine and money the cartel was handling and who were its principal players. "When we met with him, he was as respectful and complimentary of the job we had done at the trial and as motivated as we expected," Pearson recalled. "We knew he was

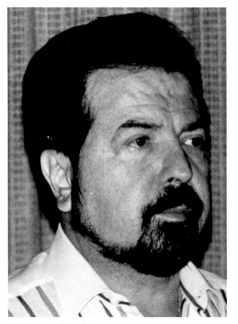

Gilberto Rodriguez.

Miguel Rodriguez.

Jose Santacruz.

Pacho Herrera.

The four drug lords of the Cali cartel. Gilberto was known as the Chess Player for this calculation and strategy. Miguel was the hands-on micro-manager. Santacruz, rugged and low key, was the most violent of the group, while the dapper Herrera was the stereotypical sharp-suited drug trafficker. *(Photos supplied by the DEA)*

An aerial view of the site of the Minden explosion in upstate New York, with the wrecked laboratory in the top left corner, which led to a concerted investigation of the Cali cartel. *(DEA)*

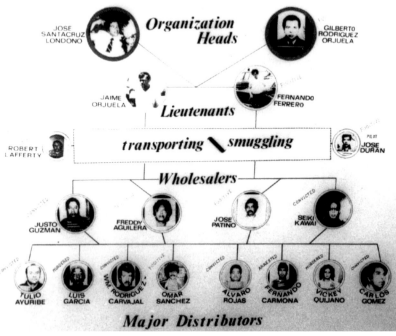

An early organisational chart of the Santacruz Londono organization. The Cali men made New York City their early base. *(DEA)*

A smiling Chepe Santacruz with his wife and children, looking every inch the successful businessman and devoted father. *(DEA)*

One of Chepe's opulent residences, with obligatory swimming pool, in Cali. The mafia made untold billions of dollars and bought numerous properties in their native Colombia. *(DEA)*

Streetwise detective Ken Robinson was one of the first to investigate the cartel's New York operation.

Harold Ackerman, Cali cartel 'ambassador' to the U.S., became a witness against his bosses after being sentenced to six life terms. *(DEA)*

What $2 million looks like: the first major money hit against the cartel after Miguel Rodriguez had taken control, seized after a high-speed chase across New York's George Washington Bridge.
(From left) Ken Spiro, Everett Pearsall, Bob Odell, Bill Mante, Frank Diaz, Mike Reeves and Captain John Burns. *(New York State Police)*

Left: Jose Gonzalo Gacha in football strip. A close ally of Pablo Escobar, the Medellin trafficker was tracked by his enemies in Cali and shot dead by Colombian security forces in 1989. *(DEA)*

Below: The corpulent body of Pablo Escobar. The brutal leader of the Medellin cartel waged war against both the Colombian state and the Cali mob until he was gunned down on a rooftop. *(DEA)*

General Rosso José Serrano, the studious but tough police commander who drove the fight against the men from Cali.

Ernesto Samper, the Colombian President accused by the U.S. of accepting Cali money for his election campaign. *(Ernesto Samper)*

DEA agents Ed Ryan (left) and Ed Kacersoky, key figures in the successful Operation Cornerstone. *(Author's photo)*

Gilberto Rodriguez being booked after his capture in June 1995.
"Don't shoot, I'm a man of peace," he told his captors. *(DEA)*

Agents posing with Miguel Rodriguez, who was caught just two months
after his brother: (left to right) Dave Mitchell, Chris Feistl, CNP Colonel
Gomez, Jerry Salameh and Ruben Prieto. *(DEA)*

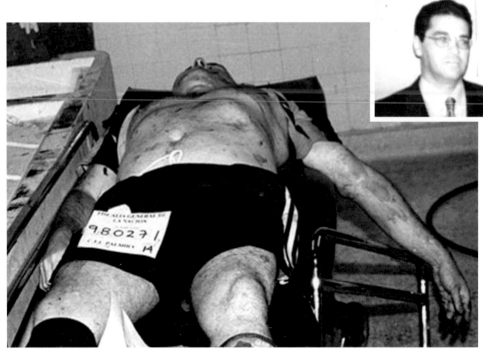

The dapper Pacho Herrera dressed like a GQ model (inset) but was shot dead while playing a football match in prison in a hit organized by a rival trafficker. *(Reuters)*

Gilberto Rodriguez, aged 65, is escorted by Colombian soldiers to a flight to Miami after his extradition to face serious drug charges in December 2004. *(Associated Press)*

intelligent. He had to be, given the responsibility he had running the dope and money operations simultaneously. We looked upon him as being the centerpiece of the case we were building against the cartel."[15] Eventually, Ackerman played a part in encouraging Raul Marti, Gustavo Naranjo, and three other former Cali associates to cooperate and in helping Naranjo find a lawyer and assisting in paying for his defense.[16]

Micromanager, always-in-control Miguel Rodriguez had a hard time handling the news of Ackerman's defection. "It was a very stunning piece of news, quite serious, and it made him physically ill," Pallomari recalled.[17] Miguel and the other godfathers held more crisis management meetings to discuss the state of their empire. All their big plans to dominate the world's illegal drug market were unraveling. They needed lots of money to keep their giant criminal multinational organization afloat, but the arrest of Ackerman and the other associates, who seemed to be falling like dominos, was drying up the pool of managers and the flow of money and disrupting distribution. Ackerman would be a tough manager to replace, but they had to find someone quick who could stop the hemorrhaging.

The cartel decided to move Carlos Torres to Miami and into Ackerman's slot, but it seemed that, suddenly, the gentlemen from Cali couldn't do anything right. They were hit with more bad news when authorities arrested Carlos Torres in April 1993 on a charge of trafficking 500 kilograms of cocaine.[18] He pleaded guilty nine months later.

Although Carlos Torres hired Stephen Golembe to act as his lawyer, his wife approached Miguel and asked for money to help pay her husband's legal fees. "Go talk to Moran," Miguel told her. When she did so, Moran informed her that Rodriguez had designated him to represent her husband, and no other lawyer was to get involved.

"Why?" Mrs. Torres asked.

"Because Mr. Rodriguez said so," was the answer. On hearing this, Torres fired Golembe.

After making his initial appearance in court, Torres met with Moran and reminded him that Miguel had promised to take care of the Torres family and his legal expenses in return for his silence. "I'm going to Colombia and I'll give him your message," Moran replied. Then Torres gave Moran a caveat. "Oh, by the way, tell Miguel to change all the beeper numbers. The police have them." Moran scribbled this important bit of information down in his notes.[19]

On May 6, Moran traveled to Cali to meet with Miguel. Two days later, Miguel gave $105,300 to Moran, who then returned to Miami. The next day, Moran went to see Torres in the Miami Correctional Center. "Okay, Mr. Rodriguez will pay your wife $5,000 a month if you don't talk to the authorities," Moran told Torres. The next day, Moran arranged for $10,000 to be delivered by courier to Torres's wife. Soon after she received the money, however, the authorities arrested Mrs. Torres and deported her to Colombia.[20]

Moran also made arrangements to pay Torres's attorney's fees and managed to obtain a $250,000 bond for Torres. Moran faxed a letter to Miguel asking that the money posted for the bond come from "their" money.[21] The U.S. government appealed the court ruling on the bond and won. Torres remained in jail. To keep his former cell head happy, Miguel arranged for a money order of $100 to be given to Torres for his concession fees at the prison.[22] In the coming months, the cartel continued to pay Torres's concession expenses and his wife's hush money.

But Torres fired Moran because the FBI and an assistant attorney general had moved to disqualify Moran from representing him. "Torres worried that Moran was drawing more attention than he, Torres, needed," said Pearson. "Torres knew, too, that he could never cooperate – that is, if he ever wanted to – with Moran as attorney."[23]

Torres rehired Golembe but fired him after Golembe filed a statement with a probation officer that implicated Miguel Rodriguez. Torres then hired Francisco Laguna and Donald Ferguson, a former federal prosecutor. Laguna submitted on behalf of Torres a statement regarding the charges he faced.[24] In January 1994, Torres was convicted of drug trafficking in the United States District Court of the Southern District of Florida. Not long after, Laguna and Ferguson delivered $8,300 to Carlos Torres's family.[25]

The cartel was doing what it had promised, but Torres later agreed to cooperate and became a valuable witness against the very person the cartel had hired to represent him – William Moran. Miguel Rodriguez had been taped while threatening Torres, which, according to Pearson, the U.S. government was able to use in court "because it supported our theory that the attorney's fees and the family subsistence money was hush money and that the attorneys served as the funnel through which those monies were paid."[26]

For the Cali godfathers, watching the drug distribution network that they had spent twenty years building fall apart was agonizing enough, but they also had to keep a nervous eye on legal developments to ensure that they wouldn't be extradited to the United States. The godfathers could buy the Colombian legal system, but they knew that all their millions wouldn't help them one iota in a U.S. court. They believed in strategic planning and were always looking for ways to insulate themselves against the legal system. That's why Miguel had talked with attorney Joel Rosenthal to get his opinion about the possibility of setting up a dialogue with the U.S. government. That the U.S. would agree to such a deal was wishful thinking on his part, but it showed how worried he was about their legal situation.

Now, Miguel had another brainwave. Why not approach the U.S. government with a proposal that could dramatically change the direction of the War on Drugs? In return for amnesty, the Cali cartel would agree to cut the flow of cocaine out of Colombia by sixty to seventy percent. Miguel put Abbell in charge of the project, responsible for finding intermediaries who could approach U.S. and Colombian officials on the cartel's behalf.

In June 1994, Michael Abbell and Francisco Laguna traveled to Colombia and met with Miguel Rodriguez and one of his attorneys, Bernardo Gonzalez. A few days later, Abbell and Laguna talked with Colombia's Prosecuting Attorney General, Gustavo De Greiff, to see if they could resolve Miguel's legal situation in Colombia and discuss the proposal that Miguel wanted to present to the U.S. government.[27] De Greiff was a prominent legal figure. He had been in private law practice for more than twenty years before becoming Colombia's prosecuting attorney general in April

1992. He made a name for himself defending Jaime Michelsen Uribe, a former financier who laundered money for the Medellin cartel before he fled the country.[28] The Colombian Supreme Court appointed De Greiff to the position from a list of three names submitted by President Gaviria, although he had no experience in penal law.

In the beginning, De Greiff had good relations with the Bush and Clinton administrations. The U.S. media described him as an effective drug-fighter, noting that "he had long enjoyed a reputation for integrity in the struggle against the drug barons." The honeymoon ended in November 1993, when he appeared at a symposium in Maryland with Kurt Schmoke, the mayor of Baltimore and an outspoken critic of U.S. drug policy, and gave a speech that detoured sharply from the party line on the War on Drugs. De Greiff declared his support for drug legalization.[29] No matter how many traffickers are put behind bars there will always be more of them because there is so much money to be made, De Greiff argued. So the consuming countries should introduce some form of legalization to take the profits out of trafficking.[30] "I said that legalization, which is not an invitation to consume, is the best strategy to destroy the narco-traffickers' business and the corruption associated with it," De Greiff recalled. "I also said that the consuming problem should be fought at the same time through educational campaigns and medical treatment of individuals."[31]

The comments by Colombia's legal point man on the War on Drugs caused a firestorm. The title of a New York Times article said it all: "A Captain in the Drug War Wants to Call It Off."[32] United States officials were angry and bewildered by De Greiff's change of view. "Something happened to him," said Robert Gelbard, the U.S. assistant secretary of state for Latin American affairs during this period. "People who have know him for years said his personality changed."[33] Bob Nieves, the DEA's chief of international operations at the time De Greiff made his comments supporting legalization, recalled, "When De Greiff arrived in office, he came out and said the right things about the War on Drugs. We thought we had a good partner. Then he sits down with Kurt Schmoke and starts talking about legalization and goes ahead and negotiates with the Cali cartel. What's going on?"[34]

Ethan Nadelmann, executive director of the Drug Policy Alliance, said that De Greiff's change of position didn't happen overnight. He recalls being on a panel with De Greiff at a conference at UCLA, which took place months before his speech in Maryland. "De Greiff gave a speech in which he raised a lot more questions and doubts about drug policy," Nadelmann said. "You would think that a top legal official from Colombia would be wary about making such comments at a drug policy conference in the U.S."[35]

The Clinton administration moved to get De Greiff back in line. Prior to De Greiff's controversial appearance in Maryland, Janet Reno, the U.S. Attorney General, arranged a meeting with him to discuss some legal issues of mutual concern to their governments. In the past, relations between the two had been cordial, and on occasion they had even embraced before meeting.[36] But this time Reno began by lecturing De Greiff about how wrong he was in his views on the drug war and how much damage they could cause. De Greiff didn't like her tone. Reno was talking to him in a manner often used by the U.S. government when speaking with officials of Third World states. "What were you doing talking about legalization?" Reno demanded. "Don't you realize you're sending a message to narco traffickers that they can deal in drugs but eventually they will be pardoned. Do you want drugs to be at the disposal of American youth?"[37] De Greiff didn't have a chance to respond, because Reno left the meeting abruptly, leaving him with her deputy assistant attorney general. De Greiff tried to explain his views to Reno's subordinate, but he recalled, "The discussion was very nasty and inconclusive, since I maintained my position and [the] deputy, his."[38]

Prominent Colombian officials thought De Greiff's drug views were "misguided," although they recognized he was trying to make a sincere attempt to address the problem of trafficking in Colombia. "Mr. De Greiff is a very intelligent man, but he also made a lot mistakes," Carlos Lemos, former vice-president of Colombia in the Ernesto Samper administration, explained in an interview in his comfortable but well-guarded home in Bogota. "Like a lot of Colombians, De Greiff was in denial. He really believed they could deal with the Cali cartel in good faith and turn them into a nice group."[39]

By the time De Greiff starting to support legalization publicly, his relations with President Gaviria were deteriorating. De Greiff had successfully led the legal aspect of the hunt for Pablo Escobar, and his relations with Gaviria during that period were good, but Colombia's president has a curious administrative relationship with the country's prosecuting attorney general.[40] In Colombia, the Prosecuting Attorney General's Office is a branch of the judiciary and completely independent of the presidency.[41] In short, the president of Colombia has no oversight of the country's top prosecutor.

De Greiff began to go his own way in dealing with the Cali problem. He wanted to convince the leaders to surrender, believing it would be the best way to reduce or eliminate the massive corruption and widespread violence associated with the cartels. So he came up with a "submission to justice" plan that he hoped would entice the godfathers to give up their criminal ways. The plan included the following conditions: When the Prosecuting Attorney General's Office had evidence, the drug trafficker would be offered a one-third reduction from the highest penalty set by the Colombian law (approximately a fifteen-year sentence). For a trafficker against whom the office had evidence that he was involved in trafficking but not enough evidence to confront him in court, he would receive a reduction of one-half of the maximum penalty. For the rest (traffickers unknown to both De Greiff's office and other government agencies), the minimum penalty under the Colombian penal code would be applied.[42]

Although independent of presidential authority, De Greiff did try to keep both Gaviria and the U.S. government informed of developments with his plan. In early 1994, De Greiff presented his plan to Morris Busby, the ambassador to Colombia.[43] "I also made an effort to keep the DEA office in Colombia informed about the negotiations," De Greiff said.[44] De Greiff called Joe Toft, head of the DEA office in Colombia from 1988 to 1994, and they would meet often, Toft confirmed, but added, "We had a complex relationship. De Greiff was meeting with some [Cali cartel] people behind the scenes, but he kept that from me.

I don't blame him for not telling me everything. We [the U.S. government] would have been all over him, and later we were."[45]

De Greiff also met with Gaviria and some of his key aides, including Dr. Francisco Sintura, the deputy assistant attorney general; Dr. Andres Gonzalez, minister of justice; Dr. Fernando Brito, head of the Colombian Intelligence Department; and Dr. Carlos Gustavo Sarrieta, the Procuador [Prosecutor] of the Republic. Meanwhile, De Greiff was meeting with the Cali cartel attorneys to work out the conditions under which the drug lords would surrender. In the first week of August 1993, De Greiff met with American lawyers, who said they represented an organization of some sixty traffickers from the Valle del Cauca. "They came to be instructed on the rules for the surrender of drug traffickers, and I explained to them the entire legal framework of the policy on surrendering to justice authorities," De Greiff told *El Espectador* newspaper. Miguel Rodriguez's attorneys first proposed that Miguel's home be assigned as his jail, and then they said Miguel would accept being put in jail if it was in the Valle del Cauca Department, where his family could visit him.[46] Neither proposal went anywhere.[47] The Gaviria administration certainly didn't want to provoke the wrath of Uncle Sam by appearing to be soft on drug trafficking.

United States government officials had reason to suspect that there was more to De Greiff's relationship with the Cali cartel than met the eye. De Greiff's name had appeared with that of Gilberto Rodriguez Orejuela in documents relating to an airline, indicating the two were co-owners.[48] De Greiff denied ever meeting either Gilberto or Miguel Rodriguez, but during the Cornerstone trial in 1997, Pallomari testified that De Greiff met with the Rodriguez brothers at the Cali home of Alberto Giraldo twice in 1993 to discuss the surrender deal. Under Colombian law it is illegal for an official in De Greiff's position to have contact with anyone whom the police are investigating.[49] In January 1994, De Greiff issued documents equivalent to safe-conduct passes to Cali traffickers Pacho Herrera and Juan Carlos "El Chupeta" ("Lollipop") Ramirez Abadia, declaring that there was not enough evidence to arrest them.[50] Today, in reference to the charges he had ties to the Cali cartel, De Greiff says bluntly:

"This is a lie," and he continues to insist he has never met the Rodriguez Orejuela brothers.[51]

De Greiff had already gone public with his surrender policy when the press reported that informal public opinion polls suggested he and his ideas had the support of a large section of the Colombian population. President Gaviria and his advisors became increasingly vocal in their opposition to what they viewed as a "sell out."[52] A U.S. embassy communiqué assessed the situation thus: "The public differences between Gaviria and De Greiff have started to become a public embarrassment to Gaviria in his finest hour, as Colombians saw De Greiff publicly challenging the President's authority. Some pundits are openly expressing doubt as to how this relationship will play out with regard to future GOC [Government of Colombia] counter-narcotics efforts."[53]

Years later, sitting in his spacious office in the Organization of American States (OAS) building in Washington D.C., Gaviria, who has been secretary general of the OAS since 1994, described his view of De Greiff's plan for submission to justice. "I thought it was a silly idea, but he was obsessed with the policy. As the fiscal [prosecuting attorney general], he was a very important man and he tried to do the plan without us. He actually thought we could put the Cali cartel leadership under house arrest."[54]

When rumors about their differences surfaced, Gaviria, De Greiff, and ministers and government officials quickly denied them, but *Semana*, a weekly magazine, revealed the differences for the first time in mid-February. De Greiff sent an indignant letter to *Semana*, protesting the news report, and Gaviria told *El Tiempo* that "there are no differences with De Greiff."[55] According to De Greiff, he had good relations with Gaviria until May 1994, but in March 1994 (two months earlier), *Semana* was writing about the "increasingly obvious two-month confrontation between the Prosecutor General's Office and [the] Gaviria government in which the Gaviria administration was considering the possibility of accusing De Greiff of collaborating with drug trafficking."[56]

In March 1994 the U.S. government stopped sharing information with De Greiff about major drug dealers, charging that he had become too lenient in prosecuting them.[57] By now, several prominent U.S. officials were publicly blasting De Greiff for his views. Both Janet Reno and John Kerry, the powerful senator from Massachusetts, charged that De Greiff wanted to cut deals that were favorable to Colombian drug traffickers. The senator was saying that the United States didn't trust the prosecuting attorney general.

That didn't deter De Greiff; in fact, he publicly called Kerry a liar.[58] In recalling that turbulent period of U.S.-Colombian relations in the War on Drugs, Senator Kerry said, "There were more than a few heated confrontations with members of the Colombian government, most of which had to do with what I felt were feeble excuses that ran counter to the reality of what we knew was happening on the ground in Colombia and the real problem of dealing with a government that often provided lip service to our demands for cooperating, transparency and the rule of law. You'd have an intelligence briefing, then have Colombian officials act as if all was hunky dory or the problems were beyond their control."[59]

The intense criticism of De Greiff continued through the rest of his term and up until December 1994, five months after he had left office and the time when the U.S. Attorney's Office began considering whether obstruction of justice charges should be brought against him. The U.S. charges revolved around the case of Daniel Munoz-Mosquera, the accused mastermind of the 1989 bombing of an Avianca airline passenger flight that killed 110 people, including an American citizen. The U.S. authorities were able to try Munoz-Mosquera, a Colombian citizen, for two reasons. First, he was arrested in New York, and also Congress had passed a law granting the United States jurisdiction in crimes in which a U.S. citizen was killed. However, Munoz-Mosquera's first trial had ended in a hung jury.[60]

In a letter dated March 28, 1994, De Greiff wrote the judge who presided at a second trial that his office had a confession about the bombing from another Medellin cartel hitman, but did not have any evidence linking such a person to the crime.[61] De Greiff's letter infuriated the U.S. State Department officials, who looked upon it as undermining their case against Munoz-Mosquera. The U.S. government sent a protest letter to the

Colombian government, charging that De Greiff's letter called into question the sincerity of De Greiff and his continuing commitment to the United States' goals in combating illegal drugs.[62]

In May 1994 De Greiff announced that there were no arrest warrants for Gilberto Rodriguez, but was immediately contradicted by the Colombian attorney general, who noted that the National Police had seven warrants for the arrests of both Gilberto and Miguel on charges ranging from murder to homicide.[63]

By now, the U.S. government had given up on the Gaviria administration, which had become much too independent on drug issues for Uncle Sam's taste, and was looking forward to working with a new Colombian president. On June 19, 1994, forty-four-year-old Ernesto Samper, the Liberal party candidate, beat his conservative opponent Andreas Pastrana by a close, 2.1 percent margin. There were rumors that Samper's campaign had been tainted by drug money, and U.S. officials had strong suspicions that he had longtime ties to drug cartels. The Clinton administration, though, wasn't concerned. Yes, Ernesto Samper had some baggage, but that could be used to mold a more dependable drug-fighting ally of the United States. It certainly couldn't get any worse.

Chapter 12

The Narco Cassette Scandal

We already got ourselves a president.
                    – Miguel Rodriguez, Cali cartel godfather

That the U.S. government thought it could work with Ernesto Samper was a graphic sign of how badly relations with Colombia had deteriorated over the issue of dealing with the Cali cartel. Many Colombia experts in the U.S. government had no illusions about the political animal with whom they might possibly have to work. Both American and Colombian officials who knew Samper describe him as a capable, experienced, charismatic, and highly intelligent politician.[1] An economist by training, he began his career as director of economic research at the Bank of Bogota from 1970 to 1974, before moving on at the tender age of twenty-five to head the National Association of Financial Institutions for six years. He entered politics in 1981 as the national coordinator of Alfonso Lopez Michelsen's presidential campaign. Running for president on the Liberal party ticket, Samper survived an assassination attempt at Bogota's El Dorado airport in 1989, and still carries the scars from the bullets that hit him. The assassin killed Jose Amquera, the secretary of the Patriotica Union party, and Samper believes the shooting was accidental, although he was shot several times.[2] He served in the presidential administration of Cesar Gaviria, first as minister of economic development from 1990 to 1991 and then as ambassador to Spain from 1991 to 1993.[3]

Any U.S. official reviewing Samper's impressive resumé would have concluded that he had the right stuff to be president of Colombia, but, as they routinely do with emerging leaders of Third World countries, U.S. intelligence agencies began collecting information on him in the 1970s. What they uncovered showed a different side to Samper's background. Samper first came to the United States' attention in 1978 when, while heading the National Association of Financial Institutions, he advocated a controversial policy that has dogged him politically ever since. Samper proposed that the government buy and burn the country's marijuana crop to protect the livelihood of poor farmers. So long as there was demand for marijuana in the United States and other countries, Samper claimed, suppression wouldn't work. All it really did was encourage criminality in Colombia and distort the country's economy. Today, Samper says he no longer holds that view, but in conversation U.S. State Department officials mention Samper's support for legalization, an indication that they have never really trusted him on the drug issue since 1978.[4]

Even worse, much of the U.S. government's intelligence linked Samper to drug traffickers. One report revealed that in 1981 Samper joined presidential candidate Alphonso Lopez Michelsen in a suite at Medellin's Hotel Intercontinental to talk with Pablo Escobar, Carlos Lehder, Jorge and Fabio Ochoa, and some other prominent traffickers about the country's drug trade. It was later rumored that Michelsen's campaign received a "donation" of from $300,000 to $400,000 from Escobar and his associates, an amount equal to the Liberal party's campaign budget. According to journalist Simon Strong, Michelsen stayed about ten minutes at the meeting, but Samper's discussions with the traffickers lasted nearly half an hour.[5] A year later Samper denied the meeting had ever happened, but in a 1983 interview, Escobar called Samper a hypocrite for "attacking certain types of financial assistance and at the same time receiving them." Carlos Lehder later claimed there were more than fifteen witnesses who could verify that the meeting took place and that Samper was there.[6]

When authorities arrested Gilberto Rodriguez in Spain in 1984,

Samper's private Colombian phone number was found in Gilberto's little black book.[7] On June 6, 1985, the general manager of the radio chain El Grupo Colombiano notified Samper that his boss, Miguel Rodriguez, had approved free airtime for Samper to use for campaign purposes. Four years later, a DEA informant said she watched the Cali godfathers give Samper $300,000. At about the same time, a drug trafficker in a U.S. jail claimed to have met Samper while he was an envoy for the Cali cartel.[8]

And as the 1994 presidential election drew near, the U.S. government had credible information that Samper's campaign had solicited funds from the Cali cartel. One informant told the DEA in 1993 that the cartel had refused to give money to a congressional campaign because they were already backing Samper.[9] But why would Samper solicit drug money? He was involved in a closer than expected race with Andres Pastrana, the Conservative party candidate and former hostage of the Medellin cartel. At the end of the first electoral round, polls indicated that Samper, the favorite, trailed Pastrana. Several political action groups had contributed to Samper's campaign in the first round, expecting him to win easily, but that didn't happen. So many of them decided that backing Samper would be like betting on a losing horse. Samper was from a prominent political family, but it had no money and his means were modest compared to his rival, Andres Pastrana, the son of a former president.[10] Samper's campaign was broke and desperate. It had to find money somewhere and quickly.

The United States was in a dilemma. Samper was still the odds-on favorite to be Colombia's next president, and the U.S. would have to work with him if he got elected. It was felt important to work out an understanding with Samper before he took office, for the sake of the War on Drugs, as well as U.S.-Colombian relations and U.S. interests in Latin America. Key officials worried that the Cali cartel power and influence was such that, if they bought the presidency, Colombia would be turned into a "narco democracy," that is, one dominated by the drug traffickers' money.

Then U.S. officials had an idea. They decided to confront Samper to let him know that they knew what was happening in his campaign and to push him into making a commitment to get

tough with Cali. Myles Frechette, who succeeded Morris
D. Busby as U.S. ambassador to Colombia in July 1994, recalled,
"We were worried about the Cali cartel's corrupting influence on
the country's political system, because we estimated that it had
intimidated or had on its payroll 75 members of the Colombian
Congress."[11]

The State Department learned that Samper would be coming
to Washington, D.C. in the spring of 1994 with two of his top
aides, Fernando Botero and Rodrigo Pardo. After some internal
discussion and debate, the department devised a strategy. They
decided to go ahead and set up a meeting with Samper, telling
him that they knew his campaign was tainted with Cali cartel
money and that he would have to stop taking it immediately.
Furthermore, they would impress upon him his need to perform
in the War on Drugs, once he was in office. "The idea was to
shake him up," recalled Robert Gelbard, who was at the time the
assistant secretary for Latin American Affairs. "I was designated to
do it privately, one-on-one."[12]

Ambassador Alex Watson, the State Department's top official
for inter-American affairs, chaired the meeting. After some
discussions on political and economic topics, Samper was invited
to have the private meeting with Gelbard, a diplomat with a
reputation for toughness. Gelbard laid out the choices for Samper.
"Our relationship, if you are president, will be based on whether
your campaign stops soliciting and receiving drug money from
the Cali cartel," Gelbard told Samper. "Once in office, you will
have to prove all those things you've been saying about fighting
drugs and taking serious action against the Cali cartel."[13]

According to Gelbard, Samper was nervous coming into
the private showdown, as if he knew what was on the agenda.
Gelbard recalled Samper saying, "No, none of it's true." Gelbard
responded: "Yes it is. You took the money."[14] The meeting
happened, Samper confirmed, but he has a different recollection
of what transpired. He described himself as being calm during the
meeting and surprised by the charges Gelbard leveled at him. "I
thought I did a good job assuring Gelbard that the corruption
charges were groundless," he recalled.[15] It was a private meeting
and no one else was present to confirm its details, but it did show

one thing to U.S. officials: Given his deep state of denial, Samper could be a big problem for the United States if he became president.[16]

While the U.S. was pressuring Samper, the Cali cartel was hard at work launching the "Champagne Project," which was designed to elect a president favorable to its interests. The cartel didn't believe in taking chances, so it tried to corrupt the election warchests of both candidates. Pastrana, however, turned down its offer of support. According to Pallomari, "I heard from Mr. Miguel Rodriguez ... that Alberto Giraldo had made several attempts on various occasions to convince Mr. Andres Pastrana to accept monies from the Cali cartel ... Mr. Andres Pastrana rejected it firmly and he never accepted any of it."[17] The cartel, therefore, was forced to put its money on Samper. In 1991, it had achieved its goal of getting rid of the extradition law that could have sent its members to a tomb in the United States. It was now working with Prosecuting Attorney General De Greiff on a "submission to justice" plan. The problem was that President Gaviria strongly opposed it. If they could buy Samper, he would be obligated to support the plan, which would further the godfathers' interests and long-term ambition – their transformation into legitimate businessmen and respected members of society.[18]

The godfathers held several planning meetings to discuss the best way to implement the Champagne Project and achieve their objective – submit to justice and receive a five-year sentence, which, given time for good behavior, would amount to only three years in jail. Alberto Giraldo and Eduardo Maestre were assigned the job of contacting Samper and arranging a meeting to discuss the cartel's offer and plan. According to Pallomari, Samper quickly agreed to accept the cartel's money and to help with its surrender plan. Miguel was ecstatic. "We already got ourselves a president," he exclaimed. Miguel also had a dinner party for Samper before the first round of the elections, which he used to stress to the presidential candidate the importance to the cartel of its surrender to justice project.[19]

The Cali cartel not only gave money to Samper's campaign but also played an active role in it. For instance, at the request of

Humberto Calle, Samper's vice-presidential running mate, the cartel bought T-shirts bearing the name of Ernesto Samper and the number ten, which were distributed to members of Samper's campaign and to other Colombian politicians who were helping him. The number ten was the candidate number associated with Samper on the election ballot. El Pibe Valderama, the most famous soccer player in Colombia at the time, even appeared on television wearing the T-shirt. One of the cartel's planes was used to ship the T-shirts all over the country.[20]

Miguel Rodriguez set up a front company and opened an account in the Cali branch of the Banco de Colombia. Other traffickers, in addition to those connected to the Cali Cartel, would benefit from the Champagne Project, and the cartel expected them to contribute to it. "All those deposits were carefully recorded in order to make sure . . . they kept track in detail as to whom contributed what," Guillermo Pallomari, the cartel's chief accountant, later testified.[21]

The money for Samper's campaign was deposited into account LTD and then converted into cash through the main branch of the Banco de Colombia in Cali. Each transaction amounted to the equivalent of about $500,000 in U.S. dollars. The cash was put into boxes, wrapped in gift-wrapping paper, taken to a private plane belonging to Pacho Herrera or Elmer Buitrago, and then flown to a farm near Cali. There, another plane would be waiting to fly the money to Bogota, where Alberto Giraldo would turn it over to Santiago Medina, the treasurer of Samper's presidential campaign team.[22]

Yet even the best-laid plans in corrupt politics can go astray. On June 15, Andres Pastrana was on a campaign swing through Cali when an unidentified man handed him several cassette tapes containing some extraordinary conversations obtained from wire intercepts.[23] On one of the tapes, Alberto Giraldo could be heard saying, "It's in your hands . . . that's curious isn't it?" Giraldo was obviously discussing the transfer of funds to Samper's presidential campaign.[24] On another tape, Giraldo and Miguel Rodriguez talked about Santiago Medina, who, said Miguel, had visited him. "Look, the reality is that they need five billion pesos [at the time, about $6.25 million] of which they have hold of two. They need three from you." Miguel answered: "It's already there. That's dealt with."[25]

The tapes provided irrefutable proof to Pastrana that the Cali cartel was financing his opponent's campaign. The next day, he and his close associate, Luis Alberto Moreno, delivered copies of the tapes to President Gaviria and to the U.S. embassy. Gaviria turned the tapes over to Rodrigo Pardo, his defense minister, and asked him to confirm their authenticity. They are for real, Pardo told his president. Gaviria was now in a tough position. He had to decide whether to make the tapes public. If he did, Samper, his Liberal party colleague, might lose the election. If he didn't, his decision might later come back to haunt him politically.

Gaviria decided to turn the tapes over to Prosecuting Attorney General De Greiff. It was the right thing to do, Gaviria believed. De Greiff's office was the appropriate legal channel, but would De Greiff do anything?[26] De Greiff said he did a lot when Gaviria turned over the narco cassettes to him. For instance, he took statements from the people involved in Samper's election campaign and checked out their bank accounts. He added, "I found no evidence of wrong doing, but I left open the possibility that the investigation could be re-opened in the future if evidence was found. My successor [Alphonso Valdivieso] did not find anything wrong with what I did."[27] Meanwhile, Moreno met with U.S. Ambassador Busby and urged his government to make the tapes public. Pastrana couldn't release them himself. At this late stage of the election, it would look too suspicious to the electorate and it could backfire at the polls.[28]

When Moreno left, Busby listened to the tapes. Their content was shocking, but they confirmed what the United States already knew about the drug-tainted corruption in Samper's presidential campaign. The ambassador passed them around to other officials in the embassy – political analysts, the DEA, and the CIA.[29] Joe Toft, the head of the DEA office in Colombia, was one of them. Toft's outspoken public comments about the corruption of Colombian society by drugs and the cozy relationship of the country's political elite with the traffickers had not endeared him to the locals. Toft went to Busby and urged him to make the tapes public, but the ambassador said he needed to go to the higher-ups in the State Department to find out what he should do. The word came back: The tapes are too delicate. Don't release them. We can't interfere in Colombian politics.[30]

Two days later, on June 19, Ernesto Samper won the presidential election by a scant 2.1 percent margin, the closest vote for a president in Colombian history.[31] In another two days, the existence of the tapes became public. Joe Toft had decided to leak them. Colombia was abuzz with rumors about what they revealed.[32]

Privately, the U.S. government was upset by the appearance of the narco cassettes, but publicly it moved to control the damage they could cause to its relations with Colombia. President Clinton wrote a letter to President Ernesto Samper in which he stressed the need for a strong bilateral relationship, but made no mention of the cassettes.[33] Myles Frechette, the incoming U.S. ambassador, also downplayed the scandal as he promoted the Clinton administration's message: "My instructions are to work as hard as possible with the new president once he takes office August 7 in order to increase cooperation, and I will do this," Frechette said.[34] Samper adamantly protested his innocence, denying he had taken money from the Cali cartel and saying he would welcome an investigation to clear his name. Alberto Giraldo backed Samper's claim of innocence, telling the press that the Cali godfathers had offered money to both Samper and Pastrana, but they both had turned it down.[35]

U.S. officials learned that Ernesto Samper was coming to New York City in late June. It would be a working vacation, Samper told the Colombian press, but Pastrana's supporters said his trip was actually a move to escape the wicked glare of negative media attention.[36] He was going to stop in New York because he had promised his children that he would take them there, Samper explained. "I really didn't want to go to New York City because I was trying to find out what had happened in my campaign," he recalled.[37]

The U.S. government pressed Samper for another meeting. Samper wouldn't travel to Washington, so the White House agreed to meet Samper in New York. On June 29, Michael Skol and Crescencio Arcos, deputy assistant secretary in the State

Department, and Ann M. Wells, a State Department Colombia Desk officer, met Samper in Manhattan at the 57th Street office of the Colombian ambassador to the United Nations, Luis Fernando Jaramillo. Samper came to the meeting with Ambassador Jaramillo, Rodrigo Pardo, Nestor Humberto Martinez (another Liberal politician), and Gabriel Silva, Colombian ambassador to the United States.[38]

The meeting was intense and lasted two hours.[39] As it had done for its previous meeting with Samper, the State Department worked out a plan and chose its team carefully. Crescencio Arcos would be the tough-talking diplomat who hammered Samper when needed. Skol would be the moderate "good guy" who really believed that the narco cassettes were inconclusive, and Wells would be the neutral observer.[40] "The whole point of the meeting was to reiterate our message," explained Skol, who headed the U.S. delegation. "We wanted to let Samper know that we had very strong information, if not evidence, that the Samper campaign had knowingly solicited and received money, and this was putting U.S.-Colombian relations at risk."[41]

Once again, Samper denied the charge. Skol marveled at how cool Samper acted, given the pressure of the moment. He was the coolest politician Skol had ever met. Still, the diplomat thought Samper was lying, although it was conceivable that some of the other Colombians at the meeting didn't know what was going on.[42] Then the American delegation gave Samper a list of demands. They weren't happy with the Gaviria administration policy toward the Cali cartel. They expected better from him. He had to get tough with the cartel and act to put its godfathers in jail.[43]

Samper objected to the charges and the manner in which the U.S. delegation leveled them. He was going to be president of Colombia and deserved better treatment.[44] But the United States wasn't through yet. Crescencio Arcos hammered Samper with an ultimatum. There would be no compromise, he said. Get the Cali cartel or else. You won't have to admit guilt about the cartel money in your campaign, so long as you get tough on drug trafficking.[45] When the meeting ended, Skol felt that Samper had gotten the message. The ball was now in his court, and it would be up to him to avoid a rupture with the United States.[46] Samper wanted the United States to issue a public statement acknowledging that there was no truth to the charge that his campaign took money from the Cali cartel. The State Department refused.[47]

In July, the powerful U.S. Senator Jesse Helms introduced the Helms Amendment, which prohibited the use of U.S. funds as foreign aid for Colombia until President Clinton certified to the U.S. Congress that its administration was taking serious steps to "significantly disrupt the operations of the drug cartels." The election of a corrupt president was only the coup de grace to a series of victories for the cartel, according to the amendment, which went on to state, "Their recent successes in subverting Colombia's Congress [have] been so great that, in the words of a former member of the Cali Cartel, it is now a narco democracy."[48]

Samper quickly fired off a letter to Helms, assuring his harsh critic that "we know who the bosses of the Cali Cartel are and we will capture them."[49] As proof that the drug barons hadn't corrupted him, Samper pointed out in his letter that "the four bullets still lodged in my body are a constant reminder of the 1989 cartel attempt to assassinate me at the Bogota airport."[50] Now embroiled in a corruption scandal and with the United States twisting his arm, Samper acknowledged that drug traffickers had enormous influence on Colombia. He vowed to work to reform the Colombian Congress.[51] To observers, Samper appeared to be deftly healing the political damage.

When Samper took office in August, it looked as if he was heeding the United States' admonition. He promised to implement legislation that would make money laundering a crime in Colombia and to increase prison sentences for drug traffickers who surrendered through plea bargaining.[52] "The way Gaviria fought against drug terrorism, my goal is to fight against drug corruption," Samper said.[53] Also in August, Fernando Botero, now Samper's defense minister, moved to break the links between the Colombian police and the cartel. Forty-eight police officers were fired, as were the entire personnel of the judicial police and the airport police. General Fabio Campos Silva, the CNP's deputy director, said charges would be brought against those in the police suspected of accepting bribes from the Cali cartel.[54]

Following the election, Alphonso Valdivieso, the new Prosecuting Attorney General (whose office is popularly known as the *Fiscalia*), launched an investigation of the narco cassettes and the election campaign scandal. The post of *fiscalia* was created in 1991 as a response to the increased corruption of the judicial system. The U.S. government had high expectations for the first head of the *fiscalia*, law professor Gustavo De Greiff, but his views on drug legalization and his lenient "surrender to justice" program had enraged both U.S. and Colombian officials and strained relations between the two countries. De Greiff had made many enemies and was forced to retire in August 1994.[55]

A former senator and education minister, the 5'2" Valdivieso was low-key, mild-mannered, and wore a fixed, sleepy expression. He did not look like the tough government official who could successfully lead a legal attack to break the Cali mob's grip on the country's political system. Valdivieso, however, had a good reason to launch an aggressive anti-drug mafia campaign. He was the cousin and close friend of Luis Carlos Galan, the prominent Liberal party leader whom drug traffickers assassinated in 1989 while he was on the campaign trail for the presidency. Galan had taken a strong position against trafficking and his death had a great impact on Valdivieso. During Valdivieso's two-and-a-half years as Colombia's top criminal prosecutor, a huge picture of his cousin hung on his office wall to remind him of his mission as he pursued the drug corruption trail.[56]

It would not be an easy mission. "The United States didn't trust anybody in the office when I assumed my position, so I didn't have a good relationship to build on," recalled Valdivieso in an interview at his office in the Colombian Mission to the United Nations in Manhattan. "But they had intelligence on me. They took a look at my record and saw that I was a man of integrity. I also gained their confidence by terminating a number of officials in my office whom I suspected of being on the Cali cartel payroll."[57]

Valdivieso used the records the CNP had taken from the office of Guillermo Pallomari, the cartel's accountant, on July 8, 1994, to launch his investigation, which became known as *Ocho Mil* (8000). Pallomari was freed the next day, but the records documented the many ties between the cartel and the political establishment that needed investigating. During the next year, the Colombian authorities launched hundreds of raids on the properties of the cartel's godfathers and added to their cache of information that provided leads and evidence.[58] Valdivieso became one of the United States' two closest allies in the Colombian government in its war against Cali. The other – General Rosso José Serrano – would lead the police attack beginning in late 1994. "With those two individuals in place, we saw that we finally had the opportunity to do something in Colombia," recalled Tom Constantine, DEA administrator from 1994 to 1997.[59]

Joe Toft also decided it was time to do something more about the corruption he saw destroying a country he loved. Colombia had a lot of things going for it, Toft believed, but as the events surrounding the narco cassette scandal showed, its people were in a state of denial. Obviously, the release of the narco cassettes hadn't made an impact. At this point, the DEA agent really had nothing to lose. He was retiring from the DEA and leaving for the United States, where he expected to live a quiet life as a private citizen.[60] This would be his last chance to wake up the Colombian people. So on September 28, 1994, the day he finished his seven-year term, Toft appeared on national television and spoke his mind. Your country is a narco democracy and not a single institution has escaped infiltration by drug traffickers, Toft told Colombians. Furthermore, he charged, "the people prefer to close their eyes and look the other way." Then Toft got on a plane and left the country for good.[61]

The U.S. government and the Samper administration were finally on the same side of an issue when they both agreed that Joe Toft's remarks were out of line. Clinton's office issued a statement calling Toft's remarks "offensive," and Myles Frechette, the U.S. Ambassador to Colombia, said, "I would have expelled him from the U.S. mission, if he hadn't left Colombia."[62] Many DEA agents felt ambivalent about Toft's remarks and still do. As one active agent put it: "Joe spoke the truth about what was going on in Colombia, but I don't know if he should have gone solo with it."[63] In a national television address, Samper charged that Toft had "denigrated a nation that had made the most sacrifices in the fight against drugs."[64] Arriving in New York City a week later, Foreign

Minister Rodrigo Pardo said Toft's remarks had created a climate of distrust between the two countries, but added, "I believe that we, Colombia and the United States, can analyze the situation quickly, revise the conditions and make the changes that must be made, if deemed necessary."[65]

Both the U.S. and Colombian governments at this point were more content to shoot the messenger than heed his message. But the attack on Toft could not obscure the reality: for Colombia it was not going to be the same situation as usual. Samper was corrupt until proven otherwise in the eyes of Uncle Sam, and he would have to go all out against the Cali cartel to prove his innocence. Meanwhile, the *Fiscalia* had begun a far-reaching investigation of the ties between the Cali mafia and the country's elite. In a short while, the CNP would get a makeover and prepare for the inevitable offensive against the cartel. It was just a matter of time.

Chapter 13

A Man of Peace

We knew that the godfathers had constructed special hiding places [in the safe houses] called *caletas*, which had been especially made for them. Their design was incredible, and you really had to appreciate the craftsmanship that went into them.
– Jerry Salameh, DEA agent assigned to the
Cali cartel investigation

The narco cassette scandal rocked U.S.-Colombian relations, but in the long run it actually furthered Uncle Sam's objectives in the War on Drugs. The Clinton administration had viewed President Cesar Gaviria's surrender policy and numerous concessions to the Cali cartel as evidence that his administration was soft on drugs. In his campaign leading to the 1994 presidential election, Samper's public statements showed he had no intentions of pursuing a more aggressive antidrug policy than his predecessor. Revelations that his election campaign may have taken millions of dollars from the Cali cartel, however, forced Samper into a position of having something to prove. As Colombian expert Randall Crandall explained, "Knowing that critics in both Colombia and Washington were highly dubious about Samper's willingness to fight the War on Drugs, Samper was forced to go further than he or the United States had ever imagined. Thus we have the paradoxical situation whereby this supposedly narco-compromised president ended up, whether he liked it or not, being a reliable and predictable ally with Washington vis-à-vis the drug war."[1]

As a prime suspect involved in shady dealings with drug kingpins, Samper was in no position to defy the Clinton administration when it began putting pressure on him to fire General Guillermo Diettes, the director of the Colombian National Police (CNP). United States officials didn't trust General Diettes and suspected that he was on the Cali payroll. When Diettes was chief of the Metropolitan Police Force in Cali, a retired army captain, who was believed to be the head of the Cali cartel's security, was switched for another person in his prison cell and escaped police custody.[2] Journalist Simon Strong described the switch: "The retired captain, Jorge Rojas, was young, bearded and white; the stand-in who was presented by the police to the public prosecutor's office the following day was elderly, beardless and black."[3] "In looking at the intelligence we had on Diettes, we had absolutely no confidence that he could lead an effective campaign against the Cali cartel," said Robert Gelbard, the U.S. assistant secretary of state for International Narcotics Matters during this period.[4]

Before the narco cassette scandal, Samper would have treated such a matter as an issue of national sovereignty. His stance would have been: I am president of an independent country, and the United States has no business telling me who I can appoint to office. However, soon after his election, Samper sent Fernando Botero, his trusted minister of defense, to Washington, D.C., to talk to some key Clinton administration officials and try to defuse the tense political relationship. In a meeting with Gelbard, Botero said, "We want to make things right. What message do you want me to bring back to President Samper?"

Gelbard didn't mince his words. "We want police commander Diettes out."

"Whom do you want to replace him with?" Botero asked.

Gelbard had already talked to the DEA about a replacement for General Diettes. "General Serrano," Gelbard said. "We trust him and can work with him."[5]

General Rosso José Serrano was a career police officer with many friends in high places in Washington, D.C., and he had built a solid reputation as a dedicated and honest warrior in the War on Drugs. The DEA, in fact, had come to trust the general like few other officers in the Colombian police force.[6] Bob Nieves, the DEA's chief of international operations from 1989 to 1995, vividly remembers meeting Serrano for the first time in the 1980s when he was a major. "I was impressed with him," Nieves recalled. "The general is mild-mannered in disposition and he doesn't project an image of a tough mafia fighter, but he is a studious, meticulous, strategic analytical thinker, who can create teams to get the job done."[7] A deeply religious man, Serrano kept a small shrine, with icons and paintings of a sacred heart and saints, out of sight of the main work area on the fourth floor office at police headquarters in Bogota.[8]

The general was a man of action, but he had considerable political skills evident in his remarkable ability to get along with people from a wide variety of professions. Politicians, bureaucrats, and military personnel, who otherwise couldn't stand to be in the same room together and even detested each other, had one thing in common: they considered General Serrano their friend. Samper called him a friend and recalled how he and the general played tennis regularly during his administration.[9] On occasion, Joe Toft, who also considered Serrano a friend, recalled chiding the general for getting too chummy with a president suspected of being corrupt. "He is my president, and I have to respect the office," was Serrano's answer.[10]

The general joined the Colombian police in 1960 after graduating from university with a law degree. On June 30, 1990, he was appointed by Gaviria to head Colombia's Narcotics Police.[11] But Samper had shuttled Serrano off to Washington, D.C., to serve as an attaché in the Colombian Embassy. The Clinton administration officials leaned on Samper. They threatened him: Don't appoint the general head of the CNP, and the World Bank (the world's biggest money lender to Third World countries) might view Colombia unfavorably when it needs loans. They reminded him, Your administration will have to pass its first certification test in a few months and getting a passing grade won't be automatic.[12]

In late 1994 Samper relented and recalled Serrano from Washington so he could be his new CNP chief. Today, Samper maintains he didn't cave in to U.S. pressure, and he could have fired Serrano anytime he wanted. United States officials say that was not an option. Samper was in no position to defy the United States because there would have been serious political repercussions.[13]

Serrano took over a demoralized, unprofessionally trained, and outfitted police force crippled by corruption, and quickly made changes. He began to clean house after a police raid on a cartel member's house uncovered lists of police officers who were being bribed and bought off. In October, 174 officers were fired, including forty-eight captains and other high-ranking officers for having links to the Cali mafia. Another twenty-seven officers were suspended for three months, 881 were fined, and 968 were cited for unprofessional conduct. Only 605 out of the 2,685 officers investigated were clean.[14] In the coming months, Serrano fired thousands more police officers, while using his contacts in the U.S. government and military to get training for his men from the DEA, FBI, United States Marine Corps and Army Special Forces to help mold them into professional units.[15] Getting rid of those men, many of whom had been career officers, was not a difficult decision for Serrano. "We had no chance of victory against the Cali cartel unless I attacked the corruption hard," Serrano explained.[16]

Samper continued to act tough publicly. In September, the Colombian Justice Ministry announced that at the Summit of the Americas that coming December, Colombia would propose a comprehensive plan to attack money laundering. Samper had previously announced he would make money laundering a crime in Colombia.[17] In December, Samper launched Operation Splendor, which involved fumigating crops in coca-growing departments of Guaviare and Putumayo in southern Colombia. The government's action touched off protests by thousands of campesinos (peasants) who depended on the coca crops for their livelihood. Samper had to call in the military after campesinos occupied several oil-pumping stations and bombed 40,000 barrels of oil imported from Ecuador.[18]

Samper appeared to be making the right moves and saying the right things, but rumors persisted that he was going to cut a deal with the Cali cartel. In October, a week after he had resigned from the DEA, Joe Toft took another swipe at Colombia, warning that the cartel had carefully orchestrated a deal that would allow them to surrender to the government while keeping their fortunes. "What we are going to see in the next six months to a year is Colombia is going [sic] to declare a victory because the Cali cartel members are going to surrender and the whole world is going to applaud Colombia and everybody's going to pat them on the back," Toft predicted.[19]

A few weeks before Toft's remarks, Gilberto Rodriguez offered to sweeten the surrender proposal he made to the Colombian government the previous March. In an exclusive interview with *Time* magazine, which took place in a high-rise apartment in the center of Cali, an area where the police were supposed to be looking for him, Rodriguez said that not only would he and his brother surrender, but they would also bring in hundreds of others members of their cartel. "My brother and I want to surrender to justice, but by no means to injustice," Gilberto explained to the reporter. "We want to do this according to the Colombia constitution and the penal codes."[20] The Chess Player added that the United States would have to endorse any surrender deal.[21] The U.S. government had repeatedly stated it would not negotiate with the cartel, but the Cali leadership still had the delusion that it could finagle its way out of the drug trade with the United States' blessing.

Three days later, the U.S. government canceled the visas of the family members of Gilberto Rodriguez. Ambassador Myles Frechette told the press that there would be no surrender deal unless the Cali cartel members turned themselves in to U.S. authorities.[22] That, of course, would have meant extradition for the surrendering drug lords and guaranteed jail for life in the United States. Despite the United States' opposition to any surrender deal, negotiations between the cartel and the Samper administration continued for several months. As late as June 29, Alphonso Salamanca, the deputy prosecuting general of Colombia, admitted that lawyers for the drug kingpins had been in communication with Colombian justice officials. Salamanca refused to call them negotiations and insisted that the lawyers had simply come to "ask about the legal situation of their clients and wanted to know the Prosecuting Attorney General's view on a possible surrender."[23]

Today, Samper remains convinced that a deal with the Cali cartel could have been worked out. "De Greiff was very close to making that deal, but he was forced into retirement and replaced by Valdivieso, who said he had no intentions of talking directly to the cartel," Samper explained.[24] At the end of 1994, Samper concluded that trying to work out an agreement with the Cali cartel wasn't practical, and he told his advisors to devise a new strategy, one that would put more pressure on the cartel. "The United States knew every step we took," Samper recalled. "I kept Ambassador Frechette informed."[25]

The United States however did not trust Samper and U.S. officials were unwilling to share important information with his administration, although they did concede that some of Samper's underlings were trying hard. United States officials began working directly with General Serrano, who managed to maintain a nice balancing act between the Clinton administration, which provided the support, and the president whom he served.[26] "Sure, Samper was making noise and enacting legislation that made him look like he was serious about drug trafficking," explained Myles Frechette, U.S. ambassador to Colombia at the time. "But behind the scenes [Horacio] Serpa [Samper's vice-president] was attaching 'micos' or amendments to the legislation to slow it down or mess it up in the process."[27]

The Colombian government had moved the headquarters to Cali and assigned 500 soldiers and police to focus exclusively on taking down the cartel. In early 1995, the Search Block conducted a series of raids designed to make life difficult for the godfathers, who just a year before had been able to move about freely without fear of arrest.[28] In March, police began conducting operations not only in Cali but also in other cities in the Valle del Cauca and even Bogota.[29] The government tried to show they meant business by having its police generals, including General Serrano himself, conduct the raids. "We, policemen, must be on the streets, not in the office," Serrano told the press.[30]

The raids were full of sound and fury but had little impact, and all the security forces had to show for their operation was small trophies. One of them was the capture of Jorge Elicer Rodriguez, the forty-seven-year-old younger brother of Gilberto and Miguel, in early March, as he sat in a parked car in front of a house in Cali waiting to see a fortune teller. A prostitute had tipped off the authorities.[31] Desperate to show some results from their offensive, the authorities touted the arrest as a "decisive blow against the Cali cartel," but, while the U.S. Embassy was upbeat about the arrest, it was careful to identify Jorge Rodriguez as a mid-level lieutenant. In 1991, Rodriguez had been indicted in New York City on cocaine trafficking charges, but because of the Colombian law on extradition, there was no chance he would be extradited.[32]

In the same month, 2,000 members of the security forces launched a massive operation in the northern Valle del Cauca department, searching farms; setting up roadblocks; impounding 516 vehicles, 416 firearms, and 118 UAF communications radios; arresting 180 suspects; and seizing sixty kilograms of cocaine at a roadblock. A reporter asked Serrano if he could capture Gilberto and Miguel Rodriguez. The general replied cautiously, his answer not exactly exuding confidence, "We are making a great effort. We are committed to the task and we have the operational and intelligence capability. Hopefully, we shall be lucky."[33]

Many times the Search Block would show up at an apartment, house, or business, only to learn that a godfather had just fled. Chepe Santacruz, for instance, had two narrow escapes, including one on March 14, when police burst into an apartment building in Cali and discovered that he had left a few minutes earlier. Two days later, approximately 150 Search Block members raided a house in Cali's well-to-do southern suburbs after receiving a phone tip that Herrera was there. Pacho escaped via a secret door.[34]

Despite Serrano's efforts, corruption in the CNP and security forces persisted and continued to be a big problem. In early April, the government had to abolish Cali's special police intelligence department because it found an extortion network within the department that was blackmailing owners of houses where they had found documents implicating them in the drug trade. A judge, a prosecutor, and twenty police captains were arrested in connection with the scandal.[35]

The corruption was an incurable cancer spreading throughout the political body. In early January, the CNP, DAS (Administrative Department of Security), the army, and top government officials advised Valdivieso's office that many of their phones were being tapped. When authorities raided the telephone company offices in Cali and Bogota, they found that hundreds of phones lines had been illegally tapped. Incredibly, the administration had to declare a state of emergency for the telephone lines of the entire national government.[36] The following month, Argemiro Serna, the head of the antidrug police, was fired after police under his command failed to stop and arrest two pilots of a Boeing 727 linked to drug shipments.[37]

Several prominent U.S. politicians and critics of the Samper administration, led by Senator Jesse Helms, kept calling for the United States to bypass the Samper administration and undertake direct action against the Cali cartel, but ambassador Frechette, the Clinton administration's point man in Colombia, downplayed the idea and publicly described the Colombian government's efforts as "excellent." United States officials praised the statistics the Colombians released – the seizure of two tons of cocaine, eighteen tons of coca leaf, and thirty-one kilograms of heroin and the arrest of 590 traffickers in the first three months of 1995.[38]

Yet, despite its accolades, the Clinton administration decided that Colombia's antidrug effort in 1994 was not good enough. In its annual report to Congress on March 1, 1995, which assessed the efforts of various nations in combating drug production and distribution as part of its certification process, the United States downgraded Colombia's rating as a U.S. antidrug partner. The Clinton administration declared it would continue to certify Colombia as a cooperating country in the drug war because the country was "vital" to U.S. interests, but for the first time, Colombia received less than unqualified certification. The Samper administration reacted angrily, complaining that in its certification review, the United States had not taken into account "the human toll that the drug war has exacted on Colombia and that the U.S. needs to do more to relieve the demand for narcotic drugs within its own borders."[39]

The acrimony between the Samper administration and

Washington reached the eruption point when Rodrigo Pardo sent Frechette a list of nine "conditions," which, in effect, would limit DEA activity in Colombia. Included in the list was the requirement that DEA agents had to inform the Colombian government of its activities in Colombia. The brashness of the Samper administration, which was hanging on for dear life amid a spreading corruption scandal, angered U.S. officials.[40] The letter led to a heated exchange between Gelbard and Pardo in a meeting. "Tempers flared," Pardo recalled. "We felt that we should have more control over what the DEA did in our country."[41]

Tearing at the U.S.-Colombian relationship was the fact that it had been about a year since the DEA and CNP had joined together and moved to apply all their resources to capture the Cali cartel's top leaders, and still there had been no capture of a kingpin. The Colombian government had set up a special command at the Military Bloque base on the outskirts of Cali, which included elements of the Colombian police, the army, and the Search Block. The DEA was given a house on the base, and it began to send agents to Cali to do intelligence work. "We [and the Colombians] worked well together as a team," recalled Ruben Prieto, special agent in charge of the DEA's Bogota office, who had taken Joe Toft's place after he retired. "Everyone knew their role."[42]

The Colombian press was reporting that more than 500 DEA agents were in Cali trying to develop intelligence that could lead them to the capture of the Big Four godfathers (the Rodriguez brothers, Jose Santacruz and Pacho Herrera), but there were never more than two or three agents in the city at any one time.[43] The DEA essentially assigned four agents to help the Colombian authorities track the Rodriguez brothers, who were the two top targets on the hit list.[44]

The agents usually worked in pairs, and, as far as looks and backgrounds went, the two pairs of agents could not have been more different. Prieto, a stocky Mexican American, had extensive experience working the U.S.-Mexican border area. A former boxing champion in his native Mexico and a martial arts expert, Prieto had a reputation for bluntness that was not always appreciated by his superiors and allies in the Colombian military.

Prieto was assigned to work with Jerry Salameh, a slender, soft-spoken Palestinian American who looked Spanish and spoke the language fluently. For no particular reason, the two referred to themselves as Batman and Robin. The other pair was Dave Mitchell and Chris Feistl, two blond, six-foot-plus All-American agents barely out of their twenties who didn't exactly blend in with the local surroundings. In fact, the two looked young enough to have just graduated from the academy. Mitchell had served with the 82nd airborne before joining the DEA as a special agent in January 1988, while Feistl was a former police officer in Virginia Beach who had joined the DEA in 1988. Mitchell and Feistl arrived in Bogota in July 1994 about the same time. Although Feistl and Mitchell hadn't worked together, they knew each other from their assignments in Miami.[45]

The DEA brass in Bogota had set up a "Cali cartel program," which included some other agents besides the two pairs, but they inadvertently had their photos taken and published in the local media and could no longer travel to Cali on assignment.[46] "I know some agents, who were a lot more Latino-looking than we were, questioned how effective we could be working under-cover, but we didn't have any problems operating in Cali," Mitchell recalled.[47] Mitchell and the other three agents were assigned to DEA Bogota's office's Group One Task Force, which was focused on investigating the Cali cartel.

The DEA knew it would be tough to get good, reliable intelligence information on the whereabouts of their targets. The godfathers had safe houses strategically spread out all over the city waiting to be used once or perhaps twice while they stayed on the run. Catching one of them would be like trying to find the proverbial needle in the haystack, and, even if they did, locating the target inside the safe house would be another challenge. "We knew the godfathers had constructed special hiding places built especially for them [the safe houses], called caletas," Salameh revealed. "Their design was incredible, and you really had to appreciate the craftsmanship than went into building them."[48] Compounding the difficulty of apprehending the godfathers was the cartel's now-legendary intelligence network that encompassed hotel clerks, corrupt police, street vendors, and 5,000 taxi drivers who served as the cartel's eyes and ears in the city. Taxis outside the Military Bloque base were waiting, watching, and ready to relay messages instantly, once police units began leaving the base in pursuit of the cartel.[49]

The continuous pressure and the raids, however, began to have some effect on the cartel's communications network and its cash flow. With rewards of as much as $1.9 million for Miguel and Gilberto Rodriguez and $625,000 for Santacruz and Herrera, the godfathers had to constantly worry about informants and betrayal. The authorities applied pressure by dropping hundreds of "wanted" leaflets on Cali. The supposedly kinder, gentler cartel wasn't going to take any chances and have somebody rat them out.[50] In one six-week period, about seventy-five dead bodies, some showing signs of torture, turned up in the city.[51]

As Search Block hunted for the godfathers, the DEA rotated its two pairs of agents in and out of Cali. While in the city, they took appropriate precautions, keeping a low profile and not going out at night. The rewards led to numerous tips – some promising, most bogus – about the godfathers' whereabouts. The four DEA agents spent much of their time tracking down every possible lead. The DEA did have confidential informants who were providing tidbits of information, although none of it was really leading anywhere.

The DEA, however, began hearing from its CIs about an assistant to Gilberto nicknamed Flaco ("Skinny"). His real name was Alberto Madrid Mayor and he worked as Gilberto's accountant and personal secretary. About thirty-five years old and 5'8" tall, Madrid was known as an impeccable dresser. He had worked for Gilberto since the mid-1990s.[52] Find and follow Flaco, the informants were telling the DEA, and he will lead you to Gilberto.[53]

One day in May, Prieto read a routine cable, which consisted of brief reports from DEA offices around the world. One of the reports from the office in Quito, Ecuador, identified a "Flaco" from Cali who had worked for the cartel. Prieto called the Quito office and talked to agent Nelson Gonzalez about the report and the Flaco from Cali.

"Is that the same Flaco who is supposed to work for Gilberto Rodriguez?" Prieto asked Gonzalez.[54]

"I don't know," the agent said. "Do you want to talk to the CI who gave us the information? He's living here in Quito."

"That sounds like a good idea," said Prieto. "Why don't you and your CI meet me here in Bogota. I'll pay the expenses."

The CI turned out to be Andres Ruiz Rios, who had begun work for the DEA in the mid-1990s. As an expert money launderer Rios worked for some of the most powerful drug traffickers in the Valle del Cauca. In one three-month period, he washed about $50 million. As part of his work, Rios traveled throughout South America, including Ecuador, and that's where the DEA discovered him. The DEA gave Rios a choice: work for us or get extradited to the United States. Rios opted to become a CI, and, working under Nelson Gonzalez, he became one of the DEA's most valuable informants.

Prieto spent two days with Rios and agent Gonzalez in an Embassy Suites hotel room in Bogota. The CI was a cocaine crackhead, but, after questioning him for two days about Flaco and Gilberto Rodriguez, Prieto concluded that he had the "right stuff" and knew the Flaco who worked for Gilberto. Prieto promised him a reward if he helped capture Gilberto. The DEA might finally have a solid lead in their hunt for the Chess Player. In describing Flaco, the CI said two of his features stuck out: he was skinny and walked like a duck with his feet turned out.

"Could you go to Cali and find him?" Prieto asked. "I'll come down and you can point out Flaco to me."

The CI agreed to do it and Prieto got authorization to give him the money for a plane ticket to Cali. "I'll give you two days to find Flaco," Prieto told the CI. "Locate him, call me and we'll take it from there."

Prieto waited two days, but the call never came. So he hopped a plane and went to Cali looking for the CI. Prieto found him in the second-floor apartment of a dumpy complex populated by seedy-looking gangster types. The CI answered the door in his underwear, looking messed up and high on crack. The CI got agitated. "What are you doing here?" he yelled at Prieto. "You are going to get me killed. Flaco is going to be here any minute!"

"You didn't call me, you son-of-a-bitch," Prieto shot back angrily. "I've been waiting like an idiot for you to call." Prieto paused. "So you say Flaco is going to be here in a minute? What kind of car is he driving?"

"Red Mazda," replied the CI.

Prieto left the apartment, and as he hurried down the balcony, he passed a skinny man walking like a duck They both glanced over their shoulders at each other. Prieto stayed calm, but he got excited as he reached the front door. "We've found Flaco!" Prieto told Salameh, who had accompanied Prieto and was sitting in the car. Flaco came out of the apartment building and the two agents tailed him to his place. The authorities finally had the key to finding Gilberto. The next day, the DEA held a meeting at the police base and made plans to set up surveillance of Flaco.[55]

For the next month, a team of seven to ten CNP members and DEA agents began tailing Flaco, hoping he would lead them to Gilberto Rodriguez. It was not the easiest of assignments. The surveillance team was sure that Flaco didn't know he was being followed, but he took paranoiac precautions. Each day he would vary his route. Sometimes he would literally walk in circles. He caught taxis. He would enter a building, come out, go back in, and then come out again. "Flaco used every counter-surveillance measure you could think of," Salameh recalled.[56]

At times, the surveillance team would spend all night planning the morning's surveillance only to lose Flaco two minutes into the surveillance the next morning. "It was frustrating and we would get on each other's nerves," Salameh recalled. "We would point the finger at each other. 'You lost him!' 'No, you did!' "[57] The surveillance team couldn't follow Flaco too far in a day or he might get suspicious and spot its surveillance. But each day, bit by bit, they would add a little more area covering Flaco's route to his final destination. After a week into the surveillance, the team had four to five miles of Flaco's route covered. He was heading into the middle-class barrio of Santa Monica, but there was still no final stop. They kept losing Flaco at Street 35 North.

In early June, Flaco took another circuitous route into a neighborhood and disappeared. The surveillance team figured he must have gone up a very steep flight of stairs. For the next three days, a group of women CNP officers, whom the CIA had trained, jogged routinely up and down the stairs anticipating that Flaco would lead them to Gilberto. Finally, he showed, walking like a duck past the joggers and up the stairs and disappearing down a street with a group of five townhouses on a hill. The surveillance team was certain that he went to one of those houses, but which one?

General Serrano was in Cali that day, and Prieto arranged a briefing meeting with him at the DEA's house on the police base. "Where are we now?" Serrano wanted to know. Prieto gave the general a synopsis of what had happened with their surveillance of Flaco the past week.

"We keep losing him in this neighborhood," Prieto said, pointing to a map of Cali he had laid out on the desk. "We are pretty certain he is in one of these five townhouses."

Prieto added that he had information Gilberto's people were going to move him. "'We'll have to start from scratch, if they do that," he said. "He could be anywhere in Cali. It might take months of more hard work before we get another shot at him again."

"So what do you think?" Serrano asked.

"We don't have a choice," Prieto said candidly. "We need to make a move now, or it could be never."

Serrano mulled Prieto's assessment. "So what are our chances if you go in now?" he asked.

Prieto looked hard at the general. "Less than fifty percent," he answered "That's about the best we will ever have of getting Gilberto."

Prieto had a plan and laid it out for Serrano. If Search Block did a typical operation and swept into the neighborhood, Gilberto would be tipped off by one of his spies at the base. Serrano had a heavy escort that included a covered truck taking him back to the Cali airport for his flight to Bogota. The escort would have to go past the neighborhood with the five townhouses. Members of the attack team could hide in the back of the truck, and as the escort moved past the neighborhood, they could jump out of the truck, move quickly to the street where the five townhouses were, and begin their search. Meanwhile, they called in a military helicopter to monitor the neighborhood and ensure that no one could escape. "We would have the element of surprise," Prieto told Serrano.

In the early afternoon of June 9, the plan was put into operation. Once the attack team got close to the townhouses, the big challenge became finding the right one. Prieto surveyed the neighborhood and spotted an old lady standing in a doorway of a nearby house.

"Lady, stay inside!" Prieto ordered.

The woman signaled to Prieto as if she had a secret to share. "No, no. Come here!"

Prieto walked over to the woman. She leaned over and took the agent into her confidence. "I know who you're looking for," she whispered.

"Who are you talking about, lady?" Prieto blurted, getting impatient.

"Those people in that townhouse," she said pointing to the one in the middle. She leaned closer to Prieto, and her tone of voice revealed that she was about to educate her listener. "I've lived here all my life and I know everybody in the neighborhood, except the people in that townhouse. They have only been there a month, month-and-a-half."

"So what else do you know about them?" said Prieto, realizing he was on to something.

"They keep their windows shut and they never come outside."

"Okay, lady, please get back inside. We'll handle this."

Prieto went to the colonel in charge of the operation and told him to search the townhouse in the middle. The helicopter was brought in closer, and the soldiers rushed to the door. They were about to kick in the door when a young woman opened it. Prieto could see Flaco standing inside. "This is the place! He's here!" Prieto shouted, his heart racing. Inside with Flaco and the young woman, who turned out to be the maid, was Gilberto's girlfriend, Aura Rocio Restrepo, all of them doing poorly at trying to look calm. The search party took a quick look around, but no Gilberto. They fanned out through the townhouse, guns drawn, checking the rooms and closets.

An hour dragged by and the search team was getting tired. Prieto had made his way to the main bedroom on the second floor, where a large-screen television sat against the wall. A young, scrawny soldier was trying to move it without success. Prieto went over and gave the television a yank. Behind it was a small door leading to a vaulted closet. The door was ajar, and there in his underwear, with no shoes, money scattered all over the floor, gun in each hand, attempting to hide, was the Chess Player – Gilberto Rodriguez Orejuela.

Prieto had no gun, just a camera around his neck. Unlike other agents working in Colombia, Prieto never carried a gun or wore a bulletproof vest. Gilberto was quivering with fear, and pointing a shaky gun at him. Prieto froze, realizing that the drug lord might panic and shoot. But Gilberto turned out to be a real chess player. He made the right move, having the presence of mind to drop the guns just as other search team members rushed into the bedroom.

Prieto heard a loud noise – one long click of automatic weapons being readied for fire. He glanced behind him. He was standing directly between Gilberto and his pursuers. A chilling thought flashed across the agent's mind. "Jesus, they're going to kill me!"

"Don't shoot?" Gilberto pleaded, looking as if he had just seen the ghost of Escobar. "I'm a man of peace."[58]

Chapter 14

Exit the Señor

How did the police know where to look? There has to be a snitch among us.

      – William Rodriguez, son of Miguel Rodriguez

The police did not shoot the Chess Player. Prieto stood in the way. Still, in arresting Gilberto Rodriguez, Colombia and the United States garnered their first major victory against the Cali cartel. General Serrano, who had not yet left Cali, returned to the townhouse to see the prize catch and escort him on a flight to police headquarters in Bogota.[1] Colombian television showed footage of the helicopter landing and heavily armed police hustling an unshaven and handcuffed prisoner out of the airport. It was a festive occasion at the CNP headquarters when Gilberto's escort arrived. Workers cheered as if they were at a soccer game and threw confetti on law officers who gathered to announce the arrest.[2] The Colombian government was ecstatic. "For the first time, the world could clearly see that we were serious about defeating the Cali cartel," recalled President Ernesto Samper. "This arrest sent a signal to the other narco traffickers that their insidious crimes would not be allowed to destroy the fabric of our people."[3] Based on interviews with Clinton administration officials, the *New York Times* reported that "the capture of the most influential leader of the world's largest drug trafficking gang in Colombia . . . was the best news United States officials had gotten in years in the long running battle against drugs."[4]

Rodriguez faced up to twenty-four years in prison on drug

trafficking and illegal enrichment charges, and there were several indictments against him in various U.S. cities. Still, if his stable of high-powered lawyers could gain for him the full benefits available under the Colombian penal code, he would have to spend no more than five years in jail.[5] The Chess Player's extradition to the United States was not even a remote possibility, since the authorities had no evidence that he committed any crimes after December 17, 1997, the date the latest extradition law went into effect.

In captivity, Gilberto continued to play his innocence charade, rejecting the charges against him and denying he ever led the Cali cartel, which he said was an invention of the DEA.[6] The day after his arrest, a bomb ripped through a street festival in the Parque San Antonio in downtown Medellin, killing twenty-one people and wounding more than 200. Anonymous telephone callers, claiming to be drug traffickers, said they carried out the bombing in reprisal for Rodriguez's arrest.[7] The bomb was a chilling flashback to the worst terrorism of the Escobar era, and an anxious public wondered if it was déjà vu.[8]

No terrorist bombing, however, was going to distract the Colombian authorities, who were fired up by their sudden victory over the Cali cartel and now focused on Miguel Rodriguez, the real Señor, or boss. Operation Cornerstone, which was reaching fruition after forty-four arduous months of investigation, had the key to apprehending Miguel. Three days before Gilberto's capture, a federal grand jury in Miami indicted fifty-nine people, including three former federal prosecutors (William Moran, Michael Abbell, and Donald Ferguson) as part of a broad racketeering case against the cartel. The indictment charged the defendants with drug trafficking activities stretching back to 1983, which resulted in the smuggling of 440,000 pounds of cocaine into the United States.[9]

Since Ackerman became a witness against his former bosses, other key players decided to cooperate with the authorities, including the sphinxlike Gustavo Naranjo in Texas, who had a change of heart after three years in captivity. "We brought him to Miami, and he was scared to death," recalled Ed Ryan, U.S. assistant attorney for South Florida. "We sat him down and had a heart-to-heart talk with him. He had been in jail for a while and listened to us. He had nothing left to lose."[10]

Arrests continued to deplete the cartel's management pool, and sixty-eight-year-old George Lopez had to leave Colombia for Miami to take over Ackerman's job after the latter was arrested in April 1992. But Lopez, too, was caught in July 1994, and when he turned against his bosses, federal prosecutors were well on their way to putting together their indictment.[11] Prosecutors included cartel lawyer Joel Rosenthal in the indictment, but he pleaded guilty to money laundering charges and was cooperating with authorities. In interrogating Rosenthal, customs agent Ed Kacerosky learned that he had struck up a friendship with Jorge Salcedo while in Cali on cartel business. Salcedo was the cartel's future chief of security and the mastermind behind its failed mission to buy a bomb in Nicaragua that could be dropped on La Catedral prison to kill Pablo Escobar. Salcedo had confided to Rosenthal that he was disgusted with his life as a criminal, and, if he could find a way to get out of the drug trafficking business, he would. Kacerosky felt that Salcedo could be an important key to turning the tide against the cartel. What better informant than a highly placed mole inside the mafia? With Salcedo on their side, the authorities would considerably increase their chances of capturing Miguel. Kacerosky, however, wondered who in the DEA office in Colombia did he know and trust to approach with this information?[12]

One might ask, why should "trust" be an issue in such an important investigation? After all, the DEA, Customs, the FBI, and the intelligence agencies were on the same side, weren't they? Wasn't the mission to take down the bad guys from Cali? Once again, though, the ugly head of interagency turf rivalry was a potential obstacle in a major criminal investigation. The intense Kacerosky was a controversial law enforcement figure in the war against the Cali cartel. Many of those who knew and worked with the customs agent describe him as a talented, hard-working and dedicated professional.[13] He had detractors, though, especially in the DEA, and they viewed him as a publicity hound and a cowboy who was not a team player.[14]

Kacerosky had some other ideas about how to capture Miguel,

but they would also have to be played out in Colombia. He knew that Chris Feistl, the DEA agent he had worked with on a couple of small cases in Miami, was now based in Bogota. They hadn't become drinking buddies, but Kacerosky had come to like and respect Feistl as a law enforcement professional. "In this job, it is very difficult to trust people, if you don't know them well," Kacerosky explained. "I got along well with Chris, and Bill Pearson spoke very highly of him, so I decided to approach him."[15]

At Kacerosky's request, Bill Pearson called Feistl in Bogota. "Would you be interested in talking with Kacerosky about some of the ideas he has on how to capture Miguel?" Pearson asked. Yes, he would, Feistl said. He was familiar with Operation Cornerstone, and he respected the work Kacerosky and fellow DEA agent Lou Weiss had done. "I talked to them often about the Cornerstone investigation, and they passed on the information that helped me pursue leads in Cali," said Feistl. "They provided whatever I asked of them."[16]

The two agents talked on the phone. Kacerosky congratulated Feistl on the DEA's capture of Gilberto Rodriguez, but he pointed out that anyone investigating the cartel knew Miguel was its real boss. But how should they proceed? Miguel was totally underground and getting him would be a tougher operation than the hunt for his brother.

"Could you and the Cornerstone team help us out?" Feistl asked.

"What do you need?" replied Kacerosky.[17]

"Can you interview all the individuals who were cooperating in the Cornerstone case and ask the same questions to find out what they knew about Miguel?" Feistl elaborated, "Ask the CIs who were the people closest to Miguel? Where were the houses or places where he liked to stay? Who could agents in Colombia follow in Cali to get to Miguel? Who might be willing to cooperate? What's the best plan to go about arresting Miguel?"[18]

Kacerosky responded by sending Feistl a ten-page handwritten letter, outlining what he thought were the most viable options law enforcement had available for capturing Miguel. The assessment was based on what investigators had found in the Operation Cornerstone investigation. The first option was to follow Jesus

Zapata (aka "Mateo"), Miguel's personal secretary, but Feistl and his partner Dave Mitchell had been following him for some time without any results. The second option involved having the CNP follow and wiretap Guillermo Villa Alzate, a former Colombian government lawyer. According to at least two of the convicted and cooperating individuals in Operation Cornerstone, Villa was handling Miguel's legal affairs.[19]

Number two looked like a good option, but number three – getting Jorge Salcedo, the cartel's head of security, to cooperate, with the help of Rosenthal – piqued Feistl's interest the most. "Why don't you contact Salcedo to see if he is serious about defecting?" Feistl suggested. Kacerosky agreed to do it and promised to get back in touch. On July 8, Kacerosky called Feistl with some good news. Salcedo wanted to cooperate. "Let me talk with Salcedo directly?" Feistl asked. "We are both in Cali. A face-to-face meeting will avoid any confusion."[20]

Kacerosky checked with Salcedo. "It's okay with Jorge," Kacerosky said. "Call him at this number." Feistl and Mitchell arranged to meet face-to-face with their new CI.[21]

Meanwhile, it became apparent to the authorities that not killing Gilberto in the *caleta* on June 9 was one of the best moves the security forces had made. As Mitchell explained, "The cartel's leadership thought the security forces would kill them, as they had Escobar and Rodriguez Gacha, if they were caught. But Gilberto lived, and this encouraged other drug traffickers to negotiate their surrender. They realized they could work with the government."[22] Four days after Gilberto's capture, Mario Del Basto, the cartel's head of security, who had brought Sean on board, was captured after the CNP had received intelligence he was on his way to a meeting in Cali. "This opened the door for us," said Feistl. "Sean took over Del Basto's position and this put him right next to Miguel."[23]

Ten days after Gilberto's capture, Henry Loaiza, the "Scorpion," became the first Cali godfather to surrender. Described as "the Cali cartel's minister of war," the Scorpion was no gentleman. Rather, he was a ruthless killer, who once directed his underlings to use chain saws to carve up 107 people suspected of being union sympathizers. Tiberio Jesus Hernandez, a local priest, complained of the atrocities, and, a few days later, his decapitated body was also found floating in the Cauca River.[24]

On June 24, Victor Patino, the cartel's reputed number-five figure who was suspected of being in charge of its *sicarios*, turned himself in at a military base in Bogota. Patino feared for his life and thought it wise to come in out of the cold and answer the accusations against him, Defense Minister Fernando Botero later told reporters.[25] Three days later, in the northern city of Vallendupar, police nabbed Fanor Arizabaleta, one of the top seven leaders. Then on July 4 at 8:05 P.M., at the Carbon de Polo restaurant on 199th street and Carrera 19 in northern Bogota, the authorities caught another big-name trafficker, none other than Chepe Santacruz. He was reportedly dining in the company of three associates when two police officers spotted him. According to the official story in the press, Serrano knew that El Gordo liked to eat, so he ordered his men to stake out several good restaurants in northern Bogota. But no explanation has ever been given for why the authorities decided to target restaurants in northern Bogota and not Cali, Medellin, or Boise, Idaho, for that matter, or why Chepe was dining in Bogota at eateries so close to Serrano's residence. One source close to the investigation said that Chepe was actually turning himself in, but he was double-crossed by police who wanted the $625,000 reward for themselves.[26] Other law enforcement sources described this scenario as far-fetched.

Feistl and Mitchell finally met with Salcedo at 8 P.M. on July 12 in a cornfield at an agricultural station about forty-five minutes from Cali and an hour from where the two DEA agents had a safe house in the city's extreme south end. Salcedo chose the station because the cartel had no security in the area, and it was common to see gringos who were associated with the agricultural station.

In their phone conversation, Salcedo had been clear about one thing. "Don't come with any Colombian police," he told the agents. "I want to see two gringos from the American embassy." As head of the cartel's security, Salcedo knew how corrupt the security forces were and he didn't trust them.[27] The DEA agents were wary, too. Meeting a top Cali associate, especially one involved with security, in the middle of nowhere had its risks. So the agents decided to arrive early, poke around, and make sure their rendezvous wasn't actually an ambush. The agents found nothing that set off alarm bells.

Feistl and Mitchell saw the familiar Mazda 626 with the tinted windows inching slowly down the dusty dirt road. Out stepped a mustachioed Colombian, about six feet in height, with a medium build, who moved with a gentle gait. To Feistl, Salcedo looked like an ordinary-looking Colombian citizen who he might pass on the street without a second glance.[28] They shook hands, and Mitchell cracked a joke to ease the tension. "Well, Jorge, can you tell we are two gringos from the embassy?"[29]

Jorge smiled, sized them up, and seemed to relax. For the next two-and-a-half hours, the agents pumped their new CI for information.[30]

"Do you know where Miguel is hiding?"

"I don't know what building, just the area," Salcedo replied.

Mitchell was curious about his impression of the DEA in Colombia. "Does the cartel consider the DEA a serious threat?" he asked.

"No, because you can't do anything in Colombia without getting the approval of the Colombian police first, and they are corrupt," was Salcedo's straight answer.[31]

"Can you tell us about Miguel's habits . . . anything that can help track him?"

"Miguel likes to stay up late at night. He normally uses two black maids. His current driver is Jorge Castillo [aka Fercho]. The car he's driving is a white four-door Mazda 626 with Cali tag BBW-712. Oh, yes, the Señor is sickly . . . a kidney ailment."[32]

They discussed the details of their arrangement. The DEA appreciates your help, the agents told Salcedo, and you will be nicely rewarded. Be assured that we will get you and your family out of Colombia.[33] Their first meeting went well and they agreed to get together again the next evening at 5 P.M. "I will try to dig out more information about Miguel's exact whereabouts," Salcedo said. Back at their apartment, Feistl and Mitchell assessed what Salcedo had told them. They agreed it could be a clever ploy by the cartel to plant disinformation with their pursuers, but their gut feeling was that Salcedo could be trusted. He truly wanted out of the cartel.[34]

The agents met with "Sean," the codename they now used to identify their CI, several times over the next two days, and Salcedo continued to provide valuable information.[35] He said that Miguel was hiding in apartment 402 or 801 at 3rd West Avenue, Number 13–86, in a barrio known as Santa Rita. Look for that white four-door Mazda 626 I mentioned in our first meeting, Sean said. It will be parked in the parking space for the apartment in which Miguel is hiding. On July 14, Sean pulled all the security personnel he had under his command around Santa Rita so Feistl and Mitchell could ride through it and conduct surveillance. You have one hour, Sean informed them.[36] Now it was time to do the raid. They had the best information they were going to get on Miguel's whereabouts, Feistl and Mitchell agreed. Besides, Sean said there were rumors he would be moved again.

Prieto also had a CI, who was close to the Rodriguez family, and he insisted that Miguel was hiding in the middle of the city. "No, that's just a relay station in case Miguel has to move," Sean had told Feistl and Mitchell. The agents asked Prieto not to raid that place because it might disrupt their effort to search the Santa Rita apartment. We believe our source is more credible, they told their supervisor.[37] Prieto was persuaded and gave them the go-ahead for the raid.[38]

Feistl and Mitchell coordinated the raid's details with the DEA's Bogota office, the CIA, the Colombian navy, and the CNP, whose personnel were sent overland directly from Bogota so as not to arouse the suspicions of the cartel's intelligence network. Sean had briefed Feistl and Mitchell on the details of cartel security in the area.[39]

At 5:30 A.M. on July 15, a team of police officers and DEA agents moved to the target in two rented chicken trucks, specifically chosen as the mode of transportation because Sean said they would not attract attention. The police locked down the neighborhood to prevent escape. They were accompanied by prosecutors who came to ensure that no human rights were violated nor laws broken.[40] Upon arriving, Feistl immediately went to the garage. There was the Mazda Sean said should be in one of the parking spaces for the two targeted apartments. The search team would hit 402 first, then 801.[41]

Just as they were about to launch the raid, however, the prosecutor announced that he had failed to bring a search warrant with him. It took the prosecutor two hours to get one, giving Miguel, if he was inside the apartment, plenty of time to hide in his *caleta*. The DEA agents were pissed, but what could they do? Only in Colombia.

The prosecutor returned with the warrant and gave the search team permission to break in. Salameh took a sledgehammer and with a couple of hard swings battered the front door down. Sitting nervously on the living room couch were Jorge "Fercho" Castillo and Lucipida Zuniga, the maid . . . a white maid. The apartment was modest by Miguel's standards – a rather smallish, quietly furnished three-bedroom apartment. There were ten to twenty phone lines, fruit in the refrigerator, and Panasonic phones, which the DEA knew Miguel preferred. "We felt pretty certain Miguel was there," Feistl recalled.[42]

Salameh took Fercho and Zuniga outside the apartment into the hallway, away from the intimidating presence of Miguel, who, in all probability, would overhear any conversation in the apartment. Salameh tried to convince them to cooperate. "You aren't in trouble," the agent assured them. "Think of the $1.5 million reward. We will guarantee your security and that of your family." But the two employees were petrified and all the pesos in Colombia wouldn't get them to squeal on Mr. Miguel Rodriguez.[43]

The search team began looking at every switch, pin, and hook in every nook and cranny they could find . . . anything that suggested a secret compartment. They checked out every air space and gap. They went to some of the other apartments in the building and compared the airspaces in them with that of 402. It had taken the search team an hour to find Gilberto, but here they were five to six hours into the search and still no Miguel. The Colombian police had a tendency to give up after fifteen minutes into a raid and they were getting bored. They kept grumbling – why are we still here?[44]

The DEA agents pressed their Colombian partners to continue the search. Outside in the street, Feistl stayed in constant contact with Sean through his Skytel pager. When Sean left a coded number on the pager, Feistl and Mitchell would head for a pay phone at a pizza shop about a mile from the apartment and make contact. "Don't leave!" Salcedo kept urging the agents. "He's still there. Keep looking."[45]

There was a frantic edge to Sean's calls. He was with Miguel's anxious son William, who had learned security forces were searching his father's apartment in Santa Rita. Sean would go to the bathroom to make the calls while William was close by in the living room. The agents marveled at Sean, who would have to return to William's company and play out his role of loyal security chief. William was not exactly the second coming of Cool Hand Luke, nor was he considered particularly bright by the cartel's lofty standards. He was screaming orders to underlings, and in his desperation, Salcedo hoped that Junior would inadvertently reveal the old man's hiding place.[46]

Feistl and Mitchell would feed Sean's information to Salameh and a CIA supervisor who would come out of the apartment periodically to see what additional info the CI had provided. Sean made contact several more times. "You need to keep looking." "There is a hidden compartment in the desk." "There is a letter from [Fernando] Botero to Miguel, requesting funds for Samper's campaign." Finally – "He's in the bathroom behind the wall." By now, the four DEA agents were all in the apartment, sensing that they might be close to the capture.[47]

Salameh noticed that the bathroom's entrance door hit the toilet bowl and couldn't open all the way. That's strange. The wall must have been built toward the door to accommodate more space in the air shaft. It had obviously been designed with a purpose. Mitchell also found something odd. He pulled out a yellow hose that went into the wall. This had to be where Miguel was hiding, the DEA agents agreed. The drilling in the bathroom wall began.[48]

"How do you know he's hiding there?" one CNP officer asked Mitchell. "Who told you?"

"Can't you see there's a space that's not accounted for," Mitchell answered, in a tone that indicated he thought he was talking to a moron. Then he checked himself from providing any more information. Mitchell's instincts were sharp. Later it turned out that the officer was corrupt and on the cartel payroll.[49]

Then, all of a sudden, the prosecutor rushed into the room. "Stop! You must stop right now!" he ordered. "You are involved in illegal operations in Colombia."[50]

"You got to be kidding," Prieto said with a laugh. "What kind of illegal operation?"

The prosecutor ignored the question and commanded: "You can't leave! I need your names and some additional information."[51]

"Don't give it to him," Feistl told Prieto, as his blood started to boil. "That's bullshit! Here we are helping you, and you're trying to get us for an illegal search. Tell him you're Donald Duck, Ruben."[52]

The prosecutor ordered the raid's commander to lock the apartment with the four agents inside and to make sure none of the tools they needed to drill into the bathroom wall were left behind.

An hour-and-a-half later, the prosecutor returned. "So are we under arrest?" Prieto asked.

"No," the prosecutor answered curtly, shaking his head.

"So we are free to leave?" Prieto asked.

"No."

"So you are holding us against our will?" Prieto persisted sarcastically. "Can I make at least one phone call."[53]

The prosecutor consented and Prieto called Tony Seneca, his supervisor at the U.S. embassy, to explain the absurd situation they were in. "Sorry, Ruben," Seneca said, "the U.S. embassy can't do anything. We are operating in Colombia, and the prosecutor is within his authority to detain you."[54]

Finally, a regional prosecutor arrived, and he allowed them to leave. It was nearly twelve hours after the search of apartment 402 had begun. So close and yet they were being forced to leave. They could almost smell Miguel behind that bathroom wall. Prieto called General Serrano on his cellphone and urged him to station some of his men at the apartment. "Miguel is in there and he is going to try to escape the area when we leave," Prieto warned. He would consider the suggestion, Serrano assured him, but inexplicably, he didn't follow through.[55]

When the search team spilled out into the street, the news media were waiting and they chased the gringos in the group down the street.[56] In the following days, the four DEA agents were identified in the media as having conducted an illegal search in Colombia.[57] The charge wasn't true, but it added insult to the search team's failure to get Miguel.

The next day, the search team returned to the apartment. They found Miguel's *caleta* under the sink in the bathroom. Inside was an oxygen bottle, a bloody towel, a bag, water, some snack food, and other items.[58] After the search team left the apartment, a captain and another security officer had returned to the apartment to help Miguel escape, hustling him down the back stairwell into a garage, where a car was waiting to take him to safety. For their services, the captain reportedly received $50,000 and his assistant, $25,000. "Miguel apparently got some flak from his brother Gilberto because the police were doing him a big favor and he was so cheap on the payoff," Salameh recalled with a laugh. "It was typical Miguel."[59]

The bloody towel helped to grow the legend of Miguel Rodriguez, as the authorities told the press that the search team may have drilled into his shoulder.[60] "Ruben [Prieto] said the drill hit Miguel in the leg," Mitchell recalled. "I find that hard to believe. Even Miguel would be screaming if a drill hit him in the leg."[61]

The raid wasn't a complete failure. Sean had told Feistl and Mitchell about some documents in a hidden compartment in the office desk. They lifted up the top of the desk and inside was a big wooden box containing several briefcases full of documents and a laptop computer.[62] One of the documents was a list of 2,800 names – politicians, police, journalists, congress members, state governors, and military personnel – all of whom were on the take for the Cali cartel. The total payroll added up to nearly $5.6 million a month, according to TV Hoy, a Colombian television news program, which broke the story.[63] The list of names illustrated how widespread the cartel-related corruption had penetrated in Colombian society and what security forces were up against in trying to take down the syndicate. Salameh also found the letter Sean told them about – from Botero to Miguel, requesting funds for Samper's campaign. This was a discovery so shocking that Samper's Liberal party temporarily suspended its annual convention. The documents found at apartment 402 later became valuable evidence for prosecuting attorney general Valdivieso's Case 8000 investigation.[64]

Feistl and Mitchell took the plane back to Bogota that evening. The agents were tired and frustrated. They agreed that the failure at Santa Rita was the lowest point of their young professional careers. By not catching Miguel, they had let down Sean, who had taken incredible risks so he could pass information on to the DEA. "It was our fault that we didn't find Miguel, but Sean was going to pay the price," Feistl recalled. "Sooner rather than later, Miguel would figure out that it was Sean who was passing on the information to us."[65]

William Rodriguez was indeed suspicious. A corrupt member of the search team had called him immediately when the documents in the desk were found. "How did the police know where to look?" William screamed. "There has to be a snitch among us!"[66] Only a handful of people, in addition to himself, could have known where Miguel was hiding: his driver, his maid, and the head of security. Sean was given security information on a need-to-know basis, but William strongly believed he was the traitor. After Miguel escaped from apartment 402, William threatened Sean with a gun while they were sitting in a car, trying to unnerve him and get him to confess. Sean, however, kept his composure and didn't buckle, insisting he was loyal to the boss. The son talked to dad, trying to convince him his head of security was the mole, but to no avail. Miguel liked the security job Sean had done since he replaced Del Basto. Besides, no one else in the organization had Jorge's knowledge of computers and technology. Miguel dismissed his son's suspicions.[67]

Two days after the raid on apartment 402, Salcedo called Kacerosky. He was angry and couldn't understand why the agents didn't apprehend Miguel. Did the DEA agents he was working with know what they were doing? How could they blow it? Kacerosky tried to calm him down.[68] Operation Cornerstone investigators knew they had to move quickly to restore their informant's confidence. They also had a stake in seeing that Miguel was apprehended.[69] On July 18, Kacerosky arranged a phone conference with Salcedo, Ed Ryan, Bill Pearson, and Lou

Weiss. The Cornerstone team was on the road, staying at a crummy hotel in rural Pennsylvania, and preparing to interrogate witnesses for the first trial against the cartel lawyers. They listened to Salcedo's complaints and concerns and tried to reassure him that what happened at Santa Rita wouldn't happen again.[70]

But it wasn't going to be that simple. Tension had started to build between the Cornerstone team and the DEA office in Miami. The warriors were singing the same old song in the War on Drugs. "It was difficult to be able to promise him [Salcedo] anything because we had to hand off responsibility to the DEA agents in Colombia and they, in turn, had to hand off responsibility to the Colombians, who were of questionable integrity," said Ryan. "Also the DEA agents in Miami who were working with Lou [Weiss] didn't think too highly of Eddie [Kacerosky]. At one point, Eddie was screaming for Lou to get DEA Miami to help us out and do something and a message came back from the group supervisor to in effect: 'Tell Kacerosky to enjoy his round of golf and relax.' We were making promises to Salcedo, but we had no control over delivery."[71]

But Salcedo had crossed his personal Rubicon and he didn't really have a choice. It was either continue helping the authorities catch Miguel – and help catch him quickly – or face the imminent prospect of being tortured, having a bag put over his head, and having his body dumped in the Cauca River. Six days after the failed raid on Santa Rita, Sean called Feistl on his pager. "I'm okay; let's go ahead. Miguel has moved again. I haven't seen him, but, if we work together, we can find and get him."[72] Feistl warned Sean to be careful. "If we screw up a second time, you're going to be the suspect."[73]

By now, the DEA was working closely with Colombia's navy seals, who had a reputation for being good on surveillance. Despite the purges conducted by Serrano and as the raid on Santa Rita showed, the Cali cartel still continued to corrupt the CNP with ease, and the DEA had even less reason to trust the security force. "Sean found out that even Serrano's pilot was on the take," Feistl revealed. "Every time the general came to Cali, the cartel's security was put on high alert because they knew something was up."[74] The fact was, the American agents didn't trust anybody in the

Colombian military. "We didn't share any intelligence with the navy," said Feistl. "When we were about to make the raid the second time around, they were shown the apartment building and told the target. That was it."[75]

On July 21 Feistl and Mitchell talked with Sean on the telephone. The CI had a good lead to Miguel's new hideout. Three days later, they talked again, and Sean told them he was sending the agents a package containing a map and a photo of the apartment where he thought Miguel was hiding now: Hacienda Buenas Aires, West Street, Number 5A-50. The new location looked a lot more upscale than apartment 402. Each floor contained one apartment of about 3,000 to 4,000 square feet, certainly a lot more area to cover in searching for Miguel's *caleta*. The next day a DEA employee went to the airport to pick up the package.[76]

On August 1, Feistl, Mitchell, and Salameh traveled to Cali to begin the surveillance of Hacienda Buenas Aires. Upon arriving, Feistl and Mitchell headed to the cornfield for an 8 P.M. meeting with Sean, while Salameh went to a square high on a hill, about 1,000 yards away from the apartment. The agents planned to meet up later that night. But a taxi cab was stolen in the vicinity of the agricultural station, and the area was crawling with police. The agents and Sean decided to go deeper in the cornfield to have the debriefing. It was just their luck that two CNP officers appeared and began to ask questions. "It became obvious they weren't going to leave us alone," recalled Mitchell. "We didn't want to reveal who we were for fear of Sean's life. We also had photos of the apartment underneath the driver's seat of our rental car."[77]

Mitchell had some money on him and he offered the cop a bribe. They wanted to know why he was offering the money if he didn't do anything wrong. "Here," Mitchell told the cop. "Take this and leave us alone." Fortunately, the cop was more greedy than curious. He took the bribe, and left the area with his partner.[78]

The agents knew Miguel was a night owl who liked to stay up until the early hours of the morning, so they began the surveillance about ten at night. They figured there would be a good chance that the last light to go out in the building would identify the apartment in which Miguel was hiding. Sean said the two black maids were definitely with Miguel this time. Hopefully they would spot them. During the next four days, the agents conducted surveillance of the apartment. The assignment actually turned out to be fun. The square was a hangout for the locals, a place where they could buy beer and candy. The agents sipped on beers and watched the burning cane fields in the distance. No one could tell that they were actually spying on the tall building in front of them.[79]

The last apartment's lights to go off were on the tenth floor, but they couldn't see anybody in it. Then on August 4, when the agents were about to call it a night, the lights in the tenth-floor apartment came on again at 2 A.M. There they were! Feistl spotted the two black maids doing something in the kitchen . . . cooking and washing dishes. The authorities could now make their move.

Colombian and U.S. officials huddled and decided the raid would happen on August 6.[80] The success of the operation would depend on the element of surprise – getting into the apartment before Miguel could get into one of those amazing *caletas*. There were two avenues of approach to the apartment: the road in front of it and a canal or drainage ditch behind it. To get to the canal, the search team had to climb a steep hill of about 100 yards. The plan was for the navy team to go up and down the hill, run through the drainage ditch, and surprise and neutralize the security guards so they couldn't sound the alarm. Mitchell and Feistl rented a dump truck that could carry in the back the police personnel conducting the search. There was a great deal of construction in the area at the time and a dump truck would not arouse suspicion. To coordinate the raid, the two units communicated by cellphone.[81]

This time, the operation moved like clockwork. At four in the morning, the two attack teams converged on the front door of Miguel's apartment. The DEA had made sure the search team had legal permission from prosecuting attorney general Alfonso Valdivieso to knock the door down, so there would be no delay or problems in quickly entering the apartment. A navy sailor battered the door down with a sledgehammer. Once inside, the team immediately spotted Jesus "Mateo" Zapata, Miguel's personal secretary and driver; Miguel's first wife, Ampara Arbalaez; and two black maids – but no Miguel. The team raced through the apartment. It was beautiful and much bigger than 402: nice marble floors, a pool table, an exercise bike. There were numerous phone lines coming in, the sure sign it was a safe house. And then a young navy officer spotted Miguel trying to climb into his *caleta*, a five-door file cabinet built into the wall. He grabbed Miguel.

"I got him! I got him!" he yelled.[82]

Miguel was in his boxer shorts, barely awake. He had tried to scurry to his hiding place, which had all the comforts of home: snacks, bottled water, an oxygen tank to breathe, a stool, and a copy of Colombia's penal code. Miguel's reaction was one of total disbelief. Who found me? How did they do it? When he spotted the gringos, his attitude changed and he seemed resigned to his fate. He even sat calmly for a trophy photo with the DEA agents and a CNP officer.[83]

Half an hour later, police put Miguel in a jeep and took him to the police base. Miguel's escort was so excited that they went much too fast for his liking. "Slow down!" Miguel barked, acting as if he was still the CEO of a multi-billion-dollar crime multinational. "What's the rush? You already got me."[84]

Chapter 15

Takedown

When Pacho arrived at the base, he looked as if he had just left a *GQ* fashion show. He wore an expensive suit, a tie, and aviator-style glasses and looked more like a businessman than a drug trafficker facing several indictments in the United States.
                                      – Dave Mitchell, DEA agent

Miguel Rodriguez Orejuela was fingerprinted and booked in the cavernous CNP headquarters in Bogota. Unshaven, bedraggled, he looked like a criminal who had been on the lam for some time. The police made him available to the media, and a horde of reporters began shouting questions. Surprisingly, Miguel wanted to answer them.

The horde demanded an answer to the big question: "Did Mr. Samper take money from the Cali cartel?"

The weary drug lord gave a firm answer: "No, Mr. Samper is an honest man. That's an invention of Santiago Medina [Samper's former campaign chairman]."[1]

No one in Colombia played charades better than the Rodriguez brothers. Still, with Miguel's capture, six of the top seven leaders of the Cali cartel were now behind bars, while the seventh, Pacho Herrera, was desperately trying to negotiate the best deal he could for his surrender.[2] Their empire was in shambles, and the age of the drug combine who had the money and the firepower to challenge the state was ending with a whimper, U.S. and Colombian officials boasted to the media.[3] "Although drug traffickers will continue operating in Colombia, they will never rise to the level of the Cali cartel," predicted Thomas Constantine, head administrator for the DEA. "They will be less sophisticated, [they will have] less technology, they won't have the international connections and they will be a heck of a lot easier to identify and arrest."[4]

Jorge Salcedo, the mole who provided the information that helped authorities to catch Miguel, made it safely out of Colombia with his family and a $1.7 million reward.[5] Still in jail, Miguel must have thought long and often about son William's suspicions of Sean and why he didn't listen to him. Salcedo is now buried deep in the Federal Witness Protection Program, no doubt wary of every move he makes, knowing that Miguel and Gilberto have long memories.[6]

In the months following the capture of the Rodriguez brothers, Colombian authorities continued their assault on the cartel's infrastructure, confiscating more than 100 properties worth around $50 million.[7] In May 1996, U.S. federal antinarcotics agents broke up what they described as an alliance between the Cali cartel and the Mexican Federation. The investigation, known as Operation Zorro, led to the arrest of fifteen people in several U.S. cities and the seizure of six tons of cocaine, which had a wholesale value of $100 million.[8]

A month later, the DEA, with the help of the Marine Corps, raided a cocaine-processing plant in Cali. A gun battle broke out and one marine and three traffickers were injured. The raid was praised by President Bill Clinton, but some members of Congress questioned the use of American military forces in Colombia. It was a harbinger of the heated debates that later ensued during the implementation of Plan Colombia by the military during the Andres Pastrana administration (1998–2002) and over the role of the United States in the War on Drugs in Colombia.[9]

In the fall of 1995, the U.S. government introduced a new tactic against drug trafficking. President Bill Clinton issued an Executive Order 12978, which blocked the assets of individuals and corporations with alleged ties to the Cali cartel.[10] In a keynote speech before the United Nations on October 22, Robert Gelbard, the assistant secretary of state for international narcotics matters, announced sanctions against people and businesses believed to be collaborating with the Cali cartel. The following March, the U.S. government designated 130 individuals and sixty companies as narcotics traffickers, and it banned U.S. citizens from doing business with them.[11] The government continued to add to the list, and by June 1998, more than 496 business and individuals had their assets blocked under the 1995 Executive Order.[12]

The new order in the underworld that Tom Constantine referred to was already taking shape during the hunt for the Cali godfathers. Encouraged by the weakened state of the most powerful cartel, many seasoned drug traffickers from the Valle del Cauca who had operated in Cali's pervasive shadow began jockeying for a larger share and role in the drug trade. They included traffickers like Archangel de Jesus Henao-Montoya, the head of a group out of the northern Valle del Cauca region, who had a reputation for violence and was believed to be closely linked to Carlos Castano, a powerful paramilitary leader; Diego Montoya-Sanchez, who worked closely with the Mexicans; and Alexandro Bernal-Madrigal (aka Juvenal), a Bogota-based "transportation coordinator," as the DEA described him, who collaborated with Colombian and Mexican traffickers.[13]

The clash of the old guard and the new Turks led to a minor version of the "War of the Cartels," which raged for several months after Miguel's capture. In one twelve-month period between 1995 and 1996, forty percent of the 468 murders in the Valle del Cauca and the 400 murders committed in Cali were attributable to this power struggle.[14] One vicious rival who emerged to challenge the Cali cartel was the mysterious "Overalls Man," the trafficker believed responsible for the hit on Miguel's son, William, who police suspected was shuttling orders back and forth from the imprisoned Gilberto and Miguel to their underlings.

The leadership had felt so secure in their home base of Cali that they allowed their security measures to become increasingly lax as they moved about the city.[15] But times had changed. William was dining with his bodyguards in Rio D'Enero, a fancy Brazilian restaurant, when *sicarios* rushed in and machine-gunned his party, killing six of Miguel's bodyguards. William took six bullets but survived thanks to one of the dead bodyguards, who shielded him and took thirty-six of the assassins' bullets.[16]

After Pacho Herrera surrendered, police were able to tape a conversation between him and the Rodriguezes. Pacho revealed that he had talked to the Overalls Man, urging him to keep innocent family members out of the dispute because it would lead to much mayhem in the underworld. Reports identified the Overalls Man as forty-year-old Orlando Sanchez, who had emerged as the main rival of the Rodriguez brothers for control of the Cali cartel empire.[17]

The turf war spread to the United States, where authorities discovered the bodies of more than twenty high-level Colombian drug traffickers. In one gruesome incident, a corpse was found stuffed in a suitcase, bound with duct tape, and its mouth gagged with a rotting apple.[18] There was a power shift underway in New York's drug underworld, police officials confirmed.

In the weeks following the arrest of Miguel Rodriguez, the street prices of cocaine soared as the supply dwindled. In Detroit, the DEA reported an increase in the wholesale price from $22,000 to $32,000 per kilogram in August and September alone.[19] In October, the DEA reported that the wholesale price of cocaine in Philadelphia rose from $20,000 to $30,000.[20] DEA officials were quick to point out that these increases were mere blips. "We felt they're capitalizing on the events in Colombia as a way to make more money," said Dana Seely, a DEA spokesperson. "We have reports of an artificial price inflation at all levels, retail through wholesale."[21] By April 1996, the DEA was reporting that the wholesale price of cocaine had decreased from the $25,000 a kilogram it had cost four months previously to $21,000, a sign that supplies had been replenished and the market stabilized.[22] Police officers who worked drug investigations in New York City at the time said events relating to the Cali cartel's takedown in 1995 did not have much of an impact on distribution in the city. "There was a much bigger impact when Luis Galan was killed in 1989," said Bill Mante, former New York State Police investigator.[23]

The authorities were having their way with the cartel since the capture of the Rodriguez brothers, apprehending several lesser godfathers, confiscating assets and crippling the syndicate's infrastructure. But they suffered a setback on January 11, 1996, when Chepe Santacruz escaped from the maximum-security wing of Bogota's La Picota prison with the help of a group of associates who posed as interrogators. Prosecutors had visited the prisoner earlier in the morning and left at midday. Another car arrived with the "interrogators" about midday under the ruse of continuing the inquiry, but they whisked Chepe away to freedom. Military and intelligence units combed Cali and Bogota, but they found no leads as to his whereabouts. The Colombian government offered a \$2 million reward for Chepe's recapture.[24]

What happened next remains uncertain. The official report was that Santacruz was killed in a shootout with police on August 5, 1996. The DEA agents who saw the autopsy photos, however, say Chepe's body showed signs of torture.[25] Santacruz's family called for a second autopsy after its lawyer, veteran Cali cartel house counsel Guillermo Villa, charged that the police "converted deterrent orders into physical execution orders." Serrano defended the forensic examination conducted in Medellin by experts and countered that Villa "should not be exercising his profession with the background he has." Chepe was buried in a Cali cemetery without the second autopsy.[26]

Many sources remain skeptical of the official account. "Although there were bullet holes in the car, you would have to imagine other persons would have been killed if there was a police shootout," said Ken Robinson, the "dean" of Chepe chasers and a retired DEA agent. "This was the first thing I thought about after I originally heard he had been killed in a police shootout and no one else was killed on either side."[27] A DEA agent close to the Cali investigation believes that Santacruz escaped from prison to exact revenge on the security officials who had double-crossed him. Santacruz was at the restaurant in Bogota on January 11, 1996, to turn himself in, but he was double-crossed and arrested for the reward, according to this source.[28]

In a *Semana* interview, paramilitary leader Carlos Castano said that he had learned through a mutual friend of his and Chepe's that Chepe had made contact with *FARC* militias in Medellin. According to Castano's story, *FARC* had captured one of Chepe's associates from Cali, and he had retaliated by kidnapping some relatives of Pablo Catatumbo, a *FARC* commander. In the subsequent negotiations for the hostages' release, they agreed on a mutual respect and "a connection began to be formed." "We knew that Santacruz had already gone over to *FARC*," Castano explained. "We also discovered . . . that among the plans that he had for being received in the *FARC* in the event of their negotiations with the government . . . was turning in one of the Castano brothers. We were quite disappointed, because we had not done anything to Santacruz."[29]

According to Castano, Santacruz was unaware that he found him out. Castano tracked him to an estate in the vicinity of La Ceja, east of Medellin, then called Serrano's office in Bogota and asked to speak to him. The general declined, so Castano spoke to a colonel instead. "I identified myself because they had intercepted my calls and could compare my voice," Castano explained. "I gave him all the information: the car in which he was traveling, the time and everything necessary."[30]

The DEA said that Castano had something to do with Chepe's death and had provided details about the drug traffickers he collaborated with to do it. Orlando Henao-Montoya contacted Chepe and Pacho Herrera to set up a meeting to discuss "serious matters." Pacho didn't trust Henao-Montoya and refused to go, but he did send his chauffeur and boyfriend John Gavi Valencia to accompany Chepe. Jairo Wilmer Varela, an enforcer for the Henao-Montoya organization, and Efrain Hernandez, another leading drug trafficker and close associate of Henao-Montoya, were with Henao-Montoya.

Henao-Montoya made arrangements with Carlos Castano to take custody of Santacruz and Valencia. Castano and his people tortured Chepe and Valencia trying to find where Chepe had his money stash. Castano was in cahoots with Danilo Gonzalez, an ex-CNP Colonel and very close associate of General Serrano's. Castano and Gonzalez killed Santacruz and Valencia and turned over his dead body to Serrano. Danilo Gonzalez and Carlos Castano split the reward money that the CNP gave for the capture of Chepe.[31]

By the time of Santacruz's death, the Rodriguez brothers were seeing Santacruz as a liability and were beginning to dissociate themselves from their longtime friend and ally.[32] In an interview with the Bogota-based *Semana* magazine, Castano said he received a letter from Miguel Rodriguez two weeks after he had sent him a cassette and some documents "proving" Santacruz was a traitor and that he acted properly. According to Castano, Rodriguez wrote back: "I would have done the same thing."[33]

With Santacruz dead, the only major Cali drug lord still free was Pacho Herrera. Through the first eight months of 1996, the Colombian police continued to raid several addresses in Cali associated with him, including one in May at which they seized about 2,000 pages of documentation, almost all of it from his attorney. Among the material were legal documents, including a 100-page bound presentation of his case, various versions of a possible surrender deal, and an outline of expectations from Colombian authorities if he turned himself in.[34]

On September 1, 1996, after months of negotiation, Pacho Herrera arrived at Bloque de Busqueda police base in Cali to surrender directly to General Serrano. DEA agent Dave Mitchell was at the base, and Serrano allowed him to debrief Pacho after the drug lord asked to see him. "When Pacho arrived at the base, he looked as if he had just left a *GQ* fashion show," Mitchell recalled. "He wore an expensive suit, a tie, and aviator-style glasses and looked more like a businessman than a drug trafficker facing several indictments in the United States. He was very friendly but evasive in our interview, and didn't really tell me anything."[35] But Herrera did turn informant, implicating thirty-five people, including some of his own family members, in being cartel members.[36] In return, Herrera received a sentence of six years and eight months and a fine of one million dollars for the crime of drug trafficking.[37]

On November 5, 1998, Pacho was playing a game of football in the maximum security area at the Palmira prison when a well-dressed man, posing as lawyer, strolled up to him, embraced him warmly, and then pulled out a gun and shot him six times in the head. Eight days later, Pacho's paraplegic brother, who was also in prison, fired shots from his electric wheelchair and killed another inmate, Orlando Henao-Montoya, the same drug trafficker who was responsible for Chepe's death and who was believed to be the architect of Pacho's killing.[38]

By the time of Herrera's death, the Colombian authorities had captured the remaining key figures of the Cali cartel: Juan Carlos ("El Chupeta"; surrendered, March 16, 1996); Juan Carlos Ramirez Abadia (surrendered, March 10, 1996); Arnaldo "Lucho" Botero (captured, January 1998); Nelson Urrego Cardenas (captured February 1998).[39] In September 1999, Rodrigo Espinosa, the head of communications during the cartel's glory days, was gunned down on a street in Cali. Authorities arrested Espinosa in 1997, but released him in early 1999 after working out a plea bargain in which he agreed to cooperate with the police.[40]

While the government was successfully pursuing the remaining Cali leaders, Miguel and Gilberto lived more like guests than criminals in La Picota prison, thanks to the incorrigibly corrupt Colombian penal system. The brothers used cellphones and a suspected communications network run through a pay phone at the prison to oversee their business interests.[41] The brothers' families and lawyers came and went as they pleased, carrying their messages to and from the prison. In one week, Gilberto received 123 visits from his lawyers.[42] Their prison cells looked more like upscale apartments and included cable television, expensive stereo sound systems, carpeting, and adjoining private bathrooms. Imagine an incarcerated John Gotti or Carlos Lehder having their meals especially prepared for them in an American prison, but that's the type of cuisine the Rodriguez brothers were able to enjoy.[43] In one search of the prison section in which the Rodriguez brothers were held, police found four bottles of French wine and twelve bottles of Scotch. Miguel operated a small kiosk, called "Poor Miguel's Shop," which sold shortbread, aspirins, Cote d'Or chocolate from Belgium, and soft drinks over the counter to visitors. For being an entrepreneur within prison walls, Miguel could actually have his sentence reduced by as much as a third.[44]

In January 1997, Gilberto and Miguel were finally convicted for their crimes by a so-called faceless judge. Through plea-bargaining by their lawyers, Gilberto received ten-and-a-half years and Miguel, nine years. The sentences were far short of the twenty-four-year maximum that the court could have handed down or the life sentence without parole they would have surely received if they had been extradited to the United States.[45] Still, it was only the first criminal ruling against the brothers; they still had four more cases pending. The next month, Miguel was sentenced to twenty-three years in jail for a 330-pound cocaine shipment to Tampa in 1989 for which he had refused to accept responsibility. Radio and television reports revealed that the judge in the case was offered a million dollars to let Miguel off the hook.[46] In May 1998, an appeals court judge added five years to the jail sentences of Gilberto and Miguel.[47]

Ernesto Samper never had to resign or go to jail for Colombia's version of the Watergate scandal. In fact, he turned out to be the biggest survivor of the Cali cartel era of hegemony and downfall. It was a remarkable achievement, given that key members in his election campaign turned against him. Two weeks after the arrest of Miguel Rodriguez, Santiago Medina, Samper's campaign manager, blew the lid off the narco cassette scandal when he testified in secret testimony that both Ernesto Samper and Defense Minister Fernando Botero were directly involved in soliciting campaign contributions for the cartel. Among the evidence Medina presented were documents connecting Botero to a bank account believed to be funded by the cartel.[48] According to documents that the United States sent to Valdivieso, the monthly average of deposits in Botero's bank accounts in the United States went from $70,000 to $963,000.[49]

Samper began maintaining a public position vis-à-vis the scandal that he still maintains today. Yes, the drug cartel money entered his campaign, but he knew nothing about it. Later, Samper would claim that Botero and Medina used the money for their benefit.[50] On December 10, Samper had a five-hour private meeting with Botero in which he reportedly offered to take care of him, including the charges against him, for his silence.[51] Despite the revelations, the U.S. Senate Foreign Relations Committee concluded in February 1996 that there was no smoking gun proving conclusively Samper personally knew that his campaign took money, although there was no doubt that the "Samper campaign received $6 million from the Cali cartel."[52]

When Botero decided to talk on January 22, 1996, Valdivieso

believed he had enough evidence to bring the case to the attention of the Indictment Commission of the Colombian Congress, the only government body that had the authority to investigate the Colombian president and request that Samper be prosecuted. But with eleven of the eighteen members suspected of receiving drug money for their electoral campaigns, the commission found Samper innocent in June 1996 in a vote of fourteen to one. The decision left it up to the plenary assembly of the Congress to decide Samper's fate, but Samper's Liberal party held a large majority of its membership. So it was no surprise when the Congress found Samper innocent on June 12, 1996.[53]

Samper began referring to himself as "the quake-proof president" because he survived so many calls for his resignation.[54] Ironically, as the United States dug deeper into the corruption surrounding his election campaign, Samper continued to fight the War on Drugs aggressively. Under his watch, the Colombian legislature increased sentences for drug trafficking and related crimes. His government signed a multiyear loan agreement for $90 million with the Inter American Development Bank to implement the government's PLANTE project, an alternative development program that enrolled 17,000 families who were formerly involved in cultivating illegal crops.[55]

Samper still resents the fact that the Clinton administration did not give him credit for the Cali cartel takedown. Interestingly, some U.S. officials say that Samper does deserve more credit than he has received.[56] "We would not have been able to take the Cali cartel down as quickly and decisively as we did without Samper's aggressive leadership," said DEA agent Ruben Prieto.[57]

One of Samper's major contributions was pushing a bill through Colombia's House of Representatives that repealed the 1991 national ban on extradition of Colombian nationals for trial in the United States. As happened in 1991, death threats were made against key officials, including President Samper, Alma Beatriz Rengifo, his justice minister, and Myles Frechette, the U.S. ambassador.[58] There were reports that a four-man hit squad consisting of drug traffickers and guerrillas had been sent to Bogota to assassinate General Luis Enrique Montenegro, the head of DAS.

The bribe was in, and some Liberal party congressmen confessed to being on the Cali payroll. Ramon Elias Nader, a former president of the lower House, admitted receiving $500,000 from front companies between 1993 to 1995.[59] Police taped conversations between Miguel Rodriguez and his lawyers in which they discussed how the campaign against extradition was going. In one conversation, the lawyers said they needed more money to take care of the Congress.[60] Carlos Lemos, vice-president in the Samper administration, recalled that the cartel was offering $25,000 per vote to any congressman and congresswoman who voted against extradition.[61]

In November 1997, the Colombian Chamber of Representatives gave final approval to the extradition bill. Critics of the measure charged that it would make it impossible for the Rodriguez brothers and other godfathers to be extradited to the United States for trial. The law stipulated that extradition could not be applied to Colombian nationals for crimes committed before December 17, 1997. But after the debate, the bill was pushed through the legislature when three senators, for unknown reasons, changed their vote at the last minute.[62] According to Rengifo, the Samper administration didn't support the retroactivity clause in the bill, but "it was a big improvement over the 1991 law and advanced the battle against drug trafficking."[63]

Despite Samper's efforts, the United States decertified Colombia a second time on March 1, 1996. "The Samper administration lacked the kind of commitment needed to help eliminate the drug trade," the U.S. government concluded.[64] Four months later, the United States revoked President Samper's visa, the first time it had been done since 1987, when the United States stripped Kurt Waldheim of his.[65]

While the Cali drug-trafficking empire lay in ruins and its powerful kingpins were in jail or dead, U.S. federal prosecutors doggedly pursued the Operation Cornerstone investigation that had started with the cartel's first major blunder, the loss of cocaine in its 1991 cement-post shipment. Guillermo Pallomari, the cartel's chief accountant, became the key witness for Operation Cornerstone prosecutors. When Jorge Salcedo began talking to

U.S. investigators, he had expressed concern about the safety of his friend, Pallomari, and his family. The prosecutors had assured Salcedo that they would do their best to protect his friend from the mafia's murderous intentions.[66]

By the summer of 1995, Pallomari had become the Man Who Knew Too Much. As the cartel's chief accountant, he had sat in on most of its important meetings and kept track of hundreds of legal and illegal documents.[67] At the end of March 1995, he turned over his position to William Rodriguez, and the following month the Colombian government called him for questioning for the crime of serving as a frontman for a criminal enterprise.[68] Miguel Rodriguez thought Pallomari was going to crack and knew time was short. If police caught Pallomari, he would be a devastating witness against him. Miguel put a contract out on his former accountant's life, but Pallomari had time to go underground in Cali.

Pallomari realized his only chance to stay alive was to defect, so he called the U.S. embassy in Bogota to make arrangements. His wife Patricia Cardona agreed to join him, but first she needed to take care of some business matters. The DEA's agents Mitchell and Feistl visited Cardona and urged her to turn herself in to the U.S. embassy. "We have intelligence that your life is in danger," they told her.[69] In August, Pallomari arrived in Bogota at the U.S. embassy and met with the DEA to arrange details about his surrender and cooperation. In return for his testimony, Pallomari would join the witness protection program. The day after the DEA agents had visited Cardona, Pallomari tried calling her at their home, her office, and her family's residence. She was nowhere to be found, but her sister-in-law had received a call from the Cali cartel when she wasn't home. There was no message.[70]

The cartel tracked Pallomari to the U.S. embassy, and Bruno Murillo, one of its *sicarios*, called him. "Your wife has been kidnapped because you have not obeyed Miguel's orders," was Murillo's chilling message.[71]

Pallomari became frantic. "What can I do to get my wife back?" he pleaded.

"Go to the Cali cartel. Don't cooperate with the authorities.

Don't participate or get involved with the DEA," were the cartel's specific instructions.[72]

But that was now impossible, given Pallomari's commitment to surrender. He never saw his wife again. On August 16, 1995, Cardona and Freddie Vivas Yangus, her employee, vanished without a trace. They were never seen again, although there is a record that Cardona left Colombia and traveled to Lima, Peru.[73] "That's a tough task for a dead person," said DEA agent Chris Feistl. "Actually, the cartel was up to its old tricks. They were kidnapped from Cardona's business, tortured, and eventually killed."[74]

A few days later, Pallomari and his two sons made their way to an undisclosed location in the United States via a commercial airline with the DEA's assistance. He was brought before a judge in Miami, and on December 15, 1998, he pleaded guilty to racketeering conspiracy and money laundering charges. He cooperated with U.S. authorities and was placed in the Federal Witness Protection Program.[75] One senior administration official told the Washington Post, "he may turn out to be the biggest witness of international drug trafficking that we've ever had."[76]

The DEA spent days debriefing Pallomari. The U.S. attorney general's office wanted him to work with their prosecutors in cases involving the Cali cartel. A tug of war ensued over who would have first crack at debriefing him. Assistant U.S. attorney generals Bill Pearson and Ed Ryan were constantly on the phone trying to get access to Pallomari for their work on Operation Cornerstone.[77]

In the weeks after arriving in the United States, Pallomari worked long hours decoding the financial records taken from an office of Jose Santacruz Londono on May 18, 1994. The authorities also confiscated from Chepe's office an IBM AS/400 computer worth one million dollars, the most sophisticated piece of technology the DEA had ever taken from drug traffickers. The DEA computer experts spent months trying to break into it. When they finally did, they found computer files containing information on thousands of bribes the cartel paid to Colombians from all sectors of society, as well as telephone and motor vehicle records of the cartel's real and potential enemies, including the

U.S. embassy and the DEA's offices in Colombia. Stunned DEA analysts found that the supercomputer contained Colombia's entire motor vehicle records.[78]

"If you were a Colombian and wanted a U.S. visa, you might call the embassy in Bogota once or perhaps twice for information," explained Steve Casto, a DEA intelligence agent who did analysis on the computer. "But what if you were an informant and were calling once or twice a month? The Cali cartel could find this pattern by analyzing the telephone records. Its computer analysts could go to the telephone records without leaving Santacruz's office and find out more information on the caller. Then the cartel could wiretap the calls that the person was making to the U.S. embassy."[79]

Finally, in July 1997, Pallomari testified in the trial of lawyers William Moran and Michael Abbell. He told the court how the Cali cartel spent millions to pick a president of Colombia who would be to their liking and confirmed the veracity of statements made by Samper's close associates, Santiago Medina and Fernando Botero.[80] Pallomari also testified about the rampant corruption in the Colombian political system, how the smugglers moved drugs, how it was structured, and what it did with its money. He confirmed that the 1992 capture of Harold Ackerman forced the cartel to change its shipping routes to the United States and align itself with the Mexican smugglers. On December 15, 1997, Pallomari was sentenced to seven years in prison for racketeering and laundering $400 million for the Cali cartel.[81]

The previous October, Moran and Abbell had been acquitted of the more serious charge in the indictment – that they had crossed the line and had actually joined the cartel to help traffic drugs. The district judge, however, declared a mistrial after jurors deadlocked on four other charges. Prosecutors said they would retry Moran and Abbell.[82] Moran and Abbell were eventually convicted and are now serving prison sentences.[83]

If Gilberto and Miguel Rodriguez had been extradited to the United States to face charges after their capture, their story would be all but over. The brothers, no doubt, would be locked up in some maximum security prison for the rest of their natural lives and then some, living under spartan conditions with no color television, private bathrooms, fine champagne, lawyers, and family members visiting them at all hours of the day and no chance to escape or buy their way out. But they were incarcerated in Colombia, where the justice system has never recovered from the assault and battery it has experienced at the hands of the country's powerful drug traffickers during the past two decades.

On November 7, 2002, a Colombian court shook the nation by ordering Gilberto Rodriguez's early release from prison, despite intense pressure from President Alvaro Uribe.[84] Incredibly, the Chess Player had spent less than six years in prison for his crimes. When elected in May 2002, Uribe had publicly vowed to stop the early release of the Rodriguezes. He pushed for Miguel's conviction on a bribery charge for which he had been earlier acquitted, and succeeded in keeping the drug lord in jail when a court added four years to Miguel's sentence.[85] A judge had ordered Miguel to be set free with Gilberto. In releasing Gilberto, the judge cited the Chess Player's good behavior while in jail and participation in a work-study program.[86] Suspecting a bribe, the justice minister ordered a criminal investigation of the judicial officers involved in Rodriguez's release, but the Supreme Court condemned the move as undermining the judiciary's independence.

United States law enforcement officials shook their heads at the thought of Gilberto Rodriguez walking out of prison a free man. They had seen this happen many times before in Colombia. During Escobar's war with the state, the Ochoa brothers – Jorge, Fabio, and Juan David – escaped with their lives and fortunes intact in 1991 when they turned themselves in to the authorities and served a few years in jail. They were released, but Fabio couldn't resist the life of crime. He was arrested again as a part of the Operation Millennium investigation and extradited to the United States to face drug trafficking charges. On August 26, 2003, a Miami court found Fabio Ochoa, Jr., guilty and sentenced him to thirty years in prison.[87]

"Once a criminal always a criminal. Believe me, we will get another crack at Gilberto," predicted DEA agent Ruben Prieto, who retired from the DEA in January 2003.[88] Other investigators who had spent years tracking the Cali cartel weren't so sure. "I expect Gilberto to retire," Ken Robinson said.[89] Asked if there was any chance of getting Gilberto extradited to the United States, Ed Ryan said, "We are working awfully hard at it."[90]

Then four months after releasing the Chess Player from jail, the Colombian government filed new charges against him – his alleged involvement in a 1990 shipment of 330 pounds of cocaine from Colombia to the United States. Gilberto Rodriguez was back in jail.[91] U.S. officials insist the Colombian government made the move on its own initiative.[92]

As the drug trade turned, the last chapter of the Cali cartel story had still to be written.

Part IV
The Epilogue

Chapter 16

Endgame

The Colombians have a term for what we have been doing to the Rodriguez Orejuela family and their associates. They call it 'Civil Death.'
– Official with the U.S. Treasury, Department Office of Foreign Assets Control

Gilberto Rodriguez's release from the Combita Boyaca maximum-security prison in Tunja, a town about sixty miles from Bogota, stunned U.S and Colombian officials. Shortly before midnight on November 7, 2002, the weary-looking drug lord, dressed casually in a light white sweater and dark dress pants and accompanied by one of his lawyers, picked his way through a crowd of reporters to a waiting bulletproof limousine. Dozens of police and soldiers surrounded the prison. Attorneys for Gilberto and brother Miguel revealed that their clients had requested protection from the government because of fears that drug rivals might try to kill him.[1]

As family and friends cheered, the Chess Player told journalists, "I feel very well, very well."[2] With the clock ticking down to Gilberto's release, officials had frantically looked for a way to stop it. "Some documents have arrived from the U.S. that officials are evaluating, and they could stop the release," Ricardo Galan, a spokesman for President Alvaro Uribe, told the Associated Press.[3] But the government's desperate effort was to no avail, and the Chess Player walked free after serving just seven years of a fifteen-year sentence.

The day after Gilberto's release, an embarrassed President Uribe vowed to defeat "the empire of crime." "Colombia needs its citizens, all its state institutions, to be committed to adapting a criminal policy which is capable of defeating criminals," Uribe said at a military ceremony.[4]

In May 2002, the forty-nine-year-old Uribe had won the presidency in a landslide by campaigning on a law and order platform. He would get tough on the drug traffickers and tough on the guerrillas, Uribe promised the Colombian electorate. In winning by more than twenty percentage points over his nearest rival, Liberal Horacio Serpa, Uribe became the first presidential candidate to win outright on the first ballot in a Colombian election. Boyish looking and educated at Harvard and Oxford, Uribe, with his wire-rimmed glasses, looked more like a bookworm than an ambitious politician. A close examination of his resumé, however, would reveal a determined candidate who had an ultra-right-wing philosophy and had exhibited paramilitary sympathies in the past.[5]

In August 2004, the National Security Archive in Washington, DC, announced that it had obtained a newly declassified Department of Defense intelligence report dated September 1991, which listed more than 100 people, including Uribe, who were believed to be associated with the Medellin cartel.[6] The U.S. government, which needed a strong and stable Colombia as an ally in its War on Drugs, moved into damage control mode. "What I can tell you is that this was a report that included information . . . based on input from an uncorroborated source," said a State Department spokesman. "It's raw information . . . not fully evaluated intelligence, and my understanding from Department of Defense [DOD] colleagues is that it did not constitute an official DIA [Defense Intelligence Agency] or DOD position."[7]

Written at the top of the report was a note cautioning that not all the intelligence had been "finally evaluated," but the report also stated, "Uribe is a close personal friend of Pablo Escobar Gaviria. He has participated in Escobar's political campaign to win the position of assistant parliamentarian to Jorge [Ortega]. Uribe has been one of the politicians, from the senate, who has attacked all forms of the extradition treaty."[8]

In 1983, *FARC* guerrillas gunned down Uribe's father at the family ranch in Antioquia province. Uribe denied that he held any grudges against the guerrillas, but during the 2002 election, he vowed to end the country's thirty-eight-year-old civil war by destroying their movement. In the six months prior to his election victory, *FARC* put a contract on Uribe's life and tried to assassinate him at least three times. In one of the attempts, Uribe was traveling in the coastal city of Baranquilla when a bomb exploded, killing three people and wounding sixteen others passing by. The armor from Uribe's vehicle saved his life.[9]

At the age of twenty-six, Uribe became mayor of Medellin, at a time when the city was the capital of the Colombian drug trade. According to reports, Mayor Uribe launched two programs, "Civic Medellin" and "Medellin Without Slums," both of which where financed by drug lord Pablo Escobar.[10] From 1980 to 1982, Uribe served as Colombia's Director of Civil Aviation, having, among other duties, responsibility for granting pilot licenses. According to investigative journalist Fabio Castillo, Uribe "granted most of the licenses to the mafia pilots when he was Director of Civil Engineering."[11] While in that position, Uribe had as his deputy Cesar Villegas, an associate of the Cali cartel, who was later sentenced to five years in prison for accepting several millions of dollars from the cartel during Ernesto Samper's 1996 political campaign.[12]

Despite these explosive revelations, the question of whether Uribe had ties to drug traffickers has never been definitively answered. Writing in her book *More Terrible than Death: Massacres, Drugs and America's War in Colombia*, Robin Kirk noted that no one had been able to prove Uribe had such links "beyond the inevitable contact that anyone living in Antioquia during the 1980s might have had, particularly if that person had interest in land and politics."[13] Kirk is the main researcher in Colombia for the U.S.-based Human Rights Watch.

Even if it could be proven beyond doubt that Uribe had narco links, it would not have mattered to the U.S. government. Alvaro Uribe was their key ally in the War on Drugs and a welcome successor to the corrupt Samper and the soft-on-guerrillas Pastrana. Despite questions about his past views towards extradition, no Colombian president has sent more traffickers to the U.S for trial than has Uribe. In the first ten months of 2004 alone, Colombia extradited close to 250 individuals for drug-related crimes.[14] Uribe also had no problem with having large numbers of U.S. military personnel in Colombia. In April 2004, 400 U.S. military personnel and another 400 U.S. contractors were operating there, but Uribe asked the U.S. to double the number. Delighted officials agreed. "We are building on success," enthused Roger Pardo-Maurer, the U.S. Deputy Assistant Defense Secretary for Western Hemisphere Affairs. "President Uribe has really done all the right things. The Colombian people are backing him . . . and his military has an eighty-seven percent approval rating."[15]

All of Uribe's power and popularity, however, could not keep Gilberto Rodriguez in jail. Uribe tried to stall the court decision, ordering a stay on the release of Gilberto and his brother Miguel, both of whom got time off for good behavior and for participating in work-study programs.[16] The Uribe administration accused Judge Pedro Suarez of obstructing justice, and its prosecutors questioned the judge as part of an investigation into his decision. Colombia's legal profession did not take kindly to Uribe's interference. The National Judicial Employees Associations filed criminal charges against Uribe for the offense of "perverting the course of justice, abuse of authority and fraud regarding a court ruling."[17] There was one consolation for the Uribe administration, though. Judge Amanda Moncada declared that Gilberto's brother Miguel would stay in jail to serve another four years for bribing a judge.[18]

The Colombian government and its U.S. allies did not give up. On March 12, 2003, police arrested Gilberto as he was leaving his house in Cali. The authorities had been hard at work digging up new charges against the Chess Player. This time they charged him with being involved with the trafficking of 330 pounds of cocaine to the U.S. from Costa Rica in 1990. The drug lord could not be extradited on this charge because the alleged crime had occurred before December 17, 1997, but at least they could put him behind bars in Colombia. The authorities transferred the Chess Player from Cali to police headquarters in Bogota, where he gave testimony. Once again, U.S. officials began looking for a way to extradite him.[19]

The authorities had jailed the Rodriguez Orejuela brothers in 1995, and criminals had killed Chepe Santacruz Londono in 1996 and Pacho Herrera in 1997. Yet the U.S. government never relented in its aggressive pursuit of Cali cartel money and assets. The Office of Foreign Assets Control (OFAC) in the U.S. Department of the Treasury became the lead agency in the financial investigation of history's richest trafficking organization. The use of economic sanctions against the cartel's assets would be its punitive tool.

The history of OFAC and the use of economic sanctions dates back almost to the beginning of the United States. Prior to the War of 1812 between Great Britain and the United States, the Secretary of the Treasury was charged with the responsibility for administering sanctions against Britain for the its harassment of American sailors. During the Civil War, Congress enacted the Trading with the Enemy Act, giving the Treasury similar sanctioning powers against the Confederacy. Congress amended that act in 1917 so that sanctions could be administered during World War I. Following Germany's invasion of Norway in 1940, OFAC's predecessor, the Office of Foreign Funds Control, was established to administer the American program of economic sanctions against the Axis powers of Germany, Japan, and Italy.

In December 1950, President Truman created OFAC in an effort to block all Chinese and North Korean assets when China entered the Korean War.[20] Today, OFAC is best known for its role in the U.S's imposition of economic sanctions against Cuba, but since the end of the Cold War it has played an important role in both the War on Drugs and the War on Terrorism. "We believe in keeping a low profile," said one OFAC official, who requested anonymity. "We don't hand out business cards and say, 'This is what we do.' It's to our advantage that the good guys don't know who we are and what we do. It's well known in Colombia that we are called *la nube* [the cloud] because the Cali cartel doesn't know how to get its arms around us. They have figured out the procedure and techniques of the DEA, FBI and Customs, but we are like a cloud to them."[21]

OFAC's main legal instrument was executive order (EO) 12978. According to R. Richard Newcomb, OFAC's former director, the office's primary mission is to "administer and enforce economic sanctions against targeted foreign countries, and groups and individuals, including terrorist organizations and narcotics traffickers, which pose a threat to the national security, foreign policy and economy of the United States."[22] In implementing the executive order, President Clinton announced that he was declaring a national emergency because he found that "the actions of significant narcotics traffickers centered in Colombia, and the unparalleled violence, corruption and harm that they cause in the United States and abroad, constitute an unusual and extraordinary threat to the national security, foreign policy and economy of the United States."[23]

OFAC gains it authority from general presidential wartime and national emergency powers, as well as specific legislation, such as the International Emergency Economic Powers Act (IEEPA). According to Newcomb, "Economic sanctions are intended to deprive the target of the use of its assets and deny the target access to the U.S. financial system and the benefits of trade, transactions and services involving U.S. markets."[24]

In January 1995, President Bill Clinton used IEEPA authority to implement Executive Order 12947, which is designed to deal with U.S. foreign policy and nuclear security threats posed by terrorists who threatened to disrupt the Middle East peace process. Later in the late 1990s, OFAC used IEEPA to impose an executive order on Osama bin Laden's al Qaida organization and other individuals and groups providing "material or financial support" to the terrorist group.[25] "The Attorney General [Janet Reno] looked at that authority and asked OFAC, 'Why can't the U.S. government use it against narcotics traffickers?'" said one OFAC official. "We said, 'Yes, it can be used', and then we began looking for ways to do it. On the fiftieth anniversary of the United Nations' founding, President Clinton signed the Executive Order (EO) 12978, and it became an important tool in the U.S.'s war against drug trafficking. We quickly began to focus on Colombia and the Cali cartel."[26]

Through EO12978, which is officially entitled "Blocking Assets and Prohibiting Transactions with Significant Narcotics Traffickers," President Clinton declared a "national emergency to deal with the threat." The EO further stated, that "with certain exceptions, no property or interest in property of a specifically designated narcotics trafficker that are within the United States, or that are or hereafter come within the possession or control of United States persons, including their overseas branches, may be transferred, paid, exported, withdrawn or otherwise dealt in."[27] Made a part of the Federal Registry in October 1995, EO12978 was later amended by EO13286 in February 2003.

OFAC identified the four Cali cartel kingpins as targets: the Rodriguez brothers, Chepe Santacruz and Pacho Herrera. "President Clinton told us to go and find the front companies and the people related to them," explained one OFAC official. "Even though the Rodriguez Orejuela brothers were in jail at the time, we began to go after their finances, identify their assets, name their companies and family members who controlled them."[28] OFAC was not starting from scratch. "The FBI, DEA and other government agencies had been investigating the Cali cartel for years and had files and files," said one official. "We started our investigation by going to those government agencies and asking them: 'What do you know? What can you tell us? What can you share with us?' Before long we had a mass of information and could tell what belonged to Miguel, what belonged to Pacho... Then we began to build on that information."[29]

According to the indictment resulting from the OFAC investigation, which was filed against Gilberto and Miguel in Southern District Court of New York in February 2004, OFAC learned that the cartel was involved in "all aspects of the cocaine trade, including production, transportation, wholesale distribution and money laundering. From about 1982 to 1995, the Cali cartel transported and sold at least 30,000 kilograms of cocaine and ultimately amassed an illicit fortune with $1 billion."[30] U.S. officials concede that the amount of money stated in the indictment is not close to the amount the Cali cartel actually garnered from the drug trade. "The amount is a conservative figure, but it's an amount that's beyond dispute in terms of the Cali cartel's assets," said one U.S. Department of Justice official close to the probe.[31]

The Cali cartel invested the billions of dollars it earned from the drug trade in what looked like legitimate companies, particularly those involved in the production and sale of pharmaceutical drugs, including Laboratorios Kressfor of Colombia and Penta Pharma. Once the Rodriguez brothers began to be identified in public documents as partners in these companies, they tried to hide their ownership and control as a way of avoiding their seizure by law enforcement authorities. About 1989, Gilberto and Miguel began arranging for their companies to be held under the names of family members and trusted associates. In reality, the brothers Rodriguez owned them and told their associates what to do.[32]

It took a few years for the cartel money-laundering plan to gain momentum. "Guillermo Pallomari stated in civil court in South Florida in the late 1990s that about 1991 the Rodriguez Orejuela brothers asked him to start transferring assets out of their names," said one OFAC official. "By 1992 and 1993 the plan was actually being implemented."[33] Another OFAC official said that the ultimate objective of the laundering scheme was to create a family dynasty. "The idea was that the Rodriguez Orejuela family would live off the money generated by the legal businesses for generations to come," he explained.[34] The children of the Rodriguez brothers played key roles in the scheme.

They included Humberto Rodriguez Mondragon, Gilberto's third son; his older brother Jaime and first cousin Juan Carlos Rodriguez Obadia; Humberto's sister Maria Alexandra; and William, Miguel's oldest son who was a lawyer in Cali and would eventually play a major role as a courier for his father and uncle as they operated their empire from prison. In a 1996 interview with a *Newsweek* magazine reporter, the young members of the clan claimed they knew nothing about Gilberto's and Miguel's illegal business dealings. "We have never had an open conversation about their involvement in the business," Maria Alexandra told reporter David Schreiberg. "Do you think they came to us and said, 'We are traffickers'? No, not even now."[35] Jaime Rodriguez Mondragon recalled growing up. "There was always somebody who said, 'Hey, your father is a drug trafficker.' We'd argue with them, call them liars."[36]

In describing the young Rodriguez clan members who sat down for an interview with him, Schreiberg wrote: "They are tastefully dressed, well-educated Latin America yuppies. They are hospitable and good humored and – up to a point – candid. They believe in God and family, the values drilled into them by the stern patriarchs of their clan: Gilberto and Miguel Rodriguez Orejuela, the reputed godfathers of the Cali cocaine cartel, and the masterminds of one of history's greatest crime syndicates."[37]

While the family circled the wagons and tried to present a picture of innocence and legitimacy to the world, the OFAC investigation was inexorably destroying their best-laid plans. As one official explained, "The Rodriguez Orejuela brothers loved to look legitimate, but we chipped away at that facade and made them pariahs in Colombia and abroad."[38] Another OFAC official described what happened when EO 12978 started hitting home. "We have stopped the Rodriguez Orejuelas brothers from getting their money out of country, but we are also having a big impact in Colombia as well," he said. "Colombians have a term for what we are doing to the Rodriguez Orejuela family and their associates. They call it 'Civil Death'."[39]

He explained how the death sentence worked: "Within a week of us putting one of the family members or a close associate of the brothers on the designated list, they would get a letter from the bank saying, 'We don't want your business anymore. We are closing your banking accounts. Pay up your credit cards and cut them up because you won't need them anymore.' The financial institutions in Colombia would no longer have anything to do with that person. So they have a problem servicing their mortgage, paying off their cars or getting a loan because no one in the financial system wants anything to do with them for fear they would be accused of helping the individual avoid U.S. sanctions. Being totally isolated now, the individual begins to feel a lot of pressure. We void the U.S. visas of not just the drug trafficker, but of his family members. The wife can't go to shop in Miami; the kids can't go to Disney World. Now his wife, kids and relatives are all linked to the target of the sanctions, and they start complaining and asking, 'What's going on?'"[40]

Colombia may have the reputation as being one of the world's most corrupt countries, thanks in large part to its long-standing drug trade, but many government officials and business people have readily complied with the OFAC sanctions program. "When we began imposing the sanctions, the Colombian financial community had to make a choice: should we let things go on as they have or should we take measures consistent with what the U.S. government is trying to do?" said an OFAC official. "The community decided it was in their best interest to cooperate with us. So there has been widespread voluntary compliance with OFAC regulations."[41]

OFAC began using both the conventional and electronic media to bring the details of its narcotics trafficking sanctions programs to the world's financial and business communities. Bulletins are routinely sent to banking institutions in the Federal Reserve System and the Clearinghouse and Interbank Payment System. Notices are provided to the pertinent state and federal regulatory agencies, automated clearinghouses and state and independent banking houses nationwide. OFAC contacts all the major security industry associations and regulators, providing material to the embassy in Bogota for distribution to U.S. companies operating in Colombia. The Office also makes the same material available on the Internet, computer bulletin boards and fax-on-demand services.[42]

One year after issuing EO 12978, President Clinton reported to Congress on its accomplishments. The Department of the Treasury had identified seventy-six individuals involved with the Colombian drug trade, and the Treasury's Office of Foreign Assets Control had also sent 498 "alert" letters to businesses in Colombia connected to the drug cartels.[43] According to the President, "The expenses incurred by the Federal Government in the six month period from April 21 through October 20, 1996, that are directly attributed to the exercises of powers and authorities conferred by the declaration of the national emergency with respect to significant narcotics traffickers are estimated at approximately $1 million."[44]

In another message to Congress, Clinton reported that the U.S. government's sanctions were having a significant impact on the Cali cartel. He noted that of the 133 business entities designated as Specifically Designated Narcotics Traffickers (SDNTs), forty-one, or nearly a third, having a combined net worth estimated at more than $45 million and a combined income of more than $200 million, had gone into liquidation as of February 20, 1998. As a result of OFAC designations, three Colombian banks had closed about 300 SDNT accounts of nearly 100 designated individuals. One of the largest SDNT commercial entities, a discount drug store with an annual income exceeding $136 million, has been reduced to operating on a cash basis.[45] The discount drug store to which Clinton alluded was Drogas de Rebaja, the flagship company in Gilberto's and Miguel's corporate empire.

The Rodriguez brothers moved quickly to protect their assets against the OFAC offensive, removing their names from the sanctioned companies and then establishing new or reorganized companies from them. According to an indictment filed in February 2004, the entities, which included Farmacoop, Pentacoop, Dromarca y CIA ("Dromarca") and Materias Primas y Suministros ("Matsum"), among others, simply assumed the assets and continued to perform the services of previously-sanctioned companies.[46] The Rodriguez brothers then named family members or trusted associates who had not been sanctioned to manage the companies.[47]

With the noose tightening around its illicit corporate neck, the Cali cartel began arranging in early 1996 to have its pharmaceutical drugs sold by Dromarca to several companies located in Peru (Colfarma), Venezuela (C.A.V.S), Ecuador (Espibena) and Costa Rica (Jormaga of Costa Rica) and Panama (Premier Sales). Trusted assistants once again operated these foreign companies in their names for the brothers.[48] When OFAC sanctioned Dromarca in February 2000, the cartel moved to have non-sanctioned Matsum take over the services provided by Dromarca, and the company began exporting pharmaceutical drugs to Venezuela, Peru, Panama, Ecuador and Costa Rica. OFAC discovered that Premier Sales, Jormaga, C.A.V.S, Colfarma and Espibena had sent Matsum more than $1.5 million though a bank account in New York between March 2002 and January 2003. So it imposed sanctions against Matsum.[49] The irony of this corporate shell game was not lost on investigators. "Here we have history's largest illegal drug trafficking organization using legitimate pharmaceutical drugs to keep their criminal empire afloat," said one U.S. Department of Justice official.[50]

"It was a sham," said an OFAC official. "The brothers ostensibly sold all the stores and pharmacies they had in Colombia to their employees on loan terms the workers could never pay back. These new companies are called 'transformers.' When we investigated, we could see that the Rodriguez Orejuela brothers were still calling all the shots and they were managing the bank accounts of Drogas La Rebaja and other major companies tied in to their pharmaceutical empire. We caught on to the scam in 1997 when we sanctioned Copservir, the workers' cooperative which controlled the Drogas La Rebaja pharmacy chain. Besides Copservir, we named over two dozen other 'transformers' controlled by the Rodriguez Orejuela brothers which had taken the place of companies we had sanctioned in 1995 and 1996. In 1999 and 2000 we began to identify additional front companies and eventually exposed the entire network."[51]

When the Treasury Department announced in December 2000 that it had added the names of eight businesses and eight individuals to its SDNT list, the number blocked under EO 12978 had grown to 548. The list included such valuable assets as Copservir and its Drogas de Rebaja drug store chain, the America de Cali professional soccer team (Colombia's equivalent of Manchester United in the UK), the Cosmepop cosmetics company, the Farmacoop pharmaceutical laboratory, as well as investment, construction, real estate, agricultural and distribution companies.[52] Also included on the list were five more drug lords in addition to the four founding Cali godfathers: Juan Carlos Ramirez Abadia, North Coast cartel drug kingpin Julio Cesar Nassar David, and North Valley cartel drug kingpins Ivan Urdinola Grajales, Julio Fabio Urdinola Grajales and Arcangel de Jesus Henao Montoya. "By 2000 we essentially had uncovered the entire network of the Cali cartel front businesses," said one OFAC official.[53]

The Rodriguez brothers and the family members that OFAC had implicated in their front game were not going to give up without a fight. Under U.S. law, they had two recourses. First, they could file an administrative appeal with the U.S. government. "They can write OFAC and petition to have their names removed from the sanctioned list," said one Treasury Department official.[54] Given the process, however, that would be difficult to do. "The administrative appeal would move through the Treasury Department, and it would ultimately be decided by an administrative law judge assigned to OFAC," a Treasury source explained. "The plaintiff can hire an attorney to represent him, but the attorney must get a license from the U.S. government, which must be renewed on an annual basis. OFAC operates under national security guidelines, so unlike in a criminal case, where we would have to prove probable cause, we just have to show reason to believe, which is a lower standard of proof."[55] Still, OFAC must build a solid, plaintiff-proof case. "We don't want to go to court unless we have to," said the official. "So after the Treasury Department reviews the evidence, the lawyers in the Department of Justice must look at it and decide, can we defend this in court? We don't want to waste their time."[56]

The Cali cartel's second option was to take the U.S. government to court, which they did twice: in April and in November of 1998.[57] The Rodriguez brothers tried to evade OFAC sanctions by having the name of their flagship company, Drogas de Rebaja, changed to Copservir. "They wanted the U.S. court to rule that it was legal to do that," said one Treasury Department official. "We said no, Drogas de Rebaja and Copservir are the same company, which means they are both subject to sanctions. The cartel took us to court, claiming we had violated U.S. administrative procedures and their U.S. constitutional rights."[58]

The cartel lost the first case in March 2000, when the U.S. court granted the government's motion to dismiss Copservir's complaint. The plaintiffs appealed and the case went before the Supreme Court, which subsequently upheld the lower court's decision. "The Supreme Court essentially ruled that the plaintiffs had no legal standing in U.S. court because they were not U.S. persons," said a Treasury official.[59] In the second case, a group of about twenty Rodriguez Orejuela family members filed a complaint against the government asking the court to do three things: declare unconstitutional OFAC's decision to list them as SDNTs, allow the plaintiffs to engage in transactions with property subject to U.S. jurisdiction, and reverse the decision of the U.S. Department of State Bureau of Consular Affairs to deny them U.S. visas.[60] The Cali cartel lost a second time in May 2000 when the court dismissed the case.

Victorious in court, OFAC continued its relentless assault on the cartel's financial infrastructure. Beginning in 2002, OFAC's International Program Division has worked jointly with the U.S. Attorney's Office for the Middle District of Florida and Operation Panama Express, a multi-agency drug task force based in Tampa. A two-year joint investigation led to action against two new Cali cartel leaders, Joaquin Mario Valencia Trujillo and Guillermo Valencia Trujillo, and fifty of their front companies and associates. Colombia extradited Joaquin Valencia Trujillo to the U.S. after his indictment in Florida.[61]

In October 2003 OFAC designated another 134 new front companies from Colombia to Puerto Rico, Ecuador, Panama, and Peru and with ties to financial companies in the Bahamas, Virgin Islands and Spain. When OFAC designated another twenty-three businesses and 118 people SDNTs in September 2004, the total number of Colombian businesses and individuals that had their assets blocked under EO 12978 had climbed 1,094.[62] The cartel's front companies and associates make up approximately seventy percent of the list. The assets of Miguel and Gilberto Rodriguez make up about fifty percent of the total, while those of Jose "Chepe" Santacruz and Pacho Herrera add another twenty percent. Obviously, the deaths of Chepe and Pacho greatly curtailed the continued growth of their financial empires.[63]

In November 2004, one OFAC official provided this assessment of the drug trafficking assets taken down under EO 12978 since October 1995: "There have been twenty SDNT actions since the program's inception. Each SDNT either may involve several separate investigations that are combined for one complete action or the naming of new Colombian cartel leaders to the SDNT list. To date OFAC has added twelve Colombian cartel leaders from the Cali, North Valle and the North Coast drug cartels in addition to the original four Cali cartel leaders named by the president in 1995."[64]

The biggest humiliation for Gilberto and Miguel came in September 2004 when the Colombian government seized assets of theirs worth $216 million. About 4,000 police, accompanied by more than 450 prosecutors, confiscated for the state 400 Drogas de Rebaja drug stores in twenty-six cities.[65] "This is the most important seizure of assets belonging to the mafia in Colombia's history," said Alfonso Plaza, head of the National Drug Directorate.[66] OFAC officials agreed. "The death knell for the Cali cartel came when Colombian authorities seized the Drogas de Rebaja drug store chain," said one. "The move broke the back of the cartel's financial empire."[67]

The hard work put in by OFAC and its partners in their aggressive attack on the cartel infrastucture was rewarded on March 3, 2004, when R. Richard Newcomb, Director of OFAC, together with David N. Kelley, the U.S. Attorney General for the Southern District of New York, and Anthony Placido, the Special Agent in Charge of the New York Division of the U.S. DEA, announced a two-count indictment and the filing of extradition affidavits requesting that the Colombian government extradite Gilberto and Miguel Rodriguez Orejuela to New York State on money laundering charges. If convicted of all the money laundering and conspiracy charges in the indictment, the brothers face a maximum sentence of twenty-five years in prison and the forfeiture of $1 billion.[68]

In the best spirit of American jurisprudence, the U.S. government's press release announcing the indictment and extradition requests cautioned that "the charges contained in the indictment are merely accusations and the defendants are presumed innocent until proven guilty."[69] It is doubtful, though, that Uncle Sam's disclaimer will give Gilberto and Miguel any comfort.

Chapter 17

Checkmate

They were Colombia's Untouchables
> – Roger P Mackin, Department of
> Homeland Security counter-narcotics officer

The ongoing financial investigation was not the only worry keeping the Rodriguez brothers awake in their jail cells at night and scheming to avoid extradition. Operation Cornerstone had reached fruition in 1996 when a grand jury identified the Cali cartel as a racketing enterprise and close to 100 of its members were successfully prosecuted in U.S. and Colombian courts. But the U.S. Attorney's office in South Florida, U.S Customs and the DEA did not rest on their laurels, and they continued to gather evidence with the aim of one day having Miguel and Gilberto Rodriguez extradited for trial. In a deposition filed in September 2003 in a Florida court, Ed Kacerosky, the Customs agent who played a key role in Operation Cornerstone, said, "Beginning approximately four years ago, I began to receive new information and evidence from a wide variety of sources and witnesses relating to the continued criminal activities of the Rodriguez Orejuela brothers and a number of their associates, despite the incarceration of many of these individuals in various Colombian prisons."[1]

As the evidence showing that Gilberto and Miguel Rodriguez had not given up their criminal ways accrued, the U.S. government intensified its investigation. Some of the evidence they obtained came from cartel members who had been convicted as a result of Operation Cornerstone and were now cooperating as a way of reducing their sentences, actual or possible. Other evidence came from additional witnesses who had collaborated with the Rodriguezes in some way and had been located and questioned.[2] The Operation Cornerstone witnesses included Guillermo Pallomari, the cartel accountant who had worked closely with Miguel, the Patron, and was now in the federal witness protection program; Jorge Salcedo, the cartel's former head of intelligence, who provided authorities with the key information in the arrest of Miguel and is also in witness protection; Harold Ackerman, the cartel's so-called ambassador to the U.S., whom Kacerosky described in his deposition as "one of the two most knowledgeable sources developed historically concerning the operations of the Cali cartel"; and Vicky Giron, a tutor of the Rodriguez Orejuela children for several years and the wife of Carlos Giron, a cartel operative who was captured in 1992.[3] Those witnesses were able to provide valuable information on the mafia's management, organization and style. Both Pallomari and Salcedo confirmed that after March 1995, the cartel's management changed and it began to make greater use of Miguel's son, William Rodriguez Abadia, in running major aspects of its drug and money laundering operations.[4]

In addition to those four, the criminal docket, which outlines the case against Miguel and Gilberto, identifies thirteen other witnesses, including eight confidential sources. When the brothers stand trial in the U.S., the witnesses will testify that it was business as usual for the surviving Cali godfathers. Pacho Herrera and Jose Santacruz were dead and Gilberto and Miguel were behind bars, but the brothers were still planning, organizing and distributing multi-ton shipments of cocaine to the U.S. Key members of their organization kept getting arrested and imprisoned, but they had no problem filling their positions from a seemingly inexhaustible labor pool of gangsters.

Several of the witnesses who were incarcerated in La Picota with Gilberto and Miguel confirm the tremendous freedom and control the brothers exerted behind prison walls and the bribes they made to prison officers, which enabled them to have an excessive number of visitors and gave them the ability to establish communication systems to run aspects of their enterprise from jail. The stories that circulated in 1997 and 1998 about the life Gilberto and Miguel had behind bars were not wild tabloid tales after all.[5]

The 300-pound Venezuelan Fernando "Fatty" Flores Germandia was one of their most important visitors. Authorities in South Florida were hot on Flores's trail for shipping thirteen tons of cocaine in concrete posts through the port of Miami in 1990 and 1991.[6] According to investigators, Flores had helped run major smuggling routes in Venezuela for the cartel. In 1997 and 1998, while Gilberto and Miguel were imprisoned, Flores helped manage for them a currency smuggling operation that involved flying loads of cash from New York and San Juan, Puerto Rico, to Venezuela, where they were spirited across the Colombian border at Cucuta. Also during this period, Flores helped coordinate the cartel's criminal activities by delivering messages to major drug traffickers, including Victor Patino, Ivan Urdinola and Juan Carlos Ramirez and taking cash from the traffickers and bringing it to William Rodriguez Abadia at one of his offices in Cali.[7] In the testimony he gave authorities, Flores revealed that the money was used in part to reimburse the Rodriguez Orejuelas for the successful distribution of the cocaine in the U.S. and to bribe corrupt officials in the Colombian government.[8] Flores also said that some of the messages involved communication between Miguel Rodriguez and other narcotics dealers concerning consolidated loads of cocaine within the United States. According to Kacerosky's deposition, "Regarding the use of messages, Flores advised that this system was only used for the most sensitive of communications and was designed to supplement cellular phones in La Picota and a landline phone system financed by the Rodriguez Orejuelas and equipped with switching systems outside La Picota designed to thwart interception of their conversations."[9]

U.S., Colombian and Venezuelan officials conducted a lengthy hunt for Flores before capturing him on August 19, 1998, in a luxury hotel, where, according to media reports, he was hiding to avoid a $1.08 million debt to a fellow cocaine trafficker. In 1995, Flores signed a sworn statement, saying he had never met or worked with Miguel and Gilberto, but prior to his arrest, authorities had taped a conversation between Flores and the trafficker to whom he owed the money that confirmed his ties to the Rodriguezes.[10] And after being extradited to the U.S., Flores agreed to testify against them. One confidential source confirms Flores's testimony, revealing that from 1996 to 1998, he accompanied Flores on numerous visits to several drug lords, including William Rodriguez Abadia, Victor Patino Fomeque, Juan Carlos Ramirez and Ivan Urdinola, where he delivered and received money.[11]

Of the incarcerated drug barons Flores collaborated with in the service of the Rodriguez brothers, Victor Patino Fomeque, a former cop, was perhaps the most important. Patino had a long and profitable relationship with the Cali cartel leadership, which involved several of Patino's family members, according to Flores. Patino, who was responsible for ensuring the security and effectiveness of the cartel's maritime operation, surrendered in June 1995 and was sentenced to twelve years in prison, serving seven years.[12]

One confidential source, who had worked for Patino's organization from 1997 to 1999, said that Patino, while incarcerated in Colombian jails, continued to provide sea transport for the cartel.[13] According to Kacerosky's deposition, "Flores advised that after their incarceration, the [Rodriguez] brothers got involved in the purchase of cocaine from laboratories and turned the bulk cocaine over to employees of the Patino family in the Cali area for safe keeping."[14] Two days after his prison release, Colombian authorities arrested Patino on drug trafficking charges and in December 2002 extradited him to the U.S.[15]

As head of the Norte Valle del Cauca mafia, Ivan Urdinola Grajales, together with his brother Julio Fabio Grajales, organized and distributed multi-ton shipments of cocaine throughout the U.S. and expanded into the production and trafficking of heroin. According to the DEA, Ivan Urdinola was responsible for the torture and murder of more than 100 people in Colombia, although he never was charged with any of those killings. Ivan was known to kill vagabonds in the hope of bringing good luck to his syndicate. He was arrested in 1992 and imprisoned.[16] In August 2000, the U.S. Treasury's Office of Foreign Assets Control put Ivan on the list of Specifically Designated Narcotics Traffickers

(SDNTs), which makes him subject to economic sanctions under Executive Order 12978.[17] Julio Fabio surrendered to Colombian authorities in March 1997 and was imprisoned.

After Ivan Urdinola's death, a vicious gang war broke out in the Valle del Cauca, the territory that the Cali cartel dominated nearly a decade before.[18] It was the worst violent confrontation between Colombian drug gangs since Cali and Escobar went to war in the late 1980s. More than 1300 people were killed in the first ten months of 2004 alone. So serious was this "war of cartels" that the Colombian National Police sent 500 members of its elite Search Block unit to the valley to restore order.[19]

The three major drug lords involved were Diego Leon Montoya (aka Don Diego), Wilmer Alirio Varela (aka Jabon, meaning "Soap") and Luis Hernando Gomez Bustamante (aka Rasguno). They are godfathers of the Norte Valle del Cauca, an offshoot of the Cali cartel, which has been described as "the last of the big Colombian drug cartels."[20] "The world of narcotics trafficking is now in crisis," a Colombian National Police colonel told *Jane's Intelligence Weekly*. "What was once known as the Norte Valley del Cauca has now fractured into about three great blocks."[21] No one knew for sure how the drug war started, but according to the *Jane's Intelligence Weekly* report, there has been speculation that after Victor Patino was extradited to the U.S in December 2002, he "began to sell out his comrades and this led to a circle of blood letting."[22]

On March 14, 1998, hitmen believed to be employed by Miguel Rodriguez shot Varela five times as he traveled to the Palmira airport. Although seriously wounded, he somehow made it to hospital two days later, but before too long Varela checked himself out, figuring that if he stayed put, the hitmen would return to finish him off. Varela sought revenge and ordered the killing of Pacho Herrera in November 1998. Gilberto and Miguel Rodriguez retaliated by contacting Pacho's half-brother Jose and asking him to kill Varela associate Jose Orlando Henao Montoya, which he did.[23] Rumors circulated that people working for Don Diego's and Rasguno's organizations, together with associates of Miguel and Gilberto, founded a group called *Peporva* ("People Persecuted by Varela") to go after Varela.[24]

Described by the DEA as a "Cali cartel kingpin," Juan Carlos Ramirez-Abadia (aka "Chupeta') surrendered to authorities in March 1996, apparently because he feared for his life and hoped to be eligible for a shorter prison term. In December 1996, Chupeta was jailed for twenty-four years. The DEA reported that Jorge Orlando Rodriguez (aka "El Mono") assumed control of the trafficking operations of Chupeta's organization while he was in prison, although Chupeta remained involved in making major decisions. A DEA source put his net worth at $2.6 billion.[25] The U.S Treasury Department added Chupeta's name to the list of SDNTs in August 2000.[26] In May 2004, the U.S. government indicted Chupeta and eight other reputed members of the Norte Valle del Cauca drug organization under the RICO (Racketeering Influenced and Corruption Organizations) Act as operating a cocaine trafficking enterprise.[27]

William Rodriguez Abadia, Miguel's son, played a key role coordinating the Cali cartel's still formidable trafficking network while his father and uncle were in jail. According to several government witnesses, in addition to handling the money of the cartel's daily operations, William also undertook efforts to retaliate against successful law enforcement operations. Salcedo told Kacerosky that William made it known the cartel had to identify and kill anyone providing information to the authorities, especially Guillermo Pallomari, who, as a foreign national (he was Chilean), could be extradited to the U.S. and cause a lot of headaches for the cartel down the road.[28] Later, when the godfathers learned that Salcedo had betrayed them, William offered money to Vicky Giron if she helped to locate Salcedo and other members of his family so they could be murdered.[29]

Flores described William's second office on the top floor of an office building adjoining the El Coral restaurant in Cali as a "secret location . . . equipped with a false wall that accessed a hidden stairway that ran parallel to an adjoining discotheque in the building to provide an escape route for Rodriguez Abadia." Flores also stated that he received Miguel's approved monthly salary and expense payments at this office.[30] How much money was William handling for an organization thought to be defunct, or at least on its deathbed? William received millions of dollars in the first eight months alone, according to Flores.[31]

In June 2002, the Colombian police issued an arrest warrant for William with the intention of extraditing him to the U.S. The U.S. Attorney's Office, Southern District of New York, had asked Colombia to extradite William to face drug trafficking charges. In February 2004, a grand jury indicted William and three of his associates, Jairo Villegas-Amariles, Francisco Ramirez and Victor Figueroa-Molineros, for attempting to smuggle five kilograms of cocaine into the U.S. According to the indictment, William's associates met with an undercover informant working for the FBI in September 2000 to discuss the receipt and distribution of more than 100 kilos of coke, which was to be shipped from Colombia to New York City. Then, on November 7, William sent an e-mail to the FBI informant providing him with a telephone number that could be used to reach Figueroa-Molineros to discuss the pending shipment. When Figueroa-Molineros met the informant two days later in New York City to discuss the shipment, U.S. authorities had enough evidence to present to a grand jury.[32] William remains a fugitive.

If the Rodriguez brothers go to trial in the U.S., George Morales can confirm that Miguel and Gilberto had easy access to the outside world during their incarceration and no serious problems running their crime business. Morales had begun distributing cocaine in the Miami area for the cartel, but was arrested in mid-1989 for buying twenty kilos of coke from a DEA informant named Rafael Lombrano. When Miguel ordered a hitman to kill Lombrano in October 1990, he fled to Colombia where, working under an assumed name, he helped set up a coffee smuggling route for the cartel. Morales was arrested again and jailed in La Picota prison, where he continued working for Miguel, eventually helping to arrange what authorities said was a test load of cocaine for shipment in a container of pumpkins from Panama. In April 2000, U.S. Customs seized the load upon the ships's arrival in Miami.[33]

That the surviving Cali cartel founders were still significant players in the drug trade is well illustrated by one smuggling operation. In 1997, U.S. Customs and FBI agents discovered a 2,400-pound cocaine shipment inside supposedly empty chlorine gas cylinders in the Port of Houston. Julio Jo Cipriano, a Cuban-American national, had been imprisoned in La Picota with Gilberto and Miguel after his arrest in March 1995. Jo became Miguel's personal secretary, and being fluent in Spanish and English, he translated newspapers from the U.S. for Miguel, including one relating to the seized 2,400-pound shipment in Houston. Miguel revealed to Jo that it belonged to his brother Gilberto. What happened after the bust illustrates how the brothers stuck with the strategies that had helped make them history's most powerful drug cartel. Two of the suspects arrested were Luis and Mauricio Arboleda. As they had done in the past when their associates were arrested, the Rodriguezes paid the expenses of at least Luis Arboleda and maintained the Arboledas and their families on routine monthly subsistence payments to ensure their continued loyalty.

With U.S. and Colombian authorities breathing hard down their necks, the Rodriguez brothers paid hush money to several other people as well. Jo for instance, told authorities that the brothers helped defray his expenses in La Picota until he was extradited to the U.S. in late 1999. The cartel also supported Jo's family members. His mother received payments from late 1991 until her arrival in the U.S. in January 2003 on condition that her son not cooperate with authorities. Sherezada Umanzor, his girlfriend, confirmed to authorities that she received subsistence money on a regular basis from Miguel and Gilberto, extending from Jo's arrival in La Picota until his extradition to the U.S. in 1999.

Yet the strategy of using hush money had created big problems for the cartel in the past. In the two trials of the U.S. lawyers working for the cartel, held in Miami in 1997 and 1998, federal prosecutors had presented a large amount of evidence to prove that the lawyers had, on the brothers' behalf, got associates to sign false statements and depositions. As Kacerosky noted, "This same substance payment program in exchange for silence about the organization led to the convictions of several lawyers in the earlier Cornerstone investigation for money laundering and obstruction of justice."

As in Operation Cornerstone, Gilberto and Miguel were able to get access to imprisoned associates who could testify against them. After the Colombian government approved Flores's extradition request, they moved him from prison to a holding cell, where two of Miguel and Gilberto's lawyers managed to visit and tell him that the brothers needed him to sign some documents. They handed Flores a pen and paper and then dictated a series of questions and answers that Flores wrote out in his hand. Flores later told authorities that the statement he wrote and signed, saying he had no first-hand knowledge of Gilberto and Miguel committing crimes between their imprisonment and December 1997, were false. The lawyers also ordered Flores to sign eight blank sheets of paper that Gilberto and Miguel planned to use at a later date.

In December 2003, the U.S. authorities initiated a legal action that they confidently expected would lead to one of the biggest victories in their War on Drugs. They announced the indictment of Gilberto, Miguel and nine other suspected associates on three charges: drug trafficking, money laundering and the continued obstruction of justice through murder and payment of hush money to associates and their families. As part of the indictment, U.S. authorities said they would seek the extradition of all eleven suspects and the forfeiture of $2.1 billion. "A decade ago, the Rodriguez bothers were at the top of their criminal game," said Roger P. Mackin, the Department of Homeland Security counter-narcotics officer. "The drug trafficking empire netted them billions. They owned vast properties and exercised great influence. They were the Colombian Untouchables. Now, because of the commitment of President Uribe, they are awaiting extradition to America to pay for their crimes."[34]

Three U.S. grand juries had indicted Gilberto and Miguel before, but given Colombian law, the cartel's ability to corrupt and the army of top-notch lawyers it had at its disposal, the godfathers had always managed to avoid extradition. Colombian law, however, changed. The two countries signed an extradition treaty in 1997 making it possible for the brothers to be sent to the United States to stand trial for crimes committed after December 17, 1997. Colombia's President Uribe was a tough law-and-order president, and had been signing extradition orders that were sending suspected drug traffickers to the U.S. *en masse.* When Colombia sent thirteen drug trafficking suspects to the U.S. in early November 2003, Cesar Garcia, an Associated Press reporter, wrote, "So many Colombians are being extradited to the United States on drug trafficking charges that a shuttle flight of sorts is taking them to America for justice."[35] The report went on to note that Colombia had extradited sixty-three nationals to the U.S. in 2004, while another seventy-seven who faced extradition had been captured.

U.S. officials were so confident that the Rodriguez brothers would join the streaming exodus that in August 2004 they held a conference call to discuss what would be the best jurisdiction in which to try them.[36] No one doubted what the decision of America's strong ally in the War on Drugs would be, and one day after U.S. announced its indictment, Colombian prosecutors filed court papers allowing the extradition of the eleven suspects.[37]

Judgment day for Gilberto Rodriguez arrived on November 4, 2004, when the Colombian Supreme Court ruled that the government could extradite him to the United States for trial. The high court said it was up to the government to decide if it wanted to put the Chess Player on a DEA plane to Miami. That was hardly an agonizing decision for Uribe. On November 9, he announced he would approve the drug lord's historic extradition.[38]

On December 3, 2004, the Chess Player, who had outwitted authorities for more than thirty years, was taken in an armored vehicle from La Picota maximum security prison in southern Bogota to a military base adjacent to Colombia's international airport. Even now, the authorities were taking no chances. Rodriguez – who was allowed to make one last phone call – wore a bulletproof vest over his brown jacket, as about 120 police officers and soldiers and a convoy of security cars escorted him. A police helicopter hovered overhead. At the airport, Gilberto was handed over to DEA agents representing at about 9:10 pm EST and he was on his way to the United States.[39]

"Gilberto Rodriguez Orejuela is alleged to have trafficked in illegal drugs that tear at the fabric of society and draw the innocent away from safe and productive lives," said Attorney General John

Ashcroft. "Those who violate federal drug laws should never believe that drug trafficking from outside our borders puts them beyond the reach of justice. Thanks to the hard work of law enforcement officers both here and abroad, Rodriguez-Orejuela will now stand trial for his actions."[40] Daniel Marcos Jiménez, U.S. Attorney for the Southern District of Florida, added, "This is a watershed moment in our nation's war against drugs. Our prosecution puts drug traffickers on notice that no matter where they are or who they are, they will eventually be brought to justice. After more than a decade of hard work, I am extremely proud that our prosecutors in the Southern District of Florida and our law enforcement partners made this day a reality."[41]

Held in solitary confinement awaiting trial, Rodriguez faced charges that he imported and distributed more than 200,000 kilos of cocaine from 1999 to July 2002, concealed in items such as concrete posts, frozen vegetables, watermelons and ceramic tiles. He was also accused of killing or bribing witnesses and of conspiracy to launder money. The indictment sought to seize $2.1 billion, which prosecutors said represented money made from drugs and money laundering.

As the Chess Player's criminal career headed towards its sordid conclusion, the remaining question was whether brother Miguel would follow him. There was speculation that Colombia would not extradite Miguel because he was on dialysis. U.S. officials were confident, however, though as one explained the day after Gilberto's extradition, "We just have to wait for the legal procedures to continue. Unfortunately, Miguel's case has yet to be presented to the Colombian Supreme Court for final ruling so my guess is that it will likely be two to three months until his extradition . . . I doubt that the Colombian government will want to skip any legal steps to speed things up, so that everything is by the book."[42]

Meantime, the United States continues its relentless attack on the Cali cartel's infrastructure. "We finally added Maria Ximena Wilson Garcia, the wife of Miguel's son William, to the SDNT list," a Treasury official revealed. "This will, of course, put pressure on William who has been a fugitive for at least two years. It's nice to see Gilberto get off the plane in Miami in handcuffs, but we can't let up. We've seen how the Cali cartel has risen like a phoenix from the ashes before."[43]

Gilberto Rodriguez once offered a depressing but prescient take on the cocaine trade. "Economics has a natural law," he declared. "Supply is determined by the demand. When cocaine stops being consumed, when there's no demand for it . . . that will be the end of that business."[44] That end may be nowhere in sight, but it is safe to declare that at least one major battle in the War on Drugs has been won. And when the end finally comes for what's left of the Cali cartel, history's most powerful drug trafficking mafia, it will come with a whimper, not a bang.

Conclusion

What Goes Around

Pablo Escobar, Carlos Lehder, and the other Medellin cartel godfathers are called the Henry Fords of cocaine trafficking. We need to go one step further with the Cali cartel and call it the McDonald's of cocaine trafficking because its godfathers turned drug trafficking into a major corporate enterprise. The Cali cartel had a set formula and knew how to make it work.

– Lou Weiss, DEA agent

It has been less than a decade since U.S. and Colombian law enforcement took down the godfathers from Cali. Today, the DEA regards that victory as perhaps the greatest in the agency's history.[1] Agents also believe the takedown provides an important lesson for those waging the War on Drugs. "At no time can we allow a criminal organization to get as powerful as the Cali cartel did," said Bob Nieves, DEA chief of operations from 1989 to 1995. "The Cali cartel was close to turning Colombia into a narco democracy."[2]

Other sources, however, believe that the takedown of the Cali cartel has made little difference in the War on Drugs, especially in terms of reducing the level of corruption in Colombia. For drug traffickers in Colombia, it has been business as usual, they say. "The corruption of Colombia's institutions, while still pervasive, is less visible today than it was in the mid- to early 1990s," said Bruce Bagley, a professor of international relations at the University of Miami, who has written extensively on the international drug trade. "We are still seeing the corruption of all sectors of Colombian society, especially at the local level, where it is much easier to bribe and manipulate. Groups that monitor corruption worldwide still rank Colombia as one of the world's most corrupt countries."[3] United States officials who served there agree. "I have a lot of respect for the DEA and the work they do in Colombia, but the drug trafficking situation in Colombia is not much different than when the Cali cartel was operating," said Myles Frechette, U.S. ambassador to Colombia from 1994 to 1997. "The traffickers have decentralized."[4]

While the significance of the Cali cartel takedown is debatable, it's not an overstatement to say that the cartel succeeded in the drug trade like no other criminal group before or since. Its success can be attributed largely to its style of operation and its innovative approach to criminality. For nearly a decade after its big-three founding godfathers, Jose Santacruz Londono and Gilberto and Miguel Rodriguez Orejuela, began building their organization, the cartel was willing to let its chief rival from Medellin assume the high profile in the Colombian drug trade. The Medellin cartel grabbed the headlines, became a household name in Colombia, tried to become part of the political establishment, and eventually went to war with the state, in a vicious clash that spawned a new term in the political lexicon – narco-terrorism. "The Colombian government hunted down and killed Pablo Escobar because he was a terrorist, not a drug trafficker," explained Mark Eiler, a DEA intelligence analyst and expert on Colombia. "If he had been smart enough to contain his psychopathic tendencies, he might still be alive today and doing well."[5]

The Cali cartel, on the other hand, adopted a more businesslike approach and went about building its criminal empire quietly, downplaying violence and terror as the principal means of achieving its objective. It's not that the cartel eschewed violence. As this book shows, it could be as vicious as the next group of gangsters when it needed to be. Still, in pursuit of its objectives, the Cali cartel preferred to offer the bribe, gather intelligence information on its enemies, and use the latest in telecommunications technology to coordinate its activities. Its intelligence system rivaled those employed by many governments. Indeed, the cartel's intelligence was probably the difference in its successful war of attrition with Pablo Escobar. The cartel was also a pioneer in the criminal world in its use of faxes, beepers, cell phones, pay phones, encryption, and computer information systems.

At the height of its power in the early 1990s, the Cali cartel ran its commodity empire more on the model of a multinational corporation than a criminal enterprise. It treated its members like company employees, hired the best person for the job, used business strategy to market its illegal product, and shifted operations from one locale to another as economic and political conditions necessitated. "Pablo Escobar, Carlos Lehder, and the other Medellin cartel godfathers are called the Henry Fords of cocaine trafficking," said Lou Weiss, DEA agent. "We need to go one step further with the Cali cartel and call it the McDonald's of cocaine trafficking because its godfathers turned drug trafficking into a major corporate enterprise. The Cali cartel had a set formula and knew how to make it work."[6]

The godfathers from Cali didn't kill leading citizens of the state as their Medellin rivals did nor engage in narco-terrorism. So for nearly two decades the Colombian government allowed them the space to grow their criminal enterprise. As a result, the cartel was able to grab seventy to eighty percent of the cocaine market by the early 1990s, according to DEA estimates.[7] The cartel's low-key style helped it build extensive distribution networks right under the nose of U.S. law enforcement, giving it an initial advantage against its deadly adversary. Even when law enforcement discovered the cartel's existence in the mid-1980s and figured out what they were doing in their communities, it was extremely difficult for the authorities to penetrate and disrupt the mafia. The cartel operated with the compartmentalization of a terrorist organization, while its associates were willing to go to jail, fearing what could happen to them and their families if they informed. Besides, they knew that the cartel would take care of their families while they were in jail.

After law enforcement finally took down Pablo Escobar at the end of 1993, it became inevitable that the men from Cali would become the focus of law enforcement's attention. Always a little ahead of the curve, the Cali godfathers saw the writing was on the wall and realized that it was only a matter of time before they would be in a grave in Colombia or a jail cell in the United States. So they began using their legions of lawyers to negotiate their way out of the drug trade before they became law enforcement's principal target.

By the early 1990s, they had forged a crime multinational too huge to ignore. It had a global reach and thousands of employees and was involved in every aspect of the drug trade. As drug trafficking expert Rennselaer Lee pointed out, "The sheer size of mafia operations require their explicit coordination of many transactions, as well as a system of information gathering and record keeping. Cocaine syndicates are too big and too complex to escape detection, and they are too vulnerable to penetration by law enforcement agents."[8]

The Cali cartel began appearing more frequently on law enforcement's radar screen as it mushroomed into a multinational enterprise. By the time authorities discovered the huge cocaine shipment in concrete cement posts in August 1991 in Miami, law enforcement had discerned a pattern to the cartel's criminality. As law enforcement successfully investigated its operations, the cartel found it increasingly difficult to hire the talent it needed to fill the ranks of its depleted managerial pool. Given its problems, its members even began breaking some of its well-thought-out rules, evident in the move that allowed Harold Ackerman, its so-called ambassador to the United States, to wear three hats. This made it easier for law enforcement to penetrate the cartel's financial structure once Ackerman was caught.

The investigation was furthered by the enormous volume of records the cartel generated as it grew. It didn't help the cartel that the wrong CEO was running affairs at the most critical juncture in its development. Miguel Rodriguez, who took over day-to-day management about 1990, was a micromanager who couldn't seem to let go of business matters or didn't know how to delegate responsibility. Micromanaging affairs in the United States and Europe from headquarters in Cali could work early in its history when the cartel was small and law enforcement had little inkling about its activities, but not when it became the size of an IBM or General Motors. In fact, Miguel's micromanaging style became a liability. Imagine the CEO of IBM or General Motors, based in

New York City, directly trying to oversee business operations in its chief market, Colombia. Sooner or later, communication is bound to break down.

The takedown of the Cali cartel and its Medellin predecessor provided a wise lesson for other Colombia drug traffickers; namely, becoming too big and complex an organization will make you more vulnerable to a takedown. So today, we see a radically different type of Colombian drug-trafficking organization. Gone is the huge octopus as represented by the Cali cartel, which employed thousands, had a global reach, smuggled large-scale shipments and earned Fortune 500-like revenues that reached $7 billion annually.[9] Instead, we have the so-called *cartelitos* or baby cartels, which try to operate as discreetly as the Cali combine did, but don't rely on the sophisticated organizational structure and communications systems that it employed.

"Today's cartelitos have learned from the past," explained Pedro M. Guzman, a DEA special agent based in Bogota since 1999. "In the days of the Cali cartel, drug traffickers relied on the cell phone to manage their day-to-day business activities. Today's criminals are using the Internet and push to talk radios as their main means of communication. They sell directly to the Mexicans so the United States won't be able to make extradition cases against them, no matter where the cocaine ends up. They like to have face-to-face meetings, which obviously alleviates the need for micromanaging and the constant need to monitor cell phones in the United States."[10]

This change began in the early 1990s, well before the Rodriguez brothers were captured and their empire began to crumble. By July 1993, an estimated 200 trafficking groups were operating throughout Colombia, at least 100 of which were located in the Cali strongholds of the northern Valle del Cauca area.[11] Six years later, a PBS *Frontline* show reported that "the DEA and Colombian National Police believe there are more than three hundred active drug smuggling organizations in Colombia. Cocaine is shipped to every industrialized nation in the world and profits remain incredibly high."[12]

Even the Cali cartel saw the need to downsize and overhaul its structure. In April 1996, *Organized Crime Digest* magazine reported that "a major shakedown of the world's premier drug cartels has transformed the way the business is conducted in the United States. The Cali Cartel has responded to increased police pressure in New York City by replacing multi-ton shipments with smaller ones, eliminating flashy displays of wealth, hiring new operatives, and moving stash houses and communications to the suburbs."[13]

Yet, even with the downsizing, the flow of drugs out of Colombia has not diminished. As Professor Bruce Bagley pointed out, "despite the U.S. government's provision of almost one billion dollars in aid to Colombia over the decade of the 1990s, by 1999 Colombia had become the premier coca-cultivating country in the world, producing more coca leaf than Peru and Bolivia combined."[14]

The *cartelitos* have not only downsized, they've diversified, and cocaine and cannabis are not the only drug trafficked from Colombia today. As early as 1995, Colombia became the largest producer of poppies in the Western Hemisphere, producing a third more of the crop than Mexico.[15] By 1999, eighty-five percent of the heroin seized by federal authorities in the northeast United States was of Colombian origin.[16] Meanwhile, law enforcement is increasingly concerned about the growing role of Colombia in the trafficking of the popular drug Ecstasy, especially to European markets.[17] "Putting the Colombian and Medellin cartels out of business caused only minor disruptions to the flow of illicit drugs from Colombia to the U.S. and European markets," Bagley noted.[18]

One can easily assume that, because of their size, the *cartelitos* do not have as much reach as the super-cartels and experience more difficulty in moving their product to market. But that assumption is dead wrong. Their use of the latest in technology, as well as the strategic alliances that the Cali cartel largely put in place, has helped them thrive. As late as the fall of 1997, Interpol reported that the Cali cartel had forged alliances with the Russian mafia, which was supplying the cartel with military equipment, including MK-47 rifles, grenades, and helicopters, in exchange for cocaine.[19] On entering a warehouse in Bogota during a predawn raid on September 7, 2000, Colombian police were shocked to find a 100-foot submarine under construction. The submarine was a joint project of the Colombians and the Russian mob, and the plan was to use it to smuggle tons of narcotics.[20]

According to the *Los Angeles Times*, the discovery of the submarine was the first solid evidence that a close partnership exists between Colombia's new, smaller cartels and the Russian mob.[21] Intelligence analysts report, however, that Colombian traffickers had met with Russian, Chinese and Japanese criminal groups at three summits (at least) between 1994 and 1998 to discuss ways they could better coordinate their activities relating to the marketing, distribution, and smuggling of illicit drug shipments.[22] "Organized crime has gone truly global and its main criminal groups have been meeting to find ways to better divide up the planet," explained Arnaud de Borchgrave, director of the Global Organized Crime Project at the Center for Strategic and International Studies in Washington, D.C.[23]

In another important international development, the Colombians have been willing to cede more control and responsibility to Mexicans in the smuggling of drugs to their biggest market, the United States. This trend began during the Cali era in the early 1990s when law enforcement disrupted the cartel's distribution routes through the Caribbean, and so they turned to their Mexican colleagues to help to move drugs. Today, the Mexicans, who are paid a fee to move the cocaine across the Colombian-Mexican border, are no longer merely transporters for the Colombians. They now move the drugs to the point of sale and, in return, receive a commission from their Colombian suppliers.[24]

The North American Free Trade Agreement (NAFTA) has made it easier for Mexicans to move drugs across the U.S.-Mexico border. Ironically, globalization, the trend that seeks to integrate the world community financially and economically, has spurred the growth of international drug trafficking. National borders have declined in importance, and customs and security safeguards have weakened with the creation of free trade bodies such as NAFTA and the European Community. This trend has made it easier for international organized crime to move into new markets, distribute illegal goods and services, and shift their profits around the world to countries who may be eager to serve as safe havens for cash deposits and laundered transactions. It's no wonder that some DEA and customs agents working the U.S.-Mexican border have jokingly referred to NAFTA as the North American Free Drug Trafficking Agreement.[25]

As national borders decline in importance, millions of people from all parts of the world are migrating, searching for a better life, whether it is Africa, Eastern Europe, or South America, in attempts to avoid ethnic conflict and turmoil or for a variety of other reasons. With migrants come criminals who exploit immigrant communities for illegal means and use those communities as strong bases from which to launch their criminal activities.[26]

These developments show that the current strategy employed in the War in Drugs – that is, focusing on single targets – ignores the reality that when you dismantle one cartel another is bound to fill the void. The truth of the observation that, as long as there is a demand for an illegal market, criminals will try to get the illegal items to the market, is no better illustrated than by the rise and fall of the Cali cartel. But while governments may not be able to stop the drugs from reaching the marketplace, they can certainly develop a more effective strategy that makes it more difficult to do so. For starters, the United States and its allies in the War on Drugs can take a lesson from the criminals' playbook and make a more concerted effort to establish effective strategic alliances. Countries, for instance, can develop partnerships to deal with what is an international problem and the root causes of the drug trafficking problem, such as providing alternatives to farmers and others in Third World countries for whom the drug trade provides the only lifeline. As US Senator and presidential candidate John Kerry explained, "It is far easier to single out an enemy but far more difficult to forge a lasting strategy to deal with the conditions that allow those cartels to thrive and which remain in place after their leaders were removed."[27]

Colombia is a graphic example of how enterprising groups, traditionally criminal or otherwise, will always be willing to enter a lucrative market such as illegal drugs if the opportunity presents itself. The guerrillas and paramilitaries have expanded their roles in the drug trade and helped to fill the void created by the Cali cartel takedown. The FARC's 20,000-strong guerrilla force is involved in the trade, mainly in protecting drug traffickers' crops, labs, and airfields for a fee and taxing peasants who grow crops in areas under guerrilla control. By the year 2000, the guerrillas' total annual take from the drug trade was put as high as $400 million.[28] "The guerrillas have taken a direct role in the drug trade because the vacuum could easily be filled," Bagley explained. "The money they are making from the drug trade has given them the degree of autonomy they need to pursue their agenda."[29]

But there has been sharp debate about the nature of the guerrillas' role in the Colombian drug trade. Are the guerrillas drug traffickers in the true sense – that is, are they smuggling drugs internationally from Colombia? Although the Colombian government has tried to make a case for the rebel–international drug connection, many experts on the country say no strong evidence has been uncovered to support the accusation. "There are reports that the guerrillas have moved the drugs across the border into Venezuela, but we don't have any evidence that they are international traffickers of drugs," said Myles Frechette, former U.S. ambassador to Colombia.[30]

Other observers agreed. Joe Toft, head of the DEA office in Colombia from 1988 to 1995, said, "They make a lot of money from drug trafficking, but they are not traffickers as the Medellin or Cali cartels were."[31] Francisco Thoumi, author of *Political Economy and Illegal Drugs in Colombia*, said, "I have not seen evidence to suggest that FARC has developed exporting capabilities. I don't think they can move drugs beyond Colombia."[32]

The 10,000-strong paramilitary group *AUC* (*Autodefensas Unidas de Colombia*) has also financed its operations through the drug trade. In January 2000 Carlos Castano admitted on Colombian television that his militia routinely charges a tax on the coca and poppy crops that Colombian farmers grow.[33] Fueled by the drug trade, the brutal struggle between guerrillas and paramilitaries has contributed to at least 3,500 murders annually.[34] Human rights groups have criticized the U.S. and Colombian governments for focusing more attention on guerrilla involvement in the drug trade than they have on paramilitaries.[35]

But while the paramilitaries have, no doubt, profited from the drug trade, the activity threatens to tear their movement apart. In September 2002, the *National Post* reported, "Drug trafficking has fractured Colombia's paramilitary army into a collection of potent regional factions that disagree over whether the financial benefit of protecting the country's vast cocaine trade outweighs the political costs and internal corruption it has brought the group."[36]

The U.S. government has indicted the leaders of *FARC* and the *AUC* on trafficking charges, while putting their armies on its official list of terrorist organizations. In its pursuit of the War on Terrorism, Uncle Sam has downgraded the War on Drugs as a priority, but has linked the two. In August 2002, the Office of National Drug Control Policy began running advertisements that urge Americans to stop buying illegal drugs like cocaine and heroin because that can help fund the terrorists who are trying to destroy America. "If you quit drugs, you join the fight against terror in America," President George Bush declared.[37]

That message is debatable, but President's Bush's aggressive move to link the War on Dugs to the War on Terrorism does raises an interesting and timely question: Are there any lessons to be learned from the history of the War on Drugs and the takedown of Cali cartel that can help the U.S. government in its war with international terrorists? Since the mega-terrorist events of September 11, 2001, President George Bush and his lieutenants have repeatedly told the nation that the United States is involved in a conflict unlike any other in its history. The War on Terrorism does not have opposing battalions, large numbers of troops, and sophisticated technology, and the enemy can be anywhere. So fighting a new type of war requires new strategies, as well as new sacrifices from the American people, if it is to be victorious. At least that has been the message from President Bush. But the War on Terrorism, as it has been fought so far, is not new. In fact, it's much like the old War on Drugs, which has consumed America's attention, money, and resources for the past two decades.

There are interesting parallels between the long War on Drugs and the War on Terrorism as it has been fought so far. From the beginning of the War on Terrorism, the United States has attacked the supply side of the conflict. Central to U.S. strategy has been the belief that eliminating Osama Bin Laden and his terror network will substantially curb the supply of terrorists and terrorism. That strategy has been at the heart of the United States' modern War on Drugs as well. During the past two decades, the United States has tried to eliminate the Osama Bin Ladens or kingpins of drug trafficking, but even though the Rodriguez Orejuela brothers, Jose Santacruz Londono, Pacho Herrera, and other drug kingpins have risen and fallen, the supply of drugs has flowed unabated to the streets of the United States. In fact, drugs like cocaine and heroin are cheaper and more plentiful today than they were in 1982, the year Ronald Reagan launched the modern War on Drugs.

From day one of the War on Drugs, the United States has also pursued a search-and-destroy policy of interdiction that focuses on eradicating the drug problem at the source. What's happened to Colombia during the past twenty years well illustrates the result. Huge fields of coca and poppy have been wiped out with herbicides; tons of drugs, seized; hundreds of drug labs, destroyed; and thousands of drug traffickers, corrupt government officials, and the man and woman in the street, jailed. Yet, what has all this accomplished? Colombia is still at the center of the drug trafficking universe, while it teeters politically on the verge of disintegration.

Perhaps the most disturbing parallel between the two wars has been the lack of attention that the United States has paid to the demand side. In the War on Drugs, the United States has all but ignored the root issues – why many people take drugs and why some people are willing to cultivate illegal crops, despite our best interdiction efforts. Likewise, in the War on Terrorism, the United States ignores the root issues – why Uncle Sam is so hated in some parts of the world and why some people continue to gravitate to the terrorist camp. For example, the Bush administration continues to play a passive role in resolving the Palestinian-Israeli conflict, even though Osama Bin Laden has been able to fool many in the Muslim world into believing that the Palestinian cause is central to his terror network's war against the United States. Until the United States addresses the root causes, it shouldn't expect any long-term success in this "new" war. As has happened with the War on Drugs, the War on Terrorism will become just another long war with no end.

Finally, in terms of strategy, a critical lesson can be learned from law enforcement's twenty-year investigation of the Cali cartel. The godfathers from Cali had a jump-start on law enforcement, not only because of their low-key style and disciplined organization but also because of the rivalries, competition, and turf battles that plagued the investigation. As this book shows, it was only when law enforcement began to cooperate and share information that headway was made in the investigation. Some disturbing reports released early in the War on Terrorism revealed that U.S. government agencies were committing the same mistake. Fortunately, however, the Bush administration has recognized the problem.

The agencies involved in fighting terrorism must realize that the terrorist organizations are much like the Cali cartel: more sophisticated and more of a challenge than any single agency or government can handle. The U.S. government will need to widen its approach beyond the single-agency focus if it is to succeed.

The good news is that the U.S. government realizes that the experience and talent of DEA agents who investigated the Cali cartel can help out in the War on Terrorism. After all, the cartel did operate on the terrorist model, and some striking similarities exist between it and al-Qaeda in terms of their organizations.

Veteran drug mob investigators like Ken Robinson, Bill Mockler, Greg Passic, Bob Nieves, and Bill Bruton are now sharing their expertise and wisdom with the current generation of law enforcement to assist with what is perhaps its biggest challenge ever. "I hope we've learned something," Ken Robinson said. "Winning the War on Terrorism is going to take focus, cooperation, sustained interest, as well as resources. Information has got to be spread around among the agencies involved. We can't have secrets. I agree with others who say we have to fight the War on Terrorism like we attacked the Cali cartel."

If we have learned well the lessons from the Cali cartel investigation, perhaps that will be the enduring legacy of what was certainly the biggest takedown in law enforcement history.

A Chronology
of the Cali Cartel

---

500 B.C.   Earliest date assigned by archeologists to coca leaves found in Peruvian burial sites

1855   Cocaine first extracted from coca leaves

1939   Gilberto Rodriguez Orejuela born

1940   Office of Foreign Funds Control, predecessor of Office of Foreign Assets Control, established

1943   Miguel Rodriguez Orejuela and Jose Santacruz Londono born

1949   Pablo Escobar born

1950   Office of Foreign Assets Control established

1953   Amado Carrillo Fuentes born

1960   Rosso Jose Serrano joins Colombian National Police

1970   New York Drug Enforcement Task Force established

1972   August Record extradited to United States

1973   Operation Springboard concluded
        Chilean president Salvador Allende overthrown

1974   Banco de Trabajadores founded
        DEA launches Operation Buccaneer

1975   Operation Banshee launched
        Gilberto Rodriguez arrested in Peru
        September: Gilberto and Miguel Rodriguez ranked as 58th and 62nd on list of Colombia's top 113 drug traffickers

1976   Pablo Escobar arrested in possession of 30 pounds of cocaine
        U.S. government deports Carlos Lehder to Colombia

	Jose Santacruz arrested
	November: DEA agent Octavio Gonzalez assassinated
1977	U.S. fact-finding mission to Colombia
	Jose Santacruz arrested
1978	Carlos Lehder buys Norman's Cay
	March: CBS's "60 Minutes" reveals existence of "cocaine memorandum"
	Summer: DEA's New York office receives letter from concerned citizens committee of Jackson Heights, Queens
	September: CI walks into the NYDETF Office with information about drug trafficking in Queens
	NYDETF busts Nelson Gomez and launches investigation of Cali cartel
1979	U.S. fact-finding mission to Colombia
	Dadeland Massacre in Miami
	Jose and Amparo Santacruz meet Alexander Blarek in Colombia
	January: NYDETF identifies Cali associate Jose Patino
	Gilberto and Miguel Rodriguez found Colombia Radio Group (GRC)
1980	Group Five detectives go to Miami to investigate Tulio Ayerbe
	July: Jose Patino busted
1981	Authorities seize Gilberto Rodriguez's ranch in Hope Hull, Alabama
	Antonio Cervantes becomes Jose Santacruz's right-hand man for cartel's New York operation
	DEA opens offices in Medellin and Cali
	July: Santacruz hires interior decorator Alexander Blarek
	September: Group Five investigators Ken Robinson and Rich Crawford visit Blarek
	November: Marta Nieves Ochoa kidnapped
	Drug traffickers organize MAS
1982	South Florida Task Force established
1983	Antonio Cervantes arrested in Waycross, Georgia
	FARC guerrillas gunned down Alvaro Uribe's father at the family ranch in Antioquia province
1984	Rodrigo Lara Bonilla, Colombian Justice Minister, authorizes raid on Tranquilandia

Michael Abbell leaves U.S. Justice Department

Colombian president Belasario Betancourt declares "war without quarter" on country's drug traffickers

Gilberto Rodriguez and Jorge Ochoa go to Spain together

NYDETF seizes Jose Gusto Guzman ledgers

February: DEA agents from around country meet in Washington, D.C. to coordinate investigations of Cali cartel

Death of Rodrigo Lara Bonilla

March: Group Five investigators search home of Jose Gusto Guzman

June: Santacruz sends his associates to Gibsonville, North Carolina

October: Spanish police arrest Gilberto Rodriguez and Jorge Ochoa

1985   NYDETF and Troop K of the NYSP launch KNEU-86055 investigation

DEA agent Enrique Camarena murdered in Mexico

Carrillo Fuentes assumes leadership of Juarez Cartel

April: Explosion at the Minden lab

May: Cartel opens lab in Orange County, Virginia

July: Police bust cocaine processing lab in Orange County

November: Colombian guerrillas storm Colombian Palace of Justice

1986   Joseph Stroh becomes currency broker for Cali cartel

Colombian President Virgilio Barco implements extradition treaty with United States and Medellin cartel responds with narco-terror campaign

November: Colonel Jaime Ramirez Gomez assassinated

Jorge Ochoa arrested near Cali

December: Guillermo Cano assassinated

Jorge Ochoa freed

1987   March: Gilberto Rodriguez goes on trial in United States and is acquitted

September: Freddie Aquilera arrested

1988   Honduras deports Juan Ramon Ballesteros to United States

Carlos Mauro Hoyos Jiminez assassinated

Jose Gonzalo Rodriguez Gacha goes to New York City

January: Large bomb explodes outside Monaco, Escobar's

luxury apartment in Medellin, and the War of Cartels begins

February: Police arrest Luis Ramos

June: Authorities find $1.7 billion in cocaine aboard *Amazon Sky*

1989 DEA launches Operation Pisces

DEA launches Operation Green Ice

Luis Carlos Galan assassinated

Operation Offsides set up at World Cup in Rome

September: 21.5 tons of cocaine seized in Sylmar, California

Berlin Wall falls

November: Avianca airplane explodes in sky

December: Rodriguez Gacha killed

Gilberto and Miguel Rodriguez begin arranging for their companies to be held under names of family members and trusted associates.

1990 May: Cesar Gaviria elected president

June: Gaviria appoints General Serrano to head Colombian Narcotics Police

August: Gaviria makes generous offers to drug traffickers

December: Fabio Ochoa turns himself in

1991 Jorge and Juan Ochoa turn themselves in to Colombian authorities

Jose Franklin Jurado Rodriguez arrested in Luxembourg

KNEU-86055 ends

Colombian Congress votes down extradition treaty

June: Pablo Escobar turns himself in

Authorities discover concrete fence posts on ship *Mercandian* in port of Miami and Operation Cornerstone begins

September: Jorge Salcedo goes to Nicaragua to buy bomb for the assassination of Pablo Escobar

November: Ramiro Herrera Buitrago arrested

According to Guillermo Pallomari's testimony, the Rodriguez brothers ask him to start transferring assets out of his name

1992 Kingpin Strategy launched

Carlos Giron captured

Operation Wizard 11 seizes 13,000 kilos of cocaine

Operation Green Ice concludes

European trade barriers erased

January: Authorities find mutilated corpses of Moncada brothers and Galeano brothers near Escobar's prison

Ivan Urdinola Grajales arrested and imprisoned

April: Gustavo De Greiff becomes Colombia's prosecuting attorney general

Jorge Lopez arrested

May: Giovanni Falcone assassinated

July: Escobar "escapes" from prison

October: Harold Ackerman retains a lawyer who is not on Cali cartel payroll

1993   DEA and IRS launch Operation Dinero

Soviet Union dissolved

January: Escobar's narco-terror war resumed

Colombian authorities launch first raid on Cali cartel financial infrastructure

February: Pepes emerge

April: Carlos Torres arrested

August: De Greiff meets with Cali cartel lawyers

November: Gustavo De Greiff attends symposium where Karl Schmoke speaks

December: Pablo Escobar killed

1994   Samper sends Serrano to Colombian Embassy in Washington and then recalls him to serve as head of CNP

Operation Dinero shuts down

January: Carlos Torres convicted

March: Claudio Endo killed

May: Authorities find supercomputer in Santacruz's office

June: Ernesto Samper elected Colombian president

July: Alberto Ochoa-Soto arrested

September: Pasquale C. Locatelli arrested

October: Joe Toft resigns from DEA

December: De Greiff finishes term as prosecuting attorney general

Samper launches Operation Splendor

1995   In early 1995, Colombian government begins raids on Cali property

Ochoa-Soto killed

January: President Clinton implements Executive Order 11947

March: United States decertifies Colombia

Juan Carlos Ramirez Abadia surrenders to Colombian authorities and imprisoned

May: Ruben Prieto reads cable about CI who knows Flaco

June: Indictment of 59 people in Miami as part of Operation Cornerstone

Gilberto Rodriguez captured

Mario Del Basto captured

Henry Loiaza surrenders

Victor Patino surrenders

Fanor Arizabaleta captured

July: Chepe Santacruz captured

July: Chris Feistl and Dave Mitchell meet with Jorge Salcedo

Raid on apartment 402 in Cali, Miguel Rodriguez escapes

August: Miguel Rodriguez captured

Pallomari's wife disappears and Pallomari flees to the United States

September: President Clinton issues Executive Order 12978

1996 Assassination attempt on William Rodriguez

January: Chepe Santacruz escapes from prison

Juan Garcia Abrego arrested and convicted

March: United States decertifies Colombia

Julio Fabio Urdinola Grajales arrested and imprisoned

Juan Carlos "El Chupeta" Ramirez Abadia surrenders

May: Operation Zorro ends

June: Colombian Congress finds Samper innocent

August: Chepe Santacruz killed

Cali cartel arranges to have pharmaceutical drugs sold by Dromarca to companies located in several counties

Children of Gilberto and Miguel Rodriguez give interview to *Newsweek* magazine

1997 January: Gilberto and Miguel Rodriguez convicted

March: Attempted assassination on drug trafficker Wilmer Alirio Varela's life

July: Amado Carrillo Fuentes dies on operating table
Pallomari testifies in Miami
September: Pacho Herrera surrenders
December: Colombian Congress passes extradition law
Pallomari pleads guilty in U.S. court
Cali cartel commissons study to see what else they can do to avoid sanctions
U.S. authorities discover a 2,400-pound cocaine shipment inside supposedly empty chlorine cylinders in port of Houston
U.S. and Colombia sign extradition treaty

1998   January: Arnaldo "Lucho" Botero captured
February: Nelson Urrego Cardenas captured
April: Cali Cartel takes U.S. Government to court over OFAC sanctions
August: Fernando Flores Germandia captured
November: Pacho Herrera killed
Cali cartel takes U.S. Government to court a second time

1999   U.S. Customs agent Ed Kacerosky starts receiving information that that the Rodriguez brothers are still involved in drug trafficking
Fabio Ochoa arrested and extradited to the United States as part of Operation Millennium
March: Cali cartel loses in court over first case regarding OFAC sanctions
September: Rodrigo Espinosa killed

2000   August:Juan Carlos Ramirez Abadia added to list of SDNTs
September: Rodrigo Espinosa killed
Carlos Castano reveals paramilitaries involved in drug trade

2002   Four years added to Miguel Rodriguez's sentence
May: Alvaro Uribe wins presidency of Colombia in landslide
June: Colombian police issue arrest warrant for William Rodriguez
November: Judge orders Gilberto Rodriguez released from jail
December: OFAC announces that the number of assets blocked under EO 12978 has reached 548
Victor Patino extradited to the U.S. two days after his prison release

2003   March: Justice orders Gilberto Rodriguez arrested and imprisoned

December: U.S. authorities announce the indictment of Miguel and Gilberto Rodriguez Orejuela and nine associates and their intention to seek their extradition

2004   February: A U.S. grand jury indicts William Rodriguez and three associates for drug trafficking

March: U.S. government announces two-count indictment of Gilberto and Miguel Rodriguez and files extradition affidavits requesting the Colombian government extradite the brothers

May: U.S. government indicts Juan Carlos Rodriguez Abadia

August: National Security archive releases declassified document linking President Uribe to Medellin cartel

Colombian government seizes Cali cartel's flagship company, Drogas de Rebaja pharmaceutical chain

September: Total number of assets blocked under EO 12978 reaches 1094

November: President Uribe approves Gilberto Rodriguez extradition to United States

December: Gilberto Rodriguez extradited to the U.S.

Selected Bibliography

Primary Sources

Interviews (on the record)

Harold Ackerman, Peter Andreas, Crescencio Arcos, Bruce Bagley, Rick Barrett, Rand Beers, Craig Benedict, Billy Bruton, Jorge Cardona, Tom Cash, Steve Casto, Tom Constantine, John Constanzo, Ken Cook, Rich Crawford, Arnaud De Borchgrave, Jessica De Grazia, Gustavo De Greiff, Monica De Greiff, Francisco Diaz, Robert Drexler, Tracey Eaton, Mark Eiler, Juan Carlos Esguerra, Chris Feistl, Myles Frechette, Cesar Gaviria, Robert Gelbard, Ron Goldstock, Lee Granato, Robert Grosse, Pedro Guzman, Michael Horn, Pat Hynes, Al James, Feliz Jimenez, Ed Kacerosky, Michael Kane, Terrance Kelley, John Kerry, Robin Kirk, Michael Kuhlman, Skip Latson, Rennselaer Lee, Carlos Lemos, John T. Mackey, Gill Macklin, Bill Mante, Jerry McArdle, Phillip McLean, Patricia McRae, Andy Massing, Robert Michaelis, Dave Mitchell, John Moody, Ethan Nadelmann, Terry O'Neill, Rodrigo Pardo, Greg Passic, Andres Pastrana, Paul Paz y Minao, William Pearson, Javier Pena, Ruben Prieto, Alma Beatriz Rengifo, Ken Robinson, Peter Romero, Chris Rush, Ed Ryan, Jerry Salameh, Ernesto Samper, Noemi Sanin, Charles Saphos, Peter Dale Scott, Bob Sears, Rosso José Serrano, Michael Skol, Sandy Smith, Greg Szczeszek, Francisco Thoumi, Bonnie Tischler, Joe Toft, Alphonso Valdivieso, German Velasquez, Luis Velez, Doug Wankel, Alexander Watson, Richard Weber, and Lou Weiss.

Unpublished Papers

Bagley, Bruce. "Drug Trafficking, Political Violence and U.S. Policy in Colombia in the 1990s. Unpublished paper, 2002.

Bruton, Bill. "Money Laundering Is Not a Corporate Problem." Unpublished paper, 2001.

"Narco Mercantilists: Assessing the Rise of Colombian Heroin Trafficking." Unpublished paper, Department of Defense, NSA, n.d.

Archival Documents

Letters from Cesar Gaviria and correspondence between Cesar Gaviria and Gustavo De Greiff, 1994 (in possession of Cesar Gaviria).

Letters from Gustavo de Greiff, 1994–1997 (in possession of Gustavo De Greiff).

Letter from drug cartels to Juan Carlos Esguerra, 1991 (in possession of Juan Carlos Esguerra).

Memorandum from Ed Kacerosky to Chris Feistl, 1995.

The author also consulted substantial primary material released in response to Freedom of Information requests made to the DEA, CIA, FBI, Interpol and the Justice Department, as well as documents from the National Security Archive, court records, government records and the Web. Where deemed necessary these are recorded in the Notes section.

Secondary Sources

Books

Aranguren Molina, Mauricio. *Confesion: Carlos Castano Revelan Sus Secretos*. N.p.: Editorial Oveja Negra, 2001.

Barnes, Tony, Richard Elias and Peter Walsh. *Cocky: The Rise and Fall of Curtis Warren, Britain's Biggest Drug Baron*. Lancashire: Milo Books, 2001.

Bowden, Mark. *Killing Pablo*. New York: Atlantic Monthly, 2001.

Bugliosi, Vincent. *The Phoenix Solution*. New York: Star Press, 1996.

Carrigan, Ana. *Palace of Justice, A Colombian Tragedy*. New York: Four Walls Press, 1993.

Castillo, Fabio. *Los Jinetes de la Cocaina*. Bogota, Colombia: Documentos Periodisticos, 1988.

Chepesiuk, Ron. *Hard Target: The U.S.'s War on International Drug Trafficking, 1982–1997*. Jefferson, N.C.: McFarland Publishing, 1997.

——— . *The War on Drugs: An International Encyclopedia*. Santa Barbara, Calif.: ABC-CLIO, 1999.

Crandall, Russell. *Driven by Drugs: U.S. Policy Toward Colombia*. Boulder, Colo.: Lynne Rienner Publishers, 2002.

De Grazia, Jessica. *DEA: The War Against Drugs*. London: BBC Books, 1991.

Duzan, Maria Jimena. *Death Beat: A Colombian Journalist's Life Inside the Cocaine Wars*. New York: Harper Collins, 1994.

Eddy, Paul, and Hugo Sabogal, and Sara Walden. *The Cocaine Wars*. New York: W.W. Norton, 1988.

Grosse, Robert E. *Drugs and Money: Laundering Latin America's Cocaine Dollars*. Westport, Conn.: Praeger Publishers, n.d.

Gugliotta, Guy, and Jeff Leen. *The Kings of Cocaine*. New York: Simon and Schuster, 1989.

Kirk, Robin. *More Terrible than Death: Massacres, Drugs and America's War in Colombia*, Public Affairs, New York, 2003, p. 279-285.

Lee, Rennselaer. *The White Labyrinth: Cocaine and Political Power*. Brunswick, N.J.: Transaction Publishers, 1989.

McGee, Jim, and Brian Duffy. *Main Justice*. New York: Simon and Schuster, 1996.

Mills, James. *The Underground Empire: Where Crime and Justice Embrace*. New York: Doubleday, 1986.

Poppa, Terrance E. *The Life and Death of a Mexican Kingpin*. Seattle, Wash.: Demand Publishers, 1998.

Riley, Jack. *Snow Job: The War Against International Drug Trafficking*. New Brunswick, N.J.: Transaction Publishers, 1996.

Ruiz, Bert. *The Colombian Civil War*. Jefferson, N.C.: McFarland, 2001.

Serrano, Rosso Jose. *Jacque Mate*. Bogota, Colombia: Grupo Editorial Norma, 1999.

Sterling, Claire. *Octopus: The Long Reach of the Sicilian Mafia*. New York: W.W. Norton, 1991, 39.

Streitfeld, Dominic. *Cocaine: An Unauthorized Biography*. New York: St. Martins Press, 2002.

Strong, Simon. *Whitewash: Pablo Escobar and the Cocaine Wars*. London: Macmillan, 1995.

Thoumi, Francisco. *Political Economy and Illegal Drugs in Colombia*. Boulder, Colo.: L. Rienner, 1995.

Magazine and Newspaper Articles

Adams, David. "Cocaine Demand in Europe Draws Interest of Mafia." *Miami Herald*, December 23, 1992, 1A.

——— . "Colombian Cartels Unraveling," *St. Petersburg Times*, July 10, 1995, 1A.

"Amid Hints of Cartel Ties, Colombia's Leader Proposes Plan." *Money Laundering Alert*, September 1994.

Ambrus, Steven. "Colombia Arrests Brother of Cali Drug Cartel Chiefs." *Los Angeles Times*, March 4, 1995, 6A.

——— . "Colombian Raids Prompt Alleged Cali Cartel Leader To Surrender." *Los Angeles Times*, March 16, 1996, A3.

Andelman, David A. "Cleaning Up the Kingpins," *Regardies*, May–June 1994, 28.

Anderson, Curt. "U.S. Charges Nine leaders of Colombia's Biggest Cocaine Cartel." Associated Press, May 6 2004.

Associated Press. "Top Colombian Drug Leader Gets Sentenced." *Newsday*, August 27, 2003, 39.

Aversa, Jeannine, "Administration Moves against 17 Implicated in Narcotics Money Laundering, including Miami Money-changer." the Associated Press, March 21, 2003.

Baena, Javier. "His Release Delayed, Colombian Drug Lord Gets Four More Years in Prison." Associated Press, November 5, 2002.

Bagley, Bruce, "Colombia and the War on Drugs." Foreign Policy, 77 (fall 1988), 76.

"Big Decline in Colombia Cocaine." BBC News (world edition), August 11, 2004.

Blackhurst, Chris. "A Captain in the Drug War Wants to Call It Off." *New York Times*, July 8, 1994, A4.

——— . "Cocaine Trial Nearing End." *Syracuse-Herald*, May 23, 1987, 12.

——— . "Conning the Cali Cartel." *The Independent*, September 20, 1995.

Brodzinsky, Sibylla. "Drug Lord's Early Release Sparks Outcry." *Sydney Morning Herald*, November 9, 2002.

Brooke, James. "Colombia Marvels at Drug Kingpin – A Chain Saw Killer, Too?" *New York Times*, June 21, 1995, 8A.

——— . "Colombia's New Leader Vows to Crack Down on Cali Cartel." *New York Times*, August 7, 1994, IA ff.

——— . "Drug Spotlight Falls on an Unblinking Cali Cartel." *New York Times*, December 17, 1993, A8.

"Cali Anti Drug Police Shake-Up Reported." United Press International, February 21, 1995.

"Cali Cartel Boss Gilberto Rodriguez Orejuela Re-Arrested." Agence France-Presse, March 12, 2003.

"Cali Cartel Bosses Manage to Escape as Anti-Drug Force Tightens Noose." *Latin American Weekly Report*, April 6, 1995, WR95-13, 145.

"Cali Cartel Kingpin Sentenced to More Than Six Years in Prison." Associated Press, March 27, 1998.

"Cali Cartel Leader Surrenders." United Press International, December 28, 2003.

"Cali Cartel Leaders' Sentence Criticized." Los Angeles Times, January 18, 1997.

"Cali Cartel Overhauls Its Narcotics Structure." Organized Crime Digest, April 10, 1996, 6.

"Cali Cartel Suspect Arrested In Spain Over Trillion Dollar Money Laundering." Agence France Presse, February 19, 2004.

"Cali High: Colombia." The Economist, December 25, 1993, 58.

Campbell, Duncan. "Bush Links War on Drugs with War on Terrorism." The Guardian, August 8, 2002, 15.

"Cartel Looks East for New Routes." Latin American Regional Reports: Caribbean and Central America, January 26, 1995, 7.

Chappell, J. L. "The Colombia Heroin Threat: Demand and Supply." Low Intensity Conflict and Law Enforcement 5 no. 3 (winter 1996): 366.

Chepesiuk, Ron. "Kings of the Jungle." Toward Freedom, June/July 1998, 4, 19.

"Cocaine Cartel Asks Ban on Extradition." Los Angeles Times, February 5, A4.

"Cocaine Kingpin Arrested." MacLean's, March 13, 1995, 45.

and Catherine Wilson. "Colombian Drug Kingpin Faces U.S. Justice," Associated Press, December 4, 2004.

"Colombia." American Review World of Information, August 1996, 31.

"Colombia Authorizes Extradition of Four Nationals to the U.S." Xinhua News Agency, October 27, 2004.

"Colombia Crackdown: Colombia's Pursuit of Drug Lords Sparks Violence." MacLean's, July 10, 1995, 34.

"Colombia – Former Communications Head of Cali Cartel Killed." Global News Service, September 11, 1999.

"Colombia: How Drugs and Hot Money Disrupt Business." Business Week, June 12, 1978.

"Colombia: Interior Minister Implicated in Drug Trafficking." Interpress Service, June 9, 1989.

"Colombia Judicial Association Files Suit Against President, Interior Minister." BBC Worldwide Monitoring, November 16, 2002.

"Colombia Outlaws Extradition over Drugs." Toronto Star, June 30, 1991, A8.

"Colombia: President Uribe To Seek Stiffer Prison Sentences For Drug Traffickers." BBC Worldwide Monitoring, November 9, 2002.

"Colombia Seizes Cali Cartel Stores." Reuters, September 18, 2004.

"Colombian Cocaine War." *Latin American Weekly Report*, June 20, 1996, 267.

"Colombia's New Leader Proposes Plan." Money Laundering Alert, September 1994, 7.

"Colombia's Top Drug Lord Gilberto Rodriguez Goes Free." UPI, November 8, 2002.

"Colombian Daily Profiles Northern Valle del Cauca Cartel Leader Jabon." BBC Monitoring Latin America, April 27, 2004.

"Colombian Drug Kingpin Extradited to the United States." AFP, December 4, 2004.

Constable, Pamela. "U.S.-Colombian Drug War Shifts its Focus to Cali." *Boston Globe*, January 23, 1994, A13.

Cummings, Judith. "44 Pounds of Cocaine Seized along with Arms Cache." *New York Times*, July 31, 1979, 12A.

Darling, Juanita. "Submarine Links Colombian Drug Traffickers with Russians." *Los Angeles Times*, November 10, 2000.

Davies, Frank. "A Novel Proposal from a Cali Cartel Boss." *Miami Herald*, August 2, 1997, 1B.

"DEA Says Cocaine Price Hikes Not Indicative of Reduced Supply." Drug Enforcement Report, October 10, 1995, 51.

"Delatar Si Paga." *Semana*, February 1, 1997.

Dermota, Ken. "Heroin Replaces Coke In Colombia." *Times of the Americas*, October 12, 1991, 5.

Drozdiak, William. "Europe Finds Colombian Cartels Well Ensconced." April 11, 1991, 37.

"Drug Barron Rearrested." *Latin American Weekly Report*, March 18, 2003.

"Drugs: Anti-drug police deal a heavy blow to Cali cartel." IPS-Inter Press Service/Global Information Network, January 10, 1994.

"El Capo, Todo Adjedrecisita." *El Tiempo*, June 10, 1995, 1A.

"El Delator." *Semana*, February 5, 2001.

Ellison, Katherine. "Trouble Spills into Once Calm Ecuador." *Philadelphia Inquirer*, October 4, 1992, 7.

"Escobar in Prison." Latin American Weekly Report, July 18, 1991, 11.

"Ex-Cartel Leader Arrested in Colombia." Reuters, March 13, 2003; and "Drug Baron Rearrested." *Latin American Weekly Report*, March 18, 2003.

"Extradition Bill Passed By Senate." *Latin American Weekly Report*, May 27, 1997, 249.

"Extradition Setback." *Latin American Weekly Report*, September 23, 1997, 778.

"Faceless Judge Sentences Cali Drug Lord to 23 Years." *Los Angeles Times*, February 24, 1997, A7.

Farah, Douglas. "Cali's Quietly Become Number 1." *Washington Post*, October 17, 1990, A18.

—— . "Colombia Drug Barons Threaten, Bribe Congress From Jail." *Washington Post*, December 11, 1996, A36.

—— . "Colombian Drug Lords Run Empire Behind Bars." *Washington Post*, December 26, 1996, 37A.

—— . "The Crack Up." June 21, 1996, A1 ff.

—— . "Raiding The World's Crime Capitol." *Washington Post*, June 10, 1995, A1.

—— . "Violence between Colombian Drug Cartels Rises Sharply." *Washington Post*, October 27, 1990, 26.

Federko, Kevin. "Bad Neighbors," *Time*, May 29, 1995, 40.

—— . "Escobar's Dead." Time, December 13, 1993, 46–47.

Ferrer, Yadira. "Drugs – Colombia Struggles to Control Drug Traffic." United Press Service, October 31, 1996.

"Foreign Minister Says Relations with U.S. Have Worsened after Former DEA Director's Remarks." British Broadcasting Corporation, BBC Summary of World Broadcasts, Part 4: The Middle East, Africa, and Latin America, October 8, 1994, 4D.

"Former Officer Says Anti-Drug Strategy Out Of Line With New Reality In Colombia." Asia Africa Intelligence Wire, August. 8, 2004.

"Freed Drug Lord Faces Internal Quarrels, Rivalries." Deutsche-Presse-Agentur, November 8, 2002.

Garamone, Jim. "Special Operations Part of U.S.-Colombia Plan to Reinforce Success." American Forces Press Service, April 1, 2004.

Garcia, Cesar. "Colombian Elite Police Want to Crack Down on Bloody Turf War Among Drug Traffickers." Associated Press World Stream, October 20, 2004.

"Gaviria Cautious After Escobar's Death." *Latin American Weekly Report*, December 16, 1993, 581.

The General Secretariat. "Cocaine: Europe Drug of the Year." I.C.P.R., May–June 1989, 23.

"Going After Drug Cartel." *St. Louis Post Dispatch*, October 5, 1992, 2B.

Goodman, Albert. "Outlaw Strongholds of Colombia." *High Times*, July 1978, 45–48.

Graham, Patrick. "A Nation Held Hostage." *National Post*, August 21, 2002, A11.

"Green Ice Dives Deep to Undermine Cartels." Money Laundering Alert (May 1995): 3.

Guillermoprieto, Alma. "Exit El Patron." *New Yorker*, October 25, 1993, 73.

Gutkin, Stephen. "Cali Drug Cartel Faces New Challenges in New York." Associated Press, March 24, 1996.

——. "Interpol Says Cocaine Trade Moving across Jungle Borders." Associated Press, December 3, 1990.

Harris, Marlys. "Lifestyles of the Rich and Famous." *Money*, November 1989, 74.

Harvey, Tom. "Bomb Blast May Signal Start of Drug War in Colombia." United Press International, May 4, 1990.

Haven, Paul. "Elite Colombian Drug Squad Turns Up Everybody but Cartel Kingpins." Associated Press, April 12, 1995.

——. "Murder Attempt in Cartel Hierarchy Shows Rules Have Changed." Associated Press, May 31, 1996.

——. "Suspects Arrested in Colombian Bombing, Cali Brother Sought." Associated Press, June 13, 1995.

"Indictment Names Who's Who of Colombian Drug Money Launderers." *Miami Herald*, March 16, 1991.

Jackson, Robert L. J. "Lawyer Indicted on Drug Charges Recognized as Brilliant by His Peers." *Los Angeles Times*, June 7, 1995, A10.

Johnson, Tim. "Cali Kingpin"s Fate Rests With Informer." *The Gazette* (Montreal, Quebec), August 27, 1998.

Johnson, Tim. "For the Wealthy, the Living Is Easy Behind Bars." *Miami Herald*, January 6, 1997, K0566.

"Judge Sets Trial Date for Accused Cocaine Smuggler." *Daily Business Review*, February 22, 2002.

Kendall, R. E. "The Role of Interpol in the Control of Drug Trafficking." *The NARC Officer*, May 1992, 5.

Kerr, Peter. "Cocaine Glut Pulls New York Market into Drug Rings' Tug-of-War." *New York Times*, August 24, 1988, B1.

Krauss, Clifford. "Colombia Arrests Raise Price of Cocaine in New York City." *New York Times*, September 15, 1995, 1A.

"La Captura: Sus Comiezos." *El Tiempo*, June 9, 1995, 2.

LaFranine, Sharon. "150 Arrested in Six-Nation Drug Sting." *Washington Post*, September 29, 1992.

"Last Big Valle Boss Surrenders on Eve of Washington Ruling." *Latin American Weekly Report*, February 24, 1998.

"Lawyers for Cali Cartel Leaders Hold Talks on Their Possible Surrender." BBC Summary of World Broadcasts, January 7, 1995.

Lee, Rennselaer W., and Scott B. McDonald. "Drugs in the East." Carnegie Endowment for International Peace, 1993, 2.

Leibowitz, Larry. "Colombian Cartel Leaders Face New Charges." Knight Ridder/Tribune Business News, December 23, 2003.

Lennard, Jeremy, and Steven Ambrus. "Elusive Supremos Redraw Drugs Map." *The Guardian*, November 28, 1997.

Lieberman, Paul. "U.S. Says Sting Pierced Cali Operations." *Los Angeles Times*, December 17, 1994, A1.

Lupsha, Peter A. "Drug Trafficking: Mexico and Colombia in Comparative Perspective." *Journal of International Affairs* (1981): 108.

Lyons, David. "Cali Cartel Accountant, Key U.S. Witness Gets 7 Years." *Miami Herald*, December 16, 1998, 26.

"The Mafia Again." *The Economist*, March 11, 1995, 53.

"Major Governmental Changes." Defense and Foreign Affairs Strategy Policy (Sept. 1990): 47.

"Massive Search Block Operations in the Northern Valle del Cauca Give Good Results." BBC Summary of World Broadcasts, Inravision TV-A, Bogota, March 12, 1995.

Matheson, Mary. "Colombia Plans to Make Cali Cartel Pay." *The Guardian*, November 21, 1996, 15.

McDermott, Jeremy. "FARC and the Paramilitaries Take Over the Colombian Drug Trade." *Jane's Intelligence Weekly*, July 1, 2004.

McFadden, Robert D. "Drug Trafficker Convicted of Blowing Up Jetliner." *New York Times*, December 20, 1994, 7A.

McGee, Jim, and Brian Duffy. "Breaking the Cocaine Connection." *Tropic*, August 8, 1996, 9.

——. "Cartel-Related Probe Focuses on D.C. Law Firm." *Washington Post*, March 28, 1995, A1.

——. "Fake DEA Bank Stings Cali Cartel." *Washington Post*, December 17, 1994, A1.

"Measure Now Goes to the Lower House for Next Two Votes." *Latin American Weekly Report*, May 23, 1997, 249.

"Mexico-U.S.: Busting the Cali-Juarez Connection." *Latin America Weekly Report*, May 25, 2004.

Molinski, Dan. "Drug Czar Says Efforts Haven't Cut U.S. Sales." *The Sun News* (Myrtle Beach, SC) August 6, 2004, a12.

——. "New Wave of Colombia drug kingpin emerges." Associated Press, September 22, 2004.

Morgenthau, Tom, and Douglas Waller. "The Widening Drug War." *Newsweek*, July 1, 1991, 32.

Moody, John. "A Day in the Life of the Chess Player." *Time*, July 1, 1991, 34 ff.

——. "Noble Battle, Terrible Toll." *Time*, December 18, 1989, 35.

Moseley, Ray. "Cold War's End Opens Door for Mafia in Europe." *Chicago Tribune*, December 29, 1992.

"Narco Castano?" *Revista Semana*, Edicion 886, April 26, 1999.

Nesmith, Suzanne. "Colombian Government Relaunches Battle Against Former Drug Lord." Associated Press Worldstream, March 13, 2003.

Nightwine, Carson A., Jr. "Drug Warrior: The Congressman and the Colombian Cop." *Soldier of Fortune*, January 1999, 42–49, 85–86.

"174 Colombian Police Fired Due to Cali Cartel Links." AP Worldstream, October 22, 1994.

"Orejuela's Interrogation Halted Owing to Security Fears." Deutsche-Press-Agentur, June 13, 1995.

Pear, Robert. "Three Nations Stage Anti-Drug Sweep." *New York Times*, Sept. 29, 1992, A1.

Pickel Thomas, and Thomas Lippman. "Accountant of Cali Cartel Surrenders, Will Inform U.S. About Operations." *Washington Post*, September 22, 1995, 3.

"Police Arrest Cousin of Drug Dealers for Killings of Rivals." Associated Press, August 20, 1988.

"Police Capture Drug Cartel Kingpin; Group Had Supplied about Eighty Percent of the World's Cocaine." *Charleston Daily Mail*, June 10, 1995, 1A.

Post, T., and Douglas Waller. "10 Acres, Valley View, A Drug Lord's Jail." *Newsweek*, July 1, 1991, 34.

Quinn, Tom. "Lunch with a Narco Boss." *Time*, November 7, 1994, 19.

"Raids Carried Out on Suspected Drug Cartel Properties." Inravision TV-A. Bogota. BBC Summary of World Broadcasts, March 25, 1995, Part 5, Latin America and Caribbean, AL/2262/L.

Ratansabapathy, Senthil. "Narcotics Cocaine Smugglers Targeting Europe, Officials Say." Italian Press Service, February 4, 1995, 1.

"Retrial Sought for Ex-Cartel Lawyers." *Washington Post*, October 30, 1997, 13.

Reuters. "Colombian Elite on Cartel's Payroll, Seized Papers Show." *Toronto Star*, July 24, 1995, A10.

Reyes, Gerardo. "The DEA Implicated in Deal With Terrorists." *El Nuevo Herald*, October 20, 2000.

Riding, Alan. "Gangs in Colombia Feud Over Cocaine." *New York Times*, August 23, 1988, 1A.

Robles, Frances. "Release of Cali Cartel Leader Stirs Debate about Uribe's Use of Power." *Miami Herald*, Knight Ridder/Tribune News Service, November 8, 2002, K2898.

Rodriguez, Cecilia. "Jailing Feared Narco Terrorist Won't End Narco Trafficking." *Los Angeles Times*, June 9, 1991, 2M.

Royce, Knute, and Peter Eisner. "U.S. Gets Gacha." *Newsday*, May 4, 1990, 1.

"Samper Received Millions in Campaign Donations from the Cali Drug Cartel, Clinton Administration Confirms." Knight-Ridder/Tribune News Service, June 22, 1994, 0622K6037.

"Samper Unscathed by Accusations." *Latin American Weekly Report*, April 20, 1995, 173.

Scripps, Howard. "Cali Cartel Cuts Deal, Ex-DEA Agent Charges." *Plain Dealer*, October 6, 1994, 16A.

Selsky, Andrew. "From U.S. to Colombia Militia: A Bomb's Saga." Associated Press, May 30, 2001.

Shapiro, Mark. "Doing the Wash: A Colombian Cartel's Money Laundering Scheme." *Harper's*, February 1997, 56.

Schreiberg, David. "Sins of the Fathers: The Children of the Cali Cartel godfathers Can't Shake the Family's Past." *Newsweek*, August 12, 1996.

Sheehan, Maeve. "Police Trace Drug Baron's Hidden Fortune of £20m." *Sunday Times* (London), February 27, 2000.

Sheridan, Mary Beth. "Colombia Defense Minister Quits as Crisis Worsens." Knight-Ridder Tribune News Service, August 2, 1995, 802, 2K270.

Sheridan, Mary Beth, and Juan O. Tomayo. "Tainted Donations Date Back 13 years in Samper's Campaigns." *Miami Herald*, November 6, 1995, 1A.

Sheridan, Mary Beth, Christopher Marquis, and Jeff Leen. "Colombians Arrest Kingpins of Cali Cartel." *Miami Herald*, June 10, 1995, 1A.

Skerrill, Michael S. "The Narco Candidate: Newly Elected President Hit With Charges That Cali Drug Lords Helped Finance his Campaign." *Time*, July 9, 1994, 49.

"Slain Colombian Drug Suspect Buried." United Press International, March 8, 1996.

Smythe, Frank. "A New Kingdom of Cocaine: For Colombia's Powerful Cali Cartel, the Critical Connection is Guatemala." *Washington Post*, December 26, 1993, C4.

Solans, Miguel. "Cocaine Today: Cocaine Trafficking in Europe." *The NARC Officer*, April, 1992, 16.

"Spanish Police Dismantle Colombian Traffickers' Money Laundering Ring." Agence France Presse, February 19, 2000.

"Special Police Force Eliminated in Cali." United Press International, April 3, 1995.

Squier, Ted. "Colombia: Contrabandistas, Gamines, and Ejecutivos." *The Atlantic*, October 1978, 18.

"Success for Big Police Operations." *Latin American Weekly Report*, May 16, 1996, 208.

Szulc, Tad. "Colombian Gold." *New Republic*, September 15, 1979, 15.

Thomas, Ken. "Feds: Colombian Brothers Ran Large Drug Operation From Prison." *Naples Daily News* (Florida), December 23, 2003.

Thomson, Adam. "Colombia's Drug Wars." *The Economist*, November 28, 1998, 34.

——. "Drug Informer Is Shot in Jail." *Financial Times*, November 6, 1998, 4.

"Three Drug Factories Raided by U.S.: Ten Arrested, Officials See New Trend in Cocaine Trafficking." *New York Times*, July 12, 1985, 12N.

Toro, Juan Pablo. "U.S. Tries to Head Off Immediate Release of Colombian Drug Lord from Prison." *Mustang Daily*, November 7, 2004.

"Treasury Moves to Freeze Assets Tied to Cali Cartel." *Washington Post*, March 8, 1996, 28A ff.

Treaster, Joseph B. "Arrest in Colombia Heartens U.S." *New York Times*, June 12, 1995, 8A.

——. "Drug Flow Battle Termed Worsening: Experts and Officials State that the Traffickers Death May Add Difficulties." *New York Times*, December 4, 1993, 7A.

Tuckman, Jo. "Guatemalan Drug Suspect Held in Mexico: Truck Boss Herrera Had 65 Million Pound Price on his Head." *The Guardian*, April 23, 2004.

"$2 Billion Cocaine Trial to End for Mastermind of Upstate Lab." *Syracuse Herald-Journal*, August 16, 1989, 12A.

"U.S. Criticizes Colombian Anti Drug Effort." Facts on File United News Digest, April 13, 1995, 264E3.

Williams, Phil. "Transnational Criminal Organizations: Strategic Alliances." *Washington Quarterly* (Winter 1995): 6.

Wilson, Catherine. 51) "Colombian Drug Kingpin Faces U.S. Justice." Associated Press, December 4, 2004.

"Ex-Colombian Kingpin Sentenced to More Than 30 Years." Associated Press State and Local U.S., August 26, 2003.

Wilson, Scott. "Cocaine Trade Causes Rift in Colombian War." *Washington Post*, September 16, 2002, 1.

Woodruff, Cathy. "Ex-workers Say Aguilera Head of Two Cocaine Labs." *Schenectady Gazette*, May 25, 1989, 17.

Yanez, Luis. "Cocaine Seized in Concrete Posts Smuggled by Sea." *Sun Sentinel*, December 3, 1991, 1.

Notes

Intro: The Labs That Made It Snow

1. This introductory passage is based on Bob Sears, interview with author, March 2002; and Ken Cook, interview with author, March 2002.
2. Bob Sears, interview with author, March 2002; and United States of America v. Fred Aguilera-Quinjano, Juan Aldana, and Carlos Gomez, 87-CR-255, U.S. District Court, Northern District of New York, 1989, trial testimony of David Karasiewski, 79. Karasiewski accompanied DEA agents to Minden; it is DEA policy that a DEA chemist must accompany agents to a crime scene because of the hazardous nature of the chemicals.
3. Bob Sears, interview with author, March 2002; and United States of America v. Fred Aguilera-Quinjano, Juan Aldana, and Carlos Gomez, 87-CR-255, U.S. District Court, Northern District of New York, 1989, trial testimony of David Karasiewski, 79.
4. United States of America v. Fred Aguilera-Quinjano Juan Aldana, and Carlos Gomez, trial testimony of Bob Sears, 40.
5. United States of America v. Fred Aguilera-Quinjano, Juan Aldana, and Carlos Gomez, trial testimony of David Karasiewski, 79.
6. Jack Riley, Snow Job: The War against International Drug Trafficking (New Brunswick, N.J.: Transaction Publishers, 1996), 184.
7. See Guy Gugliotta and Jeff Leen, The Kings of Cocaine (New York: Simon and Schuster, 1989), 127–32 ff. for a good discussion about the bust at Tranquilandia.
8. "Case Status and Disposition of Non-Drug Evidence," Report of Investigation, DEA, March 1, 1985.
9. United States of America v. Fred Aguilera-Quinjano, Juan Aldana, and Carlos Gomez, trial testimony of Bob Sears, 40; and United States of America v. Fred Aguilera-Quinjano, U.S. Court of Appeals for Second Circuit, Docket No. 89-1422, n.d., 2.
10. United States of America v. Fred Aguilera-Quinjano, Juan Aldana, and Carlos Gomez, trial testimony of Pedro Canales, 381–83.
11. United States of America v. Fred Aguilera-Quinjano, Juan Aldana, and Carlos Gomez, trial testimony of David Karasiewski, 80.

12. Cathy Woodruff, "Ex-workers Say Aguilera Head of Two Cocaine Labs," *Schenectady Gazette*, May 25, 1989, 17. How is cocaine processed? First, the drug traffickers buy coca plants from coca growers in Peru, Ecuador, Bolivia, and Colombia. They pick the flowers and buds off the plant, which are then mashed and ground into a thick paste. The paste is extracted and taken to hidden processing labs, such as the ones at Minden and Fly Creek, where the paste is combined with other chemicals and cooked until it becomes the highly potent white powder known as cocaine. During the process, the paste is dissolved in a solvent-like acetone and ether; then a precipitate is added, such as hydrochloric acid, which causes the cocaine to crystallize and fall out of solution. Heat fans and microwave ovens are used to dry the precipitate. After the cocaine is processed, it is turned into large bricks called kilos. One brick is equal to 1,000 grams of cocaine. See also Jack Riley, *Snow Job*, 185.

13. Cathy Woodruff, "Ex-workers Say Aguilera Head of Two Cocaine Labs," 17.

14. United States of America v. Fred Aguilera-Quinjano, U.S. Court of Appeals for Second Circuit, Docket no. 89-1422, N.D., 4.

15. "$2 Billion Cocaine Trial to End for Mastermind of Upstate Lab," *Syracuse Herald-Journal*, August 16, 1989, 12A.

16. Pat Hynes, interview with author, May 2002.

17. United States v. Fred Aguilera-Quinjano, U.S. Court of Appeals for Second Circuit, Docket no. 89-1422, 5. Precursor chemicals are chemicals such as acetone and ether, which are essential to the cocaine manufacturing process.

18. United States v. Fred Aguilera-Quinjano, Juan Aldana, and Carlos Gomez, 87-CR-255, United States District Court, Northern District of New York, 1989, trial transcript, 71.

19. Ibid., 73.

20. United States of America v. Fred Aguilera-Quinjano, United States Court of Appeal for Second Circuit, Docket no. 89-1422, 6.

21. Ibid.

22. Craig A. Benedict, interview with author, May 2002.

23. United States of America v. Fred Aguilera-Quinjano, United States Court of Appeal for Second Circuit, Docket no. 89-1422, 6.

24. Testimony of James Bigelow, 321; and "$2 Billion Cocaine Trial to End," 12.

25. Ken Robinson, interview with author, April 2002. Robinson was first an NYSP Investigator, and later he became a DEA agent and investigated the Cali Cartel from 1978 to 1994.

26. "Three Drug Factories Raided by U.S.; Ten Arrested, Officials See New Trend in Cocaine Trafficking," *New York Times*, July 12, 1985, 12N.

27. United States v. Fred Aguilera-Quinjano, Juan Aldana, and Carlos Gomez, trial transcripts, 345–52 ff.; and United States of America v. Fred Aguilera-Quinjano, United States Court of Appeal for Second Circuit, Docket no. 89-1422, 8.

28. "$2 Billion Cocaine Trial to End," 12A.
29. United States of America v. Fred Aguilera-Quinjano, United States Court of Appeal for Second Circuit, Docket no. 89-1422, 8–9.
30. Tom Constantine, interview with author, May 2002.
31. Bill Mante, interview with author, January 2002.

1: Getting Started

1. US Department of Justice, Drug Enforcement Administration, Intelligence Division, South American Narcotics Traffic, January 1975, 24. The DEA was created on July 1, 1973, as the successor to the Bureau of Narcotics and Dangerous Drugs.
2. Ibid., 26.
3. Bob Nieves, interview with author, January 2002; Ken Robinson, interview with author, April 2002.
4. Ted Squier, "Colombia: Contrabandistas, Gamines, and Ejecutivos," The Atlantic, October 1978, 18.
5. U.S. Congress, House of Representatives, Select Committee on Narcotics, Abuse and Control, South America Study Mission, Hearings, 95th Cong., 1st sess., April 9–23, 1977, 11; and Albert Goodman, "Outlaw Strongholds of Colombia," High Times, July 1978, 45–48.
6. Tad Szulc, "Colombian Gold," New Republic, September 15, 1979, 15; and Peter A. Lupsha, "Drug Trafficking: Mexico and Colombia in Comparative Perspective," Journal of International Affairs (1981): 97.
7. Interview with Robert Nieves, January 2002. Nieves was head of international operations; he retired from the DEA in 1995.
8. Jessica de Grazia, DEA: The War Against Drugs (London: BBC Books, 1991), 11–12.
9. "Interim Report of the Select Committee on Narcotics Abuse and Control," March 1, 1977, 3.
10. See US Health and Human Services, US Household Survey, (Washington, D.C.: GPO, 1978).
11. "Interim Report of the Select Committee on Narcotics Abuse and Control," 3.
12. Michael Kane, interview with author, May 2002.
13. Mark Eiler, interview with author, March 2002.
14. See Ron Chepesiuk, The War on Drugs: An International Encyclopedia (Santa Barbara, Calif.: ABC-CLIO, 1999), 39–41.
15. Dominic Streitfeld, Cocaine: An Unauthorized Biography (New York: St. Martins Press, 2002), 208.
16. Ibid.
17. US Department of Justice, Drug Enforcement Administration, Office of Intelligence, A Study of the Illicit Opium, Morphine and Heroin Traffic in South America, 1973–1976, April 1, 1977, 1–3. In 1937, illegal heroin labs run by legendary Corsican gang leader Paul Carbone were discovered in Marseilles, France. In the following years, the French underworld became heavily involved in manufacturing and distributing

heroin abroad, particularly to the United States. The heroin network became known as the French Connection. Turkish poppies were sold to the French underworld and refined by Corsican gangsters in Marseille (see Ron Chepesiuk, *The War on Drugs*, 39–41).

18. U.S. Department of Justice, Drug Enforcement Administration, Office of Intelligence, A Study of the Illicit Opium, Morphine and Heroin Traffic in South America, 1973–1976, April 1, 1977, 1–3; Ron Chepesiuk, The *War on Drugs*, 3.

19. U.S. Department of Justice, Drug Enforcement Administration, Office of Intelligence, A Study of the Illicit Opium, Morphine and Heroin Traffic in South America, 1973–1976, April 1, 1977, 1–3; Ron Chepesiuk, *The War on Drugs*, 21.

20. U.S. Department of Justice, Drug Enforcement Administration, Office of Intelligence, A Study of the Illicit Opium, Morphine and Heroin Traffic in South America, 1973–1976, April 1, 1977, 1–3; Ron Chepesiuk, *The War on Drugs*, 16.

21. Dominic Streitfeld, *Cocaine: An Unauthorized Biography*, 205.

22. Kevin Jack Riley, *Snow Job: The War against International Drug Trafficking* (New Brunswick, N.J.: Transaction Publishers, 1996), 14. Actually, the FBI had identified the Cuban-Colombian connection as early as 1958, when the Italian American Mafia arranged with Colombians from Medellin to process cocaine, heroin, and morphine for distribution.

23. Francisco Thoumi, interview with author, May 2002.

24. U.S. Department of Justice, Drug Enforcement Administration, Office of Intelligence, Drug Money Laundering: Colombia, August 1991, 37; and Francisco Thoumi, interview with author, May 2002.

25. Kevin Jack Riley, *Snow Job*, 14.

26. Drug Money Laundering: Colombia, 3.

27. Francisco Thoumi, interview with author, May 2002; and Bruce M. Bagley, interview with author, April 2002.

28. U.S. Congress, South America Study Mission, 19.

29. Ibid.

30. Dominic Streitfeld, *Cocaine: An Unauthorized Biography*, 27.

31. U.S. Congress, South America Study Mission, 19.

32. Ken Robinson, interview with author, April 2002; and Rich Crawford, interview with author, February 2002. For instance, these are some of the many aliases that the three founders used: For Miguel – El Señor, Patty, Pat, Manuel, Manoto, Mike, Mauro, and Doctor (see Dept. of the Treasury, Office of Assets Control, Oct. 24, 1995, v. 60). For Santacruz Londono – Chepe, Victor Crespo, Antonio Velosa, Ramon Palacios, Jose Angel Ortiz, and Jose Bolivar Calero (Fabio Castillo, Los Jinetes de la Cocaina [Bogota, Colombia: Documentos Periodisticos, 1988], 20). Add these aliases from a secret 1983 DEA report: Joseph Useche, El Nene Martinez, Gregory Gonzalez, Robert Salas, and Gregory Gonzalez (Jose Santacruz Londono, Report of Investigation, Sept. 6, 1983, 2). For Gilberto Rodriguez: Fernando Guiterrez, Roberto

Matarra, and Gilberto Gonzales Linares (Fabio Castillo, *Los Jinetes de la Cocaina*, 20).

33. Maria Jimena Duzan, *Death Beat: A Colombian Journalist's Life Inside the Cocaine Wars* (New York: Harper Collins, 1994), 138–39.

34. John Moody, "A Day in the Life of the Chess Player," *Time*, July 1, 1991, 34.

35. Fabio Castillo, *Los Jinetes de la Cocaina*, 20.

36. United States of America v. Michael Abbell, William Moran, et al., Case No. 93-470-CR-WMR, trial transcript, July 1997, 6555.

37. "El Capo, Todo Adjedrecisita," *El Tiempo*, June 10, 1995, 1A.

38. Fabio Castillo, *Los Jinetes de la Cocaina*, 181.

39. Ibid.

40. Confidential informant, as told to Ken Robinson; related by Ken Robinson, interview with author, July 2002.

41. Fabio Castillo, *Los Jinetes de la Cocaina*, 18–19.

42. Confidential informant, as told to Ken Robinson; related by Ken Robinson, interview with author, July 2002.

43. "La Captura: Sus Comiezos," *El Tiempo*, June 9, 1995, 2.

44. Simon Strong, Whitewash: Pablo Escobar and the Cocaine Wars (London: McMillan, 1995), 27; and U.S. Justice Department, Drug Enforcement Administration, Jose Santacruz Londono, Personal History Report 27-83-0017 March 12, 1984, FOIA.

45. Sandy Hill, interview with author, March 2002.

46. Ed Kacerosky, interview with author, March 2002.

47. Cited by DEA analyst who wished to remain anonymous.

48. Simon Strong, Whitewash, *Whitewash: Pablo Escobar and the Cocaine Wars*, 270. The ELN was founded in about 1964 as a guerrilla group that relied on the strategies of Che Guevara to promote revolution in Colombia.

49. See U.S. Justice Department, Drug Enforcement Administration, Strategic Intelligence Section, The Cali Cartel: The New Kings of Cocaine (November 1994).

50. Ruben Prieto, interview with author, October 2002.

51. Sandy Smith, interview with author, March 2002; and Joseph Fuentes, "The Life of a Cell: Managerial Practice and Strategy in Colombian Cocaine Distribution in the United States." Doctoral dissertation, graduate faculty, Criminal Justice, The City University of New York, 1998, 76.

52. Fabio Castillo, *Los Jinetes de la Cocaina*, 18–19.

53. Mark Eiler, interview with author, March 2002; Sandy Hill, interview with author, March 2002.

54. "Colombian Cartel," Frontline, http//www.pbs.org/wgbh/pages/frontline.

55. Fabio Castillo, *Los Jinetes de la Cocaina*, 18–19.

56. Ken Robinson, interview with author, April 2002; Rich Crawford, interview with author, February 2002; and U.S. Justice Department,

Drug Enforcement Administration, Jose Santacruz Londono, Personal History Report, 27-83-0017, March 12, 1984, FOIA.

57. "Surrender of Last Cali Cartel Leader," DEA Press Release, September 4, 1996.

58. Fabio Castillo, *Los Jinetes de la Cocaina*, 19.

59. Castillo's book *Los Jinetes de la Cocaina* remains the most helpful book on the Cali Cartel's early history.

60. "History of the DEA, 1975–1980," DEA web site, http://www.usdoj.gov.dea-deamuseum-1975_1980.htm.

61. See Guy Gugliotta and Jeff Leen, *The Kings of Cocaine* (New York: Simon and Schuster, 1989), 9–17, for a graphic description of the Dadeland Massacre.

62. Rich Crawford, interview with author, February 2002.

2: New York, New York

1. Ken Robinson, interview with author, April 2002.

2. Ibid.

3. "History of the DEA, 1970–1975," http://www.usdoj.gov.dea/deamuseum/1970_1975.htm/. Bill Mante, interview with author, January 2002; and Ken Robinson, interview with author, April 2002.

4. Ken Robinson, interview with author, April 2002; Rich Crawford, interview with author, March 2002.

5. Jessica de Grazia, *DEA: The War Against Drugs* (London: BBC Books, 1991), 127.

6. "History of the DEA, 1975–1980," http://www.usdoj.gov.dea/deamuseum/1975_1980.htm.

7. Ibid.

8. Ibid.

9. Michael Kuhlman, interview with author, May 2002.

10. Ken Robinson, interview with author, April 2002.

11. United States of America v. Anthony Alexander Blarek and Frank V. Pallechia, U.S. District Court, Eastern District of New York, trial transcript, 1998, p. 1997; and Ken Robinson, interview with author, April 2002.

12. United States of America v. Anthony Alexander Blarek and Frank V. Pallechia, U.S. District Court, Eastern District of New York, trial transcript, 1998, p. 1997; and Ken Robinson, interview with author, April 2002.

13. The following passage is based on author interviews with Rich Crawford, Ken Robinson and March and April 2002; former DEA agent Jerry McArdle, interview with author, June 2002; United States of America v. Anthony Alexander Blarek and Frank V. Pallechia, U.S. District Court, Eastern District of New York, trial transcript, 1998, 63; and James Mills, *The Underground Empire: Where Crime and Justice Embrace* (New York: Doubleday, 1986), 896.

14. Judith Cummings, "44 Pounds of Cocaine Seized along with Arms

Cache," *New York Times*, July 31, 1979, 12A. De Grazia puts the amount of cocaine seized at forty pounds in *DEA: The War Against Drugs* (7A), while James Mills uses the forty-five-pound figure in *The Underground Empire* (898).

15. Rich Crawford, interview with author, August 2002; James Mills, *The Underground Empire*, 896; and Ken Robinson, interview with author, April 2002.

16. Naddis is a computerized file containing summaries of reports of investigations of interest to the DEA, identified through the agency's investigative reporting system. Use of Naddis is restricted to authorized personnel. (Ken Robinson, interview with author, April 2002; Bob Nieves, interview with author, March 2002.

17. Ken Robinson, interview with author, April 2002; Rich Crawford, interview with author, August 2002; and Mills, *The Underground Empire*, 897. Santacruz, of course, was actually Colombian.

18. DEA, cable from headquarters to field offices, "Victor Crespo," Identification No. 0529 165155, June 1978, FOIA.

19. Fabio Castillo, *Los Jinetes de la Cocaina* (Bogota, Colombia: Documentos Periodisticos, 1988), 20.

20. Ken Robinson, interview with author, April 2002; Rich Crawford, interview with author, August 2002.

21. "Drug Lawyers," Confidential DEA Memo, n.d., FOIA.

22. Ken Robinson, interview with author, April 2002.

23. Rich Crawford, interview with author. Pen registers capture the telephone numbers of every phone call made from a particular line. While the DEA does not have statistics available for the number of telephone numbers captured, the agency reported that in 1987, for 716 installed pen registers, over 53,000 numbers were recorded.

24. The rest of this chapter is based on James Mills, *The Underground Empire*; Ken Robinson, interview with author, April 2002; Rich Crawford, interviews with author, March and August 2002.

3: Chepe Does His Thing

1. Fabio Castillo, *Los Jinetes de la Cocaina* (Bogota, Colombia: Documentos Periodisticos, 1988), 21.

2. Ken Robinson, interview with author, April 2002.

3. U.S. Justice Department, Drug Enforcement Administration, Fugitive Status of Jose Santacruz Londono, Report of Investigation, Item Identification No. 27-83-0017, October 19, 1985, 1, FOIA; U.S. Embassy, Drug Enforcement Administration, Jose Santacruz Londono, Memo, Item Identification No. C9-83-0014, September 7, 1983, 1, FOIA; and U.S. v. Blarek-Pellechia, U.S. District Court, Eastern District of New York, trial testimony of Alfredo Cervantes, February 2, 1998, 13.

4. U.S. Justice Department, Drug Enforcement Administration, Jose Santacruz Londono, Report of Investigation, Item Identification No. C9-83-0014, March 7, 1984, FOIA.

5. U.S. Justice Department, Drug Enforcement Administration, Personal History Report, Item Identification No. 6B-82-X015, March 12, 1984, FOIA.

6. The passage concerning Cervantes is based on U.S. v. Blarek-Pellechia, trial testimony of Alfredo Cervantes.

7. The safe was about three-and-a-half-feet high, six or seven feet long, and three feet wide.

8. Law enforcement sources interviewed for this book dispute Cervantes's claim, saying the shifts on Saturday or Sunday were no thinner than for any other day of the week.

9. Jessica de Grazia, *DEA: The War on Drugs* (London: BBC Books, 1991), 183.

10. Ibid.

11. U.S. v. Blarek-Pallechia, trial testimony of Alfredo Cervantes.

12. Bill Mante, interview with author, January 2002; and Ken Robinson, interview with author, April 2002.

13. U.S. Justice Department, Drug Enforcement Administration, Operation Calico-SEWO-497, Report of Investigation, File No. C1-83-2004, March 5, 1988, FOIA.

14. Bill Mante, interview with author, October 2002.

15. Bill Mante, interview with author, October 2002; and U.S. v. Blarek-Pellechia, trial testimony of Alfredo Cervantes.

16. U.S. v. Blarek-Pellechia, trial testimony of Alfredo Cervantes.

17. Ibid. See also chapter 6 of this volume, "Dirty Laundry," for more information on the Black Market Peso Exchange.

18. "The Decorators," *60 Minutes II*, CBS News Transcript, October 11, 1999.

19. See Elaine Shannon, "The Kings of Coke" 28–33, for an interesting description of Chepe Santacruz's operating style.

20. U.S. versus Blarek-Pallechia, trial testimony of Alfredo Cervantes.

21. Ken Robinson, interview with the author, December 2002.

22. In his trial testimony, Cervantes had mistakenly identified the Dupont product as a pesticide named "Manob-60." See U.S. versus Blarek-Pallechia, trial testimony of Alfredo Cervantes.

23. The court sealed the indictment.

24. U.S. Justice Department, Drug Enforcement Administration, Fugitive Status of Jose Santacruz Londono, Report of Investigation, Item Identification No. 27-83-0017, October 19, 1985, FOIA; and U.S. Justice Department, Drug Enforcement Administration, Case Closing Report, Item Identification No. G9-83-0014, March 8, 1993.

25. U.S. Justice Department, Drug Enforcement Administration, Case Status, Report of Investigation, Item Identification No. C1-76-0194, September 2, 1983, 3, FOIA.

26. U.S. Justice Department, Drug Enforcement Administration, Case Closing Report, Item Identification No. G9-83-0014, March 8, 1993.

27. U.S. Justice Department, Drug Enforcement Administration, Opera-

tion CRISP Travel Authorization, Item Identification No. RO819542, February 7, 1984.

28. Ken Robinson, interview with author, April 2002; and Rich Crawford, interview with author, February 2002.

29. Ken Robinson, interview with author, April 2002; and U.S. v. Blarek-Pallechia, trial testimony of Frank Blarek.

30. U.S. v. Blarek-Pallechia, trial transcript.

4: Growing The Criminal Enterprise

1. "Colombia: How Drugs and Hot Money Disrupt Business," *Business Week*, June 12, 1978.

2. Bruce Bagley, interview with author, April 2002; and Francisco Thoumi, interview with author, April 2002. See also Bruce Bagley, "Colombia and the War on Drugs," Foreign Policy 77 (fall 1988): 76.

3. Peter A. Lupsha, "Drug Trafficking: Mexico and Colombia in Comparative Perspective," *Journal of International Affairs* (1981): 108; Fabio Castillo, *Los Jinetes de la Cocaina* (Bogota, Colombia: Documentos Periodisticos, 1988), 27; and U.S. Congress, House, Select Committee on Narcotics, Abuse and Control, Hearings on South America Study Mission, 95th Cong., 1st sess., April 9–23, 1977.

4. Peter A. Lupsha, "Drug Trafficking; Mexico and Colombia in Comparative Perspective," 107.

5. See U.S. Congress, Select Committee Narcotics Abuse and Control, Fact Finding Mission to Colombia and Puerto Rico, 96th Cong., 1st sess., 1979.

6. U.S. Congress, Select Committee Narcotics Abuse and Control, Fact Finding Mission to Colombia and Puerto Rico, 96th Cong., 1st sess., 1979. It's a sentiment that the Colombian government has had from the 1970s to the present day.

7. See U.S. General Accounting Office, Drug Control in Latin America Having Limited Success: Some Progress but Problems are Formidable (Washington D.C.: Government Printing Office, GGD-78-45, March 29, 1978).

8. Richard B. Craig, "Colombian Narcotics and United States – Colombian Relations," *Journal of Inter American Studies and World Affairs* 3, no. 3 (August 1981): 243. See also CBS Television Network, "The Cocaine Memorandum," *60 Minutes*, April 2, 1978.

9. Richard B. Craig, "Colombian Narcotics and United States – Colombian Relations," 252.

10. Tad Szulc, "Colombian Gold," *New Republic*, September 15, 1979, 15.

11. Robert Coram, "The Colombian Gold Rush of 1978," *Esquire*, September 12, 1978, 34.

12. Ted Squier, "Colombia: Contrabandistas, Gamines, and Ejecutivos," *Atlantic Monthly*, October 1978, 18.

13. U.S. Congress, House, Select Committee on Narcotics, Abuse and

Control, Hearings on South America Study Mission, 95th Cong., 1st sess., May 9–23, 1977, 10.

14. Robert Nieves, interview with the author, January 2002.

15. Ron Chepesiuk, *The War on Drugs: An International Encyclopedia* (Santa Barbara, Calif.: ABC-CLIO), 686–89.

16. Ibid.

17. Ibid., 205.

18. Patricia McCrae, "The Impact of the Illegal Narcotics Trade on Economic and Legal Institutions Colombia: Chapter Three. Historical Evolution of International Narcotics Trafficking in Latin America," http://historicaltextarchive.com/mcrae/ch3.html/, 7.

19. Former DEA agent Ken Robinson, interview with author, April 2002.

20. Maria Jimena Duzan, *Death Beat: A Colombian Journalist's Life Inside the Cocaine Wars* (New York: Harper Collins, 1994), 58.

21. Ibid.

22. Sandy Smith, interview with author, September 2003; and Chris Feistl, interview with author, August 2002.

23. Chris Feistl, interview with author, August 2002; Ken Robinson and Bill Mante, interviews with author, September 2002; and Jerry McArdle, interview with author, September 2002.

24. Ken Robinson, interview with author, September 2002.

25. Chris Feistl, interview with author, August 2002; and observations from tour of Cali by the author in August 2002.

26. DEA analyst Sandy Smith, interview with author, September 2003; DEA analyst Mark Eiler, interview with author, March 2002.

27. Rennselaer Lee, *The White Labyrinth: Cocaine and Political Power* (Brunswick, N.J.: Transaction Publishers, 1989), 9.

28. Michael Kane, interview with author, May 2002.

29. Simon Strong, *Whitewash: Pablo Escobar and the Cocaine Wars* (London: McMillan, 1995), 52.

30. Rich Crawford, interview with author, February 2002.

31. Simon Strong, *Whitewash*, 64.

32. Fabio Castillo, *Los Jinetes de la Cocaina*, 58.

33. Ibid., 82.

34. See Guy Gugliotta and Jeff Leen, *Kings of Cocaine* (New York: Simon and Schuster, 1989), 191–96; and Paul Eddy, Hugh Sabogal, and Sarah Walden, *The Cocaine Wars* (New York: W.W. Norton, 1988), 310–12.

35. Alexander F. Watson, interview with author, March 2002.

36. Crescencio Arcos, interview with author, May 2002.

37. Former DEA agent Michael Kane, interview with author, May 2002; and former DEA agent Michael Kuhlman, interview with author, May 2002.

38. "Jose Sancruz Londono," Report of Investigation, Item No. 69-83-0014, June 19, 1984, 2, FOIA.

39. U.S. Justice Department, Drug Enforcement Administration, "Intelligence Information Regarding Santacruz," Report of Investigation, File No. ZT-83-0017, October 12, 1983, 1, FOIA.

40. U.S. Justice Department, Drug Enforcement Administration, "Compromise of Colombian National Police Wire Intercepts," Report of Investigation, Item no. ZT83-0017, April 24, 1984.
41. Ibid.
42. Rosso Jose Serrano, former head of the Colombian National Police, interview with author, August 2002.
43. Chris Feistl, interview with author, August 2002.
44. United States of America v. Michael Abbell, William Moran, et al. United States Court of Appeals, Southern District Florida, trial testimony of Guillermo Pallomari, 5843.
45. Chris Feistl, interview with author, August 2002; and observations made and information gathered by the author during a tour of Cali in August 2002.
46. Ibid.
47. Marlys Harris, "Lifestyles of the Rich and Famous," *Money*, November 1989, 74.
48. U.S. v. Blarek-Pallechia, Trial Transcript.
49. David Adams, "Colombia's Cartel Unraveling," *St. Petersburg Times*, July 10, 1995, 1A.
50. Jerry Salameh, interview with author, April 2002.
51. United States of America v. Michael Abbell, William Moran, et al. United States Court of Appeals, Southern District Florida, trial testimony of Guillermo Pallomari, 5855.
52. U.S. Embassy, Bogota, to DEA Office, Washington, D.C., Jose Santacruz Londono, Memo, Identification No. R2614382, October 26, 1983, NSA.
53. Fabio Castillo, *Los Jinetes de la Cocaina*, 110.
54. United States of America v. Michael Abbell, William Moran, et al. United States Court of Appeals, Southern District Florida, trial testimony of Guillermo Pallomari, 6245–46.
55. Fabio Castillo, *Los Jinetes de la Cocaina*, 67. In August 2002, two billion pesos was equivalent to about $1 billion U.S.
56. Fabio Castillo, *Los Jinetes de la Cocaina*, 64, 67–68; and James Mills, *The Underground Empire: Where Crime and Justice Embrace* (New York: Doubleday, 1986), 892.
57. U.S. Justice Department, Drug Enforcement Administration, Intelligence Information Regarding Santacruz and All, Report of Investigation, Identification No. ZT-83-0019, October 18, 1983, 1, FOIA.
58. Fabio Castillo, *Los Jinetes de la Cocaina*, 74.
59. Simon Strong, *Whitewash*, 212.
60. Maria Jimena Duzan, *Death Beat*, 58
61. Ibid.
62. Fabio Castillo, *Los Jinetes de la Cocaina*, 65. It should be noted that the vast majority of the press was not on the Cali cartel payroll.
63. Fabio Castillo, *Los Jinetes de la Cocaina*, 170.
64. United States of America v. Michael Abbell, William Moran,

et al. United States Court of Appeals, Southern District Florida, trial testimony of Guillermo Pallomari, 6243–44.

5: Heating Up

1. Status of Investigation, Report of Investigation, DEA, Identification No. G1-80-0170, February 7, 1983, 1, FOIA.
2. Cable, Drug Enforcement Task Force, New York, to DEA Offices, C1-83-2004, December 9, 1985, FOIA.
3. Ken Robinson, interview with author, September 2002.
4. Ibid.
5. Jessica de Grazia, *DEA: The War Against Drugs* (London: BBC Books, 1991), 135; and Ken Robinson, interview with author, April 2002.
6. Bill Mante, Louis Velez, and Francisco Diaz, interviews with author, January 2002; and tours of Queens in January and March 2002.
7. James Dao, "Land of Magic in the Heart of Queens; Others See Grit: Colombians Find Bogota on Roosevelt Avenue," *New York Times*, October 1, 1992, 10.
8. Bill Mante, Fernando Diaz, and Louis Velez, interviews with author, January 2002; Ian Fisher, "Jackson Heights Streets Familiar to Today's Cartels," *New York Times*, May 11, 1993, B2; and Clifford Krauss, "The Cali Cartel and the Globalization of Crime in New York City," in Margaret C. Graham and Alberto Vourvoulias, *The City and the World: New York's Global Future* (New York: Council on Foreign Relations, 1998), 70–78.
9. Ian Fisher, "Jackson Heights Streets Familiar to Today's Cartels," B2.
10. Clifford Krauss, "The Cali Cartel and the Globalization of Crime in New York City," 70.
11. Bill Berkeley, "Dead Right," *Columbia Journalism Review*, March/April 1993, online edition (Available: http://www.cjr/year/93/2/dead/asp/).
12. Patrcia Hurtado, "Murder Trial Up In Air," *Newsday* (Nassau and Suffolk Edition), April 20, 1999; and Joseph P. Fried, "Man Is Sentenced to 18 Years in Killing of Anti Drug Writer," *New York Times*, May 11, 1996, 25L.
13. Ken Robinson, interview with author, April 2002.
14. Ken Robinson, interview with author, April 2002.
15. Ken Robinson, interview with author, April 2002; Rich Crawford, interview with author, February 2002.
16. Rich Crawford, interview with author, February 2002.
17. United States v. Anthony Alexander Blarek and Frank. V. Pellechia, United States District Court, Eastern District of New York, trial transcript, testimony of Ken Robinson, 1998, 229–43; and Ken Robinson, interview with author, April 2002.
18. Ken Cook, interview with author, January 2002; and "NYOCTF Indicts Cali Cartel leaders in Cocaine Conspiracy," *Organized Crime Digest*, July 24, 1991, 2.
19. Tom Constantine, former head of the NYSP and former administrator,

DEA, interview with author, May 2002; Bill Mante, former NYSP officer, and Ron Goldstock, former prosecutor with the NYDETF, interview with author, March 2002.

20. Bill Mante, interview with author, March 2002; and "Governor's Remarks at the Criminal Justice Event, New York City," June 24, 1991, Public Papers of Governor (Mario) Cuomo, pp. 1144–46.

21. Bill Mante, interview with author, January 2002.

22. Ibid.

23. Ibid.

24. Louis Velez, interview with author, January 2002.

25. Ibid.

26. Terrance Kelly, interview with author, November 2002.

27. Bill Mante and Louis Velez, interviews with author, January 2002.

28. Louis Velez, interview with author, January 2002.

29. Bill Mante, interview with author, January 2002.

30. Bill Mante and Louis Velez, interviews with author, January 2002; and People of the State of New York v. Jaime Orejuela, indictment, State of New York Supreme Court, City of Queens, 1991, 10.

31. Bill Mante, interview with author, January 2002.

32. Ibid.

33. Ibid.

34. Ibid.

35. Ibid.

36. Cable, DEA headquarters, Washington, D.C., to Field Offices in New York and Miami, C1-87 1005, June 30, 1987, FOIA.

37. Robert Michaelis, interview with author, April 2002.

38. See People of the State of New York v. Jaime Orejuela and Others, indictment, 10.

39. Ibid.

40. Bill Mante, Robert Michaelis, and Ken Robinson, interviews with author, April 2002; and U.S. v. Blarek-Palecchia, trial transcript, 225–325.

41. Ken Robinson and Robbie Michaelis, interviews with author, April 2002.

42. Tom Cash, interview with author, March 2002.

43. Rich Crawford, interview with author, February 2002.

44. Rich Crawford, interview with author, February 2002; and Curtis Krueger and Milo Geyelin, "Massive Drug Load Seized in Pinellas," St. Petersburg Times, May 7, 1988, 1A.

45. Tom Cash, interview with author, March 2002.

46. Michael Isakoff, "Cali Cartel, a Rival of Medellin, Expand Reach in U.S.," Washington Post, August 29, 1989, 7.

47. Ibid.

48. See Statement of Thomas Constantine, Administrator, DEA before the Subcommittee on Legislation and National Security, U.S. House of Representatives, October 7, 1994.

49. Paul Moses and Effie Paulos, "Drug Franchises Indicted," *Newsday*, June 25, 1991, 7.

50. U.S. v. Blarek-Pallechia, trial transcript, 675.

51. Francisco Diaz, interview with author, January 2002.

52. Drug Trafficking: A Report to the President of the United States, Aug. 3, 1984, U.S. Department of Justice, Office of Narcotics Control, p. 21.

53. Francisco Diaz, interview with author, January 2002.

54. Bill Mante, Louis Velez, and Francisco Diaz, interviews with author, January 2002.

55. U.S. Department of Justice, Drug Enforcement Administration, "Traffickers from Colombia," http://www.usdoj/gov/dea/traffickers/colombia.htm/.

56. Bill Mante, interview with author, January 2002.

57. "The Supply of Illicit Drugs to the United States," National Narcotics Intelligence Consumers Committee Report, August 1995, 7.

58. Ibid.

59. Bill Mante, interview with author, January 2002.

60. Ken Robinson, interview with author, April 2002.

61. Organized Crime Task Force, 1993–94, New York State Division of the Budget, Budget Request, 1993, 10.

62. Bill Mante, interview with author, January 2002.

63. Joseph Fuentes, "The Life of a Cell: Managerial Practice and Strategy In Colombia Cocaine Distribution in the United States," (Ph.D. diss., City University of New York, 1998), 35.

64. Ibid., 36.

65. Ibid., 35 and 40.

66. Ibid., 42; and Michael Ishikoff, "Drug Raid Nets a U.S. Leader of Cali Cartel," *Washington Post*, December 7, 1991, A22.

67. Joseph Fuentes, "The Life of a Cell," p. 43. The HIDTA task forces are under the authority of the Office of National Drug Control Policy and operate in large urban drug markets. They consist of many law enforcement agencies at the federal, state, and local levels and are supported by designated assistant U.S. attorneys.

68. Michael Horn, interview with author, March 2002.

6: Dirty Laundry

1. U.S. General Accounting Office, Money Laundering: The U.S. Government is Responding to the Problem, Washington, D.C.: U.S. Government Printing Office, 1991.

2. U.S. Department of Justice. Drug Enforcement Administration. "Money Laundering by Drug Trafficking Organizations." Testimony of Harold Wankel, DEA Chief of Operations, before the House Banking and Financial Committee, February 28, 1996.

3. Drug Money Laundering, Colombia, DEA Sensitive, U.S. Department of Justice, Drug Enforcement Administration, Office of Intelligence, 6.

4. David A. Andelman, "Cleaning Up the Kingpins," *Regardies*, May–June, 1994, 28; and Greg Passic, interview with author, April 2002; and Al James, interview with author, April 2002.
5. Greg Passic, interview with author, April 2002.
6. Patricia Hurtado, "Money Laundering Trial Opens," February 3, 1998, A23.
7. Richard Weber, interview with author, July 2002.
8. Richard Weber, interview with author, July 2002.
9. Fabio Castillo, *Los Jinetes de la Cocaina* (Bogota, Colombia: Documentos Periodisticos, 1988), 22.
10. DEA Congressional Testimony: Money Laundering by Drug Trafficking Organizations, Testimony of Harold D. Wankel, 3.
11. Billy Bruton, "Money Laundering is Not a Corporate Problem," unpublished paper (in possession of Bill Bruton), 2001, 6.
12. Fabio Castillo, *Los Jinetes de Cocaina*, 83.
13. Ibid., 20.
14. Greg Passic, interview with author, March 2002.
15. Fabio Castillo, *Los Jinetes de Cocaina*, 59.
16. In his testimony, Morley said that the terms "gray market" and "parallel market" were used interchangeably with "Black Market."
17. Al James, interview with author, April 2002.
18. U.S. v. Blarek-Pallechia, United States Court. Eastern District of New York, trial testimony of Charles Morley, 1310–11.
19. United States v. Jose E. Stroh, The Indictment, United District Court, District of Connecticut, 2–3.
20. Greg Passic, interview with author, March 2002; Al James, interview with author, April 2002; Billy Bruton, interview with author, April 2002.
21. Greg Passic, interview with author, March 2002.
22. Al James, interview with author, April 2002.
23. Drug Money Laundering: Colombia, vii.
24. Robert Grosse, interview with author, January 2002.
25. "Indictment Names Who's Who of Colombian Drug Money Launderers," *Miami Herald*, March 16, 1991.
26. Bob Nieves, interview with author, March 2002.
27. Ibid.
28. Ibid.
29. Ibid.
30. Greg Passic, interview with author, March 2002.
31. Greg Passic, interview with author, March 2002; and Skip Latson, interview with author, April 2002.
32. U.S. DEA Web site, "The DEA, 1990–1994" (available: http:www.usdoj.gov/DEA/DEAmuseum/1990–1994.htm/).
33. Greg Passic, interview with author, March 2002; and Skip Latson, interview with author, April 2002.
34. Sharon LaFranine, "150 Arrested in Six-Nation Drug Sting," *Washington Post*, September 29, 1992.

35. Robert Pear, "Three Nations Stage Anti-Drug Sweep," *New York Times*, September 29, 1992, A1.
36. "Going After Drug Cartel," St. Louis Post-Dispatch, October 5, 1992, 2B.
37. "Green Ice Dives Deep to Undermine Cartels," *Money Laundering Alert*, May 1995, 3.
38. Ibid.
39. Billy Bruton, interview with author, April 2002.
40. Chris Blackhurst, "Conning the Cali Cartel," *The Independent*, September 20, 1995, 5.
41. Billy Bruton, interview with author, April 2002; and Skip Latson, interview with author, April 2002.
42. Billy Bruton, interview with author, April 2002.
43. Billy Bruton, interview with author, April 2002; and Skip Latson, interview with author, April 2002; and Chris Blackhurst, "Conning the Cali Cartel."
44. Billy Bruton, interview with author, April 2002; and Skip Latson, interview with author, April 2002.
45. Skip Latson, interview with author, April 2002.
46. "New Report," Memo to All Zones, June 6, 1995, Interpol-Washington, FOIA.
47. Billy Bruton, interview with author, April 2002.
48. "Operation Dinero," Press Conference Advisory, DEA, December 16, 1994; and Jim McGee, "Fake DEA Bank Stings Cali Cartel," *Washington Post*, December 17, 1994, A1.
49. Billy Bruton, interview with author, April 2002.
50. Al James, interview with author, April 2002.
51. Jessica de Grazia, *DEA: The War Against Drugs* (London: BBC Books, 1991), 146.
52. United States v. Michael Abbell, William Moran et al., United States District Court. Southern District of Florida, trial testimony of Guillermo Pallomari, July 1997, 5897.
53. United States of America v. Johnny Daccarat, Francisco J. Palacio et al., Docket Number 92-229, 92-6259, 1993, 3; and United States v. Johnny Daccarat, 20; and United States of America v. All the Funds on Deposit in any accounts maintained at Merrill Lynch, Pierce, Fenner, Smith and All, United States Court for the District of New York, Opinion of Judge Jack B. Weinstein, August 18, 1992.
54. Robbie Michaelis, interview with author, June 2002; and U.S. v. Blarek-Pallechia, Trial Transcript, 404–6.
55. Robert E. Grosse, *Drugs and Money: Laundering Latin America's Cocaine Dollars* (Westport, Conn.: Praeger Publishers, 105).
56. U.S. v. Blarek-Pallechia, Trial Transcript, 404–6.
57. Mark Shapiro, "Doing the Wash: A Colombian Cartel's Money Laundering Scheme," *Harper's Magazine*, February 1997, 56.
58. U.S. v. Blarek-Pallechia, 404–5; and Mark Shapiro, "Doing the Wash," 36.

59. U.S. v. Blarek-Pallechia; and Mark Shapiro, "Doing the Wash," 36.
60. See United States of America v. All Funds on Deposit in Any Accounts Maintained at Merrill Lynch, Pierce Fenner and Smith and All, LV90-2510.
61. Mark Shapiro, "Doing the Wash," 36.
62. Robert E. Grosse, *Drugs and Money*, 108–9.
63. U.S. v. Blarek-Pallechia, 1078.
64. Robbie Michaelis, interview with author, June 2002.

7: Going Multinational

1. Press Release, U.S. Department of Justice, Drug Enforcement Administration, September 28, 1992.
2. Greg Passic, interview with author, March 2002.
3. "Cartel Looks East for New Routes," Latin American Regional Reports: Caribbean and Central America, January 26, 1995, 7; and Paul Lieberman, "U.S. Says Sting Pierced Cali Operations," *Los Angeles Times*, December 17, 1994, A1.
4. Tom Morgenthau and Douglas Waller, "The Widening Drug War," *Newsweek*, July 1, 1991, p. 32
5. Ibid.
6. Frank Smythe, "A New Kingdom of Cocaine: For Colombia's Powerful Cali Cartel, the Critical Connection is Guatemala," *Washington Post*, December 26, 1993, C4.
7. Charles J. Gutensohn, "Cocaine Today: Drug Trafficking in the U.S.," August 20, 1992, 20.
8. Katherine Ellison, "Trouble Spills Into Once-Calm Ecuador," *Philadelphia Inquirer*, October 4, 1992, 7; and Steven Gutkin, "Interpol Says Cocaine Trade Moving across Jungle Borders," Associated Press, December 3, 1990.
9. David Adams, "Cocaine Demand in Europe Draws Interest of Mafia," *Miami Herald*, December 23, 1992, 1A.
10. Terrance E. Poppa, *The Life and Death of a Mexican Kingpin* (Seattle, Wash.: Demand Publishers, 1998), 185–88.
11. U.S. Congress, Senate, Prepared Remarks, Thomas Constantine, Administrator, DEA. Presentation to the Senate Foreign Relations Committee, August 5, 1995, 2; and Michael Bagley, "Drug Trafficking, Political Violence and U.S. Policy in Colombia in the 1990s," unpublished paper, January 5, 2001, 4–7.
12. Special Report, El Paso Intelligence Center (EPIC), n.d., 13.
13. Ibid.
14. U.S. General Accounting Office, Customs Service: Drug Interdiction Efforts, GAO/GGD-96–189 BR, Washington, D.C.: Government Printing Office, September 1996; and Office of National Drug Control Policy, The National Drug Trafficking Strategy, Washington, D.C.: GPO, February 1997, 49–62.
15. Ibid.

16. Prepared Remarks, Thomas Constantine, 3.
17. Ron Chepesiuk, *The War on Drugs: An International Encyclopedia* (Denver, Col.: ABC-CLIO, 1999), 131–32.
18. Ibid., 4–5.
19. Ron Chepesiuk, *The War on Drugs: An International Encyclopedia*, 80–81.
20. Ibid.
21. For additional information on Carrillo Fuentes see Ron Chepesiuk, *The War on Drugs: An International Encyclopedia*, 30.
22. Special Report, EPIC, 45.
23. Kevin Federko, "Bad Neighbors," *Time*, May 29, 1995, 40.
24. Special Report, EPIC, 44.
25. Ibid., 45.
26. Ibid.
27. Ibid., 36.
28. Terrance E. Poppa, *Drug Lord*, 186.
29. Ed Kacerosky, interview with author, March 2002.
30. Ed Kacerosky, interview with author, March 2002; and U.S. Congress. Senate. Violent Drug Mafias. Michael T. Horn, Chief, Office of International Operations, DEA, before the Senate Foreign Relations Committee. Subcommittee on Western Hemisphere, Peace Corps, Narcotics and Terrorism, July 16, 1997.
31. Tracey Eaton, interview with author, September 2002. Tony Soprano is the fictional New Jersey crime boss who appears in the popular HBO television series, *The Sopranos*.
32. Ron Chepesiuk, *The War on Drugs: An International Encyclopedia*, 30; and Tracey Eaton, interview with author, September 2002.
33. R. E. Kendall, "The Role of Interpol in the Control of Drug Trafficking," *The NARC Officer*, May 1992, 5. According to Kendall, the bulk of the cocaine seizures in Europe since 1988 until he wrote the article can be attributed to the Cali Cartel. See R. E. Kendall, "The Role of Interpol," 23.
34. Claire Sterling, *Octopus: The Long Reach of the Sicilian Mafia* (New York: W.W. Norton, 1991), 39.
35. William Drozdiak, "Europe Finds Colombian Cartels Well Ensconced," *Washington Post*, April 11, 1991, A29; and The General Secretariat, "Cocaine: European Drug of the Year," I.C.P.R., May–June 1989, 23.
36. Paul Eddy, Hugo Sabogal, and Sara Walden, *The Cocaine Wars* (New York: W.W. Norton, 1988), 203.
37. Guy Gugliotta and Jeff Leen, *Kings of Cocaine* (New York: Simon and Schuster, 1989), 90–96.
38. Tony Barnes, Richard Elias and Peter Walsh, *Cocky: The Rise and Fall of Curtis Warren, Britain's Biggest Drug Baron* (Lancashire: Milo Books, 2001), 78–9.
39. John Constanzo, interview with author, June 2002.
40. Miguel Solans, "Cocaine Today: Cocaine Trafficking in Europe," *The NARC Officer*, April, 1992, 16.

41. William Drozdiak, "Europe Finds Colombian Cartels Well Ensconced," 37.
42. John Constanzo, interview with author, June 2002.
43. Michael Horn, interview with author, February 2002.
44. Ken Robinson, interview with author, April 2002; and Rich Crawford, interview with author, February 2002.
45. John Constanzo, interview with author, June 2002.
46. Ray Moseley, "Cold War's End Opens Door for Mafia in Europe," *Chicago Tribune*, December 29, 1992.
47. General Secretariat, "Cocaine: European Drug of the Year," I.C.P.R., 23.
48. Letter from Charles B. Rangel to James A. Baker, August 23, 1991, NSA.
49. John Moody, interview with author, March 2002.
50. Rich Crawford, interview with author, February 2002; Ken Robinson, interview with author, April 2002. See also Jessica de Grazia's *DEA: The War against Drugs*, which has a detailed account of Operation Offsides.
51. Ken Robinson, interview with author, April 2002.
52. Ibid.; and Jessica de Grazia, *DEA: The War against Drugs*, 63, 65, 171.
53. "The Mafia Again," *The Economist*, March 11, 1995, 53.
54. Arnaud de Borchgrave, interview with author, July 2002.
55. Phil Williams, "Transnational Criminal Organizations: Strategic Alliances," *Washington Quarterly* (Winter 1995), 66.
56. Ibid.
57. Tony Barnes, Richard Elias and Peter Walsh, *Cocky: The Rise and Fall of Curtis Warren*.
58. U.S. Congress, Senate, Statement by Hans Ludwig Zachert, presented to the Permanent Subcommittee on Investigations of the Committee on Governmental Affairs, May 25, 1994.
59. Ibid.
60. Rennselaer W. Lee and Scott B. McDonald, "Drugs in the East," Carnegie Endowment for International Peace, 1993, 2.
61. Senthil Ratansabapathy, "Narcotics Cocaine Smugglers Targeting Europe, Officials Say," Indian Press Service, February 4, 1995, 1.
62. DEA Telegram, U.S. Embassy Bogota, 01721582, 1992, 4, NSA.
63. "Narco Mercantilists: Assessing the Rise of Colombian Heroin Trafficking," unpublished paper, Department of Defense, n.d., NSA.
64. Ken Robinson, interview with author, April 2002.
65. Ibid.
66. Ken Dermota, "Heroin Replaces Coke In Colombia," *Times of the Americas*, October 12, 1991, 5.
67. U.S. Congress, House, Heroin Production and Trafficking Trends, Testimony of Thomas A. Constantine, Administrator, DEA, for the Subcommittee on Crime and Criminal Justice, September 29, 1994.
68. DEA analyst Mark Eiler, interview with author, March 2002; and DEA analyst Sandy Smith, interview with author, March 2002.

69. "Colombia's Drug War," U.S. Embassy Cable, 01721582, n.d., FOIA.
70. Joe Toft, interview with author, March 2002.
71. Ken Robinson, interview with author, April 2002.
72. Joint Intelligence Center Pacific Report, November 14, 1991, NSA.

8: The War of the Cartels

1. Ron Chepesiuk, *The War on Drugs: An International Encyclopedia* (Santa Barbara, Calif.: 1999), 68–70.
2. Ibid.
3. Ron Chepesiuk, *Hard Target: The U.S.'s War on International Drug Trafficking, 1982–1997* (Jefferson, N.C.: McFarland 1998), 70.
4. Ibid.
5. See Ana Carrigan, *Palace of Justice, A Colombian Tragedy* (New York: Four Walls Press, 1993), for an excellent account of this chapter in Colombian history.
6. Jack Riley, *Snow Job: The War against International Drug Trafficking* (New Brunswick, N.J.: Transaction Publishers, 1996), 160.
7. Guy Gugliotta and Jeff Leen, *The Kings of Cocaine* (New York: Simon and Schuster, 1990), 78.
8. Ron Chepesiuk, *The War on Drugs: An International Encyclopedia*, 28.
9. Andres Pastrana Arango, interview with author, May 1988.
10. Rich Crawford, interview with author, February 2002.
11. Ibid.; and Jessica De Grazia, *DEA: The War against Drugs* (London: BBC Books, 1991), 139.
12. Jessica De Grazia, *DEA: The War against Drugs*, 257–58; and Paul Eddy, Hugo Sabogal, and Sara Walden, *The Cocaine Wars* (New York: W.W. Norton, 1988), 315.
13. Simon Strong, *Whitewash: Pablo Escobar and the Cocaine Wars* (London: McMillan Publishing, 1995), 165–66.
14. U.S. Congress, Senate, "Trafficking Organizations," Hearings Before the Permanent Subcommittee on Investigations, 100th Cong., 1st sess., Sept. 11–13, 1989, 130–31.
15. Ibid.
16. Simon Strong, *Whitewash*, 166.
17. Guy Gugliotta and Jeff Leen, *Kings of Cocaine*, 327.
18. "Heats Up," Memo, U.S. Embassy, Bogota, to U.S. Secretary of State, Washington, D.C., Item No. R221 56Z, August 22, 1988, FOIA.
19. Bill Mante, interview with author, January 2002.
20. DEA agent Dave Mitchell, interview with author, April 2002; DEA agent Chris Feistl, interview with author, March 2002; and Joseph R. Fuentes, "The Life of a Cell: Managerial Practice and Strategy in Colombian Cocaine Distribution in the United States," doctoral dissertation, graduate faculty in criminal justice, City University of New York, 77–79.
21. Guy Gugliotta and Jeff Leen, *Kings of Cocaine*, 338; and Simon Strong,

Whitewash, 168–69. In their account, authors Gugliotta and Leen did not mention daughter Manuela as being in the apartment.

22. Jerry McArdle, interview with author, June 2002.
23. Memo, "War Between the Cartels of Cali and Medellin Heats Up"; and "Police Arrest Cousin of Drug Dealers for Killings of Rivals," Associated Press, August 20, 1988.
24. "Police Arrest Cousin of Drug Dealers for Killings of Rivals."
25. Memo, "War Between the Cartels Heats Up."
26. Javier Pena, interview with author, March 2002.
27. Tom Harvey, "Bomb Blast, May Signal Start of Drug War in Colombia," UPI, May 4, 1990.
28. Alan Riding, "Gangs in Colombia Feud Over Cocaine," *New York Times*, August 23, 1988, 1A.
29. Alan Riding, "Gangs in Colombia Feud Over Cocaine," 1A.
30. Peter Kerr, "Cocaine Glut Pulls New York Market into Drug Rings' Tug-of-War," *New York Times*, August 24, 1988, B1.
31. Simon Strong, *Whitewash*, 165.
32. Cesar Gaviria Trujillo, interview with author, June 2002.
33. Guy Gugliotta and Jeff Leen, *Kings of Cocaine*, 338.
34. Memo, U.S. Embassy, Bogota, to Secretary of State, Washington, D.C., April 4, 1988, Item No. 042242Z, FOIA.
35. Cesar Gaviria, interview with author, May 2002.
36. Joe Toft, interview with author, March 2002.
37. "Colombia: Interior Minister Implicated in Drug Trafficking," Interpress Service, June 9, 1989.
38. Ron Chepesiuk, *Hard Target: The U.S.'s War on International Drug Trafficking*, 4–8.
39. Simon Strong, *Whitewash*, 217.
40. John Moody, "Noble Battle, Terrible Toll," *Time*, December 18, 1989, 35.
41. Robert D. McFadden, "Drug Trafficker Convicted of Blowing Up Jetliner," *New York Times*, December 20, 1994, 7A.
42. DEA agent Jerry McArdle, interview with author, June 2002.
43. John Moody, "Noble Battle, Terrible Toll," 33.
44. Javier Pena, interview with author, March 2002.
45. Knute Royce and Peter Eisner, "U.S. Gets Gacha," *Newsday*, May 4, 1990, 1. The United States also had a role to play in the downfall of the drug kingpin, according to sources. The operation involved a U.S. satellite and at least one helicopter under the control of U.S. military officials.
46. Dominic Streitfeld, *Cocaine: An Unauthorized Biography* (New York: St. Martins Press, 2002), 360.
47. Cesar Gaviria, interview with author, May 2002. See also Cesar Gaviria's biography on the Organization of America States Web site (available: http://www.oas.org).
48. Memo, Joint Staff, Washington, D.C., to DIA, Washington, D.C., Item No. 00280549, October 9, 1990, NSA.

49. Douglas Farah, "Violence between Colombian Drug Cartel Rises Sharply," *Washington* Post, October 27, 1990, 26.

50. Ibid.

51. Simon Strong, *Whitewash*, 247.

52. Ibid., 248.

53. Dominic Streitfeld, *Cocaine*, 361.

54. "Colombia Outlaws Extradition over Drugs," *Toronto Star*, June 30, 1991, A8.

55. "Cocaine Cartel Asks Ban on Extradition," *Los Angeles Times*, February 5, A4.

56. Letter from drug cartels to Juan Carlos Esguerra, 1991 (in possession of Juan Carlos Esguerra).

57. Juan Carlos Esguerra, interview with author, March 2002.

58. United States v. Michael Abbell, Williams Moran et al., Case Number 93–470–Cr–WMH, trial testimony of Guillermo Pallomari, ibid., 1997, 6156.

59. Appeal from the United States District Court for the Southern District of Florida in the United States Court of Appeals for the Eleventh District, Case No. 00–15079–G, June 1996, 46.

60. Ibid., 65.

61. Juan Carlos Esguerra, interview with author, March 2002.

62. Carlos Lemos, interview with author, March 2002.

63. Cecilia Rodriguez, "Jailing Feared Narco Terrorist Won't End Narco Trafficking," *Los Angeles Times*, June 9, 1991, 2M.

64. Douglas Farah, "Cali's Quietly Become Number 1," *Washington Post*, October 17, 1990, A18.

65. "Escobar in Prison," *Latin America Weekly Report*, July 18, 1991, 11.

66. John Moody, "A Day with the Chess Player," *Time*, July 1, 1991, 34 ff.

9: Exit The King

1. See Mark Bowden, *Killing Pablo* (New York: Atlantic Monthly, 2001), for an in-depth discussion.

2. Kevin Federko, "Escobar's Dead," *Time*, December 13, 1993, 46–47.

3. Ron Chepesiuk, *Hard Target: The U.S.'s War on International Drug Trafficking, 1982–1997* (Jefferson, N.C.: McFarland Publishing, 1997), 112.

4. T. Post and Douglas Waller, "10 Acres, Valley View, A Drug Lord's Jail," *Newsweek*, July 1, 1991, 34.

5. Alma Guillermoprieto, "Exit El Patron," *New Yorker*, October 25, 1993, 73.

6. "Delatar Si Paga," *Semana*, February 1, 1997; and with Chris Feistl, interview with author, August 2002.

7. U.S. Senate Committee on Foreign Relations, Subcommittee on Terrorism, Narcotics and International Operations, Recent Developments in Transnational Crime Affecting U.S. Law Enforcement and Foreign Policy, Superintendent of Documents, Washington D.C.: GPO, April 1994, 20–21.

8. Ed Kacerosky, interview with author, March 2002; Chris Feistl, interview with author, March 2002; and Dave Mitchell, interview with author, May 2002; and "Delatar Si Paga," *Semana*, February 1, 1997.

9. DEA agent Chris Feistl, interview with author, March 2002; Dave Mitchell, interview with author, May 2002; and "Delatar Si Paga," *Semana*, 22.

10. "Delatar Si Paga," *Semana*, 22.

11. Andrew Selsky, "From U.S. to Colombia Militia: A Bomb's Saga," Associated Press, May 30, 2001.

12. Ibid.; and Chris Feistl, interview with author, March 2002.

13. See Andrew Selsky, "From U.S. to Colombia Militia: A Bomb's Saga." One of the bombs was found in front of the offices of the Communist newspaper *VOZ*, buried under a load of bananas and oranges in the back of a pickup truck. Paramilitary leader Carlos Castano acknowledged planting the bomb.

14. Alma Guillermoprieto, "Exit El Patron," 73; and Cable, U.S. Embassy, Bogota, to U.S. Secretary of State, Identification No. 1993 Bogota 02998, February 24, 1993, FOIA.

15. Cesar Gaviria, interview with author, May 2002.

16. Alma Guillermoprieto, "Exit El Patron," 77.

17. Cable, U.S. Embassy, Bogota, to U.S. Secretary of State, Identification No. 1993 Bogota 02998, February 24, 1993, FOIA.

18. "Pepes Promise to Give Escobar A Taste of His Own Medicine," Memo from U.S. Embassy, Bogota, to U.S. Secretary of State, Washington, D.C., Identification No. 1993 Bogota 01747, February 3, 1993, NSA.

19. Cable, U.S. Embassy, to U.S. Secretary of State, February 19, 1993, NSA.

20. Cable, U.S. Embassy, Bogota, to U.S. Secretary of State, Washington, D.C., Document No. 1993 Bogota 02508, February 16, 1993, NSA.

21. Cable, U.S. Embassy, Bogota, to U.S. Secretary of State, Washington, D.C., Identification No. 1993 Bogota 05354, April 5, 1993, NSA.

22. Cable, U.S. Embassy, Bogota, to U.S. Secretary of State, Washington, D.C., Document Identification No. 1993, Bogota 06402, April 26, 1993, NSA.

23. Cable, U.S. Embassy, Bogota, to U.S. Secretary of State, Washington, D.C., Identification No. 1993 Bogota 11849, August 31, 1993, NSA.

24. Joe Toft, interview with author, February 2002.

25. Gustavo De Greiff, interview with author, May 2002.

26. Cable, U.S. Embassy, Bogota, to U.S. Secretary of State, Washington, D.C., Identification No. 07163, May 7, 1993, NSA.

27. Joe Toft, interview with author, February 2002.

28. Robert Nieves, interview with author, January 2002.

29. Ernesto Samper, interview with author, March 2002.

30. Robert Gelbard, interview with author, March 2002. In September 1995, an interview with Pacho Herrera appeared in *El Tiempo*. The reporter asked Pacho: "How did you bring down Pablo Escobar?"

Herrera's reply: "I spent a fortune on that. I paid informants so that they would pass information to the law, and the law annihilated Pablo Escobar. Personally or physically, I never contributed anything." When asked if he was a member of *Los Pepes*, Herrera responded. "No. I was never an instigator of the *Pepes* because I was not in Medellin" (see Cable 0081290, U.S. State Department, September 2, 1996), NSA.

31. Gerardo Reyes, "The DEA Implicated in Deal With Terrorists," *El Nuevo Herald*, October 20, 2000.

32. Amnesty International Web site (available: http://www.amnesty-usa.org/laws/news/20000/colombia1127/2000.html/).

33. Mauricio Aranguren Molina, *Confesion: Carlos Castano Revelan Sus Secretos* (N.p.: Editorial Oveja Negra, 2001), 167.

34. Paul Paz y Minao, interview with author, January 2003.

35. Javier Pena, interview with author, March 2002.

36. Cable, U.S. Embassy, Bogota, to U.S. Secretary of State, Washington, D.C., Identification No. 1993 Bogota 11849, August 6, 1993, NSA.

37. Ibid.

38. For a detailed account of Escobar's last days, see Mark Bowden's Killing Pablo, 203–72.

39. Ron Chepesiuk, *Hard Target: The U.S.'s War on International Drug Trafficking*, 1982–1997, 25.

40. James Brooke, "Drug Spotlight Falls on an Unblinking Cali Cartel," *New York Times*, December 17, 1993, A8.

41. Cable, U.S. Embassy, Bogota, to U.S. Secretary of State, Washington, D.C., Identification No. 18525 0222252, December 2, 1993, NSA.

42. United States v. Michael Abbell, William Moran et al., United States District Court, Southern District of Florida, Miami Division, trial testimony of Guillermo Pallomari, July 1997, 5832–33.

43. Cable, U.S. Embassy, Bogota, to U.S. Secretary of State, Washington, D.C., Identification No. 1993, December 21, 1993, NSA.

44. Cable, U.S. Embassy, Bogota, to U.S. Secretary of State, Washington D.C., Identification No. 1993 Bogota 19488, December 22, 1993, NSA.

45. "Cali High: Colombia," *The Economist*, December 25, 1993, 58.

46. Joseph B. Teaster, "Drug Flow Battle Termed Worsening: Experts and Officials State that the Traffickers Death May Add Difficulties," *New York Times*, December 4, 1993, 7A.

47. "Gaviria Cautious After Escobar's Death," *Latin America Weekly Report*, December 16, 1993, 581.

48. Cable, "Cali Cartel May Be Susceptible to Psychological Operations," Identification No. 0040099, Joint Staff, Washington, D.C., March 31, 1993, NSA.

49. Ibid.

50. Cable, Defense Intelligence Agency, Identification No. 00559403, October 7, 1993, NSA.

51. "Gaviria Cautious After Escobar's Death," *Latin American Weekly Report*, 581.

52. Cable, Defense Intelligence Agency, Identification No. 00559403, October 7, 1993, NSA.

53. James Brooke, "Drug Spotlight Falls on an Unblinking Cali Cartel," 8A.

54. "Cali High: Colombia," *The Economist*, 58; and Pamela Constable, "U.S. Colombian Drug War Shifts its Focus to Cali," *Boston Globe*, January 23, 1994, A13.

55. United States v. Michael Abbell, William Moran et al., Case Number 93-470-Cr-WMH, trial testimony of Guillermo Pallomari, ibid., pp. 5834–5840.

10: Breakthrough

1. Rich Crawford, interview with author, February 2002; and Ken Robinson, interview with author, April 2002; and Memo, NYDETF to DEA Headquarters, Washington, D.C., April 17, 1979, Item No. C1-83-2004, FOIA.

2. Lou Weiss, interview with author, April 2002.

3. Ibid.

4. Ed Kacerosky, interview with author, March 2002.

5. Luis Yanez, "Cocaine Seized in Concrete Posts Smuggled by Sea," *Sun Sentinel*, December 3, 1991, 1.

6. Ed Ryan, interview with author, September 2002.

7. Ibid.

8. Ibid.

9. Ed Kacerosky, interview with author, March 2002; and United States of America v. Miguel Rodriguez, Gilberto Rodriguez and Others, U.S. Court of Appeals for the Eleventh Circuit, Fourth Superseding Indictment, Case No. 00–15079–6, 1996, 54.

10. Ed Kacerosky, interview with author, March 2002.

11. William Moran v. the United States of America, United States Court of Appeals for the Eleventh Circuit, Case No. 0015079–6, 62.

12. Bill Mante, interview with author, November 2002.

13. United States of America v. Miguel Rodriguez, Gilberto Rodriguez and Others, U.S. Court of Appeals for the Eleventh Circuit, Fourth Superseding Indictment, Case No. 00–15079–6, 4.

14. Ibid., 58.

15. United States of America v. Michael Abbell, William Moran, et al., United States District Court, Southern District of Florida, Miami Division, Case No. 93–470–CR–WMH, 1997, trial testimony of Guillermo Pallomari, 5936–92.

16. United States of America v. Michael Abbell, William Moran, et al., United States District Court, Southern District of Florida, Miami Division, Case No. 93–470–CR–WMH, 1997, trial testimony of Joel Rosenthal, 7153, 7194; and Frank Davies, "A Novel Proposal from a Cali Cartel Boss," *Miami Herald*, August 2, 1997, 1B.

17. Robert L.J. Jackson, "Lawyer Indicted on Drug Charges Recognized as

Brilliant by his Peers," *Los Angeles Times*, June 7, 1995, A10.

18. "Massive Indictment Charges Former Justice Official and 58 Others with Racketeering," News Briefs, September 1995 (available: http://www.ndsn.org/sept95/indicts.html/).

19. Confidential DEA memo, n.d.

20. Rich Crawford, interview with author, February 2002.

21. Joe Toft, interview with author, March 2002.

22. United States of America v. Michael Abbell, William Moran, et al., United States District Court, Southern District of Florida, Miami Division, Case No. 93–470–CR–WMH, 1997, trial testimony of Joel Rosenthal, 7188.

23. Ibid., 7216–17.

24. Ibid., 7216–19.

25. Ibid., 7219–20.

26. U.S. Court of Appeals for the Eleventh Circuit, Fourth Superceding Indictment, Case No. 00–15079–G, 1996, 57–58.

27. Ed Kacerosky, interview with author, March 2002.

28. Ibid.

29. Jim McGee, "Cartel-Related Probe Focuses on D.C. Law Firm," *Washington Post*, March 28, 1995, A1.

30. Ron Chepesiuk, *Hard Target: The U.S.'s War on International Drug Trafficking, 1982–1997* (Jefferson, N.C.: McFarland Publishing, 1997). The name "Cornerstone" dates back to the original seizure of the cement posts in 1991. Because of the manner used to disguise the cocaine, some sort of reference to it was a natural, said the prosecutor who worked the case. "I remember that one of the other possibilities was Operation Cement Head," explained Ed Ryan, assistant U.S. attorney for South Florida. Ultimately, the two special agents in charge (SACs) at the time, Tom Cash and Bill Rosenblatt, settled on Cornerstone. "It was a good fit," Ryan said. (Ed Ryan, interview with author, October 2002.)

31. Ed Kacerosky, interviews with author, March and April 2002; Ed Ryan, interview with author, May 2002.

32. Harold Ackerman, interview with author, March 2002.

33. Ed Ryan, interview with author, May 2002.

34. United States v. Michael Abbell, William Moran, et al., United States District Court. Southern District of Florida, Miami Division, Case No. 93-470-CR-WMH, trial testimony of Harold Ackerman, June 1997, 2002–8.

35. Ed Kacerosky, interview with author, March 2002; Harold Ackerman, interview with author, March 2002; and Chris Feist, interview with author, November 2002.

36. Harold Ackerman, interview with author, March 2002.

37. Ed Kacerosky, interview with author, March 2002.

38. United States v. Michael Abbell, William Moran, et al., Case No. 93-470-CR-WMH, trial testimony of Harold Ackerman, July 1997.

39. Ibid.
40. Harold Ackerman, interview with author, March 2002.
41. Lee Granato, interview with author, June 2002.
42. United States v. Michael Abbell, William Moran, et al., Case No. 93-470-CR-WMH, trial testimony of Harold Ackerman.
43. Ed Ryan, interview with author, May 2002.
44. Jim McGee and Brian Duffy, *Main Justice* (New York: Simon and Schuster, 1996), 55.
45. United States v. Michael Abbell, William Moran, et al., Case No. 93-470-CR-WMH, trial testimony of Harold Ackerman.
46. Ibid.
47. United States v. Michael Abbell, William Moran, et al., Case No. 93470-CR-WMH, trial testimony of Guillermo Pallomari, July 1997.
48. Ibid.
49. Lou Weiss, interview with author, April 2002.
50. Ed Ryan, interview with author, September 2002; and Bill Pearson, interview with author, September 2002.
51. Ibid.
52. Harold Ackerman, interview with author, March 2002.

11: Submission to Justice

1. Harold Ackerman, interview with author, March 2002.
2. Ibid.
3. Harold Ackerman, interview with author, March 2002; and United States of America v. Michael Abbell, William Moran, et al., United States District Court, Southern District of Florida, Miami Division, Case No. 93-470-CR-WMH, 1997, 17.
4. Ibid.
5. United States of America v. Michael Abbell, William Moran, et al., 5.
6. Harold Ackerman, interview with author, March 2002.
7. Bill Pearson, interview with author, June 2002; and Jim McGee and Brian Duffy, *Main Justice: The Men and Women Who Enforce the Nation's Criminal Laws and Guard its Liberties* (New York: Simon and Schuster, 1996), 51.
8. Jim McGee and Brian Duffy, *Main Justice*, 51; and Jim McGee and Brian Duffy, "Breaking the Cocaine Connection," *Tropic*, August 11, 1996, 9.
9. Ed Ryan, interview with author, September 2002.
10. Ed Kacerosky, interview with author, April 2002.
11. Bill Pearson, interview with author, June 2002; and Jim McGee and Brian Duffy, *Main Justice*, 58.
12. Ed Kacerosky, interview with author; and Jim McGee and Brian Duffy, *Main Justice*, 57 and "Breaking the Cocaine Connection," 9.
13. Ed Ryan, interview with author, September 2002.
14. United States of America v. Michael Abbell, William Moran, et al., trial testimony of Harold Ackerman, June 1997, 2232–34.

15. Bill Pearson, interview with author, June 2002.
16. United States of America v. Michael Abbell, William Moran, et al., trial testimony of Harold Ackerman, June 1997, 2238–40.
17. United States of America v. Michael Abbell, William Moran, et al., trial testimony of Guillermo Pallomari, July 1997, 6001–6002.
18. United States of America v. Michael Abbell, William Moran, et al., trial testimony of Guillermo Pallomari, July 1997, 6001–6002.
19. Ibid.
20. United States of America v. Michael Abbell, William Moran, et al., Record Excerpts, Case No. 00–15079–6, vol. 2, 49.
21. Ibid.
22. United States of America v. Michael Abbell, William Moran, et al., Record Excerpts, Case No. 00–15079–6, vol. 2, 87.
23. Bill Pearson, interview with author, June 2002.
24. United States of America v. Michael Abbell, William Moran, et al., United States District Court, Southern District of Florida, Superseding Indictment, Case No. 93–470, 1996, 27.
25. United States of America v. Michael Abbell, William Moran, et al., Record Excerpts, Case No. 00–15079–6, vol. 2, 95.
26. Bill Pearson, interview with author, September 2002.
27. United States of America v. Michael Abbell, William Moran, et al., trial testimony of Francisco Laguna, 5438; and Gustavo De Greiff, interview with author, April 2002.
28. Simon Strong, *Whitewash: Pablo Escobar and the Cocaine Wars* (London: McMillan, 1995), 275.
29. "Many Events Straining Relations Between U.S. and Colombia," July 1994, 2 (available: http://www.ndsn.org/july94/colombia.html).
30. Kurt Schmoke, "Drug Policy USA: Time for a Change," News Briefs, No. 4, 1994 (available: http://www.drugtext.org/articles/94543.html/).
31. Gustavo De Greiff, interview with author, April 2002.
32. James Brooke, "A Captain in the Drug War Wants to Call It Off," *New York Times*, July 8, 1994, A4.
33. Robert Gelbard, interview with author, March 2002.
34. Bob Nieves, interview with author, March 2002.
35. Ethan Nadelmann, interview with author, May 2002.
36. Phillip McLean, interview with author, June 2002.
37. Gustavo De Greiff, interview with author, April 2002; and Phillip McLean, interview with author, June 2002.
38. Gustavo De Greiff, interview with author, April 2002.
39. Carlos Lemos, interview with author, March 2002.
40. Gustavo De Greiff, interview with author, August 2002, and Cesar Gaviria, interview with author, June 2002.
41. Ibid.
42. Ibid.
43. Gustavo De Greiff, interview with author, August 2002.
44. Ibid.

45. Ibid.
46. Joe Toft, interview with author, March 2002.
47. Gustavo De Greiff, interview with author, August 2002, and Cesar Gaviria, interview with author, June 2002; and Cable, "Cartel Lawyers Deny Clients Ties to Pepes," U.S. Embassy, Bogota, Item No. 00545827, March 17, 1994, FOIA.
48. Gustavo De Greiff, interview with author, August 2002.
49. "De Greiff Under Federal Investigation for Alleged Ties to Drug Cartels," News Briefs, January 1996 (available: http://www.ndsn. org/jan96/degreiff.html/).
50. Simon Strong, *Whitewash*, 304.
51. Gustavo De Greiff, interview with author, August 2002.
52. Cable, "De Greiff Criticized over Surrender Talks," FBIB, Reston, Virginia, to Washington, D.C., Item No. 0–0637543, March 17, 1994, FOIA.
53. Ibid.
54. Cesar Gaviria, interview with author, June 2002.
55. "De Greiff Criticized over Surrender Talks."
56. Ibid.
57. Robert Gelbard, interview with author, March 2002.
58. John Kerry, interview with author, July 2002; and Gustavo De Greiff, interview with author, August 2002.
59. John Kerry, interview with author, July 2002.
60. "De Greiff Under Investigation for Alleged Ties to Drug Cartels."
61. Ibid.
62. Ibid. In testimony at the December 1994 trial of Munoz-Mosquera, a witness testified that De Greiff had been blackmailed into letting a criminal be released from jail. De Greiff shared several letters and memoranda with the author, which appeared to prove his innocence. He sent letters to Janet Reno, which included affidavits from witnesses and other evidence which proved that he hadn't been bribed. Reno or the other recipients of De Greiff's communications never answered.
63. Simon Strong, *Whitewash: Pablo Escobar and the Cocaine Wars* (London, U.K.: McMillan Publishing, 1995), 304.

12: The Narco Cassette Scandal

1. Robert Gelbard, Myles Frechette, Rodrigo Pardo, Juan Carlos Esguerra, Michael Skol, Crescencio Arcos, and Carlos Lemos, interviews with author, March–December 2002.
2. Ernesto Samper, interview with author, March 2002; and "Biographias de Lideres Politicos CIDOB: Ernesto Samper Pizzarro, Fundacio," CIDOB (available: http://www.cidob.org/bios/castellano/lideres/s-048. htm/); and "Ernesto Samper," Newsmaker Profiles, CNNINTER ACTIVE: http://www.cnn.com/resources/newsmakers/world/samerica/ samper.html/).

3. Ernesto Samper, interview with author, March 2002.
4. Ernesto Samper, Myles Frechette. and Robert Gelbard, interviews with author, March–December 2002.
5. Simon Strong, *Whitewash: Pablo Escobar and the Cocaine Wars* (London: McMillan, 1995), 216.
6. Mary Beth Sheridan and Juan O. Tomayo, "Tainted Donations Date Back 13 Years in Samper's Campaigns," *Miami Herald*, November 6, 1995, 1A.
7. U.S. Congress, Senate, Corruption and Drugs in Colombia: Democracy at Risk: A Staff Report to the Committee on Foreign Relations, February 1996.
8. Mary Beth Sheridan and Juan O. Tomayo, "Tainted Donations Date Back 13 Years in Samper's Campaigns." In interviews with the author in March and August 2002, Ernesto Samper categorically denied having any involvement with Colombian drug traffickers, and he characterized the accusations as malicious attempts by his political enemies to impugn his character.
9. Mary Beth Sheridan and Juan O. Tomayo, "Tainted Donations Date Back 13 Years in Samper's Campaigns"; Ernest Samper, interviews with author, March and August 2002.
10. Myles Frechette, interview with author, March 2002.
11. Ibid.
12. Robert Gelbard, interview with author, March 2002.
13. Ibid.
14. Ernesto Samper, interview with author, March 2002.
15. Robert Gelbard, interview with author, March 2002.
16. United States of America v. Michael Abbell, William Moran, et al., United States District Court, Southern District of Florida, Miami Division, Case No. 93-470-CR-WMH, 1997, 6164.
17. Ibid., 6160–61.
18. Ibid., 6162–63.
19. Ibid., 6178–82.
20. Ibid., 6177–78.
21. Ibid., 6176.
22. Bert Ruiz, *The Colombian Civil War* (Jefferson, N.C.: McFarland), 206.
23. Ibid.
24. "Samper Received Millions in Campaign Donations from the Cali Drug Cartel, Clinton Administration Confirms," Knight-Ridder/Tribune News Service, June 22, 1994, 0622K6037.
25. Douglas Farah, "The Crack Up," June 21, 1996, A1 ff.
26. Ibid.
27. Interview with Gustavo De Greiff, October 2002.
28. Ibid.
29. Simon Strong, *Whitewash*, 209.
30. Ibid., 311.

31. Russell Crandall, *Driven by Drugs, U.S. Policy Toward Colombia* (Boulder, Col: Lynne Rienner Publishers, 2002), 105.
32. Interviews with various sources familiar with Colombia at the time.
33. Michael S. Skerrill, "The Narco Candidate, Newly Elected President Hit With Charges That Cali Drug Lords Helped Finance His Campaign," *Time*, July 9, 1994, 49.
34. Bert Ruiz, *The Colombian Civil War*, 209.
35. Ernesto Samper, interview with author, March 2002.
36. Ibid.; and Crescencio Arcos, interview with author, March–December 2002.
37. Michael Skol, Crescencio Arcos, and Ernesto Samper, interviews with author, March–December 2002.
38. Michael Skol and Crescencio Arcos, interviews with author, March–December 2002.
39. Michael Skol, interview with author, March–December 2002.
40. Michael Skol and Crescencio Arcos, interviews with author, March–December 2002.
41. Michael Skol, interview with author, March–December 2002.
42. Ibid.
43. Ibid.
44. Ernesto Samper, Crescencio Arcos, and Michael Skol, interviews with author, March–December 2002.
45. Crescencio Arcos, interviews with author, March–December 2002.
46. Michael Skol, interview with author, March–December 2002.
47. Ibid.
48. U.S. Congress. Senate. Foreign Operations, Appropriations/Colombia Drug Cartel Efforts. Senate Record Vote Analysis. 103rd Cong., 2nd Sess., July 15, 1994, 5–9887, no. 202, 4.
49. Ernesto Samper, interview with author, March 2002.
50. Bert Ruiz, *The Colombian Civil War*, 255.
51. Vincent Bugliosi, *The Phoenix Solution* (New York: Star Press, 1996), 93. In an interview with the author in March 2002, Samper said that the assassination had nothing to do with him.
52. "Colombia's New Leader Proposes Plan," *Money Laundering Alert*, September 1994, 7.
53. James Brooke, "Colombia's New Leader Vows to Crack Down on Cali Cartel," *New York Times*, August 7, 1994, 1A ff.
54. "Police Clean Up," *Latin American Weekly Report*, August, 382.
55. Gustavo De Greiff, interview with author, October 2002.
56. Alphonso Valdivieso, interview with author, April 2002. At the time of the interview, Valdivieso was Colombia's ambassador to the UN.
57. Ibid.
58. Ibid.
59. Tom Constantine, interview with author, May 2002.
60. Joe Toft, interview with author, February 2002.
61. Ibid.

62. Myles Frechette, interview with author, November 2002.
63. DEA agent, anonymous source, interview with author, off the record.
64. Ernesto Samper, interview with author, August 2002.
65. "Foreign Minister Says Relations with U.S. Have Worsened after Former DEA Director's Remarks." British Broadcasting Corporation, BBC Summary of World Broadcasts, Part 4: The Middle East, Africa, and Latin America, October 8, 1994, 4D.

13: A Man of Peace

1. Russell Crandall, *Driven by Drugs: U.S. Policy towards Colombia* (Boulder, Col.: Lynne Rienner Publishers, 2002), 109.
2. Simon Strong, *Whitewash: Pablo Escobar and the Cocaine Wars* (London: McMillan, 1995), 314.
3. Robert Gelbard, interview with author, March 2002.
4. Ibid. In one of our interviews, Samper said this about Diettes: "Diettes had been a hero against the Medellin cartel. He had received information from the Cali cartel. He was not an ally of the Cali cartel, but a sympathizer. So he had to be relieved from duty." Ernesto Samper, interview with author, August 2002.
5. Bob Nieves, interview with author, January 2002.
6. Ibid.
7. Major Gil Macklin, interview with author, January 2002.
8. Ernesto Samper, interview with author, August 2002.
9. Joe Toft, interview with author, March 2002.
10. General Jose Rosso Serrano, interview with author, August 2002; "Major Governmental Changes," Defense and Foreign Affairs Strategy Policy, September 1990, 47.
11. "The Drug Menace: Colombia: Crack Squad," *Police Magazine*, May 1998. The drug certification process began in 1986 and is required by U.S. law. Each year, the president makes an annual assessment of the world's 32 major drug producing countries. If a country is found not to have complied fully on drug matters, the president may withhold assistance from them. The annual assessment is released annually on March 1. See Ron Chepesiuk, *The War on Drugs: An International Encyclopedia* (Santa Barbara, Calif.: ABC-CLIO, 1999), 34–35.
12. Bert Ruiz, *The Colombian Civil War* (Jefferson, N.C.: McFarland, 2001), 212.
13. "174 Colombian Police Fired Due to Cali Cartel Links," AP Worldstream, October 22, 1994.
14. Carson A. Nightwine Jr., "Drug Warrior: The Congressman and the Colombian Cop," *Soldier of Fortune*, January 1999, 42–49, 85–86.
15. Ibid.
16. "Amid Hints of Cartel Ties, Colombia's Leader Proposes Plan," *Money Laundering Alert*, September 1994.

17. "Colombia Crackdown: Colombia's Pursuit of Drug Lords Spark Violence," *MacLean's*, July 10, 1995, 34.
18. Howard Scripps, "Cali Cartel Cuts Deal, Ex-DEA Agent Charges," *Plain Dealer*, October 6, 1994, 16A.
19. Tom Quinn, "Lunch with a Narco Boss," *Time*, November 7, 1994, p. 19.
20. Ibid.
21. "Lawyers for Cali Cartel Leaders Hold Talks on Their Possible Surrender," BBC Summary of World Broadcasts, January 7, 1995.
22. Ibid.
23. Ernesto Samper, interview with author, August 2002.
24. Ibid.
25. Robert Gelbard, interview with author, March 2002; Myles Frechette, interview with author, December 2002.
26. Myles Frechette, interview with author, December 2002.
27. Paul Haven, "Elite Colombian Drug Squad Turns Up Everybody but Cartel Kingpins," Associated Press, April 12, 1995.
28. "Raids Carried Out on Suspected Drug Cartel Properties," Inravision TV-A Bogota, BBC Summary of World Broadcasts, March 25, 1995, Part 5, Latin America and Caribbean, AL/2262/L.
29. Ibid.
30. Stephen Ambrus, "Colombia Arrests Brother of Cali Drug Cartel Chiefs," *Los Angeles Times*, March 4, 1995, 6A.
31. "Cocaine Kingpin Arrested," *MacLean's*, March 13, 1995, 45.
32. "Massive Search Block Operations in the Northern Valle del Cauca Give Good Results," BBC Summary of World Broadcasts, Inravision TV-A, Bogota, March 12, 1995.
33. Jerry Salameh, interview with author, May 2002; "Cali Cartel Bosses Manage to Escape As Anti-drug Force Tightens Noose," *Latin America Weekly Report*, April 6, 1995, WR95-13, 145.
34. "Special Police Force Eliminated in Cali," United Press International, April 3, 1995.
35. Alphonso Valdivieso, interview with author, June 2002.
36. "Cali Anti Drug Police Shake-Up Reported," United Press International, February 21, 1995.
37. "Samper Unscathed by Accusations," *Latin America Weekly Report*, April 20, 1995, 173.
38. "U.S. Criticizes Colombian Anti Drug Effort," Facts on File United News Digest, April 13, 1995, 264E3.
39. Myles Frechette, interview with author, March 2002.
40. Rodrigo Pardo, interview with author, August 2002.
41. Ruben Prieto, interview with author, October 2002.
42. Jerry Salameh, interview with author, May 2002.
43. Ruben Prieto, interview with author, October 2002.
44. Dave Mitchell, interview with author, May 2002; Ruben Prieto, interview with author, October 2002; Jerry Salameh, interview with

author, May 2002; Chris Feistl, interview with author, May 2002. See also "El Delator," *Semana*, February 5, 2001, 33.

45. Dave Mitchell, interview with author, May 2002; Ruben Prieto, interview with author, October 2002; Jerry Salameh, interview with author, May 2002; Chris Feistl, interview with author, May 2002.
46. Dave Mitchell, interview with author, May 2002.
47. Jerry Salameh, interview with author, May 2002.
48. Chris Feistl, interview with author, November 2002.
49. Mary Beth Sheridan, Christopher Marquis, and Jeff Leen, "Colombians Arrest Kingpins of Cali Cartel," *Miami Herald*, June 10, 1995, 1A.
50. Douglas Farah, "Raiding the World's Crime Capitol," *Washington Post*, June 10, 1995, A1.
51. Ruben Prieto, interview with author, October 2002, "El Delator," *Semana*, February 5, 2001, p. 33.
52. Ruben Prieto, interview with author, October 2002; Chris Feistl, interview with author, September 2003; Sandy Smith, interview with author, September 2003. The identification of Flaco's real name was based on DEA teletypes and on field reports written after his arrest.
53. Ibid.
54. This passage is gleaned from "El Delator," *Semana*.
55. Jerry Salameh, interview with author, May 2002.
56. Jerry Salameh, interview with author, May 2002; Ruben Prieto, interview with author, October 2002.
57. Ibid. Also based on author's tour of the area.
58. This extended passage is based on Ruben Prieto, interview with author, October 2002.

14: Exit The Señor

1. General Rosso Jose Serrano, interview with author, August 2002.
2. "Police Capture Drug Cartel Kingpin: Group Had Supplied about Eighty Percent of the World's Cocaine," *Charleston Daily Mail*, June 10, 1995, 1A.
3. Ernesto Samper, interview with author, March 2002.
4. Joseph B. Treaster, "Arrest in Colombia Heartens U.S.," *New York Times*, June 12, 1995, 8A.
5. "Police Capture Drug Cartel Kingpin."
6. "Orejuela's Interrogation Halted Owing to Security Fears," Deutsche-Press-Agentur, June 13, 1995.
7. Ibid.; Paul Haven, "Suspects Arrested in Colombian Bombing, Cali Brother Sought," Associated Press, June 13, 1995.
8. German Velasquez, interview with author, March 2002; Jorge Cardona, interview with author, March 2002.
9. Ed Kacerosky, interview with author, March 2002. See also United States of America v. Michael Abbell, William Moran, et al., United States District Court, Southern District of Florida, Superseding Indictment, case no. 93-470, 1996.

10. Bill Pearson, interview with author, May 2002; Ed Ryan, interview with author, May 2002.
11. Ed Kacerosky, interview with author, August 2002.
12. Ed Ryan, interview with author, October 2002.
13. Sources spoke off the record.
14. Ibid.
15. Ed Kacerosky, interview with author, August 2002.
16. Chris Feistl, interview with author, November 2002.
17. Ed Kacerosky, interview with author, August 2002.
18. Ibid.; Chris Feistl, interview with author, November 2002.
19. Handwritten memo, Ed Kacerosky to Chris Feistl, undated; Chris Feistl, interview with author, November 2002; Ed Kacerosky, interview with author, August 2002.
20. Chris Feistl, interview with author, November 2002.
21. Ed Kacerosky, interview with author, March 2002; Chris Feistl, interviews with author, March, August, and November 2002; Dave Mitchell, interviews with author, April, June, and November 2002.
22. Dave Mitchell, interviews with author, April, June, and November 2002.
23. Chris Feistl, interviews with author, March, August, and November 2002.
24. James Brooke, "Colombia Marvels at Drug Kingpin – A Chain Saw Killer, Too?" *New York Times*, June 21, 1995, 8A.
25. Ibid.
26. Law enforcement sources spoke off the record.
27. Chris Feistl, interviews with author, March, August, and November 2002; Dave Mitchell, interviews with author, April, June, and November 2002.
28. Chris Feistl, interviews with author, March, August, and November 2002.
29. Dave Mitchell, interviews with author, April, June, and November 2002.
30. Chris Feistl, interviews with author, March, August, and November 2002; Dave Mitchell, interviews with author, April, June, and November 2002.
31. Ibid.
32. Ibid.
33. Ibid.
34. Ibid.
35. Ibid.
36. Dave Mitchell, interviews with author, April, June, and November 2002.
37. Chris Feistl, interviews with author, March, August, and November 2002; Dave Mitchell, interviews with author, April, June, and November 2002.
38. Ibid.

39. Ibid.
40. Jerry Salameh, interview with author, June 2002.
41. Chris Feistl, interviews with author, March, August, and November 2002.
42. Ibid.
43. Ibid.
44. Jerry Salameh, interview with author, June 2002.
45. Ruben Prieto, interview with author, November 2002; Jerry Salameh, interview with author, June 2002.
46. Chris Feistl, interviews with author, March, August, and November 2002; Dave Mitchell, interviews with author, April, June, and November 2002. Salcedo later told the agents that a Cartel hit man was in the pizza restaurant while they were making contact with him.
47. Jerry Salameh, interview with author, June 2002.
48. Ibid.
49. Jerry Salameh, interview with author, June 2002; Dave Mitchell, interviews with author, April, June, and November 2002; Chris Feistl, interviews with author, March, August, and November 2002.
50. Dave Mitchell, interviews with author, April, June, and November 2002. Mitchell also had a bad feeling about the nosy Colombian officer. While he was staying at the Police Bloque base in Cali, the same officer asked Mitchell if he wanted to go find some girls one night. Mitchell told him he couldn't leave the base. Later, the Colombian colonel in charge of the base was photographed on a bed with a girl at the place the officer wanted to take him. The photo was released to *Semana* magazine and appeared on the front cover. Sean had arranged the tryst with the colonel and the girl and set up the hidden cameras. "Could you imagine if I fell for it and the Cali cartel had my picture – a DEA agent's photo – in a compromising position?" Mitchell said.
51. Chris Feistl, interviews with author, March, August, and November 2002; Jerry Salameh, interview with author, June 2002; Dave Mitchell, interviews with author, April, June, and November 2002.
52. Ruben Prieto, interview with author, November 2002.
53. Chris Feistl, interviews with author, March, August, and November 2002.
54. Ruben Prieto, interview with author, November 2002.
55. Ibid.
56. Ibid.
57. Jerry Salameh, interview with author, June 2002; Chris Feistl, interviews with author, March, August, and November 2002; Dave Mitchell, interviews with author, April, June, and November 2002.
58. Chris Feistl, interviews with author, March, August, and November 2002.
59. Jerry Salameh, interview with author, June 2002.
60. Jerry Salameh, interview with author, June 2002; Ruben Prieto, interview with author, November 2002; Dave Mitchell, interviews with

author, April, June, and November 2002; Chris Feistl, interviews with author, March, August, and November 2002.

61. Dave Mitchell, interviews with author, April, June, and November 2002

62. Jerry Salameh, interview with author, June 2002; Dave Mitchell, interviews with author, April, June, and November 2002; Chris Feistl, interviews with author, March, August, and November 2002.

63. Reuters, "Colombian Elite on Cartel's Payroll, Seized Papers Show," *Toronto Star*, July 24, 1995, A10.

64. Jerry Salameh, interview with author, June 2002; Dave Mitchell, interviews with author, April, June, and November 2002.

65. Chris Feistl, interviews with author, March, August, and November 2002.

66. Ibid.

67. Dave Mitchell, interviews with author, April, June, and November 2002; Chris Feistl, interviews with author, March, August, and November 2002.

68. Ed Kacerosky, interview with author, March 2002.

69. Ibid.

70. Ed Kacerosky, interview with author, March 2002; Lou Weiss, interview with author, October 2002; and Ed Ryan, interview with author, October 2002.

71. Ed Ryan, interview with author, October 2002.

72. Chris Feistl, interviews with author, March, August, and November 2002.

73. Ibid.

74. Ibid.

75. Ibid.

76. Chris Feistl, interviews with author, March, August, and November 2002; Dave Mitchell, interviews with author, April, June, and November 2002.

77. Dave Mitchell, interviews with author, April, June, and November 2002.

78. Ibid.

79. Ibid.

80. Jerry Salameh, interview with author, June 2002; Dave Mitchell, interviews with author, April, June, and November 2002; Chris Feistl, interviews with author, March, August, and November 2002.

81. Chris Feistl, interviews with author, March, August, and November 2002.

82. Ibid.

83. Ibid.

84. Jerry Salameh, interview with author, June 2002.

15: Takedown

1. General Rosso Jose Serrano, interview with author, August 2002; Ruben Prieto, interview with author, October 2002.
2. Dave Mitchell, interview with author, May 2002; U.S. Department of Justice, Memo, "Case Status – Helmer Herrera-Buitrago," DEA ZE-92–0001, April 1, 1998.
3. General Rosso Jose Serrano, interview with author, August 2002; Ruben Prieto, interview with author, October 2002.
4. "Colombian Drug Trafficking," http:infomanage.com/conflict resolution/deacali/html/.
5. "Delatar Si Paga," *Semana*, February 1, 1997, 18.
6. Ed Kacerosky, interview with author, August 2002; Chris Feistl, interview with author, August 2002; Dave Mitchell, interview with author, June 2002.
7. "Colombian Police Grab Cali Properties," United Press International, July 10, 1996.
8. "Success for Big Police Operations," *Latin American Weekly Report*, May 16, 1996, 208.
9. Stephen Gutkin, "Cali Drug Cartel Faces New Challenges in New York," Associated Press, March 24, 1996.
10. Press Briefing by Robert Gelbard, Assistant Secretary of State for International Narcotics Matters, and Richard Newcombe, Assistant Secretary of the Treasury, Office of Press Secretary. The White House, October 22, 1995.
11. "Treasury Moves to Freeze Assets Tied to Cali Cartel," *Washington Post*, March 8, 1996, 28A; "Treasury Names More Fronts of Colombian Drug Cartels," Memorandum, Office of Public Affairs, White House, June 8, 1999, RR-3192.
12. Ibid.
13. "Today's Major Drug Trafficking Organizations in Colombia," U.S. Department of Justice. DEA Web site, http://usdoj.gov/dea/traffickers/colombia.htm.
14. "Colombian Cocaine War," *Latin American Weekly Report*, June 20, 1996, 267.
15. Chris Feistl, interview with author, August 2002.
16. Paul Haven, "Murder Attempt in Cartel Hierarchy Shows Rules Have Changed," Associated Press, May 31, 1996.
17. Yadira Ferrer, "Drugs – Colombia Struggle to Control Drug Traffic," United Press Service, October 31, 1996.
18. Steve Macho, "Cali Drug Cartel under Pressure," Emergency News Service, April 1, 1996, http://www.emergency.com/calipress.htm/.
19. Clifford Krauss, "Colombia Arrests Raise Price of Cocaine in New York City," *New York Times*, September 15, 1995, 1A.
20. "DEA Says Cocaine Price Hikes Not Indicative of Reduced Supply," Drug Enforcement Report, October 10, 1995, 51.
21. Ibid.

22. Ibid.

23. Bill Mante, interview with author, November 2002.

24. U.S. Embassy, Bogota, NSA, "Brother of Paramilitary Leader Interviewed," FBIB, Item No. 00443454, July 18, 1996, Reston, Virginia.

25. Ruben Prieto, interview with author, July 2002; Chris Feistl, interview with author, March 2002.

26. "Slain Colombian Drug Suspect Buried," United Press International, March 8, 1996.

27. Ken Robinson, interview with author, November 2002.

28. DEA agent, interview with author (agent spoke off the record).

29. U.S. Embassy, Bogota, NSA, "Brother of Paramilitary Leader Interviewed," July 18, 1996.

30. Ibid.

31. Sandy Smith, interview with author, March 2002; Mark Eiler, interview with author, March 2002; Ken Robinson, interview with author, November 2002.

32. Ruben Prieto, interview with author, July 2002.

33. U.S. Embassy, Bogota, "Brother of Paramilitary Leader Interviewed," July 18, 1996, NSA.

34. U.S. Justice Department, Drug Enforcement Administration, "Investigation File Closing Report – Helmer Herrera-Buitrago," File Number 2E-92–0001, January 28, 1997.

35. Dave Mitchell, interview with author, April 2002.

36. "Cali Cartel Kingpin Sentenced to More Than Six Years in Prison," Associated Press, March 27, 1998.

37. Adam Thomson, "Drug Informer Is Shot in Jail," *Financial Times*, November 6, 1998, 4; "Colombia's Drug Wars," *The Economist*, November 28, 1998, 34.

38. "Arnaldo Botero," Intelligence Newsletter, January 22, 1998; "Last Big Valle Boss Surrenders on Eve of Washington Ruling," *Latin American Weekly Report*, February 24, 1998; Steven Ambrus, "Colombian Raids Prompt Alleged Cali Cartel Leader to Surrender," *Los Angeles Times*, March 16, 1996, A3.

39. "Colombia – Former Communications Head of Cali Cartel Killed," Global News Service, September 11, 1999.

40. Douglas Farah, "Colombian Drug Lords Run Empire behind Bars," *Washington Post*, December 26, 1996, 37A.

41. Ibid.; and Javier Baena, "Jailed Cali Leader Enjoyed Champagne Behind Bars," AP World Stream, December 8, 1996.

42. Tim Johnson, "For the Wealthy, the Living Is Easy behind Bars," *Miami Herald*, January 6, 1997, K0566.

43. Mary Matheson, "Colombia Plans to Make Cali Cartel Pay," *The Guardian*, November 21, 1996, 15, and Tim Johnson, "For the Wealthy, the Living Is Easy behind Bars," *Miami Herald*, January 6, 1997, K0566.

44. "Cali Cartel Leaders' Sentence Criticized," *Los Angeles Times*, January 18, 1997, A4.

45. "Faceless Judge Sentences Cali Drug Lord to 23 Years," *Los Angeles Times*, February 24, 1997, A7. To protect judges in Colombia against possible intimidation and assassination, they are often made anonymous as part of special tribunals that try powerful criminals. As this case showed, anonymity is not always guaranteed.

46. "Cali Sentence Increased," *Latin America Weekly Report*, May 12, 1998, 208; Reuters, "Colombia Lengthens Drug Baron's Sentence," *New York Times*, February 25, 1999, 8A.

47. Mary Beth Sheridan, "Colombia Defense Minister Quits As Crisis Worsens," Knight Ridder Tribune News Service, August 2, 1995, 802, 2K270.

48. "File 8000: The Stakes of a Political Crisis," http://www.ogd.org/rapport/gb/RP12_1_Colombia.html, 2.

49. Ibid.; Ernesto Samper, interviews with author, March and August 2002.

50. U.S. Congress, Senate, Corruption and Drugs in Colombia: Democracy at Risk: A Staff Report to the Committee on Foreign Relations, February 1996, 6.

51. Ibid., 5.

52. "File 8000: The Stakes of a Political Crisis." Interestingly, Colombia's Attorney General's Office filed "unlawful enrichment charges" against Fernando Botero in January 2001. The move came after officials uncovered evidence that Botero had moved $1 million from Samper's 1994 election campaign to his own private financial account.

53. Ernesto Samper, interview with author, March 2002.

54. "Ernesto Samper Embarks on His Last Year As Colombia's President," *Washington Times*, August 26, 1997, 3.

55. Ernesto Samper, interview with author, March 2002.

56. Ruben Prieto, interview with author, July 2002.

57. "Measure Now Goes to the Lower House for Next Two Votes," *Latin American Weekly Report*, May 23, 1997, 249.

58. "Extradition Bill Passed by Senate," *Latin America Weekly Report*, May 27, 1997, 478.

59. Douglas Farah, "Colombia Drug Barons Threaten, Bribe Congress from Jail," *Washington Post*, December 11, 1996, A36.

60. Carlos Lemos, interview with author, March 2002.

61. "Extradition Setback," *Latin American Weekly Report*, September 23, 1997, 778.

62. Alma Beatriz Rengifo, interview with author, March 2002.

63. "Colombia," American Review World of Information, August 1996, 31.

64. Ibid.

65. I asked Samper what it meant to him to be stripped of his American visa. Samper's answer: "It means I won't be able to see Mickey Mouse." (Ernesto Samper, interview with author, March 2002.) In 1997, the U.S. government stripped 253 Colombians, including Gilberto and Miguel Rodriguez and several of their family members, of their visas for involvement in drug trafficking.

66. Ed Kacerosky, interviews with author, March and August 2002; Ed Ryan, interview with author, June 2002.

67. Ed Kacerosky, interviews with author, March and August 2002.

68. United States of America v. Michael Abbell et al., United States District Court, Southern District Court, Southern District of Florida, Miami Division, Testimony of Guillermo Pallomari, Case No. 93–470-CR-WMA, July 23, 1997, 627.

69. Dave Mitchell, interview with author, May 2002.

70. United States of America v. Michael Abbell et al., Testimony of Guillermo Pallomari, 6476–77.

71. Ibid., 6480.

72. Ibid., 6492.

73. Dave Mitchell, interview with author, May 2002.

74. Chris Feistl, interview with author, November 2002.

75. United States of America v. Michael Abbell et al., Testimony of Guillermo Pallomari, 6495.

76. Thomas Pickel and Thomas Lippman, "Accountant of Cali Cartel Surrenders, Will Inform U.S. about Operations," *Washington Post*, September 22, 1995, 3.

77. Ken Robinson, interview with author, October 2002; Jerry McCardle, interview with author, October 2002.

78. Steve Casto, interview with author, December 2002.

79. Ed Ryan, interview with author, June 2002; Bill Pearson, interview with author, June 2002.

80. "David Lyons, Cali Cartel Accountant, Key U.S. Witness, Gets 7 Years," *Miami Herald*, December 16, 1998, 26.

81. "Retrial Sought for Ex-Cartel Lawyers," *Washington Post*, October 30, 1997, 13.

82. Javier Baena, "His Release Delayed, Colombian Drug Lord Gets Four More Years in Prison," Associated Press, November 5, 2002.

83. Ed Ryan, interview with author, June 2002. According to Ryan, Moran is serving his time in a federal prison in Texas and Abbell is serving his time in Allenwood, Pennsylvania.

84. Frances Robles, "Release of Cali Cartel Leader Stirs Debate about Uribe's Use of Power," *Miami Herald*, Knight Ridder/Tribune News Service, November 8, 2002, K2898.

85. "Retrial Sought for Ex-Cartel Lawyers," *Washington Post*, October 30, 1997, 13; and Ed Ryan, interview with author, June 2002.

86. "Judge Sets Trial Date for Accused Cocaine Smuggler," *Daily Business Review* (Miami, Florida), February 22, 2002.

87. Catherine Wilson, "Ex-Colombian Kingpin Sentenced to More Than 30 Years," Associated Press State and Local U.S., August 26, 2003; "Top Colombian Drug Leader Gets Sentenced," Associated Press, *Newsday*, August 27, 2003, 39.

88. Ruben Prieto, interview with author, November 2002.

89. Ken Robinson, interview with author, October 2002.

90. Ed Ryan, interview with author, June 2002.
91. "Cali Cartel Boss Gilberto Rodriguez Orejuela Re-Arrested," Agent France-Presse, March 12, 2003.
92. Ed Ryan, interview with author, March 2003; Chris Feistl, interview with author, March 2003.

16: Endgame

1. "Freed Drug Lord Faces Internal Quarrels, Rivalries," Deutsche Presse-Agentur, November 8, 2002.
2. Colombia's Top Drug Lord Gilberto Rodriguez Goes Free," UPI, November 8, 2002.
3. Toro, Juan Pablo, "U.S. Tries to Head Off Immediate Release of Colombian Drug Lord from Prison," *Mustang Daily*, November 7, 2004.
4. "Colombia: President Uribe to Seek Stiffer Prison Sentences for Drug Traffickers," BBC Monitoring Latin America, November 9, 2002.
5. McDermott, Jeremy, "Profile: Alvaro Uribe Velez," BBC News, August 7, 2002, http://news.bbc.co.uk/.
6. Lobe, Jim, "Bush Rallies Behind Colombian President, Despite Drug Allegations," Antiwar.com, August 3, 2004, and "Declassified:1991 Report from Defense Department Links Colombian President Alvaro Uribe Valez to Medellin Cartel," *Newsweek*, August 1, 2004. See also the document, "Narcotics – Colombian Narco-Trafficker Profiles," Defense Intelligence Agency, Intelligence Information Report, confidential, 14 pp., at the National Security Archive website (http://www2.gwu.edu/~nsarchiv/).
7. McDermott, Jeremy, "Profile: Alvaro Uribe Valez," ibid.
8. See "Narcotics – Colombian Narco-Trafficker Profiles," ibid.
9. McDermott, Jeremy, "Profile: Alvaro Uribe Valez," ibid.
10. Ibid.
11. Castillo, Fabio, *Los Jinetes de Cocaina* (Bogota, Colombia: Documentos Periodisticos), p. 72.
12. "Alvaro Uribe Valez: Paramilitary Candidate," ibid.
13. See Kirk, Robin, *More Terrible than Death: Massacres, Drugs and America's War in Colombia* (Public Affairs, New York, 2003, p. 279–285).
14. "Colombia Authorizes Extradition of Four Nationals to the U.S.," Xinhua News Agency, October 27, 2004.
15. Garamone, Jim, "Special Operations Part of U.S.-Colombia Plan to Reinforce Success," American Forces Press Service, April 1, 2004.
16. Brodzinsky, Sibylla, "Drug Lord's Early Release Sparks Outcry," *Sydney Morning Herald*, November 9, 2002.
17. "Colombia Judicial Association Files Suit Against President, Interior Minister," BBC Worldwide Monitoring, November 16, 2002.
18. Brodzinsky, Sibylla, "Drug Lord's Early Release Sparks Outcry," ibid.
19. Nesmith, Suzanne, "Colombian Government Relaunches Battle Against Former Drug Lord," Associated Press Worldstream, March 13,

2003; "Ex-Cartel Leader Arrested in Colombia," Reuters, March 13, 2003; and "Drug Baron Rearrested," *Latin American Weekly Report*, March 18, 2003.

20. See OFAC web site at www.ustreas.gov/offices/enforcement/ofac/.

20. Interview with OFAC official, ibid.

22. Testimony of R. Richard Newcomb, Director, Office of Foreign Assets Control, U.S. Department of the Treasury, Before the House Financial Services Subcommittee on Oversight and Investigations. Available at OFAC website at www.ustreas.gov./offices/enforcement/ofac/.

23. Ibid.

24. Testimony of R. Richard Newcomb, ibid.

25. Interviews with OFAC officials, November 2004. By June 2004, 14 Colombia drug kingpins, 35 entities and 561 other individuals associated with the Cali Cartel, North Valle and North Coast drug cartels had been designated SDNTs under EO 12978 (Testimony of R. Richard Newcomb, ibid.).

26. United States of America v. Gilberto Rodriguez Orejuela and Miguel Angel Rodriguez-Orejuela, Sealed Indictment, S4 03cr. 1465, United States District Court. Southern District of New York, February 24, 2004, p.2.

27. Ibid.

28. Interview with OFAC official, November 2002. On October 24, 1995 the Department of the Treasury issued a list containing 76 additional names of persons who met the criteria set forth in EO 12978.

29. Ibid.

30. Sealed Indictment, ibid., p. 6.

31. Interview with U.S. Department of Justice official, who requested anonymity, July 2004.

32. Sealed Indictment, ibid p. 7.

33. Interview with OFAC official, ibid.

34. Ibid.

35. Schreiberg, David, "Sins of the Fathers: The Children of the Cali Cartel Godfathers Can't Shake the Family's Past," *Newsweek*, August 12, 1996.

36. Ibid.

37. Ibid.

38. Interview with OFAC official, ibid.

39. Ibid.

40. Ibid.

41. Sealed Indictment, ibid.

42. Interviews with OFAC officials, ibid.

43. "Blocking Assets and Prohibiting Transactions With Significant Narcotics Traffickers," Presidential Documents, Federal Register, v. 60, no. 205, 60 FR 54411, October 24, 1995.

44. "Letter to Congressional Leaders Reporting on Colombia's Narcotics Traffickers," Weekly Compilation of Presidential Documents, v. 32, October 28, 1996, p. 2136 plus.

45. Interviews with OFAC officials, ibid., "Message to Congress on Narcotics Traffickers of the Cali Cartel," Weekly Compilation of Presidential Documents, v. 34, n. 18, May 4, 1998, p. 718 plus, and "Letter to Congressional Leaders Reporting on a National Emergency with Respect to Significant Narcotics Traffickers Centered in Colombia," Weekly Compilation of Presidential Documents, v. 34, i43, October 26, 1998, p. 2089.

46. "Treasury Names More Fronts of Colombian drug cartels" Press Release, U.S. Department of Treasury, December, 20, 2000.

47. See sealed indictment, ibid.

48. Ibid.

49. Interview with OAFC officials, and sealed indictment, ibid.

50. Interview with OFAC official.

51. Ibid.

52. "Treasury Names More Fronts of Colombian drug cartels," Press Release, U.S. Department of Treasury, December, 20, 2000.

53. Interview with OFAC official, ibid.

54. Interview with U.S. Treasury Department official, ibid.

55. Ibid.

56. Interview with OFAC official, ibid.

57. See Copservir v. R. Richard Newcomb and al., Civil Action, No. 98-0949-LFO, United States District Court, District of Columbia, April 1998, and Carolina Arbolaez and al. v. R. Richard Newcomb and al., Civil Action No. 98-213-LFO, U.S. Direct Court, District of Columbia, filed November 19, 1998.

58. Interview with Treasury Department official, ibid.

59. Ibid.

60. Carolyn Rodriguez Arbolaez and al v. R. Richard Newcomb and al, Order. Civil Action, 98-2813-LFL, United States District Court, District of Columbia, May 16, 2000. The U.S. Court rejected all three of the plaintiffs' complaints. (Ibid.)

61. Testimony of Richard Newcomb, Before the House Financial Services Subcommittee, ibid.

62. Interviews with OFAC officials, ibid.

63. Interview with U.S. Treasury Department official, ibid.

64. Interview with OFAC officials, ibid.

65. "Drug Lords stripped of 120 million pound fortune in prison," Telegraph, September 18, 2004, http://www.telegraph.co.uk/news; "Colombia Seizes Cali Cartel Stores," Reuters, September 18; and Colombia Takes Charge of Pharmacy Chain Linked to Cali Cartel," USA Today, September 17, 2004. http://www.usatoday.com/news/.

66. "Colombia Takes Charge of Pharmacy Chain Linked to Cali Cartel," USA Today, September 17, 2004, ibid.

67. Interview with OFAC official, ibid.

68. "United States Requests Extradition of Cali Cartel Leaders from

Colombia on Money-Laundering Charges," Press Release, U.S. Attorney's Office, March 3, 2004.
69. Ibid.

17: Checkmate

1. U.S.A. v. Rodriguez-Orejuela and al, Criminal Docket for Case #1:03cr20774-all, United States District Court, Southern District of Florida (Miami), September 18, 2003), p. 3.
2. Criminal Docket for Case #1:03c120774-all, ibid., p. 5.
3. Ibid, pp. 5–10.
4. Ibid.
5. See Chapter 15 of this book.
6. Johnson, Tim, "Cali Kingpins Fate Rests with Informer," *The Gazette* (Montreal), August 27, 1998, p. E8.
7. Criminal Docket, ibid., pp. 12–14.
8. Ibid., p. 38.
9. Ibid., pp. 37–38.
10. Johnson, Tim, "Cali Kingpin Fate Rests with Informer," ibid.
11. Criminal Docket, ibid., p. 16.
12. "Patino tiene un pie de E.E.UU.," El Pais.com, December 6, 2002, and "Narcotraficante Colombiano Extraditado EE.UU.," *Terra*, December 6, 2002, http://www.terra.com/.
13. Criminal Docket, ibid. pp. 37–38.
14. Ibid.
15. "Patino Tiene un Pie de E.E.UU.," El Pais.com, December 6, 200, ibid., and "Narcotraficante Colombiano Extraditado EE.UU.," *Terra*, December 6, 2002, ibid.
16. Marshall, Donnie, Chief of Operations, Drug Enforcement Administration, U.S. Department of Justice, "The Colombian National Police and Military in Anti-Narcotics Efforts, and the Current Initiatives the DEA has in Colombia," Statement before the Subcommittee of National Security, International Affairs and Criminal Justice, July 9, 1997.
17. Interview with OFAC official, November 2004, and "Treasury Names Colombian Drug Kingpins to Traffickers' List," Press Release, Office of Public Relations, U.S. Treasury Department, August 18, 2003.
18. "Los Cuentos de Mafia," Semana.com, November 24, 2004.
19. Garcia, Cesar, "Colombian Elite Police Want to Crack Down on Bloody Turf War Among Drug Traffickers," Associated Press World Stream, October 20, 2004.
20. McDermott, Jeremy, "FARC and the Paramilitaries Take Over the Colombian Drug Trade," *Jane's Intelligence Weekly*, July 1, 2004.
21. Ibid.
22. Ibid.
23. "Colombian Daily Profiles Northern Valle del Cauca Cartel Leader Jabon," BBC Monitoring Latin America, April 27, 2004.

24. Ibid.
25. "Colombian Drug Trafficker Surrenders to Authorities," CNN Interactive World News, March 16, 1996.
26. "Treasury Names More Fronts of Colombian drug cartels" Press Release, U.S. Department of Treasury, August, 20, 2000.
27. Anderson, Curt, "U.S. Charges Nine leaders of Colombia's Biggest Cocaine Cartel," Associated Press, May 6 2004.
28. Criminal Docket, ibid., p. 34.
29. Ibid., p. 35.
30. Ibid., p. 39.
31. Ibid.
32. This passage is based on United States of America v. William Rodruguez-Abadia and al., Indictment, S3 01 Cr. 1001 (DC), United States District Court, Southern District of New York, February 17, 2004.
33. "New Indictment Charges Leaders of Colombia's Notorious Cali Cartel with Continuing Global Drug Business from Prison," Press Release, U.S. Department of Homeland Security and U.S. Immigration and Customs Service, December 22, 2003. See also Criminal Docket.
34. Ibid.
35. Garcia, Cesar, "13 Colombians to be Extradited on U.S. Drug Charges," Associated Press, November 3, 2004.
36. Interview with U.S. law enforcement official who wished to remain anonymous.
37. "Colombia Files Papers to Extradite Drug Lords to U.S.," ABS-CBN.com/, http://www.abs.cbnnews.com/.
38. "Colombia President Approves Extraditing Drug Lord to U.S.," China View, November 9, 2004, www.chinaview.com/.
39. "Colombian Drug Kingpin Extradited to the United States," AFP, December 4, 2004, and Catherine Wilson, "Colombian Drug Kingpin Faces U.S. Justice," Associated Press, December 4, 2004.
40. Extradition of Cali Cartel Leader to Miami to face Drug Trafficking Charges Ordered by Colombian President," News Release, U.S. Attorney's Office, Southern District of Florida.
41. Ibid.
42. Interview with U.S. official who requested anonymity, ibid., December 4, 2004.
43. Interview with U.S. Treasury Department official, November 2002.
44. John Moody, "A Day with the Chess Player," *Time*, July 1, 1991.

Conclusion: What Goes Around
1. Tom Constantine, interview with author, May 2002.
2. Bob Nieves, interview with author, January 2002.
3. Bruce Bagley, interview with author, April 2002.
4. Myles Frechette, interview with author, November 2002.
5. Mark Eiler, interview with author, March 2002.

6. Lou Weiss, interview with author, June 2002.

7. Cable, Defense Intelligence Agency to U.S. Government Agencies, Item Identification No. 0058747, July 22, 1993, FOIA.

8. Rennselaer Lee, *White Labyrinth: Cocaine and Political Power* (Brunswick, N.J.: Transaction Publishers, 1989), 190.

9. See U.S. Congress, House, Testimony of Former DEA Administrator Thomas A. Constantine, presented to the House Subcommittee on National Security, International Affairs and Criminal Justice, June 6, 1996.

10. Pedro M. Guzman, interview with author, May 2002.

11. Cable, Defense Intelligence Agency, Item Identification No. 0058747, FOI.

12. *Frontline*, "Drug Wars: The Business: The Colombian Traffickers." Available: http://www.pbs.org/wgbh/pages/frontline/shows/drugs/business/inside/colombia html.

13. "Cali Cartel Overhauls Its Narcotics Structure," *Organized Crime Digest*, April 10, 1996, 6.

14. Bruce Bagley, "Drug Trafficking, Political Violence and U.S. Policy in Colombia in the 1990s," unpublished paper, 2002.

15. J. L. Chappell, "The Colombia Heroin Threat: Demand and Supply," *Low Intensity Conflict and Law Enforcement* 5, no. 3 (winter 1996): 366.

16. See U.S. Department of State, Bureau for International Narcotics and Law Enforcement Affairs, Colombia (Washington D.C.: U.S. Government Printing Office, March 2000).

17. Jerry Salameh, interview with author, May 2002; Chris Feistl, interview with author, August, 2002; and Dave Mitchell, interview with author, May 2002.

18. Bruce Bagley, interview with author, April 2002.

19. Request for Information, Memorandum, Interpol (Europe) to Interpol Washington, September 10, 1997, FOIA.

20. Juanita Darling, "Submarine Links Colombian Drug Traffickers with Russians," *Los Angeles Times*, November 10, 2000.

21. Ibid.

22. Arnaud De Borchgrave, interview with author, July 2002; Andrew Alderson and Carey Scott, "Crime Kings Meet to Carve Europe Up," *Sunday Times*, March 29, 1988.

23. Arnaud De Borchgrave, interview with author, July 2002.

24. Jeremy Lennard and Steven Ambrus, "Elusive Supremos Redraw Drugs Map," *The Guardian*, November 28, 1997; Mark Eiler, interview with author, March 2002; Sandy Smith, interview with author, March 2002.

25. DEA agent, anonymous source, interview with author, March 2002. See also Ron Chepesiuk, "Kings of the Jungle," *Toward Freedom* (June/July 1998): 4–6.

26. Chepesiuk, "Kings of the Jungle," 4–6.

27. John Kerry, interview with author, August 2002.

28. Bruce Bagley, "Drug Trafficking, Political Violence and U.S. Policy in Colombia," 10.

29. Bruce Bagley, interview with author, April 2002.

30. Myles Frechette, interview with author, February 2002.

31. Joe Toft, interview with author, March 2002.

32. Francisco Thoumi, interview with author, April 2002.

33. "Narco Castano?" *Revista Semana*, Edicion 886, April 26, 1999.

34. Patrick Graham, "A Nation Held Hostage," *National Post*, August 21, 2002, A11.

35. Paul Paz y Mino, Amnesty International, interview with author, January 2002; Robin Kirk, Human Rights Watch, interview with author, March 2002.

36. Scott Wilson, "Cocaine Trade Causes Rift in Colombian War," *Washington Post*, September 16, 2002, 1.

37. Duncan Campbell, "Bush Links War on Drugs with War on Terrorism," *The Guardian*, August 8, 2002, 15.

Index